# Financial Market Regulation and Reforms in Emerging Markets

# Financial Market Regulation and Reforms in Emerging Markets

MASAHIRO KAWAI
ESWAR S. PRASAD

*editors*

ASIAN DEVELOPMENT BANK INSTITUTE
*Tokyo*

BROOKINGS INSTITUTION PRESS
*Washington, D.C.*

*Library of Congress Cataloging-in-Publication data*

Financial market regulation and reforms in emerging markets / Masahiro Kawai and
Eswar Prasad, editors.
    p.    cm.
Includes bibliographical references and index.
Summary: "In the wake of the global financial crisis that began in 2008, offers a
systematic overview of recent developments in regulatory frameworks in advanced and
emerging-market countries, outlining challenges to improving regulation, markets, and
access in developing economies"—Provided by publisher.
ISBN 978-0-8157-0489-8 (pbk. : alk. paper)
1. Financial services industry—Management.  2. Financial crises.  I. Kawai, Masahiro,
1947–  II. Prasad, Eswar.  III. Title.
HG173.F51435  2011
332—dc22                                                                    2011005502

9 8 7 6 5 4 3 2 1

Printed on acid-free paper

Typeset in Adobe Garamond

Composition by Cynthia Stock
Silver Spring, Maryland

Printed by R. R. Donnelley
Harrisonburg, Virginia

# Contents

# Introduction

MASAHIRO KAWAI AND ESWAR S. PRASAD

The global financial crisis has necessitated the reconsideration of even basic principles of financial regulation. Meanwhile, the imperative of financial development remains as strong as ever in emerging markets, although the focus is more on basic elements such as strengthening of banking systems and widening the scope of the formal financial system, rather than sophisticated instruments and innovations. Remarkably, emerging market financial systems have in general proved to be more robust and less affected by the global turmoil compared to their advanced economy counterparts—it will be important to carefully filter out the right lessons from this outcome.

The crisis has highlighted the need for strengthening financial systems to make them more resilient to shocks. Emerging markets face particular challenges in stabilizing their nascent financial systems in the face of shocks, both domestic and external, and financial reforms are critical to these economies as they attempt to pursue sustainable high-growth paths. New paradigms for financial development and regulation will have to be suitably reframed for emerging markets, which have a number of varying institutional and capacity constraints. Low-income countries, where the breadth of formal financial systems is severely limited, pose an even greater set of conceptual and practical challenges.

Policymakers in emerging markets are grappling with a distinct set of issues, including the lessons the crisis can offer for the establishment of efficient and

We are grateful to Lei Ye for his help in producing this chapter. This book adopts some of the Asian Development Bank naming conventions used to refer to its member economies. The Brookings Institution takes no position on Taipei,China's legal status.

flexible regulatory structures, the avenues that should be pursued to enable effective regulation of financial institutions with large operations in multiple countries, and how to raise financial inclusion. A broad reconsideration of the optimal structure, and appropriate scope, of the regulation and supervision of financial institutions is needed for these economies.

In October 2009 a conference was held at the Brookings Institution in Washington, D.C., to bring together a group of academics, policymakers, and practitioners to discuss these issues and initiate an extensive research program. The conference objective was to make progress on framing the key questions in a sharper manner to enable progress on moving toward solutions. This volume brings together a selection of papers that were discussed at that meeting. The papers here attempt to outline the issues with clarity and collectively bring out the key connections among regulatory reform, financial development, and broader inclusion. They present a systematic overview of recent developments in regulatory frameworks in both advanced countries and emerging markets, and lay out the challenges to improving financial regulatory structures, functioning of markets, and access in emerging markets.

This is a joint project of the Asian Development Bank Institute, the Brookings Institution, and Cornell University. We are also grateful for funding provided by the Institute for Financial and Management Research Trust (India), International Center for Financial Regulation (U.K.), International Growth Center (U.K.), and International Monetary Fund.

A brief overview of the contents of the book follows below.

## Part I. Overview

Chapter 1 by Eswar Prasad provides a synthetic overview of the main issues concerning regulatory reforms in emerging markets. The author discusses the complex conceptual and practical challenges that emerging market economies face as they attempt to improve their frameworks for financial regulation. These economies need to balance the quest for financial stability with the imperatives of financial development and broader financial inclusion. The author argues that these objectives can in fact reinforce one another. He also discusses aspects of macroeconomic policies and cross-border regulation that have implications for financial stability and the resilience of the financial sector in emerging markets. Thus, the chapter ties together the various themes of the overall research agenda that covers financial market development, regulation, access, and other related issues.

## Part II. New Perspectives on Financial Regulation

What is the right way to approach financial sector regulation and supervision? A reconsideration of basic principles is needed to design an effective and flexible regulatory mechanism that is capable of dealing with financial innovations and systemic risks. The papers in this section provide an overview of the evolving debate on regulatory policy in advanced economies.

Chapter 2 by Viral V. Acharya, Thomas Cooley, Matthew Richardson, and Ingo Walter is on "Market Failures and Regulatory Failures: Lessons from Past and Present Financial Crises." The authors focus on four major market failures that precipitated the current crisis—excessive risk taking by financial firms under government guarantees; regulatory focus on individual institutions rather than systemic risk; lack of transparency of financial institutions; and proliferation of the shadow banking system. For each market failure, different policy options are discussed and compared. The chapter concludes with a discussion on the implications of these market failures for emerging markets, with a focus on government guarantees and systemic risk transmission. The authors stress that policymakers need to identify the source of market failure first and then design regulations to specifically address those market failures.

Chapter 3 by Douglas J. Elliott is on "Evaluating the U.S. Plans for Financial Regulatory Reform." This chapter assesses various regulatory measures adopted (and under consideration) in the United States after the current crisis and draws out the implications of these policies for emerging markets. The author outlines some widely accepted fundamental premises of the U.S. financial system, such as financial regulators' political independence and the avoidance of overregulation. The author argues that the details embodied in the new regulations will be critical to their effectiveness. Furthermore, striking the right balance among factors such as systemic risk reduction, innovation protection, and political feasibility is an important priority for the design of these policies.

## Part III. Regulatory Frameworks for Emerging Markets

Along with a reconsideration of basic principles, it will be important to think about how to adapt these principles to the particular circumstances of emerging market economies where there are significant institutional and capacity constraints. Although country-specific conditions cannot be ignored, it will still be useful to develop a framework for making progress on this issue. The papers in this section provide some emerging market perspectives—from India, China (People's Republic of China), and Indonesia—on these issues.

Chapter 4 by Rakesh Mohan is on "Emerging Contours of Financial Regulation: Challenges and Dynamics." The author frames the global financial crisis as originating from the interplay among excessive loose monetary policy in major developed economies, global imbalances, excessive risk taking by financial institutions, and lax financial regulations. The author argues that regulations were not adequate for dealing with exponential growth in derivatives and securitized credits in the past decade. The growing shadow banking industry contributed to the growing divide between the financial and real sectors. He articulates a number of policy priorities, including macro-prudential regulations that mitigate systemic risk, broader regulatory scope, greater capital and liquidity buffers, stronger international coordination, and more effective risk management.

Chapter 5 by Luo Ping is about "What Regulatory Policies Work for Emerging Markets?" The author compares and contrasts China's banking regulation and standards with that of the Basel Core Principles for Effective Banking Supervision (BCPs). The author first provides a brief overview of China's banking reforms. He then reviews major themes of the BCPs and examines China's practices in these areas. He characterizes China's practices as rules based, while the BCPs are seen as principles based. The author argues that China's regulatory standards, while significantly influenced by the BCPs, are more prescriptive and specific and that this approach is more suitable for emerging markets.

Chapter 6 by Anwar Nasution presents an overview of "Banking Supervision in Indonesia." The Indonesian banking sector faced a variety of problems in the past, such as a long period of financial repression, low transparency, and low asset quality. The author argues that further upgrades to Indonesia's market infrastructure and implementation of international standards are needed to address these issues. As a sound supervisory framework should be dynamic and reflect the realities of the financial sector for which it is created, best practices in advanced economies should be considered as a starting point for enhancing current supervisory frameworks, though one should also bear in mind that a single framework does not fit all types of financial institutions or systems.

## Part IV. Financial Market Development and Stability

The financial crisis will shift the emphasis of the financial development agenda toward the basics of strengthening banking systems, developing basic derivative markets such as currency derivatives, and increasing the depth and diversity of corporate and government bond markets. The papers in this section attempt to redefine the objectives and avenues of financial development in light of recent events.

Chapter 7 by Masahiro Kawai and Michael Pomerleano is entitled "Who Should Regulate Systemic Stability Risk? The Relevance for Asia." The authors contend that financial crises can be prevented, even if their precise timing cannot be predicted, by identifying and dealing with sources of instability. Policymakers need to complement top-down macro-prudential surveillance with micro-prudential supervision. They argue for adequate provision of liquidity during crises and a clearly defined cross-border insolvency resolution mechanism for global financial institutions. At the national level, systemic crises are best managed by a strong and comprehensive systemic stability regulator. The authors support regional initiatives to improve financial stability.

Chapter 8 by Richard Reid is on "Financial Development: A Broader Perspective." The author examines the evolution of different financial systems and attempts to draw out practical policy lessons from varied historical experiences. He lays out a framework for classifying financial development, looking not just at the size of the financial system over time but also at the composition of instruments and institutions, the structure of financial flows, and the interplay of markets. These all have important regulatory implications. The author mentions that while it is difficult to characterize the notion of an optimal financial system, efforts such as broader flow of funds analysis will help countries identify whether a particular financial system is serving the needs of the economy well.

Chapter 9 by K. P. Krishnan is on "Financial Development in Emerging Markets: The Indian Experience." The author reviews the evolution of Indian financial markets, including securities, money market, foreign exchange, debt, insurance, and banking. He highlights the dualistic development of the financial sector in India—the stock market has blossomed while other parts of the financial system have progressed more slowly. This varying pace across sectors is attributed to the differences in each market's regulatory framework and public sector presence. The author sets out a road map for the future development of financial markets in India. He makes a case for reducing overlaps and gaps in regulatory structure, increasing convergence in financial market regulation, broadening financial services provision, creating an independent debt management agency, and enhancing interagency coordination.

## Part V. Improving Financial Access in Emerging Markets

Financial inclusion is a critical part of the financial development agenda for emerging markets. A significant fraction of the population in these countries lacks access to the formal financial system. This affects economic growth and welfare in a variety of ways—by limiting access to credit (for households and entrepreneurs), sharing risks, and diversifying financial savings. Regulators sometimes see broadening financial inclusion as increasing risks to the financial system, but it could in fact be a key component of increasing rather than diminishing financial stability. The papers in this section analyze some key conceptual issues related to financial inclusion.

Chapter 10 by Suyash Rai, Bindu Ananth, and Nachiket Mor is on "Universalizing Complete Access to Finance: Key Conceptual Issues." The authors examine the issue of financial inclusion from the standpoints of welfare and financial stability and provide analytical perspectives on how potential tensions between broadening inclusion and ensuring stability can be managed. The authors discuss a variety of conceptual challenges including balancing simplicity and complexity, communicating clearly about product characteristics, and increasing proximity of access. The authors argue that customizing financial services that are tailored to each household would be more effective from the perspective of financial inclusion, as it allows for more support from providers and better takes into account behavioral biases and household characteristics.

Chapter 11 by Alfred Hannig and Stefan Jansen is on "Financial Inclusion and Financial Stability: Current Policy Issues." The overarching argument of this chapter is that financial inclusion enhances financial stability. The authors outline recent trends in financial inclusion in Asia, Africa, and Latin America. They then discuss micro- and macroeconomic evidence on the positive effects of financial inclusion, including microfinance, on individual and aggregate welfare. The authors remark that innovations in financial inclusion increase certain idiosyncratic risk but contribute relatively low systemic risk. The current crisis should be used as a catalyst to further develop financial inclusion policies that boost economies' resilience; innovations aimed at countering financial exclusion help strengthen financial systems rather than weakening them.

## Part VI. Cross-Border Regulation

The global financial crisis is likely to result in a moderation of cross-border capital flows and other aspects of financial globalization. Nevertheless, the capital accounts of emerging markets have become more open over time and it is unlikely that this trend can be reversed once the incentives for cross-border flows return. Macroeconomic policies and financial regulation in emerging markets will have to deal with this reality. The papers in this section cover how policy and regulatory frameworks can deal with complications associated with open capital accounts.

Chapter 12 by Alejandro Werner and Guillermo Zamarripa is on "Cross-Border Regulation after the Global Financial Crisis." The authors describe the origins of the crisis and the market incentives that contributed to it. They identify four sources of contagion—toxic asset losses, mismatches between assets and liabilities, the financial market's decoupling and recoupling effects, and risk aversion of large conglomerates. The authors suggest that future regulatory design should embody elements such as a global perspective, broader information exchange across emerging markets, bankruptcy resolution mechanism for international financial conglomerates, and clear assessment of sources of vulnerabilities.

Chapter 13 by Jeromin Zettelmeyer, Piroska M. Nagy, and Stephen Jeffrey is on "Addressing Private Sector Currency Mismatches in Emerging Europe." The global financial crisis highlighted the problems associated with currency mismatches on the balance sheets of emerging market borrowers, particularly in emerging Europe. The mispricing of foreign exchange risk, externalities from foreign currency exposure, and weak macroeconomic and institutional credibility all contributed to financial dollarization. The experience of Latin America is then presented as a successful case of de-dollarization. Based on such experiences and emerging Europe's own circumstances, the authors recommend for emerging Europe a set of macroeconomic and institutional reforms, further development of domestic currency and debt markets, and common application of regulation across economies.

# 1

## Financial Sector Regulation and Reforms in Emerging Markets: An Overview

ESWAR S. PRASAD

The speed and breadth of contagion from the U.S. financial crisis have dramatically demonstrated the degree to which national economies, developed and developing alike, are intertwined. Initially a problem confined to the U.S. housing market, the rapid spillover of the crisis to the rest of the U.S. financial system and then to the global economy left financial institutions in other advanced economies reeling. The crisis has highlighted the need for substantive regulatory reforms geared toward ensuring the integrity and resilience of financial systems in the advanced economies.

The macroeconomic consequences of the crisis have also affected emerging markets and other developing economies, even though these groups have rebounded more quickly and sharply from the crisis.[1] These shared ramifications have brought into even sharper relief the centrality of sound financial systems for emerging markets as well as low-income developing economies. Efficient and stable financial systems are essential for both emerging markets and low-income developing economies to achieve long-term balanced development and to absorb various types of shocks.

It is striking that the crisis emanated from the United States and hit a group of economies particularly hard, including that of the United Kingdom, that were once believed to have the most sophisticated and robust financial systems. These

The author would like to thank Parul Sharma for her comments.
1. See Kose and Prasad (2010).

developments have necessitated the reevaluation of basic principles of financial regulation. Clearly, existing regulatory models and frameworks need to be reconfigured and strengthened. The necessary paradigms are still evolving, although there appears to be a general consensus on some key principles that will be central to a major redesign of financial regulation.

Emerging market financial systems, including those in Asia, have generally proven to be more robust and less affected by the global turmoil than their more advanced economy counterparts. It will be important to carefully filter out the right lessons from this outcome. Meanwhile, the imperative of financial development remains as strong as ever in emerging markets, although the focus is more on basic elements, such as strengthening banking systems and widening the scope of the formal financial system, rather than on creating sophisticated instruments and innovations.

Emerging markets face particular challenges in stabilizing their nascent financial systems in the face of shocks, both domestic and external. These challenges occur at a basic level in emerging markets, many of which are at the point of creating sound banking systems, widening inclusion in the formal financial system, and creating and managing a broader set of financial markets (such as corporate bond markets and basic currency derivatives). Thus the regulatory challenges in these economies are more about risks emanating from underdeveloped financial systems rather than risks from sophisticated financial innovations.

New paradigms for financial development and regulation will have to be suitably reframed for emerging markets, which have a number of varying institutional and capacity constraints. Regulation in low-income countries, where the breadth of formal financial systems is severely limited, poses an even greater set of conceptual and practical challenges.

Policymakers in emerging markets will need to grapple with a distinct set of issues once the recovery in the global economy is entrenched and attention can turn to the steps needed to restore financial stability. The following are some of the key issues facing policymakers and regulators in emerging markets:

—What lessons does the crisis offer for the establishment of efficient and flexible regulatory structures? Even advanced economies have had to confront these deep structural questions, which tend to be more complex in emerging markets due to inadequate regulatory capacity and weak legal and public institutions.

—How can the regulatory and financial development agendas be reconciled in a manner that creates regulatory space for the introduction of standardized products and the development of broader financial markets while effectively managing the associated risks? The financial development agenda is an important one in emerging markets where efficient financial intermediation remains a major challenge, with implications for general economic welfare.

—Is broader financial inclusion consistent with financial stability? In general, increasing financial inclusion—extending access to the formal financial system to a greater swath of the population—is a key issue for emerging markets at this critical juncture of their economic development. Financial inclusion has many implications for allowing households to save and diversify their sources of income, enabling entrepreneurs to have access to financing, and creating a more efficient system of intermediating domestic savings into investment.

—What avenues should be pursued to enable effective regulation of financial institutions with large operations in multiple countries? Foreign banks and other financial institutions have become key players in many emerging markets and have provided a number of direct and indirect benefits to local financial systems. However, in times of externally induced crises, they may prove to be a source of contagion.

This chapter focuses on evaluating the lessons from the crisis and on designing effective strategies for maintaining the momentum of financial development and inclusion in emerging markets, with a particular focus on Asian emerging markets. It attempts to assess the implications of the financial crisis for the design of regulatory frameworks and models, taking into account the specific constraints in emerging markets. The main areas covered in this paper are:

—Basic principles of financial regulation: synthesizing evolving paradigms on the key characteristics of optimal regulatory structures to promote financial stability.

—Financial regulatory reforms in emerging markets, with a focus on emerging Asia: dealing with the challenges of limited institutional development and regulatory capacity.

—The financial development agenda: improving financial intermediation and creating space for the development of broader financial markets, including basic derivative products.

—Financial inclusion: how to increase the access of households and entrepreneurs to the formal financial system in emerging markets and considerations of whether greater inclusion is consistent with promoting sound regulation.

—Optimal macroeconomic policy frameworks to enhance financial stability: challenges in designing robust monetary policy frameworks, particularly in light of de facto increasingly open capital accounts.

—Cross-border financial regulation and, more broadly, regulation of financial institutions that have a substantial presence in emerging markets.

## Basic Principles of Financial Regulation

Before the financial crisis, the debate about optimal regulatory structures was focused narrowly on a few issues. One aspect of the debate was whether the United Kingdom's single regulator model, as embodied in the Financial Services

Authority, was better than the multiple regulator framework of the United States, where different agencies have varying jurisdictions. The crisis has exposed gaping weaknesses in both models. The Financial Services Authority was responsible for overall financial stability but appears to have regulated with a "light touch," allowing large levels of systemic risk to build up in the system. In the United States, regulatory failures were compounded by gaps in the overall framework for supervision and regulation that left some products and markets relatively unregulated and created large opportunities for regulatory arbitrage.

A different angle to this issue is the contrast between rules-based and principles-based regulation. Rules-based regulation, which emphasizes getting the regulated to obey the letter of the regulation, typically involves more direct control by the regulatory authority and has been the preferred mode in emerging markets. It had been argued that principles-based regulation, which emphasizes getting the regulated to adhere to the spirit of the regulation, is more appropriate for advanced financial markets. But it also may be relevant for emerging markets looking to develop their financial markets by opening them up to more innovation and risk taking. The crisis has shown that both approaches, which tend to be based on microprudential regulation of individual financial institutions, may be insufficient for dealing with systemic risk.

A reconsideration of basic principles is needed for designing an effective and flexible regulatory mechanism that is capable of dealing with financial innovations and systemic risks. In the wake of the financial crisis, a number of reports have been commissioned from various bodies to look into regulatory reforms. These reports generally agree on some core principles that will have to be emphasized in any set of reforms.[2]

## Higher Capital Requirements

One clear impact of the crisis has been to increase the desirable levels of capital buffers held by financial institutions. The U.S. Treasury has enunciated a set of core principles for capital and liquidity requirements for financial institutions, including the following three principles:

---

2. In the discussion in this section, I mainly draw upon the following reports: the *Report of the High-Level Group on Financial Supervision in the EU* (de Larosière Group 2009), the Group of Thirty report on financial sector reforms (Group of Thirty 2009), *The Turner Review* from the United Kingdom (Financial Services Authority 2009), the report on "Enhancing Sound Regulation and Strengthening Financial Transparency" (G20 Working Group 1 2009), the report on "Reinforcing International Cooperation and Promoting Integrity in Financial Markets" (G20 Working Group 2 2009), and the U.S. Treasury white paper on financial regulatory reform (U.S. Treasury 2009). Other relevant reports and papers are listed in "Additional Sources" at the end of this chapter.

—Capital requirements should be designed to protect the stability of the financial system, not just the solvency of individual banking firms.

—Capital requirements for all banks should be increased from present levels and should be even higher for financial firms that pose a threat to overall financial stability.

—Banking firms should be subject to a simple, non-risk-based leverage constraint and also to a conservative, explicit liquidity standard.[3]

Major advanced economies are considering a reevaluation of assets that can be counted as tier one capital as well as the use of an equity capital standard. Higher-quality forms of capital that enable banking firms to absorb losses and continue as going concerns should provide for a more effective first line of defense for those institutions and limit systemic spillovers. The Treasury report also notes that stricter capital and liquidity requirements for the banking system should not be allowed to result in the reemergence of an underregulated nonbank financial sector that poses a threat to financial stability. Determining appropriate capital adequacy standards for the shadow banking system will be a key challenge in an effective redesign of the regulatory system.

Indeed, another key challenge is to ensure that capital requirements for banks and other highly regulated entities do not result in their simply shifting activity to less regulated areas, including off-balance-sheet activities such as structured investment vehicles. This would simply encourage more risk-taking and raise systemic risk as well, since many off-balance-sheet activities could end up being effectively on-balance-sheet in times of crises.

### Countercyclical Provisioning and Acyclical Accounting Standards

In addition to higher capital requirements, the nature of capital requirements will have to be reevaluated to ensure that they do not intensify systemic financial distress. Existing risk-weighted capital requirements can sometimes exacerbate financial panics by requiring financial institutions to raise capital by selling assets into falling markets.[4] The alternative of a countercyclical capital requirement, however, creates complications in terms of defining and measuring the business

3. U.S. Treasury (2009).

4. Brunnermeier and others (2009) contend that countercyclical capital charges are essential and avoid inefficiencies related to higher capital requirements. They argue that regulators should adjust capital adequacy requirements over the cycle by two multiples: the first related to above average growth of credit expansion and leverage, the second related to the mismatch in the maturity of assets and liabilities. Kashyap, Rajan, and Stein (2008) suggest the creation of contingent capital that could be infused into an institution when it is in distress and facing higher capital needs. This contingent capital could take the form of debt issued by banks that could be automatically converted to equity when the system as a whole is in crisis and when the bank's capital ratio falls below a predetermined threshold.

cycle. Even in relatively calm periods, it is not easy in real time to distinguish between trends and cyclical movements in output, and this becomes even more difficult as a practical matter in emerging market economies where business cycles tend to be more persistent.[5]

On the other hand, the dynamic provisioning approach adopted in Spain appears to have had some success as it facilitates earlier detection and coverage of credit losses in loan portfolios. This enables banks to build up buffers against cyclical downturns, thereby increasing the resilience of individual banks as well as the banking system as a whole, a consideration that is particularly relevant for emerging market economies with bank-dominated financial systems.[6] In addition to some form of countercyclical capital requirements, accounting standards will have to be reconsidered so that they do not further intensify systemic problems. But it will be equally important to preserve some notion of forward-looking fair market value in developing new accounting standards.

### Liquidity Risk and Leverage

Following the crisis, these are concepts that will need to be given careful consideration in the regulatory process. Regulators will need to establish parameters for financial firms to manage liquidity risk and limit leverage, especially as the latter can heighten counterparty risk in the financial system. It is important in this context to note that it is not just banks but other financial institutions that—because of their interconnectedness or size—will need to have their liquidity risk carefully monitored. Constraining leverage at both the institution-specific and aggregate levels is necessary to ensure that excessive leverage at either of these levels does not create systemic breakdowns. Regulatory oversight of payment, clearing, and settlement systems can help ensure that they are not subject to failure as a result of the failure of one or two institutions with large counterparty exposures. Central counterparty clearing of large-scale transactions, rather than having all settlements take place between individual firms, could add further stability to these systems.

In assessing capital requirements on the basis of risk, it will be important to consider the broader relationship among credit, liquidity, and market risks. At times of crises, these risks can interact with and amplify each other. For instance, during the recent crisis, credit and market risks surged when liquidity dried up in financial markets. To deal with the impact of such feedback effects, capital requirements should take a broader view of risk and the relationships (and potential feedback mechanisms) among different sources of risk in the financial system. This implies that different aspects of risk must first be carefully

5. Aguiar and Gopinath (2007).
6. See Saurina (2009).

considered at the level of the individual institution and then also analyzed at a broader systemic level.

## Increasing Transparency

This is a broad concept that includes substantive issues such as bringing more derivative products onto exchanges where they can be traded in a more transparent setting and thereby can be monitored and regulated more effectively. Large over-the-counter (OTC) derivatives contracts that raise counterparty exposure can elevate the level of systemic risk. Steps should be taken to standardize derivative products to the extent possible and improve the technical trading infrastructure in order to increase the incentives for financial firms and corporations to hedge various kinds of exposures on these exchanges rather than via OTC instruments. There could still be a place for certain types of OTC products, but these also should be brought into the regulatory net, and financial firms that are involved in these products should be subject to high capital requirements.

## Macroprudential Approach to Regulation

The crisis has created a clear recognition of the need to evaluate and manage financial risks at the systemic level rather than at the level of individual institutions. In complex financial systems, where there is a high level of interconnectedness among financial institutions, institution-specific risk can quickly get transformed into aggregate-level risk. The solution is, in principle, to monitor institution-specific as well as aggregate risk. But a lot of work needs to be done on how to evaluate aggregate risk, especially in determining what sort of reporting requirements are needed to make proper assessments of the level of interconnectedness among different institutions within a system. The ultimate goal is to enable a systemwide approach for regulating systemically important institutions (based on their size, extent of leverage, interconnectedness with other institutions, and degree to which they provide financial services critical to the operation of key markets).

## Coordination among Regulators

Following from the previous point, it is clear that closer coordination among different regulatory agencies as well as a careful analysis to close gaps that exist in the regulatory framework are essential. Many financial institutions are now complex and operate under multiple jurisdictions, including in some areas where regulatory oversight might be minimal. There is an increasing impetus in different economies to put in place an institutional setup to coordinate the work of different regulatory agencies and to provide oversight of the agencies themselves. For instance, the U.S. Treasury has recently mooted the idea of a Financial Services Oversight Council while the Rajan Committee made a similar recommendation to set up a Financial Sector Oversight Agency in India, a proposal that has recently been implemented by the government.[7] There are some challenges in determining the authority of such an institution, particularly if it is subsumed under an existing regulatory institution.

As discussed in the context of capital requirements, it is important to ensure that tighter regulation in one area does not lead to regulatory arbitrage in the form of financial institutions shifting the regulated activity to less tightly regulated areas. The financial crisis has shown that operations of unregulated entities have the potential to contaminate markets and infect even highly regulated sectors in times of crises. Thus the systemic consequences of the operations of lightly regulated and unregulated entities will have to be taken into account as part of the process of overall regulatory coordination.

There are also basic conceptual and practical questions that need to be addressed in the context of setting up the broad regulatory framework, including, for instance, whether it is appropriate for the central bank to have responsibility not just for overall financial stability but also for bank regulation. Even in the United States, which ostensibly had an efficient regulatory system, there were clearly flaws in the multiple-regulator approach that allowed large and complex financial institutions to engage in regulatory arbitrage. The proposal to give the Federal Reserve Board regulatory authority over large, systemically important ("too big to fail") institutions met enormous resistance because of fears of concentration of power with the Fed as well as concerns about diluting its primary objective of ensuring price stability.

## Resolution Mechanisms for Failing Financial Institutions

Massive government bailouts of distressed financial institutions were undertaken in many advanced economies during the throes of the crisis. This has meant that even if the government now exits from direct support of these institutions, the system has become infected with enormous moral hazard, as the market will now regard every major financial institution as having implicit government backing. The problem of moral hazard is an important one that will have to be dealt with carefully as it can create perverse incentives and stifle competition.

One solution to this problem is to create a resolution mechanism whereby even a large financial institution can be allowed to fail but in an orderly manner that does not involve systemic spillovers of that institution's distress. This mechanism will need to allow for orderly unwinding of counterparty positions, disposal of assets, and resolution of creditor and other claims. For this to work effectively, however, it might be necessary to impose capital requirements on individual units of financial conglomerates (rather than just on the conglomerate as a whole).

---

7. See, respectively, U.S. Treasury (2009) and Planning Commission (2009).

There are a number of additional issues that are under active consideration as part of the Group of Twenty (G20) process. These include creating adequate statutory protection for consumers (the U.S. Treasury has created a Consumer Financial Protection Agency), monitoring and evaluating the role and performance of credit rating agencies, and restructuring compensation schemes for investment managers in a manner that does not reward excessive short-term risk taking. The regulatory landscape in the advanced economies, including the United States, is in a state of considerable flux, with even basic principles still being reformulated based on lessons learned from the crisis.

## Regulation in Emerging Markets

Along with a reconsideration of basic principles, it will be important to think about how to adapt these principles to the particular circumstances of emerging market economies where there are significant institutional and capacity constraints. Although country-specific conditions cannot be ignored, it will still be useful to develop a framework for making progress on this issue.

Many of the basic principles that are being formulated, including higher capital requirements and a focus on liquidity risk management, are as relevant for emerging markets as they are for advanced economies. For emerging markets, it is also a priority to deal with institutional and capacity constraints that limit effective regulation and hinder financial stability. Indeed, even basic microprudential regulation—the effective oversight of individual financial institutions—can be a challenge for many emerging market economies.

A basic priority in emerging markets is to strengthen the institutional framework in order to promote financial stability. This includes instituting comprehensive bankruptcy procedures for corporations and financial firms, and a more robust legal framework to enforce property rights consistently and fairly.

Whatever its benefits in terms of avoiding gaps and regulatory arbitrage, the concept of a single regulator may not be feasible for emerging markets, and, as the U.K. experience shows in a different context, may not even be desirable. A more viable approach would be to create an oversight body that effectively coordinates the work of individual regulatory agencies, ensures the absence of regulatory arbitrage, prevents large gaps from opening up in the regulatory framework, and oversees the regulation of large institutions with operations in multiple markets.

Latin American and Asian experiences show not only how valuable lessons can be extracted from crises but also how these lessons are sometimes forgotten over time. In the debt crises of the 1980s and 1990s, a number of Latin American countries suffered from problems caused by currency mismatches between their external assets and liabilities, particularly in terms of having taken on large amounts of short-term debt denominated in foreign currency. Asian economies faced similar problems during the Asian financial crisis of 1997–98.

Major Latin American and Asian economies have withstood the recent financial crisis reasonably well as a consequence of having substantially reduced their foreign currency borrowing. By contrast, the debt-financed growth of many Eastern European economies left them highly vulnerable to the latest crisis.[8] Maintaining a cautious approach to foreign-currency denominated borrowing is clearly a safe policy but one that has to be balanced against the benefits to financial institutions and corporations of borrowing abroad. A sensible regulatory approach can be used to balance the benefits of foreign-currency denominated debt against the attendant currency risk.

As noted earlier, another key constraint in emerging markets is inadequate regulatory capacity that cannot keep up with fast-evolving markets and products. This constraint is exacerbated by the challenge that competent and knowledgeable staff in regulatory bodies in these countries tend to be absorbed quickly into the private sector. Multilateral institutions can enable capacity building by providing training to country officials, synthesizing and transferring information about international best practices, and providing direct guidance in the formulation of codes and regulations.

The regulatory reform agenda in emerging markets is, in fact, closely tied to their financial development agenda. Financial instability in some of these economies is less a matter of unfettered innovation than it is about incomplete and underdeveloped financial markets. This creates its own set of regulatory challenges, but it is worth turning directly to the relationship between two core priorities—financial development and financial inclusion—to see how they tie in with regulatory issues.

## Financial Development in Emerging Markets

The financial crisis makes it imperative to refine rather than retreat from the objectives and avenues of financial development. Mobilizing savings and effectively channeling them into productive investment remains a key challenge for financial systems in emerging markets. In economies like China and India that have high private saving rates, effective financial intermediation is relevant not just for promoting growth but also for improving the welfare impact of that growth.[9]

---

8. See Kose and Prasad (2010).

9. See (Prasad 2009). These issues are more relevant to middle-income emerging market economies. Among low-income economies, the emphasis may need to be more on getting the basic elements of the institutional framework right, including the legal and regulatory frameworks, corporate governance, and accounting and auditing standards.

The crisis will shift the emphasis of the financial development agenda toward the basics of strengthening banking systems, developing plain vanilla derivative markets such as currency derivatives, and increasing the depth and diversity of corporate and government bond markets. The challenge is to create a regulatory environment that facilitates innovation in these areas without allowing financial innovation to get so far ahead of regulatory capacity that it creates systemic risks.

The key priorities related to the financial development agenda in Asian emerging markets are summarized below.

### Strengthening and Improving Banking Systems

In major Asian emerging markets, the financial systems remain largely bank-dominated. Moreover, public sector banks (PSBs) still play a dominant role in several key Asian emerging markets, including China and, to a lesser extent, India. Improving the efficiency and governance of both public and private banks is a key priority. Unfortunately, in both of those countries, PSBs are often seen as instruments of social policy, including directing credit toward favored industries. A number of other Asian countries are in a similar position.

Interestingly, the financial crisis has cast public banks in a different light. During periods of extreme financial stress, when the rest of the financial system is frozen up, public banks can obviously serve a useful function by providing credit. But reforms are still necessary to ensure that these banks turn in an adequate performance in normal times as well. While banks in many emerging markets, including China and India, meet or exceed even the higher capital requirements being proposed under the Basel III Accord, the major priority for these banks is actually to improve risk management rather than to strengthen their capital bases.

Corporatizing PSBs, which does not necessarily entail a full-scale one-shot privatization, would be one step toward improving their performance. Indeed, some PSBs have increased their efficiency and, despite their social obligations, are able to compete with private sector banks. The State Bank of India is a good example of a publicly owned bank that has become highly profitable and competes effectively with private banks, both domestic and foreign.

### Development of Corporate Bond Markets

This is necessary to broaden the scope of financial markets in order to raise financing for large-scale enterprises. Bond markets also would provide a way of disciplining firms and increasing their transparency. However, the development of well-functioning corporate bond markets is closely tied to the development of government bond markets, since the yield curve on low-risk government bonds serves as a benchmark for pricing corporate risk. In China and India, these markets are small and underdeveloped, partly because of regulatory constraints.[10] The Asian Bond Fund initiative was meant to catalyze the development of regional fixed-income securities markets, particularly bond markets, but has gained only limited traction in this dimension.

## Development of Basic Derivatives Markets

Although derivatives products have acquired a negative connotation, there is a range of plain vanilla derivatives and securitized products that have proven to be useful innovations that reduce rather than raise systemic risk when properly regulated. These include commodity derivatives, which can play a key role in many low-income countries where a significant fraction of the workforce is still connected to agriculture, as well as the extraction and processing of primary commodities. Asian countries have become increasingly open to trade, making it valuable for importers and exporters in these countries to have access to exchange rate derivatives for hedging foreign currency risk. Indeed, even during the throes of the crisis, the Asian region made progress in setting up some of these markets. In particular, currency derivatives markets have only recently been set up in both China and India; the size of these markets has expanded substantially over the past year, indicating the strong demand for these derivative products. Indian authorities have recently permitted the introduction of credit default swaps, albeit in a limited and carefully controlled manner. Nevertheless, this development shows that there is a demand for a broader range of securitization products in the large emerging markets, and that regulators are willing to accommodate this demand as long as they are reasonably certain that they can maintain adequate regulatory control over such products so that they do not elevate the level of systemic risk.

## Improving Technical Infrastructure for Trading Financial Instruments

In large emerging markets, significant progress has been made in improving the technical infrastructure for trading various financial instruments, including equities, bonds, and derivatives. Moving more securities transactions onto open exchanges and creating a viable alternative for OTC transactions would increase transparency and efficiency in these markets. Extensive oversight of the payment, clearing, and settlement mechanisms will be necessary to maintain confidence in these markets, particularly to prevent any single financial firm from playing a dominant role.

---

10. Krishnan (2009) provides an interesting overview of the factors that have governed the development of India's financial markets and discusses why Indian equity markets have done well in terms of depth and resilience while corporate bond markets and the commercial paper market have barely gotten off the ground.

Given these financial development priorities, the question is what the right approach should be to building regulatory capacity relative to fostering financial innovation and development. While it is tempting to put financial stability first and focus on minimizing risks and potential losses, there could be costs in terms of reduced growth and welfare that result from underdeveloped financial markets.

This points to a difficult tension that emerging markets face between tight regulation that limits the development of new financial markets and products, and adequate regulation that provides some space for financial innovation. Financial crises can have particularly painful effects on populations living at or near subsistence levels, so relatively poor and even middle-income countries might choose prudence over innovation and the risks that the latter entails. At the same time, holding back financial innovation and development has hidden costs if it stunts growth or makes growth less inclusive.

The solution might lie in broadening the perimeter of regulation and adapting the evolving international principles of regulation to suit the needs of newly emerging financial markets and institutions. Indeed, since nonbank financial intermediaries in Asian emerging markets are typically smaller than those in advanced economies, while also accounting for a relatively smaller share of the financial system, it should be easier for countries in the region to upgrade their regulatory frameworks to encompass all such institutions in a more robust manner.

## Financial Inclusion

This is a critical part of the financial development agenda for emerging markets. Indeed, the G20 has highlighted the importance of the need for greater "financial access" in both advanced and emerging market economies. In the latter group of economies, a significant fraction of the population lacks access to the formal financial system. This affects economic growth and welfare by limiting access to credit (for households and entrepreneurs), making it harder to share risks, and limiting diversification of financial savings.

Broadening financial inclusion is sometimes seen by regulators as increasing risks to the financial system, but in fact, it could be a key component of increasing rather than diminishing financial and macroeconomic stability. Indeed, lack of adequate access to credit for small and medium-size enterprises as well as small-scale entrepreneurs in the services sector has adverse effects on overall employment growth, since these enterprises tend to be much more labor-intensive in their operations than large scale industries.

Financial inclusion often has been seen as a social priority that should be subsidized by the government. For instance, the Indian government requires banks to dedicate a certain proportion of their lending to "priority" sectors such as agriculture. Similarly, despite the purported absence of "directed lending," Chinese banks continue to play an important role in providing financing to agriculture (and to large state-owned enterprises). Unfortunately, this makes the financial inclusion process much less effective and also reduces the overall efficiency of the financial system.

The key issue is to see financial inclusion not just as a social priority but as one that the private financial institutions should be incentivized to take up. There is a large demand for even basic financial services in underserved segments of the population in many Asian countries, particularly in rural areas. The constraint lies in achieving scale efficiencies that make it worthwhile for the private sector to reach these markets.

Technology can play a useful role here. Innovative approaches such as mobile banking (using mobile phones, which have proliferated even in rural areas in most Asian developing countries) could be used to increase inclusion in an easy manner. Automated teller machines (ATMs) can reduce the costs of setting up bank branches that may not achieve adequate scale economies to be individually profitable. Other approaches, like using retail grocers to provide small-scale retail banking services, are also being considered in many countries, including India.

In some developing economies, however, such initiatives often come up against regulatory constraints. For instance, the Reserve Bank of India has insisted that Indian banks must maintain the "know your customer" principle in all transactions, making it difficult to implement some of the approaches mentioned above. Until recently, the Reserve Bank also required each ATM installation to go through a cumbersome licensing and regulatory approval process. Such measures highlight the inherent tension that exists in regulators' minds between instituting effective regulatory oversight and broadening financial inclusion through nontraditional means. Analytical work and field experiments are needed to evaluate different approaches to broadening inclusion as well as their implications for financial stability.

A lot more work also needs to be done to harness the informal financial system that still plays an important role in low-income countries and even in some middle-income countries. There is a difficult set of issues about whether informal financial systems still have a viable and useful role, and whether they can be brought into the regulatory net in a manner that makes them compatible with overall financial stability. But the role of the informal financial sector, and the potential problems with instability associated with it, will tend to endogenously diminish in size as the formal financial system takes its place in delivering basic financial services to a broader segment of the population. Thus the financial inclusion agenda is not only compatible with but could also promote overall financial stability.

## Macroeconomic Frameworks to Support Financial Stability

The financial crisis has highlighted the intricate interplay between macroeconomic and financial policies at both the national and global levels. Without stable macroeconomic policies, financial development can be difficult. On the flip side, weakly supervised and inefficient financial systems can hamper the effectiveness of policy transmission mechanisms and make it harder to manage macroeconomic policies. Approaches to monetary policy frameworks, capital account liberalization, and related issues are being reconsidered in light of the crisis.

### Monetary Policy

Over the last two decades, many emerging markets have started adopting some form of inflation targeting in order to anchor monetary policy and move away from exchange rate targets, which have become increasingly untenable given that capital accounts are becoming more open.[11] A key issue is whether monetary policy should explicitly strive to manage asset prices. This debate has particular resonance in light of the criticism directed at central banks that targeted inflation either explicitly (Bank of England) or implicitly (Federal Reserve) and overlooked the asset market bubbles, especially in the housing market, that have come back to haunt policymakers.

There is a fundamental tension between increasing the mandates of the central bank and the independence that the central bank needs in order to adequately meet its objectives.[12] The hierarchy of complexity related to central banking in an emerging market economy can be broadly characterized as follows.

Attaining the basic objective of price stability is already a difficult challenge in emerging markets. Financial underdevelopment, weaknesses in the monetary transmission mechanism, and often profligate fiscal policies (creating fiscal dominance over monetary policy in determining aggregate price dynamics) make it difficult to consistently attain a low inflation objective with the interest rate instrument.

Adding an exchange rate objective, which many emerging market central bankers are under pressure to do, makes this yet more difficult operationally. In principle, capital controls provide a degree of freedom that insulates domestic monetary policy from the stance of monetary policy in major partner countries. But capital accounts are becoming more open in virtually every country. Even in economies like China and India where there are still many capital controls, de facto capital account openness has increased, and it has become harder to limit inflows or outflows when the incentives to bring money into or take it out of the country are large enough.

---

11. Hammond, Kanbur, and Prasad (2009).
12. See Prasad (2010).

Furthermore, in light of the crisis, central bankers around the world are now being asked to pay more attention to asset price bubbles. As in advanced economies, in emerging markets it also is difficult to identify incipient asset price bubbles. Trying to deflate them once they have grown large and are more easily identifiable engenders large social and political costs, since the collateral damage can be much greater at that point. In any event, the traditional monetary policy instrument—a short-term policy interest rate—may not be the most effective tool to deal with asset price bubbles. An alternative is to use prudential requirements and regulatory policies to deal with bubbles. This is a reasonable approach and would expand the set of instruments that central banks have. In practice, however, central banks have less control in certain asset markets, especially as they grow more sophisticated and as foreign inflows increase in volume and in terms of importance to domestic markets.

As discussed earlier, government ownership of banks can be very helpful in a crisis but creates conflict between monetary policy and regulatory objectives even in normal times. Interest rate changes to maintain price stability may not always be consistent with the stability and profitability of the banking system. This creates another layer of tension within a central bank's mandates.

In short, central banks in emerging markets face myriad challenges in fulfilling their mandates, some of which are mutually inconsistent. At the same time, in many emerging markets, central banks are often the public institutions with the best intellectual and technical capacity and robust institutional structures. So it is not surprising that they are asked to take on multiple mandates.

Such conflicting directives can reduce a central bank's effectiveness in meeting its core mandate of maintaining price stability. Indeed, it could be costly to abandon the hard-won benefits of price stability in emerging markets. Inflation is especially pernicious in these economies as it hits the poor very hard, rendering low inflation a crucial objective of monetary policy. Inflation targeting has a good track record of delivering price stability and anchoring inflation expectations, which is very valuable in emerging markets, especially those with a history of high and volatile inflation.

A key issue, which the crisis also has brought to the fore, is whether adding objectives to a central bank's basic mandate makes it more subject to political pressures and interference, thereby reducing its operational independence. There are also economic efficiency issues to be considered carefully in this context. For instance, directing the central bank to focus on asset price bubbles might prevent meltdowns, but lack of a singular focus on price stability could create smaller boom-bust cycles if inflation expectations are not well anchored by a target.

De Gregorio (2009) has argued forcefully that the best and only realistic approach for emerging market central banks is to focus on an inflation objective, using prudential requirements where possible to manage asset market bubbles (which are, in any case, difficult to identify) and letting the exchange rate serve as the adjustment mechanism. This approach is plausible, but it will not be straightforward to implement in emerging Asia, which is highly open to trade (and therefore greatly affected by large exchange-rate fluctuations) and where memories of the sharp exchange rate fluctuations during the Asian financial crisis are still raw. But it is still an important lesson to be learned from the experiences of Latin American economies. They were wracked by high inflation and crises before they moved to inflation targeting and flexible exchange rates, which have done much to promote macroeconomic stability in the region.

Perhaps this is a trade-off to think about carefully in the context of the institutional and economic environment of each country, and ultimately this is a sociopolitical choice rather than a purely economic one. Further analysis is also needed to determine what additional instruments central banks will require to effectively try to satisfy multiple objectives and to address questions such as what sort of rule can be used to keep asset prices in line, especially when there is a conflict between hitting an inflation objective and dampening asset price bubbles.

## Other Macroeconomic Policies

Fiscal policy plays an important role in financial stability. Weak fiscal policies can create a number of distortions in the economy, especially if the scale of government borrowing becomes large. In the first place, it creates monetary instability by making it difficult for the central bank to anchor inflation expectations. If the government borrowing is done through banks, as is the case in India, this can have adverse effects on financial intermediation in the economy. Large fiscal deficits can also reduce fiscal space that is available for responding to financial crises or even normal business cycle downturns. During the global financial crisis, for instance, China was able to effectively ratchet up its fiscal stimulus by a large amount, as it had implemented disciplined fiscal policies for many years, resulting in relatively low levels of explicit budget deficits and public debt.[13]

As discussed earlier, capital controls used to be an important part of developing country central bankers' toolkits, but their effectiveness and durability have eroded significantly over time. With emerging markets' rising trade and financial integration within the global economy and their de facto more open capital accounts, capital controls now simply generate distortions without any commensurate benefits in terms of providing adequate protection from volatility of capital flows or promoting stability in financial markets.

---

13. However, contingent liabilities in the state-owned banking and pension systems suggest that the implicit public debt could, in fact, be significantly higher.

## Cross-Border Regulation

The recent financial crisis is likely to result in a moderation of cross-border capital flows and other aspects of financial globalization, at least in the short run while financial systems around the world stabilize. Nevertheless, capital accounts of emerging markets have become more open over time, and it is unlikely that this trend can be reversed once the incentives for cross-border flows return. Macroeconomic policies and financial regulation in emerging markets will have to deal with this reality. An important question is how to design policy and regulatory frameworks that can deal with complications associated with open capital accounts. It is useful first to review different factors that could affect the trend in emerging markets to financially integrate with the rest of the world. In the discussion below, I focus on the case of Asian emerging markets, but the general principles are relevant for all emerging markets.

### Possible Impact of the Crisis on Financial Flows to and from Emerging Asia

For Asia a key aspect of greater financial integration relates to capital flows into or out of the region.

#### Flows from Advanced Economies

Capital inflows from advanced economies constitute the bulk of gross inflows into emerging markets, including in Asia. These flows are likely to remain at relatively low levels in the short term, as international investors remain wary of taking on risk while the global economic recovery still seems fragile. On the other hand, the relatively stronger growth prospects of emerging markets compared to those of advanced economies should have a positive effect on such flows. As a reflection of international investors' more favorable sentiments toward emerging markets, sovereign bond spreads for the major emerging markets have dropped substantially relative to their peak in November–December 2008.

An important factor that could have a longer-term effect is that many financial intermediaries in advanced economies (such as investment banks) that had specialized in investments in developing countries have been swept away by the financial crisis. This entails a significant loss of information about investment possibilities and financial markets in emerging markets, including Asia. It will take a while for this knowledge to be rebuilt and for new intermediaries to take on the role of channeling funds from advanced economies to emerging markets. Of course, emerging market economies can assist this process by making their financial markets more open and transparent, which would make it easier for foreign investors to evaluate investment possibilities and act on them.

#### Rising International Exposure of Asian Banks

The size and reach of major Asian banks have continued to expand over time. They have large deposit bases in their home countries and are at a comparative advantage now that many of their international competitors have been hit hard by the crisis while they have remained relatively immune because of their hitherto modest international exposure. Many banks in the region, particularly those headquartered in China and India, are likely to have increasing cross-border exposure and become true international banks.

### ASIAN HOUSEHOLDS' DEMAND FOR FOREIGN INVESTMENTS

As income levels in the region rise, the desire for international investments, especially for portfolio diversification purposes, is likely to increase among Asian households and corporations. As financial markets in these countries become deeper and the range of financial intermediaries increases, the quantum of financial flows that will move into foreign investments is likely to increase.

### THE ROLE OF INSTITUTIONAL INVESTORS

Institutional investors based in the Asian region, including pension funds, could serve as an important channel for private as well as official funds to flow abroad. Sovereign wealth funds that manage a portion of foreign exchange reserves are also likely to aggressively seek investments abroad when asset values remain relatively cheap, and this pattern is likely to be maintained even after global financial markets have stabilized.

## *Implications for Cross-Border Regulation*

All of the factors listed above suggest that cross-border supervision will be of increasing interest to emerging Asia as foreign financial institutions increase their presence in the region and institutions from within the region increase the scale of their foreign operations. An additional factor that is relevant in this context is that with rising trade and financial linkages among Asian countries, the scale of cross-border financial transactions within the region itself will increase rapidly. Hence regulatory authorities in the region will face multiple challenges during the process of greater financial integration both within the region and with the rest of the global financial markets. These trends will require three types of regulatory responses.

### GREATER OVERSIGHT BY NATIONAL REGULATORS OF THE INTERNATIONAL OPERATIONS OF THEIR DOMESTIC FINANCIAL INSTITUTIONS

Cross-border operations naturally involve additional risk factors, especially exchange rate risk. These various dimensions of risk that arise from larger cross-border exposures will need to be carefully monitored, both from the perspective of individual institutions and from a systemic perspective. In extending the principle of imposing capital requirements on individual units of financial institutions in order to allow for orderly dissolutions of institutions in financial distress, it may be useful to explicitly impose capital requirements on country-specific operations of each financial institution. This approach should be considered cautiously, however, as it could lead to a reduction in the provision of financial services in countries where the deposit base is weak.

### GREATER COORDINATION AMONG REGULATORS IN THE REGION
This could help promote regional financial stability. The idea mooted by the G20 of having colleges of supervisors that could coordinate, or at least share, information concerning institutions that have large cross-border operations could also be implemented at the regional level. There are a number of practical challenges, however, in terms of coordination among countries with very different levels of financial market development, institutional quality, and regulatory capacity. Regional multilateral institutions like the Asian Development Bank may have a critical role to play in fostering and facilitating this process.

### BETTER COORDINATION WITH REGULATORS FROM OUTSIDE THE REGION
Exchange of information with other national regulators via international colleges of supervisors would be essential to enhance monitoring of their domestic institutions as well as foreign institutions that have a substantive presence in the region.

In the aftermath of the financial crisis, international regulatory norms and standards are being refashioned by institutions such as the Bank for International Settlements, the International Monetary Fund, and the Financial Stability Board. Emerging market economies would ultimately benefit from the greater financial stability that will be engendered by the steps taken by these institutions. However, these international agencies are standard-setting bodies that can only provide guidance on codes and international best practices; they are unlikely to enforce international standards or to intrude into individual countries' implementation of those standards. Aligning their own regulatory frameworks with these new standards will be the responsibility of the individual national authorities, creating a complex set of challenges.

## Final Remarks

This chapter has provided an overview of the complex conceptual and practical challenges that emerging market economies face as they attempt to improve their frameworks for financial regulation. In the aftermath of the global financial crisis, these challenges are not unique to emerging markets but are heightened by the capacity and institutional constraints in these economies. Emerging markets need to balance the quest for financial stability with the imperatives of financial development and broader financial inclusion. I have argued that these objectives are not necessarily inconsistent and can actually reinforce one another. I have also discussed aspects of macroeconomic policies and cross-border regulation that have implications for financial stability and the resilience of the financial sector in emerging markets.

## References

Aguiar, Mark, and Gita Gopinath. 2007. "Emerging Market Business Cycles: The Cycle Is the Trend." *Journal of Political Economy* 115, no. 1: 69–102.

Brunnermeier, Markus, and others. 2009. *The Fundamental Principles of Financial Regulation.* Geneva: International Center for Monetary and Banking Studies.

De Gregorio, José. 2009. "Frameworks for Monetary and Financial Stability: An Emerging Markets Perspective." Keynote speech delivered at the Brookings Institution. Washington D.C., September 15.

De Larosière Group. 2009. *Report of the High-Level Group on Financial Supervision in the EU.* Brussels.

Financial Services Authority. 2009. *The Turner Review: A Regulatory Response to the Global Banking Crisis.* London.

Group of Twenty (G20), Working Group 1. 2009. "Enhancing Sound Regulation and Strengthening Financial Transparency. Final Report." March (www.g20.org/Documents/g20_wg1_010409.pdf).

———, Working Group 2. 2009. "Reinforcing International Cooperation and Promoting Integrity in Financial Markets. Final Report." March (www.g20.org/Documents/g20_wg2_010409.pdf).

Group of Thirty, Working Group on Financial Reform. 2009. *Financial Reform: A Framework for Financial Stability.* January (www.group30.org/pubs/reformreport.pdf).

Hammond, Gill, Ravi Kanbur, and Eswar Prasad. 2009. *Monetary Policy Frameworks for Emerging Markets.* Northampton, Mass.: Edward Elgar Publishing.

Kashyap, Anil, Raghuram Rajan, and Jeremy Stein. 2008. "Rethinking Capital Regulation." Paper prepared for the Federal Reserve Bank of Kansas City symposium on "Maintaining Stability in a Changing Financial System." Jackson Hole, Wyoming, August 21–23.

Kose, M. Ayhan, and Eswar S. Prasad. 2010. *Emerging Markets: Resilience and Growth amidst Global Turmoil.* Brookings.

Krishnan, K.P. 2009. "Financial Development in Emerging Markets: The Indian Experience." Paper presented at the ADBI-Brookings-Cornell conference on "Financial Sector Regulation and Reforms in Emerging Markets." Brookings Institution, Washington, D.C., October 22–23.

Planning Commission, Government of India (Rajan Committee). 2009. *A Hundred Small Steps: Committee on Financial Sector Reforms.* SAGE Publications India.

Prasad, Eswar. 2009. "Rebalancing Growth in Asia." Working Paper 15169. Cambridge, Mass.: National Bureau of Economic Research.

———. 2010. "After the Fall: Central Banking Challenges in the Aftermath of the Crisis." *Finance and Development* 47, no. 2: 22–25.

Saurina, Jesús. 2009. "Dynamic Provisioning: The Experience of Spain." Crisis Response
    Note 7. Washington D.C.: World Bank (July).
U.S. Department of the Treasury. 2009. "A New Foundation: Rebuilding Financial Reg-
    ulation and Supervision." White paper (June).

## Additional Sources

Acharya, Viral V., and Matthew Richardson, eds. 2009. *Restoring Financial Stability:
    How to Repair a Failed System.* Hoboken, N.J.: John Wiley and Sons.
Asian Development Bank. 2007. *Beyond the Crisis: Emerging Trends and Challenges.*
    Manila (www.adb.org/documents/books/beyond-the-crisis/default.asp).
Asian Policy Forum. 2009. "Recommendations of Policy Responses to the Global Finan-
    cial and Economic Crisis for East Asian Leaders." Tokyo: Asian Development Bank
    Institute (www.adbi.org/key-docs/2009/03/18/2900.policy.global.financial.crisis.east.
    asian.leaders).
Committee on Global Financial System. 2009. "Capital Flows and Emerging Market
    Economies." CGFS Paper 33. Basel: Bank for International Settlements.
Financial Stability Forum. 2008. *Report of the Financial Stability Forum on Enhancing
    Market and Institutional Resilience.* Basel: Bank for International Settlements (April).
Group of Thirty. 2008. *The Structure of Financial Supervision: Approaches and Challenges
    in a Global Market Place.* Washington D.C.
International Monetary Fund. 2009. "Detecting Systemic Risk." In *Global Financial
    Stability Report*, chapter 3. Washington D.C. (http://imf.org/external/pubs/ft/gfsr/
    2009/01/pdf/chap3.pdf).
James, William E., and others. 2008. "The U.S. Financial Crisis, Global Financial Tur-
    moil, and Developing Asia: Is the Era of High Growth at an End?" Economic Work-
    ing Paper 139. Manila: Asian Development Bank (December).
Kawai, Masahiro, and Michael Pomerleano. 2009. "Containing a Systemic Crisis: Is
    There a Playbook?" Paper prepared for the Federal Reserve Bank of Chicago and the
    World Bank conference on "The International Financial Crisis: Have the Rules of
    Finance Changed?" Chicago, September 24–25.
Lee, Jong-Wha, and Cyn-Young Park. 2008. "Global Financial Turmoil: Impact and
    Challenges for Asia's Financial Systems." Regional Economic Integration Working
    Paper 18. Manila: Asian Development Bank (April).
Prasad, Eswar, and Raghuram Rajan. 2008. "Next Generation Financial Reforms for
    India." *Finance and Development* 45, no. 3: 23–27.
Reddy, Yaga V. 2008. "Global Financial Turbulence and Financial Sector in India: A
    Practitioner's Perspective." *Reserve Bank of India Bulletin*, August.
Squam Lake Group on Financial Regulation. 2009. Various reports (www.squamlake
    workinggroup.org).
Turner, Adair. 2009. "Priorities for the Reform of Global Regulation—Challenging Past
    Assumptions." Speech at the Annual Conference of the International Organization of
    Securities Commissions. Tel Aviv, June 8–11.

PART II

# New Perspectives on Financial Regulation

# 2

## Market Failures and Regulatory Failures: Lessons from Past and Present Financial Crises

VIRAL V. ACHARYA, THOMAS COOLEY,
MATTHEW RICHARDSON, AND INGO WALTER

The severity of the financial crisis of 2007–09 has forced academics, regulators, and policymakers to rethink the contours of the current financial system. Calls for the greatest regulatory overhaul since the Great Depression have become common. Indeed, many observers, including ourselves, view the crisis first and foremost as a regulatory failure and are convinced that the current regulatory architecture—the product of many ad hoc responses to prior crises, and antiquated in the face of the evolving structure and role of financial institutions—is in need of repair. But regulation is a tricky business; the law of unintended consequences always applies. The wrong decisions may well make future crises more likely and more severe, while regulation that is too heavy handed could stifle future financial efficiency and innovation.

While the current crisis has exposed multiple cracks in the financial system, the instinctive reaction of some is to call for a paradigm shift—even blaming the nature of capitalism itself. In reality, the problem is far less dramatic. A good rule of thumb for designing effective regulation is to focus almost exclusively on the specific source of the market failures and evaluate robust ways of addressing these failures through regulatory interventions.

Some of the material in this article is based on the book *Restoring Financial Stability: How to Repair a Failed System* (Acharya and Richardson 2009b). The authors would like to thank the discussant, Marcus Miller, and are grateful to their colleagues at NYU-Stern who contributed to the book and to the thinking that has influenced this essay greatly.

History can be a good guide here. Somewhat paradoxically, even though financial crises are rare, they are recurring phenomena, just like the business cycle. Thus it is possible to think about crises—and how to respond to them—in a systematic manner. What are the common causes of crises across their recurrences? Are there lessons to be learned from the crises of the past that can be helpful in the future? What responses to crises have been most successful? And based on these, what can be done next to try to improve stability without unduly undermining efficiency and innovation?

One view of the financial crisis of 2007–09 has been that it illustrates the failure of the market-driven view of economic activity. In this view, the past decades of liberalizing markets, removing regulatory restrictions, and trusting markets to discipline themselves have had the unintended consequence of destabilizing the financial system.

A companion view is that one can best understand how markets act in terms of behavioral phenomena—like herd behavior—where market participants all move in the same direction in waves of pessimism and optimism. And indeed, if one had to describe market behavior in terms of bubbles and collapses, this turns out to be a very useful description. But there is an important distinction to be made between description and explanation. The notion of herd behavior or "animal spirits" carries with it little, if any, positive prescription for policy.

A contrasting view is an analytical market-driven view that asks what the specific market failures were that led to the crisis, and paves the way for thinking about regulatory solutions that can address these failures. We argue in this essay that such an analytical view also provides a better positive explanation of the financial crisis.

The set of institutions that today provide the architecture for the U.S. financial system—the Federal Reserve System (Fed), the Securities Exchange Commission (SEC), the Federal Deposit Insurance Corporation (FDIC), and the Commodity Futures Trading Commission—all emerged over time in response to events, most often to past crises. Regulatory institutions that survive today exist because they turned out to be useful. They are seen to have contributed to the stability and growth of the U.S. financial markets for many decades. There were many other institutions that did not meet this test, either because they were ill-conceived from the beginning or because financial innovation rendered them obsolete.

Today, there is a strong desire to reform the surviving institutions, and there is some urgency to do so because of the enormous costs to society associated with their manifest failure in the recent financial crisis. In this chapter, we document the market failures that characterized that crisis and then develop a sensible set of policy responses to reform the regulatory landscape.

The first section of this discussion reviews some of the historical precedents, panics, and banking crises that led to the present financial and economic environment and that shaped the current regulatory system.

The second section describes the recent financial crisis in terms of specific market failures as they relate to the following:

—the excessive risk-taking incentives of financial institutions when government guarantees are not priced or are mispriced;

—the regulatory focus on individual, rather than the systemic, risk of financial firms;

—opacity of financial firms and markets that created externalities from failures of individual firms; and

—the likelihood of "runs" in the shadow banking system, which relies heavily on uninsured short-term funding.

In the third section, we lay out some principles of regulation that address these failures. Specifically, we propose the following regulation to address these issues:

—Government guarantees in the system (for example, deposit insurance, too-big-to-fail status, and implicit subsidies to hybrid financial intermediaries, such as the government-sponsored enterprises [GSEs]), need to be priced to align the risk-taking incentives of financial firms.

—The systemic risk associated with actions of individual financial institutions needs to be priced, that is, firms need to be forced to internalize the costs of the negative externalities imposed by their actions on the system as a whole.

—Arguably, the leading candidate for the bottleneck that emerged in the financial system was the over-the-counter (OTC) market for derivatives; we argue for much greater transparency in this market.

—A key aspect of the crisis centered on runs in the wholesale funding markets (asset-backed commercial paper, repurchase agreements, unsecured commercial paper, and unsecured interbank lending). We argue for the imposition of liquidity requirements for financial institutions that are similar in spirit to the way capital requirements are imposed.

The last section illustrates, through a series of examples, that these principles are as relevant for emerging markets as they are to the global wholesale markets.


## Lessons from Past Crises

If one focuses for the moment on the United States during the twentieth century, it may come as a surprise to find that it has suffered a number of significant financial crises. Among them were the Panic of 1907, a severe contraction in 1921, the banking panic of the 1930s and the Great Depression, the failure of the Continental Illinois Bank and Trust Company in 1984, the savings and loan crisis of the 1980s, and the Long-Term Capital Management crisis in 1998. We discuss several of these to illustrate the relationship between market failure and financial regulation.

Table 2-1. *Description of Five Financial Crises in the United States during the Twentieth Century*[a]

| Crisis | Event | Market failure | Solution | Success? |
|---|---|---|---|---|
| Panic of 1907 | Losses due to speculation; bank run due to links across players | Uncertainty about bank insolvency and lack of liquidity | Creation of Federal Reserve and lender of last resort | Did not deal with uncertainty issue and thus bank runs |
| Great Depression | Huge macroeconomic shock, caused large losses at banks nationwide | Uncertainty about bank firm insolvency led to massive runs | Creation of FDIC and deposit insurance coupled with bank regulation | Served well for about fifty years before becoming antiquated |
| Continental Illinois (1984) | Losses due to concentrated exposure, lost access to funding | Relied on wholesale, as opposed to retail, funding | Bailout and creation of TBTF designation | Gave TBTF special status without any cost; ignored wholesale funding |
| Savings and loan crisis (1980s) | Losses throughout system due to risk shifting on the part of banks | Mispriced government guarantee created misaligned incentives | Bailout and the creation in 1991 of risk-based deposit insurance | From 1996 to 2006, premiums no longer collected due to funds being well capitalized |
| LTCM (1998) | Large hedge fund ran aground | Too interconnected to fail | Negotiated unwind | Ignored LCFI mantra |

Source: Authors.

a. Abbreviations: LCFI, large complex financial institutions; LTCM, Long-Term Capital Management; TBTF, too big to fail.

Table 2-1 provides a summary of our discussion. In brief, we argue that the financial regulation of the 1930s was successful to the extent that it addressed the main sources of market failure at the time, namely, uncertainty about which institutions were insolvent. Financial crises began to recur in the 1980s. In contrast to the 1930s, however, the problems that arose in the more recent period—runs in the wholesale funding market, excessive risk shifting, and legal barriers to winding down institutions—were not repaired by regulatory responses. In hindsight, some of these regulatory failures sowed the seeds for the crisis of today, just as poor regulatory responses today could likely sow the seeds of crises tomorrow.

*Lesson One: The Panic of 1907*

The Panic of 1907 was triggered in the "curbside" stock market that was organized outside of the formal confines of the New York Stock Exchange.[1] Investors tried to corner the market in United Copper Company by executing a short squeeze. Their scheme failed, and the price of United Copper plummeted. The same investors were also heavily involved with a number of banks and brokerages. When the United Copper play collapsed, it raised concerns about the safety of the banks that had lent money to back their scheme. The panic spread and led to pressure on other banks, forcing a number of banks to close their doors and suspend operations.

The problem that faced the banks and financial markets more broadly was the inherent contradiction of fractional reserve banking. All of the institutions involved in the panic were engaged in intermediation of one form or another, with less than 100 percent reserves. When depositors became concerned and demanded their money back, even solvent financial institutions found their cash and gold reserves insufficient to meet demand. Drained of cash, they were forced to shut their doors. The institutions that had evolved endogenously to address the problems of temporary liquidity shortages were bank clearinghouse associations that pooled resources to provide liquidity in times of stress and performed many of the functions of a central bank.[2] However, two problems emerged in the Panic of 1907. The first was that private clearinghouse associations also faced the risk of default. The second was that some companies, notably the trust companies in New York, were not allowed to be members of the clearinghouse associations due to the internecine rivalry between commercial banks and trust companies.

There are many important lessons to be derived from the Panic of 1907. First, fractional reserve banking is inherently precarious. Second, information on solvency (or lack thereof) of financial institutions is incredibly valuable but extremely difficult to gather, and at the time, no institution existed to provide it. Finally, a lender of last resort for solvent but illiquid institutions is needed for financial stability, but the private provision of that liquidity through the clearing-house associations was ineffective when it was most needed.

In May 1908 Congress passed the Aldrich Vreeland Act that created something called the National Monetary Commission, chaired by Senator Nelson Aldrich, whose mission was to study the underlying causes of the Panic of 1907 and develop proposals to make such events less likely in the future. The final report of the National Monetary Commission was published on January 11,

1. The best recent account of this episode is Bruner and Carr (2007).
2 . See Gorton (1985).

1911. For nearly two years, legislators debated the proposal, and it was not until December 22, 1913, that Congress passed the Federal Reserve Act. The bill was signed by President Woodrow Wilson on December 22, 1913, creating the Federal Reserve System.

The Federal Reserve has evolved over time and periodically has been severely challenged, notably in the 1930s and in the crisis of 2007–09. But it has quite successfully served one of the critical purposes for which it was created, that is, the need for a credible lender of last resort facility. This was only a partial solution, however, since it failed to resolve the information problem of consumers who had to decide whether or not to join a run on a bank in the first place. It took the banking panics of the 1930s to focus additional attention on sources of instability other than illiquidity.

## Lesson Two: The Banking Panics of the 1930s

There were three separate waves of banking panics during the 1930s—in 1930, 1931, and early 1933. The economic forces at work in creating and perpetuating the Great Depression have been much discussed and debated. We will not repeat those issues here except to note that there is a general consensus that the contractionary monetary policies that the Federal Reserve Board pursued at the time were a contributing factor to the banking crisis of the early 1930s.[3]

The prices of goods and services in the United States fell by approximately 25 percent between 1929 and 1933. This led to debt deflation, a phenomenon by which the collateral underlying loans shrink in value, causing the real burden of debt to rise and leading the economy to spiral further downward. In a parallel with the recent financial crisis, the collapse of the real estate bubble in the second half of the 1920s was arguably a factor contributing to the 1929 stock market crash and added materially to the solvency stresses imposed on the banks. The debt deflation of 1929–33 and the contemporaneous soaring of unemployment rates made it extremely difficult for homeowners to repay their debts. As borrowers were increasingly unable to make their payments, the underlying value of banks' assets fell, many banks were unable to meet the needs of their depositors, listed bank stocks plummeted, and a lack of confidence in the remaining banks led to a general state of panic (Bernanke 2000).

By March 1933, as Franklin D. Roosevelt took office, there was a full-fledged banking panic and cries for reform of the banking system. The responses to those pressures could have been many—for example, nationalizing the banks or relaxing restrictions on bank mergers or interstate banking (and the latter would have led to a highly concentrated banking system)—all of them solutions that had been adopted elsewhere and all actively debated at the time.

---

3. See Friedman and Schwartz (1971); Meltzer (2003, 2004).

The immediate response to the panic was to declare a "bank holiday" in order to determine, as had been the case in 1907, whether individual banks were solvent, illiquid, or liquid enough to reopen. This helped to calm the system but only restored the status quo of the post-1907 world. The fundamental market failure still existed. Banks made money by engaging in risky intermediation. Consumers had no easy way of assessing that risk, leaving intact the possibility of panics and bank runs.

The policy innovation that addressed this problem was the Banking Act of 1933, which created the Federal Deposit Insurance Corporation to provide credible government insurance for individual bank deposits and which effectively dealt with the problem of retail bank runs. The Glass-Steagall provisions of the Banking Act separated investment banks from commercial banks, in an effort to insulate depositors' savings from being used to finance high-risk investments in the financial markets. Firms that already engaged in both commercial and investment banking activities, such as the J.P. Morgan Bank, were forced to break up into commercial banks (in this case, what became the Morgan Guaranty Trust Company of New York) and investment banks (in this case, Morgan Stanley and Company). The Banking Act further stipulated that interest not be paid on demand deposits in commercial banks; those seeking returns would have to use less liquid savings deposits or securities.

The creation of the FDIC was arguably the most successful policy response to the banking crisis of the 1930s. In fact, the FDIC resulted from an amendment to the Banking Act of 1933 and had been opposed by President Franklin Roosevelt and many leading bankers in the big U.S. money centers. Nevertheless, this one institutional innovation was responsible for calming the fears of depositors and ending retail bank runs. Its creation was followed by many decades of relative stability in the financial system.

The Banking Act of 1933 required that all banks that were members of the Federal Reserve System have their deposits insured, up to a monetary limit, by the FDIC. Nonmember banks could also be covered, subject to approval by the insurer. Insured banks were required to pay premiums covering their insurance, based on their deposit size. Within six months of the creation of the FDIC, 97 percent of all commercial bank deposits were covered by insurance.

The FDIC has been a highly successful institution because it solved a well-defined problem: uncertainty about the solvency of the banks among retail depositors. More important, it did so in a way that acknowledged the contradictions and risks inherent in fractional reserve banking by making those responsible for managing the risks—the banks themselves—pay for insuring against them. These costs were passed through to bank borrowers, time depositors, and investors. Judged by the results, this was a remarkably successful piece of regulation. It stabilized the industry. Bank runs disappeared, and the number of bank failures dropped to an extremely low level compared with prior decades.

The other important regulatory innovation of the 1930s comprised the Securities Act of 1933 and the Securities Exchange Act of 1934. The main intention of this legislation was to ensure that investors receive significant (or "material") information concerning securities being offered for public sale and to redress market misbehavior. The objective was to "shine a bright light" on financial information so that investors could make informed decisions. To underscore the need for reliable information, the 1933 and 1934 acts required that public financial information be verified by independent auditors using standardized accounting rules. These rules gave a major boost to the efficiency and transparency of financial markets and deserve much credit for stimulating the flow of capital in the U.S. economy.

The important thing to note about both of these seminal regulatory innovations is that they were not attacks on the free market or on capitalism—something that could not be taken for granted since, at the time, the spread of socialism and communism was gaining momentum, and other options might well have seemed appealing. What these reforms recognized was the need for information and confidence to make the markets function better. These were attributes that only public policy could require of market participants and then provide to markets at large. The regulatory reforms also constituted a bet on the decisionmaking of the individual investor. Given enough transparency, investors were believed capable of making smart and profitable long-term decisions. These were intelligent, effective pro-market regulations that worked well for many decades.

## Lesson Three: Continental Illinois and Too-Big-To-Fail Status

From the 1930s until the 1980s, the U.S. banking system functioned fairly smoothly.[4] The lessons learned in the early part of the twentieth century and the institutions created to deal with the fundamental market failures and information frictions—the Fed, the FDIC, and the SEC (bolstered by the Investment Company Act of 1940)—led to a long period of relative tranquility in banking and financial markets. Bank failures slowed to a trickle as bank regulation focused on maintaining adequate capital and controlling risk.

There were bank failures to be sure, but the FDIC had a well-tested approach to the problem. When failure was unavoidable, the regulatory machinery worked as designed: either the regulators sold the bank successfully ("purchase and assumption"), or they liquidated the institution, made good on deposit insurance promises, and wiped out the uninsured depositors and other creditors. This set of procedures imposed a discipline on the banking system that seemed to work very well.

---

4. The following discussion about Continental Illinois relies heavily on FDIC (1997).

In 1982, however, federal regulators decided to close the Oklahoma-based Penn Square Bank, a $436-million institution that specialized in oil and gas sector loans. Penn Square originated large volumes of loans to the historically risky exploration sector of the U.S. energy industry, which began to suffer as energy prices fell in the recession of the early 1980s. The seventh-largest bank in the United States, Continental Illinois Bank and Trust Company, had invested aggressively alongside or through Penn Square and booked a large volume of Penn Square–originated loans. Continental Illinois had made many other loans to the energy sector and, at the same time, had expanded its lending to developing countries to help them finance debts incurred in the energy crises of the 1970s. In 1982 Mexico was forced to renegotiate its debt, triggering the less-developed-country debt crisis involving hundreds of bank loan syndications.

While many other U.S. commercial banks followed the same lending strategy in the late 1970s, Continental Illinois's credit exposures were compounded by a funding strategy that was unusual at the time. Traditionally, banks funded growth in their lending activities by attracting larger volumes of savings from retail depositors. Continental Illinois, however, had a limited retail presence, due in part to federal and local banking regulations that limited the number of banking outlets it was permitted to have. Consequently, Continental Illinois depended heavily on funding itself in the wholesale money markets. Indeed, by 1981 it was sourcing most of its funding through federal funds and by selling short-term certificates of deposit on the wholesale money markets. Only 20 percent of Continental Illinois's funding came from traditional retail deposits in Chicago.

Continental Illinois had pursued an aggressive growth strategy and had assumed a great deal of concentrated risk. When the energy sector turned sour and the less developed countries rescheduled, Continental Illinois was unusually vulnerable to the views of the wholesale funding markets. In 1984 investors and creditors lost confidence in the bank, and in a precursor to the crisis of 2007–08, Continental Illinois was quickly shut out of its usual sources of funding in the domestic and Eurodollar markets.

In May 1984 Continental Illinois experienced what the FDIC described as a high-speed electronic bank run. To stem the panic, regulatory agencies and the banking industry arranged billions of dollars in emergency funding for the bank. The fear was that a failure of Continental Illinois would undermine the entire banking system. More than 2,300 banks had correspondent accounts with Continental Illinois. Unlike the uninsured retail depositor runs of the 1930s, this time it was an uninsured wholesale depositor run. In an extremely controversial decision, the FDIC tried to stop the run by extending its guarantee beyond its retail deposit limits to cover uninsured depositors and creditors, as well. This was the beginning of the notion that some banks should be considered too big (or too interconnected) to fail.

The FDIC's emergency help was followed by a package of permanent measures, making Continental Illinois the largest bank in U.S. banking history to be rescued by government agencies. Unable to find a takeover partner, the FDIC ended up owning more than 80 percent of the bank. The Continental Illinois board was replaced, senior management was fired, the bank was restructured and later floated in a public offering, and subsequently was acquired by Bank of America. The FDIC's share of the bill to rescue Continental Illinois was later calculated to be $1.1 billion.

The Continental Illinois story provides a classic example of how a sharp drop in confidence can lead counterparties in the wholesale markets suddenly to withdraw funding from a wounded bank, spinning the institution into a liquidity crisis as potentially fatal as any nineteenth-century run on a bank by retail depositors—in this case, a liquidity crisis triggered by a suspected insolvency problem that turned out to be true.

It should have been a warning call that systemic risk can build up quickly in a credit expansion cycle and needs to be appropriately priced and regulated. But that was not to be. Continental Illinois should have been the canary in the coal mine. It demonstrated that the regulatory system crafted in the 1930s needed updating to account for the development of massive wholesale banking markets. Instead, and despite many warning voices, the problem was ignored.

### Lesson Four: The Savings and Loan Crisis

The most serious postwar crisis in the U.S. banking sector was the savings and loan (S&L) crisis of the late 1980s. It is often blamed (with at least some justification) on the more lax regulatory environment that evolved during the Reagan administration.[5] That is not the entire story, however, and the S&L crisis remains an episode that contains valuable lessons for the crisis of 2007–09.

Savings and loan institutions, as distinct from commercial banks, were another product of the Great Depression. They were created to serve the public policy goal of encouraging home ownership. The Federal Home Loan Bank Act of 1932 created the Federal Home Loan Bank System to provide liquidity and low-cost financing for S&Ls. There were twelve regional Home Loan Banks; these were owned by their members and were under the supervision of the Federal Home Loan Bank Board (FHLBB). The National Housing Act of 1934 created the Federal Savings and Loan Insurance Corporation (FSLIC) to provide federal deposit insurance for S&Ls, similar to what the FDIC provided for commercial banks. In contrast to the FDIC, which was established as an independent agency, the FSLIC was placed under the authority of the FHLBB. In retrospect, the FHLBB carried far heavier political baggage than did the FDIC.

5 . White (1991).

For decades, the FHLBB's examination, supervision, and regulatory capabilities were relatively poorly developed, in part because S&Ls had a narrowly defined financial intermediation role and not much scope for expanding it. S&Ls took in savings on which they paid low interest rates and lent the money at marginally higher interest rates on thirty-year fixed-rate mortgages. This model all began to change with the accelerating inflation of the 1970s, when interest rates soared. S&L deposits began to flee in pursuit of higher returns, and even when Congress lifted caps on deposit rates, the S&Ls were still being squeezed on the other end by their legacy portfolios of thirty-year fixed-rate mortgages. It was a classic maturity mismatch. They needed to find other sources of income.

In response, the FHLBB began loosening its regulations. It allowed the thrifts to begin issuing adjustable-rate mortgages. Congress also encouraged diversification and explicitly authorized the thrifts to engage in consumer lending and investments in commercial real estate. Accordingly, both federal and state thrift regulators began relaxing restrictions on the their asset allocation options, easing safety and soundness regulation, lowering capital requirements, and changing accounting rules to make it easier for S&Ls to meet their net worth requirements. All of these changes helped the thrift industry to grow dramatically. Between 1980 and 1986, 492 new thrifts were chartered in the United States. Taken together, it was a recipe for disaster.

Things began to change when inflation was brought under control early in the Reagan administration and a major recession took hold. Oil prices fell to levels that made many earlier investments unprofitable. An array of tax benefits for real estate investments was eliminated, and that made many earlier projects unprofitable. Much of the banking growth between 1983 and 1985 had been in commercial real estate lending.

By 1985 it had become clear that the thrift industry faced serious trouble. Enough S&Ls had folded or were in danger of folding that the FSLIC was insolvent. Efforts to recapitalize the FSLIC in 1986 and 1987 were bitterly opposed by the industry, which lobbied aggressively with members of Congress. Thrift failures increased during 1987 and into 1988, but the insolvency of the FSLIC meant that rescuing troubled thrifts would cost more than the FSLIC had available in its insurance fund. As a result, the regulators could not intervene in S&Ls that had more in liabilities than assets. This left many insolvent thrifts still in business. These "zombie" banks had incentives to take even greater risks in the hope that they could improve their outcomes, and many did so using an early version of brokered deposits by returns—chasing clients who hoped to be bailed out if things went wrong.

The crisis in the S&L industry was finally acknowledged and resolved after the inauguration of George H.W. Bush in 1989. Congress passed the Financial Institutions Reform Recovery and Enforcement Act of 1989, which abolished the FHLBB and shifted regulation of S&Ls to the Office of Thrift Supervision (OTS), transferred the thrifts' deposit insurance function from the FSLIC to the FDIC, and reinstituted many of the regulatory provisions that had been weakened during the previous decade. In turn, the 1989 reform act created the Resolution Trust Corporation to liquidate or restructure the insolvent S&Ls.

There are several lessons to be learned from the S&L mess. The first is that when regulatory institutions have outlived their usefulness or have been rendered obsolete by market developments, it is not enough just to eliminate the boundaries without consideration of the risks that are being created. This was the case with the thrift industry, which had been created and developed with specific goals in mind.

Another lesson is that regulators can easily be captured by the industry they regulate. This was clearly the case with FHLBB. The S&L crisis reinforces the point that moral hazard is an important and ever-present issue. It is critical to close insolvent, insured financial institutions promptly in order to minimize potential losses to the deposit insurance fund (or the taxpayer, in general) and to ensure a more efficient financial marketplace—zombie financial intermediaries extract a heavy price on financial market efficiency. Finally, resolution of failing financial institutions requires that the deposit insurance fund be strongly capitalized with reserves based on real risk assessments.

## Lesson Five: Long-Term Capital Management

An episode that deserves mention in any litany of financial crises is the collapse of Long-Term Capital Management (LTCM), the storied hedge fund that had grown so quickly between 1994 and 1998, and was so interconnected, that it was thought to be a systemically risky institution.

In 1998 LTCM collapsed in a "liquidity event." A sudden disappearance of liquidity from credit markets—associated with a Russian default on external debt on August 15, 1998—triggered a global "flight to quality." It is interesting to ponder why this enormous liquidity event did not lead to a global financial meltdown.

As it became clear that the magnitude of LTCM's liquidity problem was enormous and that unwinding its positions could put severe strains on financial markets, the president of the Federal Reserve Bank of New York, with Alan Greenspan's blessing, called a meeting of all of LTCM's major banks and prime brokers to get them to work on a cooperative solution to the problem. Reluctant banks were forcibly dragged into the workout. That is the formula that the Fed and U.S. Treasury were trying to reprise on the fateful weekend in October 2008 when they met to discuss the fate of Lehman Brothers. In 1998 what they did worked. There was an orderly insolvency and dissolution of LTCM without undue harm to the markets or the banks most directly involved.

The resolution of LTCM and the unwinding of its complicated positions were orderly because they were carried out by LTCM itself with the support of the other major financial firms and the New York Fed. The lessons of the LTCM collapse were clearly articulated in a 1999 report entitled "Hedge Funds, Leverage and the Lessons of Long-Term Capital Management."[6] It was signed by Robert Rubin, Alan Greenspan, Arthur Levitt, and Brooksley Born.

One lesson the report clearly delivers is that procedures for unwinding complicated systemic firms needed urgent attention. The report devotes an entire appendix to a discussion of the inconsistencies in the U.S. Bankruptcy Code that interfered with a private market resolution of LTCM's debt problems and derivatives contracts. It describes the extent to which existing bankruptcy procedures are not, in fact, conducive to private market solutions in complex situations involving both standard loan contracts and derivatives contracts. These were clearly failings that needed to be fixed.

The key LTCM lesson was that better mechanisms were needed for the resolution of large, systemic firms. Absent that, and absent methods for penalizing institutions for accumulating systemic risk, the system would be stuck with firms that are both too big and too interconnected to fail and to resolve at an acceptable cost to the public. Unfortunately, regulators believed that hedge funds might be the type of firm to get into trouble in a financial crisis; but in the crisis of 2007–09, it turned out to be investment banks and universal banks themselves, many of which were, in fact, running "in-house" hedge funds.

## Market Failures of the Financial Crisis of 2007–09

Financial crises have many common features. In the background real economy, there is usually the presence of an asset price "bubble" (or asset price inflation, for purists), a corresponding credit boom, and large capital inflows into that economy.[7] However, these characteristics are necessary but not sufficient for a financial crisis to develop. The severity of the crisis depends crucially on the underlying financial sector's exposure to these conditions and, in fact, the overall market's uncertainty about the financial sector's exposure to them. A key role of financial regulation is to put limits on financial institutions so as to limit this exposure. While there are many reasons for the relative calm of the U.S. financial system during the fifty years after the Great Depression, many analysts continue to give credit to the financial regulation that was enacted at that time.

As described in the preceding section, the banking acts of the 1930s solved the uncertainty problem that led to bank runs by providing deposit insurance

---

6. See President's Working Group (1999).
7. See, for example, Reinhart and Rogoff (2008).

through the creation of the FDIC. Depositors no longer had to run on insured banks because the government guaranteed deposits up to certain maximums. Of course, it was well understood that deposit insurance creates moral hazard—that is, an incentive for banks to undertake greater risk than they would otherwise without the insurance. Regulators and policymakers understood that deposit insurance could lead to excessive risk taking, so they set up a number of counteracting barriers:

—Banks would have to pay to be part of the deposit insurance system. So, at least, on an ex ante basis, regulators took into account the cost of the insurance. Deposit insurance was limited in magnitude per account, thus restricting the size of the banks.

—The risk-taking activities of banks were ring fenced to the extent that there was a separation of the commercial and, presumably more risky, investment banking activities.

—Enhanced supervision and winding-down provisions for individual banks generally centered on required minimum capital requirements, which served as a buffer against the risk-shifting incentive arising from deposit insurance.

So what happened in the 1980s that kept deposit insurance but took away these protections?

There is considerable debate about this issue, but the general consensus is that technological and other innovations changed the nature of banking—and therefore competition—in the financial sector.[8] Some of these innovations included the development of the automated teller machine, which reduced geographic ties between banks and depositors; the proliferation of money market funds and cash management accounts by broker-dealers and asset managers outside the banking system; and an increase in the types of communication channels, further reducing the ties between local bankers and depositors. In other words, the traditional lines of business of banks no longer enjoyed their previously protected status.

Keeley (1990) uses the increase in bank competition as an explanation for the S&L crisis described earlier. Prior to these technological changes, banks and thrifts enjoyed monopolistic advantages so that their bank charters had "franchise value." But once this disappeared, the value to risk shifting and exploiting the guarantees of deposit insurance increased. In general, there is ample evidence of risk shifting related to deregulation, stepped-up banking competition, and the S&L crisis.[9]

Around the same time, the institutional side of banking also changed dramatically. There was tremendous growth in the so-called shadow banking

---

8. See Kroszner (2000); Kroszner and Strahan (2007).

9. See, for example, Saunders, Strock, and Travlos (1990); Cordell, MacDonald, and Wohar (1993); Kroszner and Strahan (1996); Hovakimian and Kane (2000).

system—that is, financial institutions outside the traditional banking system that provide very similar services.[10] The shadow banking system includes derivatives—futures, options, swaps, repurchase agreements, and money market funds—securitization of loans in the mortgage, corporate, and household sectors, and an increasing emphasis on public equity and bond markets. As an illustration, the amount of assets of the financial sector held by depository institutions dropped from 60 percent in 1950 to less than 30 percent in 2006.[11]

Kroszner and Melick (2009) provide a description of two financial systems, one being the traditional model of banking, the other a modern version of banking.[12] In the old model, an individual deposits funds in a bank. The bank then uses these funds to lend to corporations or individuals. The bank pays interest on the short-term deposits using interest earned on the loans. Concern over the funding mismatch and potential solvency issues of the bank are addressed through the bank's asset-liability management process and the individual's deposits being insured. This insurance, however, comes at a cost, both in terms of premiums paid, restrictions on the bank's actions, and the requirement that a fraction of the funds be held as capital.

In the new model, the same individual now provides funds to a money market fund. This fund buys commercial paper issued by a special purpose vehicle of the bank backed by asset-backed securities. These asset-backed securities are made up of the same loans described above in the old model of banking. The money market fund rolls over the commercial paper periodically as it becomes due. In the overwhelming majority of the cases, the credit risk of the loans underlying the asset-backed securities had embedded recourse back to the banks (effectively, "securitization without risk transfer").[13] On the surface, this means that the economics underlying these two banking models are almost identical.

Yet the risk-sharing mechanics and pricing are quite different. The rate offered by money market funds is invariably higher than that for equally liquid funds at checking and savings accounts of banks. Are these higher rates due to greater efficiency? Or are the rate differentials due to credit risk and the lack of "deposit-like" insurance? Or are they due to implicit government guarantees in a framework in which these guarantees are not priced, bank actions are much less restricted, and at most, only one-tenth the capital is required for off-balance-sheet financing via the special-purpose vehicles? One set of arguments focuses on efficiency (welfare gains), and the other set of arguments focuses on risk shifting (inefficient wealth transfers).

---

10. Gorton (2009).
11. Kroszner and Melick (2009).
12. See also Acharya, Schnabl, and Suarez (2009); Gorton (2009).
13. See Acharya, Schnabl, and Suarez (2009).

Taking this background into account, we now describe the four market failures that we believe triggered and amplified the financial crisis of 2007–09.

## Risk-Taking Incentives of Financial Institutions

Given their inherently high leverage and the ease with which the risk profile of financial assets can be altered, banks and financial institutions have incentives to take on excessive risks. Ordinarily, market mechanisms would be expected to price risks correctly and thereby ensure that risk-taking in the economy is at efficient levels. However, there are two factors that have impeded such efficient outcomes.

First, with the repeal of most protections from the Banking Act of the 1933, the only remaining protection against risk shifting is capital requirements. If the guarantees are mispriced, financial firms have an incentive to skirt capital requirements and take excessive risk. One way of telling the story of the 2007–09 crisis is that financial institutions managed to exploit loopholes in the regulatory system and built up large amounts of tail risk on the economy, particularly tied to residential real estate, with little or no underlying capital.

The second mechanism that induces excessive risk taking is a failure of corporate governance involving shareholders and employees. The fact that financial institutions have become large and increasingly complex and opaque in their activities has weakened external governance that operates through capital markets (accurate prices), the market for corporate control (takeovers), and boards. Coincident with this, and to some extent a corollary to it, has been the fact that financial risks at these institutions are now increasingly concentrated in the hands of a few "high-performance" profit-risk centers, which have an incentive to produce short-run imaginary profits at the expense of long-term risks (that is, "fake alpha").

At this point, we concentrate on what we consider to be the primary factor associated with the financial crisis, namely, the accordance of the numerous government guarantees in the system—most notably deposit insurance, the implicit guarantee of "too big to fail," and the "subsidies" provided to government-sponsored enterprises (GSEs) like Fannie Mae and Freddie Mac. Together, these imply that the vast majority of liabilities in the U.S. financial system were subject to some form of safety net, with profound implications for efficiency in capital allocation, incentives, and the structure of financial intermediation.

At the same time, it is important to note that the fact that banks received "free" or underpriced government insurance does not necessarily imply excess risk taking on their part. If the franchise value of their enterprise exceeds the benefits to risk shifting, then there might be very little effect associated with moral hazard from the insurance. The possibility of material shareholder losses, and the limits imposed on banks via Glass-Steagall, did contribute to relative calm for fifty or so years after the 1930s. However, once the Glass-Steagall separation between commercial and investment banking was lifted (steadily since the 1970s), and competition dramatically increased (within and across states in the United States as well as globally), the only real protection for the financial system came from adequate capital requirements.

There were two consequences resulting from increased competition and the erosion of profits underlying the traditional lines of business of banks. First, it meant banks increasingly moved into businesses highlighting noninterest income, such as trading and fees. Second, and more important, it increased the relative value of risk shifting, since bank charter values had been eroded by deregulation. Because mispriced guarantees had effectively removed the market discipline component of governance normally reserved for creditors, risk shifting was particularly easy to do.

In the crisis of 2007–09 financial firms managed to shift risk by exploiting loopholes in regulatory capital requirements to take an undercapitalized, $2- to 3-trillion, highly leveraged, one-way asymmetric bet on the economy, particularly tied to residential real estate but also to commercial real estate and other consumer credit exposures. This bet was taken in four distinct ways.

First, the banks funded their portfolios of risky loans via off-balance-sheet vehicles (structured investment vehicles and conduits). These vehicles required about one-tenth the amount of capital of the same exposures held on the balance sheet, yet in 95 percent of the cases, the credit risk effectively had full recourse back to the sponsoring institutions.[14] Acharya and others (2010, figure 3.7) provide evidence of the remarkable growth in asset-backed commercial paper in the pre-crisis period.

Second, financial institutions bought "underpriced" protection from monoline insurers and AIG, in the sense that banks were able to pocket the difference between the spread on the AAA tranches of the securitization instruments and the monolines' premiums. Because neither AIG nor the monolines had much capital backing this insurance, and certainly not enough in a systemic crisis, the risk again was effectively shifted back to the financial institutions through the counterparty risk of the insurers.

Third, financial institutions made outright purchases of AAA tranches of nonprime securities, which were treated as having low credit risk and zero liquidity and funding risk. Together the broker-dealers, the GSEs, and the banks held more than half of the $1.6 trillion of these securities outstanding.[15] Table 2-2 shows these holdings for financial institutions in 2007. This is the exact opposite of the key objective of securitization, in which the safest parts of credit risk are

14. See Acharya, Schnabl, and Suarez (2009) for an anatomy of asset-backed commercial paper conduits.

15. See Acharya and Richardson (2009a).

Table 2-2. *Holdings of Mortgage-Related Debt by Financial Institutions, 2007*[a]

Billions of dollars, except as indicated

| Institution | Loans | HELOC | Agency MBSs | Non-agency AAA | Subordinated CDOs | Non-subordinated CDOs | Total | Percent |
|---|---|---|---|---|---|---|---|---|
| Banks and thrifts | 2,020 | 869 | 852 | 383 | 90 | . . . | 4,212 | 39 |
| GSEs and Federal Home Loan Bank | 444 | . . . | 741 | 308 | . . . | . . . | 1,493 | 14 |
| Broker-dealers | . . . | . . . | 49 | 100 | 130 | 24 | 303 | 3 |
| Financial guarantors | . . . | 62 | . . . | . . . | 100 | . . . | 162 | 2 |
| Insurance companies | . . . | . . . | 856 | 125 | 65 | 24 | 1,070 | 10 |
| Overseas | . . . | . . . | 689 | 413 | 45 | 24 | 1,172 | 11 |
| Other | 461 | 185 | 1,175 | 307 | 46 | 49 | 2,268 | 21 |
| Total | 2,925 | 1,116 | 4,362 | 1,636 | 476 | 121 | 10,680 | |
| Percent | 27 | 10 | 41 | 15 | 4 | 1 | . . . | . . . |

Source: Krishnamurthy (2008).

a. CDOs, collateralized debt obligations; HELOC, home equity line of credit; MBSs, mortgage-backed securities; GSEs, government-sponsored enterprises.

meant to be transferred from the financial sector to institutional investors and the capital markets at large.

Fourth, in August 2004 investment banks successfully lobbied the SEC to amend the net capitalization rule of the Securities Exchange Act of 1934. This amendment allowed a voluntary method of computing deductions to net capital for large broker-dealers. It permitted the investment banks to use internal models to calculate net capital requirements to market risk and derivative-related credit risk, placing them on an equal competitive footing with universal banks of Europe operating under the Basel II Accord. The net impact was essentially to double the leverage applied by investment banks.

There is strong evidence in the literature for the existence of mispriced government guarantees and the consequences arising from these guarantees. In terms of the financial crisis of 2007–09, how did these guarantees contribute to market failures?

With respect to deposit insurance, as described earlier, there is some consensus that moral hazard played an important role in both initiating and prolonging the S&L crisis. As a logical consequence, substantial reforms were enacted to address this issue, notably the Federal Deposit Insurance Corporation Improvement Act of 1991. One of the major changes in setting FDIC premiums was to make them more risk based. In theory, the FDIC assesses higher rates on those institutions that pose greater risks to the insurance fund. In practice, however, if the deposit insurance fund is well capitalized (that is, 1.25 percent of reserves to total insured deposits), no premiums are assessed to those banks considered to be of the lowest-risk category. In fact, from 1996 to 2006, more than 90 percent of all banks paid very little in deposit insurance premiums.[16] Acharya and others (2010, figure 2.1) illustrate this point by showing a reserve ratio close to 1.25 percent for this period and a small increase in fund balances.

The S&L crisis implied the need for risk-based insurance premiums to be charged to banks. In what constitutes a significant regulatory failure, the risk-based method was not applied to the extent that 90 percent of the banks fell in a single risk bucket, and indeed no insurance premiums at all were charged to the majority of U.S. banks. This effectively meant that the United States was running a free deposit insurance system with little or no protection at all at the time Glass-Steagall was repealed, and commercial banks were free to engage in all forms of investment banking and trading.

At first glance, the moral hazard inherent in depository institutions was limited in scope, since deposits were only a limited fraction of the assets (and liabilities) of the U.S. financial system. However, since the majority of assets of the financial sector were held by a small number of large complex financial institutions (LCFIs), the market discipline provided by liability holders can be considered notionally similar to that provided by depositors given the presumptive too-big-to-fail (TBTF) guarantee. Since the 1984 bailout of Continental Illinois (described in the first section), the TBTF issue had been much discussed in regulatory and academic circles.[17] Even before the financial crisis of 2007–09 made the TBTF guarantee explicit, there was ample evidence that a TBTF policy was effectively in force and that it distorted market pricing for more than two decades before the onset of the crisis itself.[18]

The case of the GSEs—Fannie Mae and Freddie Mac—illustrates the key importance of moral hazard and government guarantees. Fannie Mae was founded in 1938 in the wake of the Depression to provide liquidity and aid to the mortgage market. It became a government-sponsored enterprise in 1968,

16. This issue was only partially addressed by the Federal Deposit Insurance Reform Act of 2005 to the extent that the ratio of reserves to total deposits covered a wider range for which premiums would be collected.

17. See Stern and Feldman (2004); Ennis and Malek (2005).

18. See, for example, the empirical evidence in O'Hara and Shaw (1990); Penas and Unal (2004); Morgan and Stiroh (2005).

and shortly after, Freddie Mac was formed to compete with Fannie Mae to create a more efficient secondary market for mortgages. Both were listed companies, with shares actively traded in the market. While not explicit and often denied, there was the presumption that both the guarantor function and debt of the GSEs had full backing of the U.S. government. Fannie and Freddie sharehold-ers could be wiped out under adverse circumstances, but their debt holders fully expected to be rescued at face value by the GSE relationship with the U.S. Treasury. Indeed, GSE debt generally was priced marginally above the prevail-ing treasury rate. U.S. institutional investors (like pension funds) and foreign investors (like China's central bank) were big players, chasing a few basis points of "free lunch" and fully expecting the implied Treasury Department backstop to kick in if times got tough. An excellent bet, as it turned out.

Consider the investment function of the GSEs. For every dollar of mortgage-backed securities (MBSs) purchased with equity, there was a large amount of debt issued to purchase additional MBSs.[19] The extraordinary point is the GSEs' access to very high leverage, given that they were investing in risky mortgage securities with questionable liquidity. This provides an idea of the size of the implicit government guarantee. In fact, the empirical literature has quantified the transfer from the taxpayer to the GSEs' bondholders and stockholders to be in many billions, even before the crisis ignited.[20]

Furthermore, it has been well documented that the investment portfolio of the GSEs also became riskier over time, as both Fannie Mae and Freddie Mac began to load up on nonprime mortgages under intense pressure from both the Clinton administration (through the Department of Housing and Urban Devel-opment under Secretaries Henry Cisneros and Andrew Cuomo) and by Con-gress, to better serve the political end of housing affordability for lower-income Americans. Though the available data are sparse and somewhat controversial—with some analysts arguing that the nonprime bets were much larger—it is clear that by the mid-2000s, at least 15 percent of GSE funds were invested in subprime mortgages.[21] In contrast to prime mortgages, however, they were not hedged using corresponding interest rate swaps, making them highly vulnerable.

In their recent study, Acharya and others (2010, figure 2.3) illustrate the size of the GSE mortgage portfolios, noting the subprime holdings in the years immediately before the crisis. With the lack of market discipline from debt hold-ers due to the government's guarantee, one would expect that the GSEs would invest in riskier assets to the extent possible. It is therefore not surprising that

19. For the book and market leverage ratios of the GSEs over the period of 1993 to 2007, see Acharya and others (2010, figure 2.2).

20. See Passmore (2005); Lucas and McDonald (2006).

21. See the congressional testimony of Edward Pinto (U.S. House 2008).

as nonprime mortgages took off, the GSEs shifted risk toward these assets. As creditors did not price the risk exposures of GSEs, given the implicit guarantee, and as equity holders allowed the risky bets to maximize their option value on the guarantee, the interests of effective claimants of GSEs—the taxpayers—were marginalized in the highly politicized corporate control environment of these public-private hybrid financial institutions.

## Systemic Risk of Financial Institutions

Over the preceding two decades, there had been tremendous, sometimes unrecognized, growth in the systemic risk arising from failures of financial institutions (LTCM case, described in the first section, is the prime example). There is in essence a negative externality on the system because the systemic cost of a financial institution's collapse—which can lead to failures of others, the freezing of capital markets, or both—is not fully internalized by that institution.

With mispriced guarantees and the repeal of Glass-Steagall, the only protection the financial system had from excessive risk-taking was prudential bank regulation, primarily through capital requirements aimed at constraining financial leverage and risk. The market failure here was that regulation should have been focused on such externalities so as to curb the risks to the financial sector and the economy at large. However, prudential regulation of the financial sector has focused not on systemic risk but rather on the individual institution's risk profile. This design is seriously flawed. Regulation that ignores externalities encourages financial institutions to pass their risks in an unfettered manner throughout the system and onto unregulated entities.

For instance, as they reduce their individual risks, financial institutions are rewarded with a lower capital requirement that gives them the license to originate more risk, possibly aggregate in nature. This new risk gets passed around in the system and creates a financial sector in which any individual institution's risk of failure appears low to the regulator, but it is either hidden in the unregulated sector or has combined to form an aggregate concern—in either case, it is systemic in nature. Instead of penalizing behavior that leads to excessive systemic risk, current financial regulation appears to be rewarding it.

As we have emphasized, in this crisis financial firms loaded up on assets with low volatility and high systemic risk (and therefore high expected returns). At the risk of repeating, the best example can be found in the many large financial intermediaries that ignored their own securitization business models by holding onto the nondiversifiable credit risk associated with the AAA tranches of securitized loan portfolios. Because little capital (typically 10 to 20 percent of nominal credit exposure) was attached to these bets—that is, the transactions were highly leveraged—it can be shown that their economic properties were those of writing an extreme out-of-the-money put option on the aggregate market.[22] It is well known that writing out-of-the-money put options produces large expected returns; this is why financial institutions engaged in the trade. Large expected returns, however, go hand in hand with large aggregate risk. There is no free lunch. This is why financial institutions got into so much trouble when the negative aggregate shock to the real estate market began in 2007. Consequently, the financial sector's capital buffer to protect underperforming loans in times of recession eroded almost instantaneously, leaving the sector with no capital protection for very weak portfolios.

The failure to focus on systemic risk, as opposed to individual institution risk, extends beyond prudential bank regulation. Specifically, there are several types of systemic risk that can be generated from the failure of a financial institution, especially during a financial crisis. Past crises also provide a guide here.

The first is counterparty risk. If a financial institution is highly interconnected to many other financial institutions, then its failure can have a ripple effect throughout the system. Consider the OTC derivatives market. The main reason for systemic risk in OTC markets is that bilaterally set collateral and margin requirements in OTC trading do not take account of the "counterparty risk externality" that each trade imposes on the rest of the system, thus allowing systemically important exposures to be built up without sufficient capital to mitigate associated risks.[23] The prime example in the current crisis is AIG, which built up $450 billion of one-sided credit default swap exposure on the so-called AAA tranches of securitized products. These positions were created with little or no capital support. Because all the trades were in the same direction, once the trades lost value, AIG's failure would inevitably propagate and amplify throughout the financial system.

Another example was the rating downgrade of monoline insurers that took place in the first six months of 2008. As the major rating agencies began to downgrade the monoline insurers during 2008, their guarantees lost their AAA backing, and thousands of municipal bonds and structured products were downgraded as a consequence. The downgrades, in turn, caused financial institutions to increase capital requirements as the losses on the insured securities were forced back onto their balance sheets. Furthermore, institutions had to rebalance portfolios now that some of their underlying bonds were no longer AAA rated, putting additional downward pressure on bond pricing.

And consider again the GSEs. As one of the largest investors in capital markets, the GSEs presented considerable counterparty risk to the system, similar in spirit to LTCM in the summer of 1998, as well as to the investment banks and some insurance companies during this current crisis. While often criticized for

22. See, for example, Coval, Jurek, and Stafford (2009).
23. See Acharya and Bisin (2009), who formalize the notion of counterparty risk externality.

not adequately hedging the interest rate exposure of their portfolios, the GSEs were nevertheless major participants in the interest rate swaps market. As was characteristic of other LCFIs, the GSEs increased their swaps and derivatives positions through the years; by 2007 the total notional amount of their swaps and OTC derivatives was $1.38 trillion and $523 billion, respectively.[24] Failure of GSEs would have led to a winding down of large quantities of swaps with the usual systemic consequences.

The list could go on. But whether it was a few punters speculating in the curbside market outside the New York Stock Exchange in October 1907 who happened also to be exposed to many banks, or the 1984 collapse of Continental Illinois with exposure to over 2,000 other banks, or a failing LTCM in August 1998 with more than $1.25 trillion in notional swap positions—making it the seventh-largest institution in notional derivatives—the warning signs should have been clear. The system cannot withstand the failure of a highly interconnected institution. In the oft-cited words of Mark Twain, "History doesn't repeat itself, but it does rhyme."

The foregoing discussion also points to the second way systemic risk can enter the market, namely, spillover risk that arises as one institution's trouble triggers liquidity spirals, leading to depressed asset prices and a hostile funding environment, pulling others down and thus leading to further price drops and funding illiquidity.[25] In a distressed market, you sell what you can sell as long as liquidity remains, regardless of the underlying asset quality. In the case of the GSEs, which owned such a large (and leveraged) portfolio of relatively illiquid MBSs, their failure would have led to a fire sale of these assets that would have infected the rest of the financial system, which was holding similar assets. To the extent that the MBS market is one of the world's largest debt markets, the fire sale could have brought other financial institutions down, similar to what actually happened with the subprime collateralized debt obligations (CDOs).

The third type of systemic risk is that financial institutions operating in the shadow banking system are subject to bank-like runs. The "new model" of banking relied heavily on the short-term wholesale funding market. For example, the volume of repo transactions soared from $2 trillion a day in 1997 to $6 trillion daily a decade later in 2007, and money market funds accumulated over $4 trillion in assets, compared with the $8 trillion in deposits in the banking sector. Since these funds were rolled over on a short-term basis, sudden fund withdrawals that occur because of uncertainty about a financial institution's health can ironically cause the institution to fail. Short-term liabilities were funding longer-term, less liquid assets that the institutions could not unload in an orderly way.

24. See Acharya and Richardson (2009b, figure 4.5).
25. Brunnermeier and Pedersen (2009).

These are the same issues that exist in "old-fashioned" banking and are handled inside the bank using conventional asset and liability management—except here, the problem exists across institutional boundaries, and there is no asset-liability management process that transcends them.

When a particular institution that is engaged in maturity mismatch fails in this manner, uncertainty about the health of similar institutions can lead to an indiscriminate run, and otherwise well-capitalized firms can face withdrawals of their short-term liabilities, in turn causing a systemic crisis. While many observers point to the fall of Lehman Brothers, the forced sale of Merrill Lynch, and near failure of Morgan Stanley—and possibly Goldman Sachs—as the most telling illustration of runs in this crisis, there are others. Most notably, the collapse of Lehman Brothers and the value of its short-term debt caused the largest money market fund, the Prime Reserve Fund, to "break the buck," leading to a run on the entire system. Only the government's 100 percent backstop of money market funds reversed the slide.

More generally, consider the fact that securitization had become a primary tool to issue credit to individuals and corporations. The recent study by Acharya and others (2010, figure 3.4) demonstrates the massive growth in this market from 2001 to 2007. Of course, if the securities underlying the pool of loans via securitization were held in the capital market at large, then there would not be a systemic issue. But as we know from this crisis, many of these securities were in fact held in vehicles that had recourse back to the sponsoring financial sector firms, funded using short-term, highly mobile, asset-backed commercial paper. This funding exposed the financial institutions to runs reminiscent of those seen during the Great Depression.

Two of the more recent crises discussed earlier—the failure of Continental Illinois and LTCM—should have alerted the system and its regulators to the dangers of a new type of "bank run" (via the wholesale funding markets) and to the systemic nature of counterparty risk. These two types of failures were at the center of the current crisis.

## Opacity of Financial Institutions and Markets

One can reasonably debate the advantages and disadvantages of a more transparent financial system. On the one hand, transparency reduces the benefit of private information, which, in turn, reduces the collection of such information. On the other hand, the past crises—especially the Panic of 1907, the Great Depression, and the LTCM crisis—illustrate how information asymmetry can potentially lead to runs on the entire system, even if many of its institutions are healthy.

There are four types of institutions with different regulation and guarantee levels—commercial banks, broker-dealers (investment banks), asset management firms, and insurance companies—and mispriced guarantees and excessive risk taking for any one type can wreak havoc on the whole financial sector. This is because of the counterparty risk externality that has been largely unregulated. There are several aspects that have contributed to this externality.

First, the incentive to get too big to fail pushes institutions toward the LCFI model, the regulatory structure for which has yet to be fully articulated. The coarseness and lack of regulatory granularity of these institutions have allowed the unregulated sectors—primarily the so-called shadow banking sector and hedge funds—to thrive. Financial institutions have innovated ways to take unregulated risk exposure (for example, through prime brokerage activity) and to park their assets off the balance sheet temporarily (for example, in the form of asset-backed conduits and structured investment vehicles) so as to get relief from regulatory capital requirements and subsequently take on additional risks. The sheer magnitude of this activity —especially in the shadow banking sector— and its spillover to the financial sector have meant that systemically important pockets can easily develop in the financial system that have little or no regulatory oversight or scrutiny.

With the repeal of Glass-Steagall and the lack of market discipline due to government guarantees, the financial system's only protection was through the regulators (that is, regulatory capital requirements). However, there was no one single regulatory body responsible for LCFIs. This allowed for substantial regulatory arbitrage across regulators. The most telling example was that AIG was able to choose the OTS as the regulatory body for its holding company because it had bought a small savings and loan. The OTS clearly did not have the expertise to supervise the insurer's parent company. Indeed, it can be argued that lapses in LCFI corporate governance, laid bare during the crisis, suggest that such institutions may be too big and complex to manage and control, not to mention too big and complex for just about any external regulator to do its job effectively.

Second, innovations for sharing risk, such as credit default swaps (CDSs) and collateralized debt and loan obligations (CDOs and CLOs, respectively), which have the potential to serve a fundamental risk-sharing and information role in the economy, were designed to trade in opaque, OTC markets. While such a trading infrastructure is generally beneficial to large players and has some benefits in terms of matching trading counterparties, its opacity—especially in terms of counterparty exposures—is a serious shortcoming from the standpoint of financial stability during a systemic crisis. If financial institutions take on large exposures in such markets (for example, commercial banks with access to mispriced deposit insurance encouraging the growth of a large insurer providing credit protection), then the failure of a single large institution can raise concerns about the solvency of *all* others, given the opacity of institutional linkages.

The main problem associated with the trading of OTC derivatives (CDSs, foreign exchange derivatives, and interest rate swaps, among others) is that the contracts are bilateral, typically with collateral depending on the type of contracts and the rating of the counterparty. The advantage of OTC contracts is that they are tailor made, which is important to entities that want to be perfectly hedged. On the other hand, they are more subject to liquidity shocks and counterparty risk. Moreover, an issue that transcends these two problems is the lack of transparency within the system. Unlike in the case of a central clearinghouse or an exchange, no one knows precisely what the total exposure is, where it is concentrated, and what the value of such contracts is. These issues always exist, but they rarely surface when positions are small. However, when the sizes become large, and combined commitments are many times larger than the underlying contracts, the lack of transparency makes the system prone to information problems, converting a small shock into a systemic failure.

In the current crisis, counterparty risk concerns arose around the failures of Bear Stearns (which was a large CDS clearer), Lehman Brothers (on which CDSs were traded in significant quantity), and AIG (which had written $450 billion worth of CDSs on AAA-rated CDO tranches of mortgages, loans, and bonds). Table 2-3 illustrates the magnitude of the OTC derivatives problem in this crisis relating to AIG, showing the payments (via government aid) to its various counterparties in the autumn of 2008. The payments are broken down into collateral postings under CDS contracts, outright purchase and closing of contracts tied to CDSs on nonprime mortgage-backed securities via Maiden Lane III, and guaranteed investment agreements held by municipalities. The table shows that almost $60 billion worth of losses would have been borne by counterparties, causing possible failures elsewhere in the system and potentially leading to a meltdown.

An equally important issue is that there was essentially no regulatory oversight or jurisdiction. Currently, the Commodity Futures Trading Commission, SEC, and the Fed regulate exchange-traded derivatives in a fragmented manner, resulting in inefficiencies and arguably a waste of valuable resources. In contrast, OTC derivatives are mostly unregulated, creating a clear incentive to engage in regulatory arbitrage. This lack of regulation of OTC derivatives received a seal of approval by the passage of the Commodity Futures Modernization Act of 2000, under heavy lobbying pressure from the financial industry. In fact, a number of policymakers have argued that this act led to serious deficiencies in the system, including Enron taking advantage of the legislation in some of its fraudulent accounting practices, and perhaps more important, the unchecked growth of the CDS market. In short, growth in the size of financial institutions and in their linkages and fragility has raised the prospect of extreme counterparty risk concerns. When these concerns have materialized, financial institutions have been unable to fathom how losses resulting from a large institution's failure would travel along the complex chains connecting them. The consequence has been

Table 2-3. *AIG Financial Products Counterparty Payments,*
*September 16–December 31, 2008*

Billions of dollars

| Collateral postings under AIGFP CDS | Maiden Lane III payments to AIGFP CDS counterparties | Payments under guaranteed investment agreements |
|---|---|---|
| Société Générale: 4.1 | Société Générale: 6.9 | California: 1.02 |
| Deutsche Bank: 2.6 | Goldman Sachs: 5.6 | Virginia: 1.01 |
| Goldman Sachs: 2.5 | Merrill Lynch: 3.1 | Hawaii: 0.77 |
| Merrill Lynch: 1.8 | Deutsche Bank: 2.8 | Ohio: 0.49 |
| Calyon: 1.1 | UBS: 2.5 | Georgia: 0.41 |
| Barclays: 0.9 | Calyon: 1.2 | Colorado: 0.36 |
| UBS: 0.8 | Deutsche Zentral-Genossen- schaftsbank: 1.0 | Illinois: 0.35 |
| Deutsche Zentral-Genossen- schaftsbank: 0.7 | Bank of Montreal: 0.9 | Massachusetts: 0.34 |
| Wachovia: 0.7 | Wachovia: 0.8 | Kentucky: 0.29 |
| Rabobank: 0.5 | Barclays: 0.6 | Oregon: 0.27 |
| Total for top 20 counter- parties: 18.3 | n.a. | Total for top 20 counter- parties: 7.00 |
| Overall total: 22.4 | Overall total: 27.1 | Overall total: 12.10 |

Source: AIG (www.aig.com/aigweb/internet/en/files/Counterparties150309RELonly_tcm385-155648.pdf).

complete illiquidity of securities (such as credit derivatives) held primarily by these institutions and a paralysis of interbank markets, which, in turn, has paralyzed credit intermediation in the whole economy. It is important to realize that what may superficially appear to be a problem of illiquidity of a class of assets and markets may well be a symptom of the deeper issues of excessive leverage, risk taking, and the resulting insolvency of financial institutions fueled at least partly by mispriced guarantees.

Financial institutions, left to private incentives, do not and will not internalize this potentially severe counterparty risk externality.

## Runs on the System

As discussed in the systemic risk section of this chapter, regulated financial institutions, as well as their unregulated siblings, have fragile capital structures in that they hold assets with long duration or low liquidity, but their liabilities are mainly short term in nature. While commercial banks are not subject to large-scale runs because of deposit insurance and central bank lender of last resort support, the other kinds of institutions are vulnerable, and indeed many of them—most notably Bear Stearns and Lehman Brothers, as well as a number of managed funds in the money market and hedge fund arena—did experience "wholesale" runs during the crisis. And commercial banks still are subject to localized runs in the wholesale funding and interbank markets if they themselves are perceived to have exposure to institutions experiencing large-scale runs.

Of course, not all runs are problems that need a regulatory fix. It is not clear that the run on subprime lenders in the first half of 2007, the run on asset-backed commercial paper conduits in the second half of 2007, and the run on hedge funds post-Lehman were market failures. Take the asset-backed commercial paper market as an example. There is much discussion in academic and policy circles about the sudden inability of asset-backed commercial paper conduits to roll over their commercial paper. Some view this as a run on the system that needed to be fixed—a "buyer's strike." But this was not because of information asymmetry about the quality of the underlying asset-backed securities. Rather, there was a sudden awareness that the risk of *all* the AA- and AAA-rated tranches of the underlying asset-backed securities was systemic in nature, and that the likelihood of this risk had increased sufficiently so that these securities were no longer safe for investment portfolios. In other words, this was not a question of insolvency. If insolvency is defined as trading below par, then all these conduits were insolvent, given the fact that they lacked any meaningful capital support.

Thus the real concern is when runs are *not* affiliated with failure or insolvency. For example, during the early 1930s, the banking crisis led to runs on many solvent institutions, and likewise, during the week of Lehman's failure, the crisis led to runs on money market funds that had not "broken the buck." To the extent that such runs represent an information contagion from runs on other, less deserving institutions, they carry a systemic externality. In other words, addressing the likelihood of runs on the shadow banking sector—the uninsured parts of the intermediation sector—may be a critical ingredient to stabilizing the system as a whole.

## Principles of Financial Regulation

What implication does the financial crisis—and our assessment of market failures that led to it—have for financial regulation going forward?

The previous section outlined four market failures that are interlinked and need to be addressed collectively:

—mispriced government guarantees,
—focus on individual versus systemic risk of firms,
—lack of transparency in the financial system, and
—runs on the financial system.

We now consider appropriate regulation to deal with these failures.

## Risk-Taking Incentives and Systemic Risk of Financial Institutions

With respect to the risk-taking incentives of financial firms, much of the focus by policymakers in the United States and elsewhere has been on both the type and level of compensation contracts within financial firms. It has been argued that, in the period leading up to the crisis, bankers were increasingly paid through short-term cash bonuses based on volume and current marked-to-market profits, rather than on the long-term profitability contribution of their bets. Coupled with the fact that shareholders of the failed (or nearly failed) institutions lost most of their investments, policymakers see this as prima facie evidence of massive failure of corporate governance at the equity level (that is, between shareholders and boards, and between boards and managers). That Citigroup's board fired its CEO in 2008 without a succession plan would be astounding in any listed company whose shareholders are about to be devastated, much less a systemically critical financial conglomerate. While clearly this view cannot be completely discounted, we believe that, in the end, it is not the issue of greatest urgency or an issue where it is clear what advantage regulators have in resolving it. As outlined in the preceding section, the costliest market failure of corporate governance—one that regulators can do something about with reasonable precision and success—was at the debt and regulatory levels.

To understand this, we examine how the claim structure of the LCFIs is different from that of a regular nonfinancial firm. On the liability side, LCFIs are highly levered entities. At least 90 percent of the claim holders of an LCFI are debt holders (including depositors). Another claimant is the government as guarantor. Given this structure of claims, corporate governance mechanisms that align the manager with equity holders may deviate significantly from those that maximize firm value. Put differently, corporate governance mechanisms in LCFIs have to be designed so as to align the manager with the interests of the debt holders and the government guarantor and not just those of the shareholders.

To assess the role of regulation in this context, it is useful to think through the optimal governance system that the LCFI should have. Take the example of FDIC insurance.[26] If the FDIC insurance is properly priced, the with-guarantee value of the LCFI would be equal to the without-guarantee value of the LCFI. On the other hand, if the FDIC insurance is not properly priced, then the appropriate objective in structuring corporate governance and managerial incentives would be to maximize the without-guarantee value of the LCFI. Otherwise, the LCFI management might make value-destroying choices to take advantage of the discrepancy in the pricing of the FDIC insurance.

---

26. Note that the same reasoning holds for other types of insurance provided by the government, for instance, the implicit insurance provided to TBTF institutions.

If one were to specify a model of a banking system with limited liability in which each bank both maximizes shareholder value under conditions in which the regulator provides a safety net (that is, guarantees for creditors such as deposit insurance or implicit TBTF support) and also faces systemic risk (that is, systemwide costs in a crisis), the optimal plan would be for the regulator to "tax" (that is, charge an insurance premium) each individual bank an amount equal to the sum of two components.[27]

The first component would be the bank's *expected losses upon default*. That is, the government guarantees in the system need to be priced. Financial firms must pay for the guarantees they receive. Because the price of these guarantees will vary across firms in light of their different risk profiles, each firm will choose some optimal level of risk-taking activities consistent with the cost of the guarantees, almost surely at a more prudent level than in the absence of appropriately priced insurance. Ostensibly, the FDIC determines the level of premiums it charges on the basis of risk, although in reality, premiums are only charged when the fund is poorly capitalized. Consequently, this policy will not optimally evaluate the firm's assets, and the result will be excessive risk shifting. Hence insurance premiums need to be charged to banks on a risk-sensitive basis, and crucially, at all parts of the cycle. Premiums should not be rebated to banks in good times, as this destroys the incentive role played by premiums.

The second component would be the bank's *contribution to a systemic crisis,* that is, its marginal expected losses in the crisis, or in other words, *the contribution of each firm to aggregate losses above a certain threshold of aggregate losses.* In addition to expected losses, the systemic risk contribution also needs to be priced. In this way, the financial institutions can be made to internalize the costs of the negative externality imposed on the system by their losses and failures. Arguably, the principal failure that contributed to the 2007–09 crisis was that financial sector regulations sought to limit each institution's risk in isolation and did not focus sufficiently on systemic risk. As a result, while individual firms' risks might have been properly dealt with in normal times, the system itself remained, or was induced to be, fragile and vulnerable to large macroeconomic shocks. Consistent with economic intuition, these systemic losses increased with lower initial capital, riskier asset holdings that contributed to the interdependence of tail risks between the institution and the system, institutional and aggregate volatility, and the severity of the externality.

Charging a premium for systemic risk will cause financial institutions on the margin to hold more initial capital up front (be less leveraged) and to take less risky positions. That is, by incorporating the "tax" in exposure decisions,

---

27. For a formal treatment of such a "tax," see Acharya and others (2009); Acharya and Yorulmazer (2009).

the financial institution will organically choose to become less systemic. Putting aside the political economy of the viability of expanding FDIC-like premiums, the biggest hurdle to successful implementation is measuring systemic risk contributions and setting the proper price for the insurance. There are two main obstacles.

First, the regulator may not have the expertise to set the appropriate price. This is especially true with LCFIs, since their risk profile can change rapidly as they enter and exit markets or change the weight of various kinds of exposures. There are a number of empirical studies that use publicly available data and standard statistical techniques to evaluate whether the more systemic firms do, in fact, perform worse in crisis conditions, and the findings seem quite encouraging that systemic risk is generally measurable.[28]

An alternative solution to this first problem would be to partially privatize the systemic guarantees through private reinsurance or a public-private reinsurance scheme.[29] The idea is that private insurers would help price the insurance while the government would provide most of the underlying capital in return for a proportionate share of the premium income. While some reinsurance schemes have been considered by the FDIC, most recently in 1993, with the conclusion that the market did not seem viable, there is reason to be more optimistic today. Financial markets in general have become much more sophisticated in how they develop niche products. An example of innovative coinsurance, motivated by the events of September 11, 2001, is the Terrorism Risk Insurance Act, enacted in November 2002, that provides federal reinsurance for qualifying losses from a terrorist attack. The Terrorism Risk Insurance Act incorporates both industry loss triggers and government excess loss coverage, which helps to minimize the insurance industry's losses, yet provides insurers with an incentive to price, monitor, and reduce risks.

The second problem in charging for systemic risk contributions is perhaps more serious. The issue with moral hazard is that ex ante contracting does not lead to first-best actions.[30] Because the actions of banks are not fully observable after the premiums for the guarantees and systemic risk are set, the banks can subsequently change their behavior. While a private market such as that just described may be better able to monitor bank actions, the optimal contract in such a setting usually calls for some type of state-contingent mechanism. It often imposes a severe penalty function in bad states to get the agent (that is, the bank) to avoid excessive risk-taking activities. It involves the same underlying economics as do most insurance contracts to the extent that those contracts often have

28. See, for example, Acharya and others (2009).
29. Acharya and Richardson (2009b, chap. 13).
30. For example, John, John, and Senbet (1991); Prescott (2002).

large deductibles. Here, the "punishment" can take several forms, all with the intention of aligning incentives and thus bringing back market discipline:

—The creation of an insolvency regime for complex financial institutions that would allow the orderly failure or restructuring of insolvent firms. Under current discussion are plans to force firms to develop an ex ante way for them to unwind if they fail—a "living will." Putting aside whether this is feasible for global institutions, this type of punishment would pass the moral hazard test.

—Alternatively, one could require financial institutions to hold in their capital structure a new kind of "hybrid" claim that has a forced debt-for-equity conversion whenever a pre-specified threshold of distress (individual, systemic, or both) is breached.[31] While this has the benefit of recapitalizing financial firms in a crisis, more significantly, it brings back market discipline via creditor losses.

—A less discussed option is to institute so-called double liability for stockholders of financial institutions.[32] Under double liability, shareholders of the bank lose not only the value of the stock but are also charged an additional penalty, possibly up to the par value of their holdings. While double liability may be impractical and raises many conceptual and legal issues, it was in fact standard practice from 1863 to 1933.

Arguably less efficient, but easier to implement, would be a state-contingent plan for deposit insurance premiums that are higher in good states and thus reduce the net payoff in these states. Reducing these payoffs provides less reward to excess risk-taking activities as well. This reduction would effectively take the form of windfall profit taxes.[33] A related idea is to require that firms have a certain amount of convertible debt that dilutes shareholders' percentage ownership during good economic times, reducing the return to undertaking risky gambles.[34]

The success of the Banking Act of 1933 had two sides to it. On the one hand, it effectively put an end to runs on bank deposits. On the other hand, it managed the moral hazard problem through a combination of insurance premiums, capital requirements, and separation of investment and commercial banking. Currently, however, the general view is that insurance premiums are lowered by banks through lobbying in good times, higher capital requirements are quite costly—not just privately for bankers but also for society—and separation of bank activities by scope is no longer feasible. We explain below that these concerns are either surmountable or overstated.

31. See, for example, Doherty and Harrington (1997); Flannery (2002); Squam Lake Working Group (2009); Hancock and Passmore (2009).

32. Kane and Wilson (1997).

33. For examples of payoff structures in a stylized model of deposit insurance, see Prescott (2002).

34. See John, John, and Senbet (1991).

Consider, for instance, the case of higher capital requirements, with capital defined as core equity. The Modigliani-Miller theorem, the most basic theorem in finance, shows that the value of the firm's assets will be the same regardless of how those assets are financed when the form of financing does not distort the nature of asset investments.[35] In other words, choosing investments should be based solely on whether the return on the project's assets exceeds its cost of capital for those assets. Increasing the return on equity via leverage is just a wash and contributes nothing to efficiency in capital allocation. That the systemic costs to leverage are so high suggests that higher capital requirements will not necessarily be socially costly at all. While the Modigliani-Miller theorem is not reality, it is a useful starting point.

Putting aside the tax benefits of debt, the issue of how costly it is to raise equity depends on whether one believes the agency problems of LCFIs are due primarily to conflicts between shareholders and managers or to conflicts between shareholders and creditors or regulators. If it is the latter, as we have argued, then the relatively higher cost of equity financing versus debt financing is being driven by the mispriced guarantees that benefit the creditors. Fixing this problem—that is, charging for the guarantees and systemic risk—is tantamount to charging for higher leverage, which will, in turn, put the cost of capital for debt and equity on equal footing. While it is true that banks can alter their risks in fairly swift and opaque fashions, and this necessitates a certain amount of demandable debt for discipline, this argument has yet to be tested for complete empirical merit when favorable tax treatment of debt and mispricing of debt due to government guarantees have been properly accounted for.

Thus higher capital requirements for riskier—and systemically riskier—activities are certainly an option. However, as we have learned from the 2007–09 financial crisis, capital requirements can be gamed. So, to some extent, the financial system must rely on the power and supervisory expertise of the regulator. Furthermore, significant improvements are possible by closing major capital loopholes and relying less heavily on the rating agencies. With respect to the loopholes, a good rule of thumb is that if off-balance-sheet financing in reality involves recourse back to the banks, then the capital at risk should be treated as though the activity were on the balance sheet. Moreover, counterparty credit risk exposures to financial firms, including OTC derivatives and securities financing transactions, should also be taken into account.

While the Basel II Accord did expand the notion of risk for financial institutions, in hindsight, it chose simplicity over accuracy in the determination of how capital should be treated. It seems reasonable to consider not only the credit risk of defaultable assets but also the liquidity, funding, market, and specification

35. Modigliani and Miller (1958).

(or valuation model) risks. In retrospect, Basel II was necessary but not sufficient for preventing institutional and systemic failure. It focuses narrowly on the individual risk of institutions but ignores altogether the systemic risk. Indeed, by encouraging the use of CDSs to reduce banks' regulatory capital, it arguably encouraged the concentration of risk elsewhere (in monoline insurers and AIG, which turned out to be highly vulnerable) and propagated systemic risk.

### EXAMPLE: AAA-RATED TRANCHES OF CDOs

We can illustrate some of these ideas using the super senior AAA tranche of collateralized debt obligations relative to a more standard AAA-rated asset, say an AAA corporate bond. Specifically, assume that the probability and magnitude of losses (that is, the expected mean and variance) associated with default are similar between the two classes of securities. What are the differences?

First, there is the liquidity risk, which refers to the ability of the holder to convert the security or asset into cash. Even before the crisis started, the super senior tranches were considered to be highly illiquid and more of a hold-to-maturity type of security. The fact that these securities offered a spread should not be surprising, given that there are numerous documentations of a price to illiquidity. For instance, consider the well-documented spread between the off-the-run and on-the-run U.S. Treasuries.[36]

Second, there is the funding risk, which refers to the mismatch in the maturity of the assets and liabilities. There is a tendency for financial institutions to hold long-term assets using cheap short-term funding, a kind of a "carry trade." But this exposes the institution to greater risk of a run if short-term funding evaporates during a crisis. Indeed, some researchers have argued for capital requirements to take into account this particular funding risk.[37] These two points suggest that it would be useful to know the "liquid" assets a financial institution holds against short-term funding. One could imagine that the higher the ratio, the less an institution is subject to a liquidity shock and therefore the less risky it is.

Third, the systematic risk of the AAA tranche is much higher than that of the more standard AAA-rated asset. The AAA tranche has no idiosyncratic risk, so all of its volatility surrounding the probability and losses associated with default occurs only when the market does poorly and households' or corporations' underlying assets in the CDOs default in a correlated fashion. In other words, the losses occur when the system can least afford them. This is particularly acute in systemic crises because these correlated defaults are most likely to occur during extreme market downturns.

---

36. Krishnamurthy (2002).
37. See Brunnermeier and others (2009).

The fourth and final difference has to do with a form of risk rarely discussed, the one associated with specification error or model risk. It is important to realize that the measurement error of risk varies across assets—consider the difference between measuring the interest rate risk of Treasury securities versus the aggregate market risk of stocks. The AAA tranches, especially those involving more structured products like CDOs-squared, are mathematically equivalent to a compound option.[38] It is well known that compound options are very sensitive to the risk (volatility)—and the risk that risk will change (volatility of volatility)—of the underlying asset. For AAA-tranche CDOs, the initial parameters chosen are the correlation and volatility of the loans in the portfolio. Given the fact that these parameters are mostly unknown and likely to evolve over time in any case suggests caution in estimating the risks and treating them as known in banks' or regulators' internal risk models.

Capital requirements should be a function of the risk of the underlying assets, and these risks should be related to the above issues. To the extent that financial institutions spend considerable time and effort circumventing capital rules by searching for higher spreads and consequently engaging higher risks, appropriate accounting for these risks would help alleviate the excessive risk taking.

As a final comment on capital requirements, there is much discussion in policy circles about whether narrower banking, along the lines of the Glass-Steagall provisions of the 1933 Banking Act, would help alleviate systemic risk. Narrow banking would generally restrict the types of exposures that could be built up by institutions subject to deposit insurance and other forms of government support, such as proprietary and directional trading, equity investments using the firm's capital, and implicitly through asset management activities like mutual funds and hedge funds, as well as structured asset-backed securities intended to be passed onto the capital market at large ("pipeline or warehouse exposure"). There is some validity to this view, although it is often described as impractical in a world of global banking. Of course, if substantial capital requirements were tied to the riskier exposures, then LCFIs should, on their own, decide to engage in less of these risky activities, and functional separation of activity generating systemic risk could be achieved in an organic fashion rather than by fiat.

## Transparency

All financial crises have the common feature that opacity greatly amplifies financial shock, leading to bank-like runs and the freezing of markets. It is not clear how one could regulate LCFIs to become more transparent. Any "systemic risk" regulator that is established will undoubtedly try, most likely by requiring the

---

38. See Coval, Jurek, and Stafford (2009).

LCFI to release financial information that takes into account off-balance-sheet financing, maturity mismatch, liquid asset holdings versus short-term funding, and so on. The hope is that regulation based on correctly pricing government guarantees, a systemic risk assessment, and mandatory convertible debt would organically lead to greater transparency. The LCFIs would have incentives to let the market know it is much less complex and risky than meets the eye.

In the 2007–09 crisis, the leading candidate for the bottleneck in the financial system was the OTC market for derivatives. Its sheer size and unregulated nature meant that there was virtually no information about counterparty exposures, either at the regulatory or the market level. Fixing this key problem, perhaps after the LTCM debacle, would have gone a long way toward making the most recent crisis less severe.

Regulators should separate the economic role played by derivatives and financial transactions from shortcomings in their trading infrastructure. There is little merit in shutting down these markets (for example, prohibiting short selling), even during crises. However, the concerns arising in the case of counterparty risk due to the opaque nature of OTC derivatives need to be addressed:

—First, standardized markets, such as credit default swaps and related indexes, should be traded on centralized counterparty-cum-clearinghouses or exchanges.

—Second, smaller, less standardized markets, such as for collateralized debt and loan obligations, which also pose significant counterparty risk issues, should have at the least a centralized clearing mechanism so that a clearing registry is available to regulators to assess the contagion effects of a large institution's failure.

—Third, OTC markets can continue to remain the platform through which financial products are innovated; but to give these markets an incentive to move to a centralized registry and eventually to a clearinghouse, there should be an explicit regulator in charge of enforcing higher transparency in OTC markets—possibly in the form of bilateral information on net exposures with some time delay—and providing infrastructure for enforcement relating to insider trading and market manipulation practices.

—Fourth, in order to implement these changes, the regulator may simply have to play the coordinating role —possibly requiring some firmness with large players—to move trading onto centralized trading platforms. Also, the global nature of these markets will require a certain degree of international coordination between regulators, especially when timely counterparty information is required.

Table 2-4 summarizes some of the market mechanisms and characteristics associated with possible trading of OTC derivatives.

## Bank Runs in the Shadow Banking System

The Panic of 1907 and the banking crises of 1930, 1931, and 1933 all had in common massive systemwide runs on banks. Arguably, the most recent crisis

Table 2-4. *Summary of Different OTC Market Organizations*

| Market characteristic | Market organization | | | |
|---|---|---|---|---|
| | OTC | Registry | Clearinghouse | Exchange |
| Trading style | Bilateral negotiation | Bilateral negotiation | Bilateral negotiation | Continuous auction |
| Market participants | Large well-capitalized firms | Large well-capitalized firms | Well-capitalized counterparties only | Retail trade possible; largest trades in upstairs market |
| Flexibility and standardization of contracts | Maximum flexibility | Maximum flexibility | Flexible terms, standardized credit enhancement | Largely standardized contracts |
| Counterparty credit risk | Substantial | Substantial | Little to none | Little to none |
| Collateral and margin requirements | Bilateral negotiation and management | Consistent mark-to-market valuation of positions and collateral; required amounts set bilaterally by counterparties | Consistent mark-to-market valuation of positions and collateral; required amounts standardized and set by clearinghouse | Consistent mark-to-market valuation of positions and collateral; required amounts standardized and set by clearinghouse |
| Currently enforced ("current") levels of price information | Largely opaque; daily quotes available | Currently largely opaque; daily quotes available | More transparent; daily settlement prices publicly available | Transparent to all |
| Current levels of volume and open interest information | Opaque | Largely opaque | More transparent | Transparent to all |
| Current level of information on large trader positions | Opaque | Available only to regulators | Available only to regulators | Available only to regulators |
| Netting of cash flows | Bilateral only | Yes | Yes | Yes |
| Netting of offsetting positions | Bilateral only | Bilateral only | Yes | Yes |
| Secondary market | Only by mutual agreement between counterparties | Only by mutual agreement between counterparties | Yes | Yes |

Source: Acharya and Richardson (2009b, chap. 11).

also went pandemic when there was a run on the investment banks and money market funds after Lehman Brothers failed. But the earlier Bear Stearns episode also had the features of a run, even though the firm was neither particularly large nor particularly complex. Like past runs, the runs on investment banks and money market funds occurred because there was uncertainty and lack of information about the health of these institutions, and their funding sources were short term and highly mobile (repo and securities lending transactions for investment banks, and short-term fund flows for money market funds).

As mentioned repeatedly in this chapter, the solution in the 1930s was to create deposit insurance and a number of protections to counter risk-taking activities. In the most recent crisis, the government temporarily guaranteed money market funds and, some would argue, the creditors of investment banks, when it offered support to Goldman Sachs and Morgan Stanley after experiencing the systemic impact of Lehman's failure in the fall of 2008. The ongoing question is, what should financial regulation to contain the risk of contagious runs in the shadowbanking world look like? There seem to be two ways to go.

One surefire approach to prevent runs would be to guarantee the liabilities. But these guarantees would need to be priced, and surely the activities of these firms would need to be restrained in a Glass-Steagall manner. This regulatory approach advocated above—insurance plus scope restrictions—also calls for pricing the guarantees and systemic risk. Existing research, both ours and that of others, suggests that systemic risk (estimated from market data) is higher for firms that have a mismatch between their assets and liabilities. Thus a systemic premium for a guarantee would be one way to proceed. Financial institutions would have an incentive to lower the assessment through reducing the mismatch in funding. This reduction in funding would naturally lower the probability of a systemwide run.

A more structured approach would be to impose liquidity requirements on financial institutions that are similar in spirit to the way capital requirements are imposed. The basic idea would be to mandate that a proportion of short-term funding must be in liquid assets—ones that can be sold immediately and in quantity at current prices. This requirement might also be sufficient to prevent runs. It will, in effect, increase the cost to financial institutions of taking on carry trades and holding long-term asset-backed securities. For example, in the context of the securitization market, the business model was developed under the premise of "originate to distribute." But in this crisis, financial firms did not follow this model. Instead, firms held onto these securities and funded these purchases short term, creating a significant mismatch and making them susceptible to runs. Imposition of liquidity requirements would cause these trading activities to migrate naturally to the capital market at large (for example, pension funds, mutual funds, hedge funds, and trading accounts of wealthy individuals), where they arguably belong.

Highly regulated entities such as money market funds would be treated similarly, albeit with less reliance on the credit rating agencies. And, in accordance with our earlier arguments, regulators would need to consider not only the credit risk of defaultable assets but also their liquidity, market, and specification or model risks.

The implementation of liquidity requirements to stem runs is complicated by the fact that some institutions benefit from a government guarantee of their short-term funding (such as deposit insurance) while other firms do not. The purpose of the guarantee (at least in the case of deposit insurance) is so that banks can provide loans to the real sector of the economy without the threat of a run, not so that they can load up on illiquid, long-term securities. Of course, if the guarantees are mispriced, then banks with insured deposits will have an incentive to enter the market of managed funds and money market funds, and this regulatory arbitrage might distort prices and risks.

## Lessons for Emerging Markets

We conclude by discussing the implications of the financial crisis—and of our assessment of the market and regulatory failures that led to it—for financial stability in emerging markets. We focus on three issues: government guarantees, mostly in the form of deposit insurance; the implications of these guarantees in the current crisis; and the transmission of systemic risk.

### Government Guarantees

Explicit and implicit government guarantees such as deposit insurance and implicit TBTF status can generate significant moral hazard in the form of risk-taking incentives. Even absent other market failures, this moral hazard can lead to excessive systemic risk and financial fragility. Consider our analysis of the lessons for the United States from the current crisis. Deposit insurance enacted in the 1930s in the wake of the Great Depression had long-term success only because significant protections were put in place in terms of insurance charges, regulation (mostly in the form of capital requirements and wind-down provisions), and restrictions on bank activity. As these protections began to erode in the United States in recent years, the moral hazard problem resurfaced.

To some degree, this lesson was already known to researchers studying the moral hazard of government guarantees in emerging markets. As pointed out by Demirgüç-Kunt and Kane (2002), the number of countries offering explicit deposit insurance increased multifold from twelve to seventy-one in the thirty-year period starting in the 1970s. They argue that the key feature of a successful deposit insurance scheme is the financial and regulatory environment in which it functions. Such environmental conditions include the coverage limits of deposit insurance, the degree to which depositors take coinsurance on their balances, restrictions on certain deposit accounts, and whether the program is funded publicly or privately, among other characteristics.

Demirgüç-Kunt and Detragiache (2002) look at a large cross-section of countries in the post-1980 period and conclude that deposit insurance increases the likelihood of a banking crisis.[39] Moreover, the likelihood and severity of the crisis increase the weaker the institutional and regulatory environments are and the greater the coverage offered to depositors. The authors conclude that the incentive problems associated with the moral hazard from deposit insurance can be partially offset by effective prudential regulation and loss control features of deposit insurance. This result is completely consistent with the analysis provided here in relation to the United States.

In addition, the analysis in the first and second sections argues that opacity amplifies the financial crisis once it starts and suggests remedies for this problem. Consistent with this view, Kaufmann and Mehrez (2000) find that for a large cross-section of countries, a lack of transparency worsens financial crises. The authors conclude that regulation should focus on increasing the transparency of economic activity, government policy, and the financial sector, especially when the country is going through a period of financial liberalization.[40]

### Bailouts, the Current Crisis, and Emerging Markets

The provision of government guarantees is quite common during a crisis, and has occurred, for example, in Sweden (1992), Japan (1996), Thailand (1997), Republic of Korea (1997), Malaysia (1998), and Indonesia (1998).[41] In the current crisis, the United States guaranteed money market funds after the fall of Lehman Brothers and made explicit the previously implicit guarantees of the GSEs and the TBTF institutions.

What is the impact of such guarantees?

Honohan and Klingebiel (2003) find that unlimited depositor guarantees and regulatory forbearance increase the fiscal costs of financial crises.[42] Moreover, these actions increase the expectation that this will be the government's solution for future crises, thus undercutting market discipline and increasing the

---

39. See also Hovakimiam, Kane, and Laeven (2003).
40. This, too, is the conclusion of Demirgüç-Kunt and Kane (2002).
41. Demirgüç-Kunt and Kane (2002).
42. For further analysis and discussion of the costs of providing guarantees during a banking crisis, see also Claessens, Klingebiel, and Laeven (2004); Kane and Klingebiel (2004).

chances of risk-shifting among financial institutions. Laeven (2002) also finds that in many countries, deposit insurance is sharply underpriced, thus contributing to both the likelihood of a financial crisis and the cost of one if it occurs. Of course, as described in the second section, deposit insurance premiums were not collected from most banks in the United States from 1996 to 2005 because their funds were considered to be well capitalized. As in the discussion of government guarantees above, the lesson here is that the problems that plagued the United States are similar to those that have afflicted emerging markets.

Of course, many analysts might point to the apparent "success" of the guarantees employed in the United States during the current financial crisis, and even more so to the stellar success stories of the Indian and Chinese banking sectors and the government backing they received. Therefore we analyze these latter cases as examples in emerging markets.

Consider India first. A significant part of the Indian banking system is still state owned. While they are generally considered less efficient and sophisticated than the private sector banks, public sector banks in India actually grew in importance during the financial crisis (which for India could be considered to be the year 2008). The reason is simple and somewhat perverse: there was a "flight to safety" away from private sector banks, which have limited deposit insurance, to public sector banks, which are 100 percent government guaranteed (effectively so, as with the GSEs in the United States). This is because the relevant law (the Bank Nationalization Act) explicitly places 100 percent liability for public sector banks on the government.

Hence, when the financial crisis hit India—especially in the autumn of 2008, by which time the Indian stock market had plummeted by more than 50 percent and corporate withdrawals from money market funds threatened a chain of liquidations from the financial sector—there was a flight of deposits to state-owned banks.[43] During the period from January 1, 2008, through February 24, 2009, the public sector banks' market capitalization fell by 20 percent less than that of the private sector banks. Interestingly, this occurred even though based on a precrisis measure of systemic risk—the marginal expected shortfall measure—public sector banks were substantially more likely to lose market capitalization during a marketwide downturn than private sector banks.[44] In addition, within the private

43. In a notable incident, Infosys, the bellwether of Indian technology and a NASDAQ-listed company, moved its cash in hand from ICICI Bank, one of the largest private sector banks, to State Bank of India, the largest public sector bank.

44. Acharya and Kulkarni (2010). The marginal expected shortfall was calculated as follows. The worst 5 percent days for the S&P CNX Nifty (or Bombay Stock Exchange Sensex) were taken during the year 2007. On these days, the average return of a financial firm was measured. This average return is the marginal expected shortfall for that financial firm. The results are available from the authors upon request.

sector banks, those with higher systemic risk suffered more during the economy-wide crisis of 2008 (as the systemic risk measure would predict), whereas within public sector banks, those with higher systemic risk actually performed better! This divergence in the behavior of public and private sector banks is telling and strongly suggests a role for government guarantees in boosting weak public sector banks at the expense of private sector banks that have similar risk profiles.

The trend of benefiting the state-owned banking sector at the expense of the privately owned banking sector continues. Recent reports suggest that loan growth among private sector banks in India has not been that high in 2009, whereas loans at public sector banks have grown in many segments, such as vehicle-backed finance, by as much as 10 percent. In essence, government guarantees have created an uneven playing field, which is destabilizing for two reasons. First, it has weakened those institutions that are in fact subject to market discipline. Second, it has raised prospects that the "handicapped" private sector banks (due to lack of comparable government guarantees) may have to lend—or take other risks—more aggressively in order to maintain market share and generate comparable returns to shareholders. Bank regulation in India tends to be on the conservative side, often reining in risk-taking with overly stringent restrictions. However, the debilitating effects of government guarantees can travel quickly to the corporate sector and other financial firms reliant on banks, which are not directly under a bank regulator's scrutiny or legal mandate.

In the case of China, the Chinese government essentially employed its almost entirely state-owned banking sector to lend at large to the economy as a part of its fiscal stimulus. From July 2008 to July 2009 lending by the Chinese banking sector grew by 34 percent. While this has clearly helped the Chinese economy recover quickly from the effect of the financial crisis in the United States—and its consequent effects on global trade—much of the growth in banking sector loans mirrors the growth in corporate deposits. In other words, loans are often sitting idle on corporate balance sheets, a phenomenon that is generally associated with severe agency problems in the form of excessive investments. While some of the "excess" may be desirable as part of the stimulus, especially if it is in public goods such as infrastructure projects, estimates suggest that the excess liquidity is also finding its way into stock market and real estate speculation. It is not inconceivable that such lending through state-owned banks would be reckless and sow the seeds of asset-pricing booms and, perhaps, the next financial crisis. The moral hazard is clear: China has bailed out its entire banking system more than once before, and at far greater magnitudes than the United States has in the current crisis.

The examples of India and China highlight the classic risks that arise from government guarantees. First, they create an uneven playing field in banking sectors where some banks enjoy greater subsidies than others. This invariably leads the less subsidized players to take on excessive leverage and risks to compensate for a weak subsidy, and the more subsidized players to simply make worse lending decisions given the guarantees. Second, government-guaranteed institutions are often employed to disburse credit at large to the economy, but this invariably ends up creating distortions, as the costs of the guarantees are rarely commensurate with the risks taken. The situation in India partly mirrors that in the United States, where commercial banks enjoyed greater deposit insurance but investment banks did not; over time, investment banks expanded their leverage significantly, leading to their demise. Commercial banks suffered, too, but fared somewhat better because of their insured deposits. The situation in China is comparable to the massive credit expansion and risky betting that occurred on the balance sheets of Fannie Mae and Freddie Mac in the United States.

Both of these problems festered because of government guarantees and contributed to the financial crisis of 2007–09. India and China should not rest on their laurels because of their rapid recovery from the latest global economic crisis. Instead, they need to safeguard their financial and economic stability by engaging in a rapid privatization of their banking sectors—or at the least stop inefficient subsidization of risk-taking through state-owned banks. Government guarantees do not just weaken the banks that are guaranteed but also create systemic risk by weakening competing banks, subsidizing corporations, and fueling excessive asset speculation.

## Systemic Risk of Emerging Markets

Our earlier analysis of systemic risk described various ways a financial institution produces systemic risk when it fails: counterparty risk, fire sales, and "runs." One of the principal conclusions from that analysis is that systemic risk is a negative externality on the system and therefore cannot be corrected through market forces. In other words, there is a role for regulation in order to force financial institutions to internalize the external costs of systemic risk. The exact same analogy for financial institutions within a domestic market can be made with respect to international markets, and especially for emerging markets.

Even if a domestic regulator penalized a multinational financial firm for producing systemic risk locally, does this penalty carry through to all the international markets a firm operates in? In other words, should the penalty be more severe in such a case because failure can lead to systemic consequences elsewhere? The issue becomes even more complicated because financial institutions have an incentive to conduct regulatory arbitrage across national jurisdictions; that is, if institutions are more strictly regulated in one jurisdiction, they may move (their base for) financial intermediation services to jurisdictions that are more lightly regulated. But given their interconnected nature, such institutions nevertheless expose all jurisdictions to their risk taking. Individually, jurisdictions may prefer to offer regulation "lite" (adopt a regulation "lite" structure) in order to attract more institutions and thereby jobs.

In the current crisis, the poster child for being internationally interconnected is Iceland.[45] Iceland, a tiny country with its own currency, allowed its banking sector to grow almost tenfold in terms of foreign assets compared to the growth of its own GDP. Its huge leverage aside, Iceland's survival was completely dependent on conditions abroad. The systemic risk of the three largest Icelandic banks (Kaupthing, Landsbanki, and Glitnir) also went beyond its own borders. Because the banks had fully exploited internal expansion within Iceland, they opened up branches abroad, particularly the United Kingdom and the Netherlands, by offering higher interest rates than comparable banks in those two countries. When the Icelandic banks began to run aground and faced massive liquidity problems, in a now somewhat infamous event, the U.K. authorities invoked an antiterrorism act to freeze British assets. Essentially, Iceland as a country went into shutdown.

Of course, the most common source of systemic risk is a run. It is well known that, for many emerging markets, capital inflows are their lifeblood. There are numerous examples of capital flowing into new, emerging markets only to be suddenly withdrawn upon the occurrence of a crisis. These runs can leave the corporate and banking sectors of the developing country devastated, especially if there are currency, liquidity, or maturity mismatches between the assets and foreign liabilities. An example from the recent crisis is that net private capital flows to emerging Europe fell from about $250 billion in 2008 to an estimated $30 billion in 2009. Not surprisingly, emerging Europe has been one of the hardest hit in terms of the impact of the crisis on its GDP and internal institutions.

The current crisis has been severe for both its financial effect (for example, a spike in risk aversion among investors) and economic impact (the largest drop in global trade since World War II). Therefore it is quite surprising that compared to past banking crises, emerging markets have gotten through largely unscathed. This can be attributed in part to better (or excess!) internal planning—having a substantial stock of international reserves—and partly to liquidity funding by international government organizations such as the International Monetary Fund and World Bank. Both of these elements suggest an approach to international coordination that mirrors how one might regulate systemic risk domestically.

Emerging markets need to coordinate with their larger brethren on prudent measures such as leverage limits and currency reserves. As a reward, these markets could access international lender-of-last-resort facilities during a liquidity event and, in a systemic crisis in which there is a run on all financial institutions, employ loan guarantees and recapitalizations that are fairly priced and

45. See Buiter and Sibert (2008).

impose low costs on taxpayers. Of course, it would be necessary to shut down and resolve insolvent institutions to maintain the right incentives in good times.

If national regulators can agree upon a core set of sensible regulatory principles, then the constraints imposed by such alignment would reduce substantially the practice of regulatory arbitrage through jurisdictional choice. The central banks could present their proposals with specific recommendations to their respective national authorities and seek consensus internationally through the Financial Stability Board or committee of the Bank for International Settlements. The lessons learned from this crisis should be an especially useful aid in such discussions.

# References

Acharya, Viral V., and Nirupama Kulkarni. 2010. "State Ownership and Systemic Risk: Evidence from the Indian Financial Sector during 2007–09." Working paper. Stern School of Business, New York University.

Acharya, Viral V., and Alberto Bisin. 2009. "Centralized versus Over-the-Counter Markets." Working paper. Stern School of Business, New York University.

Acharya, Viral V., and Matthew Richardson. 2009a. "Causes of the Financial Crisis." *Critical Review* 21, no. 2-3: 195–210.

———, eds. 2009b. *Restoring Financial Stability: How to Repair a Failed System.* New York: John Wiley.

Acharya, Viral V., Philipp Schnabl, and Gustavo Suarez. 2009. "Securitization without Risk Transfer." Working paper. Stern School of Business, New York University.

Acharya, Viral V., and Joao Santos. 2010. "Systemic Risk and Deposit Insurance Premiums." *Federal Reserve Bank of New York Economic Policy Review. Special Issue of Central Bank Liquidity Tools and Perspectives on Regulatory Reform* 16 (1): 89–99.

Acharya, Viral V., and others. 2009. "Measuring Systemic Risk." Working paper. Stern School of Business, New York University.

———. 2010. "Manufacturing Tail Risk: A Perspective on the Financial Crisis of 2007–2009." *Foundations and Trends in Finance* 4, no. 4: 247–325.

Bernanke, Ben S. 2000. *Essays on the Great Depression.* Princeton University Press.

Bruner, Robert, and Sean D. Carr. 2007. *The Panic of 1907: Lessons Learned from the Market's Perfect Storm.* New York: John Wiley.

Brunnermeier, Markus K., and Lasse Heje Pedersen. 2009. "Market Liquidity and Funding Liquidity." *Review of Financial Studies* 22, no. 6: 2201–38.

Brunnermeier, Markus, and others. 2009. *The Fundamental Principles of Financial Regulation.* Geneva: International Center for Monetary and Banking Studies (www.voxeu.org/reports/Geneva11.pdf).

Buiter, Willem and Anne Sibert. 2008. "The Collapse of Iceland's Banks: The Predictable End of a Non-Viable Business Model." In *The First Global Financial Crisis of the 21st Century, Part II: June–December 2008*, edited by Andrew Felton and Carmen

Reinhart, pp. 23–26. London: Center for Economic Policy Research (www.voxeu. org/reports/reinhart_felton_vol2/First_Global_Crisis_Vol2.pdf).

Claessens, Stijn, Daniela Klingebiel, and Luc Leaven. 2004. "Resolving Systemic Financial Crises: Policies and Institutions." Policy Research Working Paper 3377. Washington D.C.: World Bank.

Cordell, Lawrence, Gregor MacDonald, and Mark Wohar. 1993. "Corporate Ownership and the Thrift Crisis." *Journal of Law and Economics* 36, no. 2: 719–56.

Coval, Joshua, Jakub Jurek, and Erik Stafford. 2009. "Economic Catastrophe Bonds." *American Economic Review* 99, no. 3: 628–66.

Demirgüç-Kunt, Asli, and Enrica Detragiache. 2002. "Does Deposit Insurance Increase Banking System Stability? An Empirical Investigation." *Journal of Monetary Economics* 49, no. 7: 1373–406.

Demirgüç-Kunt, Asli, and Edward J. Kane. 2002. "Deposit Insurance around the Globe: Where Does It Work?" *Perspectives* 16, no. 2: 175–95.

Doherty, Neil A., and Scott Harrington. 1997. "Managing Corporate Risk with Reverse Convertible Debt." Working paper. Wharton School, University of Pennsylvania.

Ennis, Huberto, and H. S. Malek. 2005. "Bank Risk of Failure and the Too-Big-to-Fail Policy." *Federal Reserve Bank of Richmond Economic Quarterly* 91, no. 2: 21–44.

Federal Deposit Insurance Corporation. 1997. *History of the Eighties—Lessons for the Future: Volume I: An Examination of the Banking Crises of the 1980s and Early 1990s* (www.fdic.gov/bank/historical/history/vol1.html).

Flannery, Mark. 2002. "No Pain, No Gain? Effecting Market Discipline via Reverse Convertible Debentures." Working paper. University of Florida.

Friedman, Milton, and Anna Jacobsen Schwartz. 1971. *A Monetary History of the United States 1867–1960.* Princeton University Press.

Gorton, Gary. 1985. "Clearing Houses and the Origin of Central Banking in the United States." *Journal of Economic History* 45, no. 2: 277–83.

———. 2009. "Slapped in the Face by the Invisible Hand: Banking and the Panic of 2007." Working paper. Yale University.

Hancock, Diana, and Wayne Passmore. 2009. "Three Initiatives Enhancing the Mortgage Market and Promoting Financial Stability." *B.E. Journal of Economic Analysis and Policy* 9, no. 3 (symposium): article 16 (www.bepress.com/bejeap/vol9/iss3/art16).

Honohan, Patrick, and Daniela Klingebiel. 2003. "The Fiscal Cost Implications of an Accommodating Approach to Banking Crises." *Journal of Banking and Finance* 27, no. 8: 1539–60.

Hovakimian, Armen, and Edward J. Kane. 2000. "Effectiveness of Capital Regulation at U.S. Commercial Banks, 1985 to 1994." *Journal of Finance* 55, no. 1: 451–68.

Hovakimian, Armen, Edward J. Kane, and Luc Laeven. 2003. "How Country and Safety-Net Characteristics Affect Bank Risk-Shifting." *Journal of Financial Services Research* 23, no. 3: 177–204.

John, Kose, Teresa A. John, and Lemma W. Senbet. 1991. "Risk-Shifting Incentives of Depository Institutions: A New Perspective on Federal Deposit Insurance Reform." *Journal of Banking and Finance* 15, no. 4-5: 895–915.

Kane, Edward J., and Daniela Klingebiel. 2004. "Alternatives to Blanket Guarantees for Containing a Systemic Crisis." *Journal of Financial Stability* 1, no. 1: 31–63.

Kane, Edward J., and Berry K. Wilson. 1997. "A Contracting-Theory Interpretation of the Origins of Federal Deposit Insurance." *Journal of Money, Credit and Banking* 30, no. 3: 573–95.

Kaufmann, Daniel, and Gil Mehrez. 2000. "Transparency, Liberalization and Banking Crisis." Policy Research Working Paper 2286. Washington D.C.: World Bank.

Keeley, Michael C. 1990, "Deposit Insurance, Risk, and Market Power in Banking." *American Economic Review* 80, no. 5: 1183–200.

Kehoe, Timothy J., and Edward C. Prescott. 2007. *Great Depressions of the Twentieth Century*. Federal Reserve Bank of Minneapolis.

Krishnamurthy, Arvind. 2002. "The Bond/Old-Bond Spread." *Journal of Financial Economics* 66, no. 2-3: 463–506.

———. 2008. "The Financial Meltdown: Data and Diagnoses." Working paper. Northwestern University.

Kroszner, Randall. 2000. "Lessons from Financial Crises: The Role of Clearinghouses." *Journal of Financial Services Research* 18, no. 2: 157–71.

Kroszner, Randall, and William Melick. 2009. "The Response of the Federal Reserve to the Recent Banking and Financial Crisis." Paper presented at the conference "An Ocean Apart? Comparing Transatlantic Response to the Financial Crisis." Rome, September 10–11.

Kroszner, Randall S., and Philip E. Strahan. 1996. "Regulatory Incentives and the Thrift Crisis: Dividends, Mutual-To-Stock Conversions, and Financial Distress." *Journal of Finance* 51, no. 4: 1285–319.

———. 2007. "Regulation and Deregulation of the U.S. Banking Industry: Causes, Consequences and Implications for the Future." In *Economic Regulation and Its Reform: What Have We Learned*, edited by Nancy L. Rose. University of Chicago Press.

Laeven, L. 2002. "Pricing of Deposit Insurance." Policy Research Working Paper 2871. Washington D.C.: World Bank.

Lucas, Deborah, and Robert L. McDonald. 2006. "An Options-Based Approach to Evaluating the Risk of Fannie Mae and Freddie Mac." *Journal of Monetary Economics* 53, no. 1: 155–76.

Meltzer, Allan. 2003. *A History of the Federal Reserve,* vol. 1: *1913–1951*. University of Chicago Press.

———. 2004. "Monetarism Revisited." *World Economics Journal* 5, no. 2: 161–64.

Modigliani, Franco, and Merton H. Miller. 1958. "The Cost of Capital, Corporation Finance and the Theory of Investment." *American Economic Review* 48, no. 3: 261–97.

Morgan, Donald P., and Kevin J. Stiroh. 2005. "Too Big to Fail after All These Years." Staff Reports 220. Federal Reserve Bank of New York.

O'Hara, Maureen, and Wayne Shaw. 1990. "Deposit Insurance and Wealth Effects: The Value of Being Too Big to Fail." *Journal of Finance* 45, no. 5: 1587–601.

Passmore, Wayne. 2005. "The GSE Implicit Subsidy and the Value of Government Ambiguity." *Real Estate Economics* 33, no. 3: 465–86.

Penas, Maria, and Haluk Unal. 2004. "Gains in Bank Mergers: Evidence from the Bond Markets." *Journal of Financial Economics* 74, no. 1: 149–79.

Prescott, Edward C. 2002. "Prosperity and Depression." *American Economic Review* 92, no. 2: 1–15.

President's Working Group on Financial Markets. 1999. "Hedge Funds, Leverage and the Lessons of Long-Term Capital Management" (www.ustreas.gov/press/releases/reports/hedgfund.pdf).

Reinhart, Carmen M., and Kenneth S. Rogoff. 2008. "The Aftermath of Financial Crises." *American Economic Review* 99, no. 2: 466–72.

Saunders, Anthony, Elizabeth Strock, and Nickolaos G. Travlos. 1990. "Ownership Structure, Deregulation, and Bank Risk Taking." *Journal of Finance* 45, vol. 2: 643–54.

Squam Lake Working Group on Financial Regulation. 2009. "An Expedited Resolution Mechanism for Distressed Financial Firms: Regulatory Hybrid Securities." Working paper. New York: Council on Foreign Relations (www.cfr.org/content/publications/attachments/Squam_Lake_Working_Paper3.pdf).

Stern, Gary, and Ron Feldman. 2004. "Too Big to Fail: The Hazards of Bank Bailouts." Brookings.

U.S. House of Representatives. 2008. "Statement of Edward J. Pinto before the Committee on Oversight and Government Reform." December 9 (http://oversight.house.gov/images/stories/Hearings/110th_Congress/Fannie_Freddie/Fannie_Freddie_Testimony_of_Edward_Pinto_12.9.08_written_submission_Full.pdf).

White, Lawrence J. 1991. *The S&L Debacle: Public Policy Lessons for Bank and Thrift Regulation.* Oxford University Press.

# 3

## Evaluating the U.S. Plans for Financial Regulatory Reform

DOUGLAS J. ELLIOTT

The administration has proposed a series of major changes to U.S. financial regulation to respond to the issues raised by the financial crisis. This chapter describes and evaluates those proposals with a particular eye toward their implications for the regulation of finance in emerging market economies. Before going into the specifics of the reform proposals, I start by reviewing the major explanations of the financial crisis, since they affect the choice of remedies, and then discuss the underlying principles of U.S. financial regulation for which there is broad agreement and therefore little pressure for change. In fact, the consensus on these points is so strong that there is very little discussion of these basics. The remainder of the chapter explains the major legislative proposals in some detail.

### Views of the Crisis and Their Effect on Regulatory Reform

People instinctively try to understand complex situations by hanging the facts on a simple story line.[1] For example, America's entry into World War I came to be seen after the fact as the result of financiers looking to protect their loans to Europe and U.S. trade flows. This attitude played a major role in the isolationism that kept the United States out of World War II until it was actually attacked. Similarly, one of

---

This chapter was written before legislation for regulatory reforms in the United States was finalized. While some of the personalities have changed and some reforms have taken more concrete shape, the analytical discussion in this chapter remains very much relevant.

1. This section draws heavily on Elliott and Baily (2009).

the earliest American theories of the Great Depression was that it sprang from the crash on Wall Street, which came to be associated with financial manipulation by bankers and rich speculators. This created much of the impetus for the separation of commercial and investment banking, and the creation of the Securities and Exchange Commission and the associated laws to protect investors. In both cases, there were many complex causes and therefore the potential for alternative story lines to have taken hold that would have led to different legislative outcomes.

There is a great body of facts about the current financial crisis but as yet no consensus narrative about the fundamental causes. In my view, there are three major story lines vying for acceptance:

—Narrative one: It was the fault of the government, which encouraged a massive housing bubble and mishandled the ensuing crisis.

—Narrative two: It was Wall Street's fault, which suffered from an abundance of greed, arrogance, stupidity, and misaligned incentives, especially in compensation structures.

—Narrative three: "Everyone" was at fault: Wall Street, the government, and the wider American society. People in all types of institutions and as individuals became blasé about risk taking and leverage, creating a bubble across a wide range of investments and countries.

I believe that narrative three comes closest to the truth, and that it matters whether that story line becomes accepted by the public. The best regulatory reforms would fix the widespread problems in both the markets and in government regulation. In contrast, public acceptance of narrative one would lead to too little regulatory change, while believing entirely in narrative two would likely encourage a stifling of markets without fixing the problems inherent in U.S. regulatory structure. My preferred narrative encourages a balanced and comprehensive set of changes.

## Caveats and Apologies

Postulating simple narratives that may take hold in the minds of the public intrinsically forces one to oversimplify and to ignore the subtleties of the analyses presented by those whose views come closest to these simplistic stories. I do not mean to imply that any of the policy analysts arguing for facets of narratives one or two fail to understand the complexities of this crisis, nor that any of them hold precisely the views described here. In addition, this chapter is considerably too short to do justice to those complexities. My colleagues and I have tried to cover some of this ground more comprehensively in several previous, much longer pieces.[2]

I should also note that I will be using the term "bubble" somewhat loosely, in the manner in which it has come to be used in popular discussion. It will refer to

---

2. Please see Baily, Litan and Johnson (2008); Baily and Elliott (2009).

any situation in which asset prices become substantially overvalued as a result of psychological factors, including an unsustainably large decline in the premium investors charge to take on a given level of risk. I generally will not attempt to distinguish between over-optimism about future prospects and a willingness to take a correctly estimated risk for an unusually low premium.

## The Three Story Lines

This section lays out the three narratives in greater detail.

### Narrative One: Government at Fault

The government created the crisis by inflating a housing bubble and mismanaging the resulting risks and problems, especially in regard to Fannie Mae and Freddie Mac. This narrative is popular among conservatives, particularly since it argues for a smaller increase in regulation than the other story lines.

The core of the story is that the crisis was the result of a housing bubble of unprecedented proportions, which wreaked havoc because of the central role of housing in the financial system and the economy. This effect was significantly magnified because Fannie Mac and Freddie Mac were effectively encouraged by the government to take on $5 trillion of housing exposure with minimal capital to cover the risk.

The government bears prime responsibility for the housing bubble because it strongly pushed a substantial increase in home ownership rates. Not only did this encourage millions of families to own homes without having strong enough finances to handle the commitment, but the various methods used to make home ownership easier led millions of others to buy larger homes than they could afford or to speculate by buying houses purely as investments. The massive increase in demand for housing led to sharply higher prices, increasing the risks for everyone who bought at the inflated prices. The bursting of the bubble destroyed so much wealth, especially at financial institutions, that it led to all the other problems of which everyone is so aware. Proponents of this narrative often accept that there were other financial imbalances and even bubbles, but believe that without the housing bubble the other problems would have been much easier to handle, leading to a mild recession at worst.

### Narrative Two: Wall Street at Fault

Wall Street created the crisis through reckless behavior, greed, and an arrogant belief in its own ability to understand and manage excessively complex investments. These behaviors were encouraged and magnified by perverse incentives that encouraged both wild risk-taking and activity that bordered on the fraudulent—or even crossed that border. This narrative is popular with the left wing but is accepted significantly more widely, including in much of the media.

The housing part of the crisis is viewed as principally resulting from financiers pushing naïve consumers into taking on mortgages bigger than they could handle and which were structured to hide large fees and interest rates that would jump after a few years. Financiers knew the loans were too risky, but they did not care, since they could package them into mortgage-backed securities and sell them to investors who relied on the evaluations of rating agencies that were essentially tools of Wall Street. Financiers further took advantage of the silent complicity of the rating agencies by creating collateralized debt obligations (CDOs) that owned the less attractive parts of mortgage-backed securities, and even CDOs that owned portfolios of other CDOs (CDOs-squared). At heart, these instruments were meant to obtain excessively high ratings for most of the tranches of these risky instruments in order to sell them to investors who relied almost purely on ratings. However, perverse incentive compensation structures even led traders to commit their own banks' capital to owning many of these risky securities since, in most years, they would perform well and produce big bonuses for the traders. The worst that could happen is that a bad year would lead to no bonus but also no repayment of excessive past compensation.

Outside of housing finance, Wall Street created many other excessively complex financial instruments in the areas of derivatives and securitization, often to give the appearance of holding less capital or more capital per unit of risk. In the end, most of these risks, both those related to housing and those that were not, eventually blew up and created the mess being cleaned up now.

## Narrative Three: Everyone at Fault

Everyone is responsible. Not literally everyone, of course, but virtually every major type of institution and class of people is considered to have failed. Wall Street made the kinds of mistakes and bad actions that lie at the heart of narrative two. The government and regulators made the kinds of mistakes described in narrative one, plus they failed to control, or often even recognize, Wall Street's excesses. The ratings agencies messed up in numerous ways.

Individual consumers and investors are also hardly blameless in this narrative. Some people were cheating the system by obtaining mortgages under false pretenses or while knowing that they were taking crazy risks, assuring themselves that they could always walk away from their tiny equity investments in the houses on which they were speculating. Many other homebuyers willingly accepted the fantasy that house prices could only go up. Similarly, large parts of the middle class over-invested in the stock market, including those who went into retirement with portfolios consisting almost entirely of common stock.

According to narrative three, the principal underlying cause of this widespread behavior was a major decline in risk aversion resulting from roughly twenty-five years of strong performance by the financial markets, encouraged by and associated with the "great moderation" in the macroeconomy, whereby business cycles seemed almost to vanish. This showed most tellingly in the stock market. The Dow Jones Industrial Average bottomed out at roughly 800 in 1982 and went up by a factor of almost twenty over the ensuing quarter of a century. There were a few bumps along the way, such as the crash of 1987, but the troubles were generally relatively short term and not usually that severe.

People "learned" that it was good to take financial risks. Not only would one expect on average to be rewarded, as the textbooks tell us, but actual experience showed it almost always paid off much more handsomely and with less pain than the theories said. Individuals learned a similar lesson with housing, which did experience some declines but generally produced very satisfactory results. Since home owners were usually highly levered through mortgage debt, a fairly steady and decent return became a very attractive levered return. The returns on housing, of course, shot up even further as the bubble inflated during the first decade of the twenty-first century.

This decline in risk aversion worked in dangerous combination with the "easy money" conditions of the mid-2000s. Investors working in institutions or acting as individuals found that they could easily fund their purchases of investments whose risk they were significantly underestimating. The combination was highly intoxicating and seemed to produce great risk-adjusted returns, since the risks were not fully apparent.

Each of these narratives is simplistic, but different players in the political and policymaking process tend toward different story lines, even if no one accepts them as entirely accurate and all encompassing. Congressional Republicans tend fairly heavily toward narrative one. After all, it has considerable truth, matches their original view of the world, and is politically convenient as a way to oppose the Obama administration. The liberal wing of the Congressional Democrats leans heavily toward narrative two for similar reasons. There is also considerable truth in this alternative story line, it matches their preconceptions, and it allows them to align with a populist fury that much of the public feels.

The administration is made up of many individuals and institutions with diverse and complex views. However, it is probably fair to say that the average view is closer to narrative three than to narrative one or two, although there are significant aspects of narrative two that color the administration's proposals. The net result, in my view, is that the administration is looking for reforms in a wide range of institutions and sets of rules rather than assuming that there is a clear villain. However, considerably more emphasis is being placed on curbing

Wall Street (consistent with narrative two) than on reforming the way regulators operate (which would be more consistent with narrative one.)

## Retaining the Basics of Regulation and Supervision

When officials in emerging market economies examine the moves being considered by other countries, such as the United States, they take note of what is not being changed as well as what is. Some of the more important aspects of regulation may be so strongly accepted in a country that they do not really enter into the public debate, which tends to focus on areas of controversy. This section will focus on some of these basic areas of agreement in the United States.

The most basic point is that the U.S. economy functions on the basis of the rule of law and that regulators are intended to operate within a fairly tight set of legal constraints in order to restrain their discretion and maintain predictability of outcomes. One implication is that there is an implicit separation between "safety and soundness" and consumer protection issues, on which regulators are allowed to intervene, and ordinary business decisions, on which they are required to let financial institutions operate as they wish. An important recent example of this relates to the "toxic asset" problem at the banks. It appears that regulators generally would have preferred banks to sell these assets in order to remove their valuation uncertainty; however, many banks were sufficiently sound that they could stick with a business decision to hold these assets and wait for rising prices, since they had the capital to absorb potential further losses. Another implication is that regulators generally do not review individual transactions but conduct supervisory exams after the fact to determine if the general approach and situation of a financial institution is sound.

On a related note, there is a strong belief that participants ought to be able to structure financial transactions as they wish, as long as this will not violate laws or specific prudential rules, and assuming that the two parties have relatively equal access to the relevant information to make decisions. This does not preclude a considerable body of laws and regulations intended to protect consumers, which are based on the assumption that financial institutions have much better information than do consumers, as well as a superior ability to draw conclusions from that information. Nor does this preclude requirements for standardization of certain types of contracts or the outright prohibition of others, where safety and soundness issues enter into the picture. For example, regulators now believe that the huge "over the counter" market in derivatives, particularly credit default swaps, poses systemic risks. As a result, they are proposing requirements to use exchanges or clearinghouses, where possible, for these instruments, as discussed below.

The U.S. approach implicitly places considerable emphasis on the avoidance of overregulation, which might hinder efficient operation or useful financial innovations. Even after the deepest financial crisis in many decades, fears of blocking innovation remain a powerful political argument within the U.S. Congress as debate proceeds on financial regulatory reform. This is a sentiment that may not be shared in emerging economies. Even in the United States, there are some academics who argue that financial innovation has done more harm than good, although this is not a belief that I share.

The U.S. system also places great emphasis on the political independence of financial regulators. There has been a fear that a lack of independence would create pressures to push banks to lend more in total, or to lend to politically favored groups, or would force regulators to allow unsound behaviors by banks with political clout. In order to avoid this outcome, regulators are substantially shielded from political oversight of their decisions by law, organizational structure, and custom.

In general, regulators and politicians are discouraged from pushing financial institutions to allocate credit in a particular manner, except where it is perceived that there has been discrimination. One of these exceptions is the Community Reinvestment Act, which was passed in large part to reduce perceived discrimination against minorities. Governments do provide positive incentives to favor certain types of lending, such as guaranteeing many loans to small businesses, but using the "carrot" of incentives is viewed differently than is using the "stick" of regulation.

An implicit but important difference between the United States and many other countries is that regulators and politicians here are comfortable with a system in which most credit is allocated via financial markets rather than directly by banks. Most countries in the world have financial systems dominated by banks, whereas nonbanks and financial markets in the United States are substantially larger than the banks. Although this was not necessarily an explicit goal of previous governments and regulators, it could not have arisen without a regulatory system that made it possible.

This touches on another point where there is some debate in the United States but little likelihood of action. A few prominent voices, such as former Federal Reserve chairman Paul Volcker, have called for a division of financial groups between those that do traditional banking and those that perform more risky activities, somewhat similar to the division between commercial banks and investment banks that existed under the old Glass-Steagall law. Although this has some appeal for many people, there is no broad support for such a change, and it is virtually a dead issue politically. My own belief is that the U.S. financial system is much too complex these days to be able to usefully divide activities into the two groupings. For example, I do not know how to tell the difference between a "loan" and a "security" now that most large loans can be, and are, traded. Without some of these basic distinctions, it becomes impossible to implement a Glass-Steagall-like division, even if one felt it were worthwhile. Perhaps it would be more practical in emerging economies, which have less developed markets.

Finally, despite the acceptance of a large role for financial markets in the United States, banks are considered to play a critical role in the economy that cannot easily be fulfilled by other means. This role is important enough that banks have been chartered on a special basis by governments since the founding of the republic. Banks fund themselves in large part by accepting deposits, from individuals and companies, that can be withdrawn on short notice but which tend, on average, to remain for much longer periods. Under normal conditions, the "stickiness" of the deposits allows banks to make loans and investments that are much longer term in nature than the very short-term nature of the deposits. This "time intermediation" function is important to the economy, as otherwise a great deal of savings would have to be employed in such short-term undertakings that it would provide little value.

As a result, banks hold large amounts of funds that individuals and companies cannot afford to lose and to which they could need access on short notice. Before the advent of deposit insurance, a bank failure would do immediate harm to the depositors. They would likely suffer losses and often had funds tied up for some time. Even worse, this result was disruptive enough to cause runs on other banks, as depositors who could not be sure of the solvency of those banks would rush to avoid the possibility of suffering a similar fate. In order to mitigate these problems, the United States, like most other countries, has created a deposit insurance system that is implicitly guaranteed by the government. In exchange for guaranteeing deposits, the government also stepped in with a wider range of regulation in order to protect the deposit insurance fund. This guarantee role is the implicit or explicit reason for much of the safety and soundness of the regulation in the United States, as well as the existence of a specialized insolvency regime for banks. Even before the institution of deposit insurance, the Federal Reserve System (Fed) was created in large part to serve as a lender of last resort that could lend banks funds against solid collateral if they faced a liquidity crisis, as in the case of a bank run. Such a role was not intended to deal with a solvency crisis where there would be insufficient good collateral to offer the Fed.

Other financial institutions in the United States, such as money market funds and investment banks, have taken on some of the intermediation role of banks. However, at least until this crisis, banks enjoyed a privileged basis in terms of the government efforts to protect their solvency and liquidity.

## The Administration's Financial Reform Proposals

The administration has offered many detailed proposals for the reform of financial regulation, covering a wide range of topics. The remainder of this chapter focuses on what I believe are the key points, including:

—higher capital requirements for financial institutions,

—stronger liquidity requirements for financial institutions,

—greater focus on systemic risks,

—tougher regulation of systemically important financial institutions,

—expanded "resolution authority" for regulators to take over troubled financial institutions,

—modest consolidation of regulatory functions,

—new regulations for securitizations,

—new regulations for derivatives,

—stronger consumer protections led by a new Consumer Financial Protection Agency, and

—greater international coordination.

### The Process

Before walking through the substance of the proposals, it may be worth reviewing the process that will determine what actually becomes law. In the U.S. system, laws originate in the legislative branch. This is Congress, made up of two equal chambers, the Senate and the House of Representatives, each of which must pass an identical bill before it goes to the president, the head of the executive branch, for signature or veto. The administration's proposals are suggestions for legislation to be initiated by Congress. In practice, the two chambers are generating their own legislative bills that overlap considerably with the administration's proposals but do differ in significant ways.

In each chamber, the process starts with the appropriate committee drafting and voting on legislation. In the House of Representatives, this is the Financial Services Committee, formerly chaired by Representative Barney Frank. Senator Chris Dodd chaired the Banking Committee in the Senate as of this writing. After each committee approves a bill, it moves on to the floor of the full chamber for debate and a vote. The bills passed by the House and Senate will undoubtedly differ, which will require the appointment of a conference committee, composed of selected members of both chambers, who will work out a compromise bill to propose back to the two chambers. Assuming this compromise bill can generate sufficient support, each chamber will separately approve the measure, and it will go on to the president. Theoretically, the president could veto the legislation and force a new vote requiring a supermajority for passage, but it is virtually certain that in this instance the president would simply sign the measure, and it would become the law of the land. President Obama was of the same party as the majorities in both chambers, so there was little likelihood of a reform package out of Congress that would be simply unacceptable to him.

This process is significantly lengthier than the legislative processes in many countries and was likely to take until well into 2010 before being finished. (The U.S Constitution was designed to force careful deliberation and consensus on important issues, at the expense of speed or certainty of action.)

## Higher Capital Requirements

The current crisis has reinforced the importance of a strong level of capital at banks and other key financial institutions. In its purest form, capital represents the portion of a bank's assets on which no one has a claim except the owners of the bank—the holders of the common stock (or "ordinary shares" as they are called in many countries.) The common stockholders' role is to absorb any losses, in exchange for which they receive any profits. The accumulated value of their original investment, plus any retained profits or losses, is known as "common stockholders' equity."[3] This common stockholders' equity is available to pay for mistakes and misfortunes that, as has been vividly demonstrated, are a real possibility in this business. The more capital held, the greater the level of errors and bad luck that can be tolerated.

In addition, certain other types of securities, generally in the form of preferred stock, are also considered capital, usually up to a limited percentage of total capital. (Preferred stock falls between debt and common stock. It has a fixed dividend rate, like debt, but failure to pay the dividend is not grounds to force a firm into bankruptcy. Preferred stock ranks below debt in bankruptcy priority.)

The criteria for being considered capital relate to how closely the instrument mimics the key features of common stock: the residual nature of the claim, the perpetual term of the instrument, and the lack of any requirement to make periodic payments. For example, a junior preferred stock whose claim in bankruptcy ranks below everything except common stock, whose term is thirty years or more, and whose dividend can be skipped without incurring a long-term obligation might easily be considered a form of capital only modestly weaker than common stock.[4]

There is a strong consensus, both in the United States and internationally, that the recent crisis has demonstrated a need for higher total capital and for

3. This can be thought of as the accountants' estimate of the value of the firm's assets that would be left over after all other claims are paid off. However, this value can differ considerably from the actual liquidation value and from the market value of the common stock, since accounting rules are fairly mechanical and backward-looking and strive to minimize the role of estimates of future values.
   4 . See Elliott (2009a).

more of the capital to be in the form of common stock. There are, however, some who disagree. Generally, they pursue one or both of two lines of argument. First, virtually everyone accepts that higher capital requirements will make lending more expensive for banks, leading to at least a modest increase in loan pricing and a corresponding decrease in loan volume. Opponents of higher capital contend that the effect on credit will be too painful to be warranted by what they see as only a small increase in the safety of the banking system. Second, some observers believe that the banks will find ways to "game" the system by use of devices such as off-balance-sheet entities, which will allow them either to retain most of the risk without raising more capital or to increase their risk-taking in proportion to their new capital, leaving the safety margin no higher than before. In addition, even advocates of substantially higher capital requirements usually support a significant transition period so that banks are not forced either to try to raise large sums of capital quickly in these difficult markets or to cut back on their lending.

The administration has made clear that it supports substantially tougher capital requirements, to be agreed upon by the end of 2010 and implemented by the end of 2012. (Implementation might, of course, include a transition period. The administration has been silent on this.) It has not provided specific suggested changes but listed eight core principles that will be incorporated into a detailed proposal from the Treasury. These are:

—Capital requirements should be designed to protect the stability of the financial system (as well as the solvency of individual banking firms).

—Capital requirements for all banking firms should be higher, and capital requirements for tier one financial holding companies (FHCs) should be higher than capital requirements for other banking firms.

—The regulatory capital framework should put greater emphasis on higher-quality forms of capital.

—Risk-based capital requirements should be a function of the relative risk of a bank's exposures, and risk-based capital ratios should better reflect a bank's current financial condition.

—The pro-cyclicality of the regulatory capital and accounting regimes should be reduced, and consideration should be given to introducing countercyclical elements into the regulatory capital regime.

—Banking firms should be subject to a simple, non-risk-based leverage constraint.

—Banking firms should be subject to a conservative, explicit liquidity standard.

—Stricter capital requirements for the banking system should not result in the reemergence of an under-regulated nonbank financial sector that poses a threat to financial stability.

ASSESSMENT

The administration has outlined very sensible principles for capital reform but has not provided the detail to truly judge their specific proposals. The public will have to await the fuller proposal, which was supposed to come out in December of 2009, but has been delayed. In terms of principles, I strongly agree that capital requirements need to be lifted fairly sharply and that most, if not all, of the increase should be in the form of common equity rather than weaker forms of capital. My preliminary analysis strongly suggests that concerns about the effects of higher capital on lending are generally being overstated. It appears that a four-point increase in the ratio of common equity to total assets might be achievable with only a 0.2 percentage-point increase in loan pricing and a very modest tightening of loan conditions. Although counterintuitive to some, this result makes sense when one considers three key factors.

First, banks are highly levered, meaning that there just is not that high a level of equity backing each loan. As a result, even though equity is much more expensive than bank debt, only about a fifth of the cost of an average loan is required to pay for the equity allocated to it. Second, investors in common stock lower their return requirements when they perceive lower risk, which would clearly be the case when capital levels are raised significantly. Third, banks have multiple ways of adjusting to higher capital costs, not just the single lever of loan price. Using these various means in combination, including reductions in compensation and other expenses, allows for a less harsh increase in loan pricing.[5]

Substantially higher levels of capital should make the system significantly safer, a benefit that outweighs what looks to be a relatively modest change in credit conditions. I hope that the administration sticks to its plans and works with the regulators and the international community to provide sensible, uniform increases in capital requirements across the globe and across types of financial institutions. I do agree, however, that a significant transition period may be necessary to avoid any chance of helping send the economy back into recession.

One way to soften the effects of higher capital requirements would be to allow a portion to be in the form of "contingent capital," as many academics and policymakers have proposed. In its simplest form, this would be a debt instrument that the holders have agreed in advance would be swapped for common equity in the financial institution in the event that the institution runs into serious trouble, which would be specifically defined up front. This essentially guarantees a "debt for equity swap" if it is needed at some future point and specifies the terms in advance. This instrument should not be used as the main form of capital but could be a useful supplement that would be significantly less costly for banks to raise, given that investors would generally price it much more like

5. See Elliott (2009c).

a debt instrument than an equity instrument, since under the large majority of circumstances it would remain debt.

## IMPLICATIONS FOR EMERGING ECONOMIES

It seems likely that emerging economies may also need to increase their capital requirements, since they have often been set using principles similar to those employed in the more established financial markets or have been calibrated directly with respect to those levels. The logic of the analysis would be very similar to that applied to developed economies but would depend on the individual circumstances of each country.

## *Higher Liquidity Requirements*

As discussed earlier, banks classically have borrowed short term and lent long term. This brings with it the danger that funds will be demanded in a panic in greater amounts than can be raised without "fire sale" liquidations of long-term assets that would result in major losses. Banks in the United States are relatively cushioned from this concern by the existence of deposit insurance backing much of their funding. However, even a bank can get into a precarious liquidity situation if it relies too much on other forms of funding that are short term in nature, such as borrowing overnight from other banks in the "fed funds" market or through commercial paper. One of the roles of the Fed is to act as a lender of last resort to provide liquidity in exchange for loans using bank assets as collateral. One of the ways the Fed does this is by offering liquidity through its "discount window," which is also used on occasion as a matter of convenience in more ordinary times.

The liquidity problem is potentially much worse for nonbanks, which by definition do not have access to insured deposits and traditionally did not have access to the Fed's discount window or other lender of last resort functions. Bear Stearns, for example, got into the habit of borrowing a large portion of its needs overnight or for very short periods, which held down the average cost of its funds but made it very vulnerable to a loss of confidence. The issue of nonbank liquidity has become much more of a problem as such financial institutions have increasingly taken on economic functions that mimicked those of banks to some extent, but without the same degree of government protection, involvement, and regulation.

The administration supports tougher liquidity requirements, as do most other governments and central bankers. Indeed, the industry has also recognized the importance of such measures, even if it argues about the need for government enforcement and its precise form.

The administration has not released a detailed liquidity proposal, but it gave a good summary of the principles on which that liquidity should be based in the same paper in which it outlined its goals for a revised capital regime. The paper indicated that,

> liquidity regulations should be designed to accomplish two goals: (i) enhancing the short-term resiliency of banking firms by requiring them to hold a pool of unencumbered, liquid assets sufficient to cover likely funding shortfalls in the event of an acute liquidity stress scenario; and (ii) reducing longer-term structural asset-liability maturity mismatches at banking firms. The core attributes of a desirable liquidity regulation include simplicity; comparability across firms and across countries; conservative assumptions about the liquidity of assets during times of types of liabilities, collateral calls by derivative counterparties, draws by borrowers on committed credit facilities extended by the banking firm, and implicit support that would be provided to vehicles sponsored and advised by the banking firm.[6]

The paper goes on to describe how liquidity requirements need to be considered at the systemic level as well, as liquidity problems in one part of the financial sector can feed into other parts. Finally, there is discussion of the interplay between liquidity and capital requirements, with the suggestion that it is worth considering having higher capital requirements for less liquid financial institutions.

ASSESSMENT

The principles outlined by the administration are both comprehensive and sound. However, it is difficult to assess their effectiveness without considerably more detail.

IMPLICATIONS FOR EMERGING ECONOMIES

As with capital requirements, there may be considerable overlap with the considerations that apply to the more established financial markets. The issue is worth serious reexamination at a minimum.

## Systemic Regulation

Regulation in the United States has largely focused on ensuring that each financial institution is sufficiently sound in its own right, with less attention paid to how the dominos could fall if a major institution fails. Unfortunately, banks and other financial institutions are now so interconnected that problems at one can lead to problems at others, which are then magnified throughout the entire system. The level of systemic risk before this crisis was much higher than had been appreciated, spurring the government into significantly more extreme responses than one would have expected to be necessary.

---

6. U.S. Department of the Treasury (2009, p. 12).

There are two key questions about systemic regulation. First, who will act as the regulator? Second, what power will the systemic regulator have to respond if it perceives developing problems?

There is a dual response in the proposals to the need for more systemic oversight. In both cases, the Fed is intended to play a key role. It is nominated to be the lead regulator identifying emerging risks to the system. The Treasury Department, however, would head a new Financial Services Oversight Council (FSOC), whose role would be to oversee what the Fed does in that regard as well as to coordinate regulatory activities in general. In addition, the Fed would have regulatory power over individual, systemically important financial institutions of all types, as discussed later.

This dual approach appears to be a political compromise. The administration's initial impulse was apparently to give the Fed sole authority over systemic risk regulation, both at the system-wide level and over individual, systemically important financial institutions. There would have been the usual consultation with its peers, but nothing close to a veto power wielded by the other regulators. However, Congress is not happy with the Fed at the moment. The Fed's role in the bailouts, especially of AIG, has annoyed many in Congress. This has magnified concerns about the huge financial power of the Fed and its dramatically expanded role in the credit markets, where it operates with little congressional oversight.

In addition to the obvious issues of divvying up power between institutions and trying to match competences with responsibilities, there is also a concern that many have expressed that a strong role in regulating the financial system could cause conflicts with the Fed's other responsibilities. One concern is that the Fed might compromise monetary policy in order to aid the financial system, or that it might go the other way, and nudge banks and other financial institutions to offer credit freely or act in ways that aid monetary policy but hurt the financial system. It should be noted, of course, that if monetary and overall economic goals conflict with the stability of the financial system, these issues will not go away simply by placing them in the jurisdictions of separate institutions. There will still need to be some method for balancing the different concerns. The best argument for separation may be that having the goals overseen by one institution may keep them from being fully argued out in public, whereas separate institutions would be likely to defend their viewpoints in the open.

There is also a concern about maintaining the relative independence of the Fed, which is largely a matter of custom rather than law. (Congress has the ability to alter how the Fed operates and has done so on a few occasions in the past.) Most observers believe that monetary policy is best executed by an independent agency operating with relative freedom from political constraints, since halting inflation often requires short-term sacrifices that are difficult for politicians to support. Mixing the Fed into the politically sensitive area of systemic regulation, with the potential requirement to support tough action to halt a popular asset bubble, could make Congress more inclined to place additional limits on the Fed that might also affect its independence on monetary policy.

Moving to the second question, it is not clear what powers the Fed or the FSOC would have once they have identified a systemic problem. At one end of the spectrum, they might only play a role as "systemic monitor," simply warning the administration, other regulators, Congress, and the markets that there is a problem that will require action. It would then be up to the individual parties to act with whatever degree of coordination they voluntarily chose. At the other end of the spectrum, the systemic regulator could forbid or restrict certain activities or raise capital requirements on them in order to discourage them and provide greater protection if they do go wrong.

ASSESSMENT

It makes sense to have a regulator responsible for watching over risks to the system as a whole, but there is a real limit to how effective it can be, because it would be asked to do something extremely difficult. Ideally, the regulator would spot problems before they spawned bubbles whose bursting would cause great economic pain afterwards. However, it is not necessarily easy to spot a bubble in advance, no matter how clear it seems in retrospect. Some things that may appear to be bubbles reflect true long-term changes in the economy. Other trends may be bubbles but seem as if they are not. For example, what happens if commodity prices go up further and oil reaches $100 a barrel again? Is that a commodity bubble or a natural response to tight energy supplies in a recovering world economy? Bubbles almost always start as a reasonable response to changing circumstances; the problem comes when they accelerate beyond reason as investors pile into a rising market.

It is worth pondering Alan Greenspan's famous observation about the "irrational exuberance" of the stock market in the mid-1990s. This was widely interpreted to mean that he perceived the existence of a stock market bubble, at least in its initial stages. Even in retrospect, one cannot know if such a concern was correct. On the one hand, the stock market went up considerably after that for several years, suggesting that perhaps there was not really a bubble at the time he spoke. On the other hand, the compounded growth rate of stock prices since then has been quite lackluster, and there are concerns that even now the market has returned to overvaluation. Such low returns may mean that over a decade has been spent working off a bubble that Greenspan correctly identified in its early stages.

The actual powers of the FSOC in practice will matter, as will its approach to using them. At one end of the spectrum, the FSOC's authority could effectively be little more than the power to warn about danger, which could be useful but might not make much difference. At the other end of the spectrum, there could be solid authority to force changes, perhaps by raising capital standards or even limiting certain activities outright. Ironically, the stronger the power, the harder it may be to use. Bubbles grow because there is a widespread belief in the underlying thesis driving the market and investors are profiting from following that belief. Thus there will be strong resistance to any regulator who argues against the prevailing belief, especially if the exercise of that authority is perceived as threatening a profitable market opportunity, one that will be defended as beneficial to society at large. For that reason, there is little risk in practice of a systemic regulator acting too strongly or too soon, although this does remain a theoretical possibility.

Despite the risks of ineffectiveness, it is better to have a regulator responsible for leaning against the wind when market forces are pushing too hard in a particular direction. Warnings and the threat of specific actions may still help rein in at least some of the excesses associated with bubbles, even if the regulatory actions themselves are thwarted. It would be better, however, to have a single regulator play this role rather than a council. The need to win a consensus across all the regulators, with their different views, constituencies, and institutional interests, is likely to make it excessively hard to achieve the desired systemic safety.

## IMPLICATIONS FOR EMERGING ECONOMIES

Every financial system and economy is subject to systemic risk. Emerging economies should reexamine their approaches to ensure that they have not focused excessively on supervision of individual financial institutions at the expense of watching over the system as a whole, and that they have the best tools available for considering issues affecting the wider system.

### Tougher Regulation of Systemically Important Financial Institutions

Along with most observers, the administration appears to believe that as things stand now, certain financial institutions are so large or interconnected with other key market players that they cannot be allowed to fail. In practical terms, this means that there is an implicit government guarantee covering those institutions and therefore a potentially large cost to taxpayers if they begin to fail. This is often referred to as a policy of "too big to fail."

Almost everyone who believes that some institutions are too big to fail would like to see this situation change. However, there are strong disadvantages to each of the approaches that might achieve this goal. For example, one could place sufficiently stringent absolute limits on the size and range of activities of financial institutions so that the system could handle their demise. In practice, this would likely require breaking a Citigroup or J.P. Morgan into ten or more pieces, which is politically infeasible. Even were it practical, most observers believe that the economic costs would outweigh the benefits by a considerable degree. In addition to the large transitional costs of breaking up such a bank, many believe that the global, complex, and interconnected nature of business requires that at least a few U.S. banks have this kind of scale to operate effectively.

A second approach to eliminating the too-big-to-fail scenario is to change the way that financial institutions operate, are supervised, and are liquidated so that the economic costs of failure to the public would be acceptable. Virtually everyone supports the attempt to achieve this, but there is a great deal of doubt that the various changes will add up to enough of a solution to make it acceptable.

The administration is careful not to argue that there will always be financial institutions that are too-big-to-fail, but its proposals appear consistent with such a belief or, at the very least, to acknowledge that it would be very difficult to eliminate all too big to fail institutions. Therefore, the administration has proposed to regulate the largest and most interconnected financial institutions substantially more stringently, in order to reduce their chances of failure still further and to lower the cost of any taxpayer rescue that might be needed in the future.

A newly designated group of tier one FHCs would be established by the Fed in consultation with the FSOC. These entities would be required to hold more capital and perhaps bear additional restrictions not applicable to other financial institutions. The higher capital requirements will be very important but are difficult to judge at this point, given that there have been no concrete proposals. Nor has there been much specified about how activities might be restricted, if at all. Clearly, the intention is that the treatment of tier one FHCs would be substantially more stringent, but currently little more than that is known.

ASSESSMENT

I am of the camp that does not see a cost-effective method for eliminating the problem of too-big-to-fail institutions. Therefore, I favor the approach of making them substantially safer. It is reasonable to take regulatory steps to reduce the risk of failure for those institutions below the level of risk for less significant operations. Those restrictions may also reduce the temptation for smaller institutions to find a way to become too important to fail and thereby gain the same implicit federal guarantee. In addition, it makes sense to reduce the potential cost of any necessary taxpayer bailouts, including the use of expanded "resolution authority," discussed next, which is a key element of regulation being proposed for tier one FHCs.

IMPLICATIONS FOR EMERGING ECONOMIES

This issue may or may not be directly relevant to a given emerging economy. Sometimes rules and procedures have already been established that focus principally on the largest financial institutions, in which case there may be no need for additional action.

## Expanded Resolution Authority

U.S. regulators have available an elaborate set of powers to deal with banks that have fallen into trouble, powers that allow intervention well short of when a bank becomes formally insolvent. There is a set of "prompt corrective action" steps that regulators can require banks to take once they become undercapitalized or hit other severe problems. Federal regulators have much less authority to deal with troubled financial institutions of other types, with the level of authority falling to zero for insurers or hedge funds. (Insurers are regulated at the state level while hedge funds are largely unregulated.)

Under current law, most types of financial institutions are subject to the same bankruptcy rules and procedures as apply to ordinary corporations. This has three major implications. First, the government has very little authority to take preemptive actions to try to head off an insolvency, unlike the situation of the banks, where the prompt corrective action rules are broad and strong. Second, in the event of bankruptcy, the rules do not provide an effective avenue for the government to influence the resolution process in a manner intended to serve the public good. Bankruptcy procedures are essentially a means to maximize the remaining economic value from an insolvent firm and to divvy up the losses between the economic parties most immediately involved, such as creditors, stockholders, and employees. Bankruptcy judges can take account of the public good under limited circumstances, but that is a secondary consideration. Third, bankruptcy processes tend to be time consuming, especially as they invite extensive negotiation among the affected parties and provide many avenues to try to block actions that are opposed by any of the principal parties.

In contrast, bank resolution procedures give the regulators great powers, including preemptive ones, and encourage quick resolution to avoid excessive disruption to the bank's customers and the overall economy. The current crisis has underlined the key role played by financial institutions in the economy and the many ways in which financial troubles can spread to the "real" economy. The crisis has also shown that the weak tools the government currently has to deal with problems at systemically important nonbank financial institutions can steer interventions into paths that are more difficult and costly, as has been demonstrated with AIG and Lehman. In the latter case, the Fed and the Treasury Department have argued that the limitations made it impossible for them to keep the firm out of bankruptcy, with all the pain that ensued.

The administration is proposing to give the Federal Reserve and the Federal Deposit Insurance Corporation (FDIC) powers over systemically important financial institutions, including bank holding companies and tier one FHCs that are not bank holding companies, which are similar to the prompt corrective action powers already enjoyed by bank regulators. The Fed would be principally

responsible for using these powers while the financial institutions remain solvent, with the FDIC taking over any institutions that actually fail, employing a
resolution process in which the FDIC would have great control.

## Assessment

This would be a major and controversial change to existing regulation and insolvency laws. Regulatory powers similar to the prompt correction action authorities for banks seem clearly necessary in regard to bank holding companies, which
are standard corporations covered by regular bankruptcy rules but which are so
bound together with their bank subsidiaries as to form one integral whole.[7]

There is also a good case for extending bank-like resolution authority to
insurers, finance companies, and securities firms that are affiliated with tier one
FHCs, although the answer is not as clear-cut as with bank holding companies.
Here the arguments for resolution authority are tied quite closely to the basic
premise for tougher regulation of tier one FHCs in general. If a separate class
of tier one FHCs is established, it will be implicitly guaranteed by the government, giving the taxpayer a greater stake in the health of those institutions. It is
therefore necessary to optimize a way to deal with such entities if they become
insolvent, including, preferably, establishing rules and authorities that make it
less likely that they will reach insolvency. The prompt corrective action requirements used with banks are a sensible way of doing this.

There are two broad arguments against extending resolution authority, as well
as numerous more technical concerns. First, some analysts do not think that the
separate status should be established in the first place. In part this is because it
makes them view it as more likely that taxpayers will have to subsidize failures,
and in part because it could give an unfair competitive advantage to the largest competitors, leading them to become bigger still. Second, there are fairness
issues involved in changing the insolvency regime for investors who have held
bonds of the affected institutions for years under the clear understanding that
they would be protected by regular bankruptcy law in the event of insolvency.

I do not believe that expanded resolution authority would increase the probability of a taxpayer rescue. Arguably, creating the tier one FHC status could
create this problem, although I think that investors already believe that these
institutions will be rescued as needed, meaning the "moral hazard" problem
already exists. Whether or not this is true, I do not believe that once this status
is conferred the expanded tool kit for dealing with those entities that become
troubled would lead to more rescues; rather, I think it would reduce the likely
cost of those rescues that do occur.

7. For a discussion of some of the serious difficulties in dealing with a bank and its holding
company under different legal bases, see Elliott (2009b).

I am, indeed, concerned about the fairness issues inherent in changing insolvency regimes in a major way when there are long-term bondholders who made commitments years ago assuming that longstanding bankruptcy rules would remain in place. However, I do not see a way to avoid this. Perhaps there can be transition rules or procedures to ease this problem, but some fairness may have to be sacrificed to better stabilize the financial system for the common benefit.

There are also analysts who assert that the existing bankruptcy system for nonbank financial institutions can be preserved while making the necessary changes to allow early intervention, consideration of the public good in the resolution of an insolvency, and the assurance of speedy decisions. There are good arguments for this, but it seems to me that by the time all the necessary changes have been made, such an arrangement will just look like a clumsier version of the bank-like resolution mechanism that the administration proposes. Therefore, I prefer the clarity of the administration's proposal.

IMPLICATIONS FOR EMERGING ECONOMIES
This issue is very specific to the United States and may not resonate in any of the emerging economies. The general lesson is simply to ensure that governments and regulators have the tools they need to deal optimally with troubled financial institutions.

## Consolidation of Regulatory Functions

There are many different bank regulators in the United States. Different banks and bank-like institutions are regulated by the following entities: state regulators, the Office of the Comptroller of the Currency, the Federal Reserve, the Office of Thrift Supervision, the National Credit Union Administration, and, for certain important purposes, the FDIC. Early on it appeared that the administration would propose significantly reducing the number of bank regulators, perhaps to as few as a single regulator. This idea appears to have died in the face of intense opposition by many in Congress and elsewhere. Senator Dodd, the previous chairman of the Senate Banking Committee, had revived the idea of going with a single regulator, but the idea still faces very strong opposition that makes it unlikely to pass. The Office of Thrift Supervision is the only regulator that appears to have lacked the institutional support to retain its separate existence. The administration has proposed merging it with, and effectively into, the Office of the Comptroller of the Currency.

No one would design the banking regulatory system the way it is now if they were starting from scratch, but it is extremely difficult to eliminate an existing institution in Washington. There are always interests who are comfortable with the present system and will fight to preserve it. Furthermore, the system of government in the United States is deliberately designed to make change difficult, through the famous sets of "checks and balances" that spread the decision-making power among multiple institutions, such as the two houses of Congress.

## ASSESSMENT

Effectively eliminating the Office of Thrift Supervision makes sense but does not provide anywhere near the advantages that broader consolidation would have brought. Different regulators will inevitably have different approaches, especially as they are generally given substantial independence in order to reduce the politicization of regulatory decisions. These differing approaches can reduce the effectiveness of systemic regulation, in part by opening up the possibility of "regulatory arbitrage," in which financial groups put their various activities under the oversight of agencies that have the softest regulatory requirements. It is true that tighter regulation of consolidated groups at the holding company level will reduce the ability to arbitrage the regulators, but it is unlikely to entail supervision as detailed as that which will occur at the level of the regulated subsidiaries.

Outside of bank regulation, there are two financial market regulators, the Securities and Exchange Commission and the Commodities Futures Trading Commission. It makes compelling sense to combine them, but the politics are apparently too difficult. (For one thing, the agriculture committees of the two houses strongly wish to retain authority over a robust Commodities Futures Trading Commission.)

Nor has insurance regulation been touched. This has historically been the preserve of regulators in each of the fifty states, with virtually no federal role. I believe that federal regulation of at least the largest insurers is important, because it will be increasingly difficult to draw a line between insurers and other financial institutions and activities. A given package of financial rewards and risks, whether related to housing, the equity markets, or commodities, can be structured as a security, a derivative, an insurance policy, or a bank product. The more fragmented the regulatory structure, the worse the potential problems. State regulation of insurance is often quite weak and magnifies this potential for harmful regulatory arbitrage.

## IMPLICATIONS FOR EMERGING ECONOMIES

The regulation of emerging economies is usually new enough to have avoided these legacy problems. The United States can serve as a good object lesson for the importance of not fragmenting regulation excessively in the future.

### New Regulations for Securitizations

Many of the losses by financial institutions and other market players came from problems with securitizations of mortgages and other assets or from problems with derivatives, particularly credit default swaps. The administration proposes greater regulation in both areas.

The biggest change to securitizations would be a requirement that the originators of the loans underlying the securities retain at least 5 percent of the risk. The administration is also proposing other steps related to securitization, including greater transparency about the assets backing the securities, clearer guidance from the rating agencies about the differences between asset-backed securities and regular corporate debt and changes to the compensation structure for the parties involved in securitization.

### ASSESSMENT

The idea of "keeping some skin in the game" is intuitively appealing and should help. However, it is important not to take excessive comfort in this change. Banks will indeed pay more attention to the quality of the assets they securitize if they retain even a small fraction of them. But the financial incentives in a bull market for those assets will still push banks toward taking greater and greater risks, since they will immediately gain most of the benefits through securitization while only having a future risk on a small fraction of the asset pool. Also, banks are not immune to the euphoria that grips the larger markets during an asset bubble. The banks, to their regret, actually retained much of the mortgage risk from the bubble period, sometimes even buying more in the open market.

The other proposed changes are also sensible, but the devil will be in the details, and it is difficult to fully judge them yet.

### IMPLICATIONS FOR EMERGING ECONOMIES

Regulators would be well advised to better understand how securitization impacts their financial markets and institutions. The lessons may be very different from those drawn in the United States, where securitization is hugely important and long established. I would suggest avoiding one potential lesson, which is that securitization is harmful. Although difficult to prove definitively, securitization has been a powerful force for good in U.S. financial markets, which is why there are virtually no proposals for its abolition.

## New Regulations for Derivatives

The administration is pushing for all standardized derivatives to be traded through an organized exchange or cleared through a clearinghouse or both. An exchange is a centrally organized marketplace for the purchase and sale of financial products. The best known is probably the New York Stock Exchange, but there are also several prominent exchanges that do a major business in derivatives already. Exchanges confer a real benefit through transparency about the pricing and volume of trades, as well as by making it easier for regulators to track trading positions of major parties. In contrast, much of the trading volume in derivatives now takes place "over the counter," between two counterparties who are not generally required to report details of the trade and who take each other's credit risk in regard to the transaction. This credit risk is often mitigated by requiring collateral, but it is clear in retrospect that this process was not well managed in many cases, leaving a large number of institutions very exposed to the credit risk of AIG, for example.

The major exchanges dealing in derivatives use central clearinghouses that act as the counterparty to both sides. If A sells an option to B on the exchange, the clearinghouse interposes itself, buying from A and selling the option on to B. The sole purpose of this interposition is to eliminate B's credit exposure to A. If the option becomes valuable over time, B needs A to make good on its promise. If A doesn't, the clearinghouse makes good, protecting B. Such clearinghouses can also handle trades that were done off of an exchange, which will be an allowed alternative in certain cases.

It should be noted that using a clearinghouse does not eliminate counterparty risk altogether. The clearinghouse could become insolvent itself if enough of its counterparties fail to meet their obligations. This should still represent a diminution of the total credit risk in the system since clearinghouses are well capitalized and operate in a clearly defined business that is easier to manage than a broader business. However, there could be extreme circumstances where a government rescue would be required.

The big controversy surrounding derivatives is the question of what to do about customized derivatives. The use of derivatives by sophisticated corporations to manage risk is pervasive. Sometimes those derivatives are significantly cheaper or more effective if they cover the exact risk rather than using one or more standard derivatives to approximate the desired protection. The administration is trying to preserve those efficiencies by allowing the continuation of the current system for customized derivatives, but there is a fear that financial firms will deliberately sell slightly nonstandard derivatives in order to avoid the tougher rules on standardized ones. The administration attempts to mitigate this in two ways. First, any derivative that an exchange is willing to trade or a clearinghouse to clear must be traded or cleared in that manner, rather than done as an over-the-counter transaction with the customary clearing procedures. Second, customized derivatives will carry significantly higher capital charges, in the hopes both of reducing the risk level by holding a higher buffer and of steering customers and banks away from customized derivatives where there is no compelling economic case.

## Assessment

Virtually everyone agrees that more use of exchanges and clearinghouses would be a good thing for standardized derivatives. However, this is another area where the devil is in the details. The trick will be to provide incentives or requirements to use standard derivatives where possible, while leaving the ability to use customized ones where they serve a genuine need. The administration's proposal attempts to strike this balance. It will be interesting to see what comes out the other end of the legislative process, given the high degree of public anxiety about derivatives combined with a lack of understanding of this complex topic by many who are voicing opinions about the proper course of action.

## Implications for Emerging Economies

The implications here are similar to the ones for securitization: examine your specific situation and think carefully about it. Try to avoid jumping to the conclusion that derivatives are not worth the trouble, as they too have been a powerful aid to modern financial institutions and markets.

### Stronger Consumer Protections

The administration has proposed creating a Consumer Financial Protection Agency (CFPA), responsible for all aspects of regulating mortgages, credit cards, and other consumer-focused financial products, with a few exceptions such as mutual funds, which are left with the Securities and Exchange Commission. The proposed CFPA appears to be a fairly powerful agency, with the power, for example, to set binding regulations, conduct supervisory exams, and impose fines. It would be specifically authorized to impose an obligation to offer "plain vanilla" products, such as a standardized thirty-year fixed-rate mortgage, with the possibility that consumers who wish to make another choice will have to specifically waive their right to the standardized product. (This aspect of the proposal appears likely to disappear in the face of staunch opposition, although there may remain an attempt to encourage plain vanilla products without requiring them.)

There has been intense opposition by the banking industry to the creation of the CFPA. It has been portrayed as creating another layer of bureaucracy and a potentially conflicting source of regulation alongside that of the existing bank regulators. There is also the fear that the CFPA will be so focused on consumer protection that it will impose unreasonable constraints on the banks, especially if it is allowed to develop and push plain vanilla products. Another bone of contention is that the administration's proposal would allow individual states to impose more stringent consumer protection requirements, from which national banks are currently immune due to federal preemption of state consumer protection laws as they apply to nationally chartered banks. For their part, the existing regulators generally argue that while they may not have been perfect in the past, they will do a much better job of protecting consumers in the future, and therefore there is no need to change the existing structures.

## Assessment

There have been many bad practices that developed in the bubble period that harmed consumers, especially those related to subprime mortgages. It would be useful to have a clear regulatory focus on eliminating those problems and avoiding others in the future. The critical issue will be the extent to which the CFPA is able to find the right balance between promoting consumer safety and allowing innovation. Everyone can agree on the need for transparency. What is harder is when there are both risks and rewards to a given product from the consumer's viewpoint. How much will the CFPA try to protect consumers from taking risks that might actually be legitimate in light of the potential rewards?

Another key issue that will be determined by a combination of legislative wording and regulatory choices over time is the extent to which the CFPA will move out of products that are clearly consumer products into a wider range of financial products. For example, would the CFPA ever find itself imposing regulations on derivative products, perhaps on the basis that some individuals do invest in them? This appears not to be the intent of the proposal, but there will doubtless be gray areas in practice.

In general, I fear that leaving consumer regulation with agencies that also focus on the financial safety of the banks and of the financial system would inevitably cause consumer protection to become a lower priority over time. There are disadvantages to a separate consumer protection agency, but these appear to be more than offset by the benefit of focus. That said, it would be important to get the details right and to strike the best balance between protection and innovation.

IMPLICATIONS FOR EMERGING ECONOMIES
Consumer protection is very important. Unfortunately, it is easy for regulators to focus instead on safety and soundness issues. It is critical to make sure that consumers are not given short shrift in designing and running regulatory structures. Not only would that be bad for the many individuals who would suffer, but it can help to produce massive systemic problems.

*Greater International Coordination*

Finally, the administration has also highlighted the need for greater international regulatory cooperation. The idea is to have comparable capital and liquidity requirements across the world, as well as similar regulatory changes related to derivatives and securitization, among other areas.

ASSESSMENT
This would indeed be useful, particularly if the United States develops tougher rules in some areas than currently exist elsewhere. However, it is not likely that this international cooperation will have a large effect on U.S. policy. As has already been seen with the failure to propose significant regulatory consolidation, financial regulation in the United States is a very parochial affair, with entrenched interests fighting for control of their corner with relatively little regard for what is going on in the rest of the world.

The short-term dangers of differing policies among some of the major financial centers in the world may not be terribly large. However, the risks grow over time. For example, if one significant jurisdiction has substantially laxer rules on capital levels, there is a strong likelihood that more and more business would migrate to that jurisdiction. Thus the average level of regulatory rigor around the world would deteriorate, creating increasingly large risks over time.

## Implications for Emerging Economies

Do not count on this or any future administration to be able to take the regulatory actions that are globally optimal. Administrations will generally place a higher priority on this than Congress will, since the administration is charged with the day-to-day running of the country in a truly globalized world in which U.S. domestic actions have consequences overseas. Congress tends to focus much more on the parochial issues on which citizens are focused in their own districts or states. As a result, international cooperation is a low priority for the legislature.

## Postscript

Congress passed the Dodd-Frank Act in the summer of 2010, incorporating the great majority, although not all, of the administration's proposals as well as including some revisions and additions (for more details, see Elliott 2010). Among the significant additions, there is the so-called "Volcker Rule," which forces commercial banks and their affiliates to sharply cut back on proprietary trading activities. Another set of changes force commercial banks to stop doing certain types of derivatives transactions, although they can still be done by affiliates of the banks. Perhaps the most significant revisions were in the area of resolution authority. Regulators were indeed given the power to take over non-banks in a manner somewhat similar to their powers over banks, but the details were greatly changed and substantial restrictions were put in place to avoid the charge that Congress was setting up future "bailouts," which are so despised by the American public. In general, however, the administration gained the great bulk of what it asked for and the comments in the body of this paper still apply.

## References

Baily, Martin Neil, and Douglas J. Elliott. 2009. "The U.S. Financial and Economic Crisis: Where Does It Stand and Where Do We Go from Here?" Initiative on Business and Public Policy Paper. Brookings (www.brookings.edu/papers/2009/0615_economic_crisis_baily_elliott.aspx).

Baily, Martin Neil, Robert E. Litan, and Matthew S. Johnson. 2008. "The Origins of the Financial Crisis." Fixing Finance Series Paper 3. Brookings (www.brookings.edu/~/media/Files/rc/papers/2008/11_origins_crisis_baily_litan/11_origins_crisis_baily_litan.pdf).

Elliott, Douglas J. 2009a. "Bank Capital and the Stress Tests." Initiative on Business and Public Policy Paper. Brookings (www.brookings.edu/papers/2009/0303_bank_capital_elliott.aspx).

————. 2009b. "Pre-emptive Bank Nationalization Would Present Thorny Problems." Initiative on Business and Public Policy Paper. Brookings (www.brookings.edu/papers/2009/0325_bank_nationalization_elliott.aspx).

————. 2009c. "Quantifying the Effects on Lending of Increased Capital Requirements." Paper. Brookings (www.brookings.edu/papers/2009/0924_capital_elliott.aspx).

————. 2010. "The Danger of Divergence: Transatlantic Cooperation on Financial Reform." Paper. Brookings (www.brookings.edu/reports/2010/1007_atlantic_council_elliott.aspx).

Elliott, Douglas J., and Martin Neil Baily. 2009. "Telling the Narrative of the Financial Crisis: Not Just a Housing Bubble." Initiative on Business and Public Policy Paper. Brookings (www.brookings.edu/papers/2009/1123_narrative_elliott_baily.aspx).

U.S. Department of the Treasury. 2009. "Principles for Reforming the U.S. and International Regulatory Capital Framework for Banking Firms," September 3 (www.treas.gov/press/releases/docs/capital-statement_090309.pdf).

# PART III

# Regulatory Frameworks for Emerging Markets

# 4

## Emerging Contours of Financial Regulation: Challenges and Dynamics

RAKESH MOHAN

In 2008–09 the world experienced the most severe financial and economic crisis since the Great Depression. Although the crisis originated in the subprime mortgage market in the United States, it spread to Europe and later to the rest of the world. The speed of the contagion that spread across the world was perhaps unprecedented. What started off as a relatively limited crisis in the U.S. housing mortgage sector turned successively into a widespread banking crisis in the United States and Europe, the breakdown of both domestic and international financial markets, and then later into a full-blown global economic crisis. Interestingly, however, although the emerging market economies in Asia and Latin America also suffered severe economic impacts from the crisis, their financial sectors exhibited relative stability. No important financial institutions in these economies were affected in any significant fashion. So it really should be dubbed the North Atlantic financial crisis rather than a global financial crisis.

The severity of the crisis can be gauged through a number of metrics. From an average annual growth rate of 4.1 percent between 2001 and 2008, world GDP growth fell to –0.8 percent in 2009 and was projected by the International

The author gratefully acknowledges the assistance of Anand Sinha, Prashant Saran, P.R. Ravi Mohan, T. Gopinath, and Muneesh Kapur in the preparation of this chapter. The chapter has also benefited from the Group of Twenty Working Group 1 report on "Enhancing Sound Regulation and Strengthening Transparency."

Monetary Fund (IMF) to recover to 3.9 percent in 2010.[1] That the world was taken by surprise by the developments in 2008 and 2009 is shown by the fact that as late as July 2008, the IMF expected world GDP to grow by 3.9 percent in 2009.[2] The reversal in expectations was so sudden that exactly a year later the forecast had been reversed to −1.4 percent for 2009.[3] Similarly, the growth forecast for 2010 was as low as 1.9 percent in April 2009; the speed of the recovery that took place in 2010 was also unexpected.[4]

Optimism regarding the world economy continued until mid-2008. In fact, global market capitalization fell by 53 percent between the end of October 2007 and the end of March 2009, and in April 2009 losses on U.S.-originated credit assets were estimated by the IMF to amount to $2.7 trillion. As economies have contracted, unemployment has increased to levels in excess of 10 percent in North America and Europe, and there is as yet little sign of recovery in employment. The decline in property prices has led to a severe reduction in household wealth. Global credit write-downs were estimated by the IMF at $2.8 trillion in the October 2009 Global Financial Stability Report.[5] Of these only about $500 billion were outside the North Atlantic advanced economies.

Almost all governments and central banks around the world were busy during 2008 and 2009 trying to contain the effects of the crisis through both fiscal and monetary policy measures, respectively. The fiscal effort, which has been largely successful in containing the economic effects of the crisis, has been massive. Fiscal expansion of the Group of Twenty (G20) countries, relative to their 2007 levels, was approximately 6 percent of their GDP in both 2009 and 2010; U.S. fiscal expansion has been much higher, at just under 10 percent of its GDP. In containing the emerging North Atlantic financial crash in 2008–09, the total support given to the financial sector in advanced economies was approximately $7 trillion, including capital injections into financial institutions by governments, the purchase of assets by treasuries, central bank liquidity injections, and other upfront government financing. Some of these expenditures will, of course, be recovered.[6] So the cost of this crisis has been massive for the global economy, and its fiscal effects will be felt for some time to come. Just as the global nature of the crisis has been unprecedented, so has the global nature of the response, as exemplified by the G20's commitment to coordinated action.

Along with the coordinated fiscal and monetary policy actions, a comprehensive re-examination of the financial regulatory and supervisory framework is also

1. IMF (2010b).
2. IMF (2008).
3. IMF (2009a).
4. IMF (2010b).
5. IMF (2009b ).
6. IMF (2009d, 2010a).

under way around the world. Consequent to all the rapid and exceptional policy actions taken around the world, some degree of normalcy returned to global financial markets in 2009–10. Given the very heavy, worldwide costs of the recent financial crisis, it is essential that governments and regulatory authorities do not succumb to the natural temptations of complacency that such a return to normalcy could entail.

Against this backdrop, this chapter attempts to analyze the emerging contours of regulation of financial institutions, with an emphasis on the emerging challenges. The first section provides a broad overview of the global developments that contributed to the current global financial crisis. The next section presents the ongoing discussion and debate at the international level regarding the shortcomings of the extant regulatory framework. This is followed by an analysis of proposals for reforming the regulatory framework, and the chapter concludes with a discussion of the potential difficulties in implementing the regulatory proposals.

## Evolution of the Crisis: What Went Wrong?

What are some of the identifiable sources of market failures that led to the current financial turbulence? The recent financial crisis is attributed to a variety of factors, such as developments in the subprime mortgage sector, excessive leverage, lax financial regulation and supervision, and global macroeconomic imbalances.[7] At a fundamental level, however, the crisis also reflects the effects of a long period of excessively loose monetary policy in the major advanced economies during the early part of this past decade.

### Accommodative Monetary Policy

After the dotcom bubble burst in the United States around the turn of the decade, monetary policy was eased relatively aggressively in the United States and then in other advanced economies. In the United Kingdom, long-term real interest rates (yield on twenty-year treasury bonds) averaged about 3.5 percent between around 1985 and 1997, and then declined to about 1 percent by 2007.[8] Policy rates in the United States reached 1 percent in 2002 and were held around this level for an extended period, longer than was probably necessary.[9] Excessively loose monetary policy led to excess liquidity and consequent low interest rates worldwide; furthermore, the burst of financial innovation during this period amplified and accelerated the consequences of excess liquidity and rapid

---

7. Scott, Shultz, and Taylor (2010).
8. Financial Services Authority (FSA 2009b).
9. Taylor (2009); Yellen (2009).

credit expansion.[10] At one time, investors in fixed-income instruments, such as pension funds and other risk-averse institutions and individuals, could expect adequate risk-free real returns of around 3 percent, even in the long term. However, with long-term interest rates declining to 1 percent and short-term rates even lower, investors were now reduced to seeking higher yields through investment in riskier instruments in both equity and debt, as well as in increasingly complex derivatives.

What is interesting about this episode is that despite the persistent accommodative monetary policy and the associated strong worldwide macroeconomic growth, it did not result in measured inflationary pressures in goods and most services.[11] Consequently, central banks in advanced economies, particularly in the United States, did not withdraw monetary accommodation for an extended period. The excess liquidity worldwide did show up in rising asset prices and later in commodity prices, particularly oil. It was only then that measured inflation did start rising and central banks began to tighten monetary policy, though belatedly.

With significant increases in both investment and consumption, along with declining savings, aggregate demand exceeded domestic output in the United States for an extended period, leading to persistent and increasing current account deficits as the domestic savings investment imbalance grew.[12] This large excess demand in the United States was supplied by the rest of the world, especially by China, which provided goods and services at relatively low cost, leading to corresponding current account surpluses in China and elsewhere. The surpluses generated by the oil-exporting countries added to the emerging global imbalances.

Large current account surpluses in China and other emerging market economies (EMEs) and equivalent deficits in the United States and elsewhere are often attributed to the exchange rate policies in China, other EMEs, and oil exporters. Given the fact that U.S. demand exceeded output, it is apparent that with unchanged domestic macroeconomic policies, the U.S. current account deficit would have continued at its elevated levels. In the event of a more flexible exchange rate policy in China, the sources of imports for the United States would have been some countries other than China. Although the lack of exchange rate flexibility among the Asian EMEs and oil exporters did contribute to the emergence of global imbalances, it cannot fully explain the large and growing current account deficits in the United States, particularly since Europe as a whole did not exhibit current account deficits at the same time.

---

10. De Larosière Group (2009).

11. Borio (2009).

12. The U.S. personal saving rate hovered only slightly above zero from mid-2005 to mid-2007 (Yellen 2009).

## Search for Yields

As noted, accommodative monetary policy and the corresponding existence of low interest rates for an extended period encouraged the active search for higher yields by a host of market participants. The significant fall in real interest rates on low-risk instruments induced many institutional investors to look for ways and means to achieve uplift in their returns, both in their home economies and also through cross-border investments. Thus, as a manifestation of the search for higher returns, capital not only flowed toward financial innovation but also surged into EMEs; however, such flows could not be absorbed by these economies in the presence of either large current account surpluses or only small deficits, and thus largely ended up as official reserves. These reserves were recycled into U.S. government securities and those of the government-sponsored mortgage entities such as Fannie Mae and Freddie Mac. Thus, while accommodative monetary policy kept short-term interest rates low, the recycled reserves contributed to the lowering of long-term interest rates in the advanced economies, particularly in the United States.[13] Such low long-term interest rates contributed to the growth in demand for housing mortgage finance and the consequent rise in housing prices.

Furthermore, the stable macroeconomic environment, relatively stable growth, and low inflation in the run-up to the crisis led to sustained underpricing of risks and hence excessive risk-taking and financial innovation in the major advanced economies. It may be ironic that the perceived success of central banks and increased credibility of monetary policy, which led to enhanced expectations with regard to stability in both inflation and interest rates, could have led to the mispricing of risk and hence enhanced risk-taking. Easy monetary policy itself may have generated a search for yields that resulted in a dilution of standards in assessing credit risk, leading to the erosion of sound practices.[14] Lower yields encouraged excessive leverage as banks and financial institutions attempted to maintain their profitability. Lacunae in financial regulation and supervision allowed this excessive leverage in the financial system. Assets were either shifted to off-balance-sheet vehicles that were effectively unregulated, or financial innovation synthetically reduced the perceived risks on balance sheets.

The sustained rise in asset prices, particularly house prices, on the back of excessively accommodative monetary policy, and lax lending standards coupled with financial innovations, resulted in the high growth in mortgage credit to households, particularly to low-credit-quality households. Due to the "originate and distribute" model, most of these mortgages were securitized. In combination

13. Borio (2009).
14. Mohan (2007); Borio (2009).

with strong growth in complex credit derivatives and with the use of credit ratings, the mortgages, inherently subprime, were bundled into a variety of tranches, including AAA tranches, and sold to a range of financial investors looking for higher yields.

Beginning in 2004, as inflation started creeping up, the U.S. Federal Reserve did start to withdraw monetary accommodation. Consequently, mortgage payments started rising with the increasing interest rates, while housing prices started to ease. Low-to-negligible margin financing and low initial teaser rates incentivized default by the subprime borrowers. Although the loans were supposedly securitized and sold to the off-balance-sheet structured investment vehicles, the losses were ultimately borne by the banks and financial institutions, wiping out a significant fraction of their capital. The uncertainty about the extent of the likely bank losses led to a breakdown of trust among banks. Given growing financial globalization, banks and financial institutions in other major advanced economies, especially Europe, were also adversely affected by losses and capital write-offs. Interbank money markets nearly froze, and this was reflected in very high spreads in money markets and debt markets. There was an aggressive search for safety, which resulted in very low yields on Treasury bills and bonds. These developments were significantly accentuated following the failure of Lehman Brothers in September 2008, which led to a complete lack of confidence in global financial markets.

The deep and lingering crisis in global financial markets, the extreme level of risk aversion, the mounting losses of banks and financial institutions, the elevated level of commodity and oil prices (until the third quarter of 2008), and the sharp correction in a range of asset prices combined to lead to the sudden, sharp slowdown in growth momentum in the major advanced economies, especially since the Lehman failure. Global growth for 2009, which was projected at a healthy 3.8 percent in April 2008, is estimated by the IMF to have contracted by 0.8 percent.

Thus the causes for the global crisis reflect the interaction of monetary policy, the choice of exchange rate regime in a number of countries, and important changes within the financial system itself, along with lax regulation arising from the belief in efficient markets and light-touch regulation.[15] To recap, low interest rates together with increasing and excessive optimism about the future pushed up asset prices, from stock prices to housing prices. Low interest rates and limited volatility prompted the search for yield down the credit quality curve, and under-estimation of risks led to the creation and purchase of riskier assets. Central banks, focused on measured consumer price inflation and aggregate activity,

15. See the de Larosière Group (2009); Bank for International Settlements (2008).

while neglecting asset price movements, did not perceive the full implications of the growing risks until it was too late.[16]

## Shortcomings in Financial Regulation and Supervision

There have been calls for a fundamental rethinking on macroeconomic, monetary, and financial sector policies to meet the new challenges and realities; many of these ideas entail a structural shift in the international financial architecture and a potentially enhanced degree of coordination among monetary authorities and regulators. A review of the policies relating to financial regulation needs to address both the acute policy dilemmas in the short run and a fundamental rethinking of the broader frameworks of financial and economic policies over the medium term.[17]

There has been a great deal of very active discussion internationally about existing regulatory practices and the future of financial regulation and supervision. It is also perhaps correct to say that there is an emerging consensus on how financial regulation and supervision needs to be changed. The intensity of discussion is reflected in the plethora of reports that have been issued by authoritative sources:

—*Report of the High-Level Group on Financial Supervision in the European Union;* chairman: Jacques de Larosière (de Larosière Group 2009).

—*The Structure of Financial Supervision: Approaches and Challenges in a Global Market Place;* chairman: Paul Volcker (Group of Thirty 2008).

—*The Fundamental Principles of Financial Regulation,* also known as the Geneva Report (Brunnermeier and others 2009).

—*The Turner Review: A Regulatory Response to the Global Banking Crisis* (Financial Services Authority of the United Kingdom [FSA] 2009b).

—The report of Working Group 1 of the G20 on "Enhancing, Sound Regulation and Strengthening Transparency" (G20 2009).

—*Report of the Commission of Experts of the President of the United Nations General Assembly on Reforms of the International Monetary and Financial System,* also known as the Stiglitz Report (UN 2009).

—The U.K. Treasury report, *Reforming Financial Markets* (H.M. Treasury 2009).

—The U.S. Treasury report, *Financial Regulatory Reform: A New Foundation* (U.S. Department of the Treasury 2009).

—The report of the Warwick Commission, *The Warwick Commission on International Financial Reform: In Praise of Unlevel Playing Fields* (University of Warwick 2009).

16. IMF (2009c).
17. Reddy (2008).

What is common among all these reports is the acknowledgment that regulation and supervision in the advanced economies were clearly too lax, and that considerable re-evaluation is needed, which could lead to stronger and perhaps more intrusive regulation and supervision in the financial sector. There is a clear recognition of serious regulatory and supervisory failures.

At the root of such rethinking is really the questioning of existing intellectual assumptions with respect to the functioning of markets and the nature of financial risk. To quote the *Turner Review:*

> At the core of these assumptions has been the theory of efficient and rational markets. Five propositions with implications for regulatory approach have followed:
>
>> (i) Market prices are good indicators of rationally evaluated economic value.
>> (ii) The development of securitized credit, since based on the creation of new and more liquid markets, has improved both allocative efficiency and financial stability.
>> (iii) The risk characteristics of financial markets can be inferred from mathematical analysis, delivering robust quantitative measures of trading risk.
>> (iv) Market discipline can be used as an effective tool in constraining harmful risk taking.
>> (v) Financial innovation can be assumed to be beneficial since market competition would winnow out any innovations which did not deliver value added.
>
> Each of these assumptions is now subject to extensive challenge on both theoretical and empirical grounds, with potential implications for the appropriate design of regulation and for the role of regulatory authorities.[18]

What were the specific developments in the financial system that arose from these broadly accepted intellectual assumptions that led to the ongoing global financial crisis?

## Recurring Financial Crises: Buildup of Excessive Leverage

Financial and banking crises have a long history as old as the existence of the financial sector itself.[19] All liquid markets can be susceptible to swings in sentiment that can produce significant divergence from rational equilibrium prices. However, boom and bust in equity prices have surprisingly small consequences

---

18. FSA (2009b, p. 30).
19. Kindleberger and Aliber (2005); Reinhart and Rogoff (2009).

relative to boom and bust in credit instruments, unless investment in equity instruments is itself derived from heavily leveraged borrowed resources. What is common among almost all crises is the buildup of excessive leverage in the system and the inevitable bursting of the financial bubble that results from such leverage. What is interesting about the current crisis is that this excess leverage occurred over a period when, through the Basel process, greater consensus had developed on the need for and level of adequate capital required in banking institutions across all major jurisdictions.

Furthermore, it was assumed that sophisticated financial risk management capabilities also had been developed within large financial institutions during this period of unusually rapid growth in both the magnitude and sophistication of the financial system. This had some perverse results. First, because of the perceived increase in sophistication in the measurement of risk, high-quality risk capital in large banks could be as low as 2 percent of assets even while complying with the Basel capital adequacy requirements. Second, large financial institutions could maintain lower high-quality capital because of the assumption that they had better risk management capacity than smaller, less sophisticated institutions.

With financial deregulation in key jurisdictions like the United States and the United Kingdom, as well as in most other countries, financial institutions also grew in complexity. Financial conglomerates began to include all financial functions under one roof: banking, insurance, asset management, proprietary trading, investment banking, brokerage, and the like. The consequence has been inadequate appreciation and assessment of the emerging risks, both within institutions and systemwide. What were the factors that led to this emergence of excessive systemwide and institutional risk?

## Growth in Securitized Credit and Derivatives

Among the notable developments of the last decade has been the unprecedented, explosive growth of securitized credit intermediation and associated derivatives.[20] "The wreckage on Wall Street stems in part from the explosive growth in complex and mispriced securitized mortgages, which the banks both issued and themselves held."[21] For example, the issuance of collateralized debt obligations (CDOs) tripled between the first quarters of 2005 and 2007, reaching a peak of $179 billion in the second quarter of 2007, before collapsing to $5 billion by the fourth quarter of 2008. The issuance of residential mortgage-backed securities doubled from $1.3 trillion to $2.7 trillion between 2001 and 2003. The assumption underlying this development was that it constituted a mechanism that took risk off the balance sheets of banks, placing it with a diversified set

20. Yellen (2009).
21. Committee on Capital Markets Regulation (CCMR, 2009, p. 19).

of investors and thereby serving to reduce banking system risks. The opposite actually transpired. As late as April 2006, the IMF's Global Financial Stability Report noted that this dispersion would help "mitigate and absorb shocks to the financial system" with the result that "improved resilience may be seen in fewer bank failures and more consistent credit provision."[22]

This assumption has already proven erroneous, although simple forms of securitization have existed for a long time. Among the key functions of banks is maturity transformation: they intermediate shorter-term liabilities to fund longer-term assets in the nonfinancial sector. Banks are typically highly leveraged, and hence trust and confidence are crucial to their functioning and stability. Traditionally, therefore, banks exercised sharp vigilance over the risk elements of their assets, which were typically illiquid, to ensure constant rollover of their shorter-term funding liabilities. Securitization turns illiquid assets into liquid ones, which in theory then disperses risks from the banks' balance sheets and also reduces their required banking capital. Assets themselves came to be seen as liquid short-term instruments and began to be funded by ultra-short-term liabilities, including even overnight repos whose volume increased manifold in recent years. The majority of holdings of securitized credit, however, actually ended up on the books of highly leveraged banks and bank-like institutions, and hence risk was concentrated rather than dispersed. Systemic risk increased, because traded instruments are inherently more susceptible to price swings in response to changes in market sentiment. What emerged was a "complex chain of multiple relationships between multiple institutions" and hence a higher risk of contagion within the financial sector.[23] Furthermore, liquidity risks in such markets were not understood adequately. It was assumed that these liquid markets would always exist, and so securitized assets were assumed to be inherently less risky than illiquid long-term credit assets.

Financial innovation arising from the search for yields compounded this problem as second-order derivatives proliferated and as their valuation increasingly depended upon model valuation and credit ratings rather than on observable and transparent market valuation; hence such derivatives inherently became more opaque. Thus, when problems arose in these markets and prices were not visible, valuation of the assets of banks and the shadow banking system became unobservable. Consequently, trust and confidence evaporated and markets froze.

Compounding these problems was the emergence of the shadow banking system that took assets off of banks' balance sheets, thereby reducing the latter's capital requirements. The complexity and magnitude of intrafinancial sector transactions exploded over this past decade. For example, issuance of global

22. As quoted in the Turner Review (FSA 2009b, p. 42).
23. FSA (2009b).

credit derivatives increased from near zero in 2001 to over $60 trillion in 2007; foreign exchange (forex) trading activity rose tenfold from about $100 billion to $1,000 billion in the twenty years between 1987 and 2007, and doubled after 2002; over-the-counter (OTC) interest rate derivatives grew from around zero in 1987 to about $50 trillion in 1997 and $400 trillion by 2007; global issuance of asset-backed securities went up from about $500 billion in 1997 to over $2 trillion in 2007; and trading in oil futures increased from an equivalent of about 300 million barrels in 2005 to 1,000 million barrels in 2007, more than ten times the volume of oil produced![24] Thus the financial sector was increasingly separated from the real economy.

Given the explosive increase in financial transactions unrelated to developments in the real economy, the financial sector exhibited high profits and growth while doing relatively little for the nonfinancial sectors of the economy, which, in principle, the financial sector exists to serve. The debt of financial companies increased to levels exceeding the GDP of leading economies: in the United Kingdom, for example, financial sector debt increased from 40 percent of GDP in 1987 to 200 percent in 2007, and in the United States, from a similar 40 percent in 1987 to over 100 percent in 2007.[25] Thus, in the process of taking risks off balance sheets through securitization, these risks returned to the extended banking system itself, belying the original rationale for securitization. Rather than reducing systemic risk, the development of complex securitization and associated derivatives only served to increase it. Moreover, it became increasingly difficult to trace where the risk ultimately lay.

The regulatory system was clearly behind the curve in accounting for these developments. The procedures for calculating risk-based capital requirements underestimated the risks inherent in traded securitized instruments, thereby adding to the incentive for banks to securitize assets into traded instruments, which bore lower risk weights. The trading of these instruments has largely been in OTC markets that exhibit little transparency. As a result of this overall process, banks became effectively undercapitalized, and the leverage ratios of the unregulated shadow banking system and investment banks reached unsustainable levels. A good deal of the ongoing discussion on change in regulation is focused on this issue through mandating increased capital requirements for such activities.

With the existence of low interest rates, mispriced low-risk perceptions, and inherent incentives to originate lending and distribute securitized instruments, household indebtedness increased to unprecedented levels, particularly for housing. In both the United States and the United Kingdom, the household debt-to-GDP ratio increased from an average of around 60 percent between the

24. Turner (2010).
25. FSA (2009a).

mid-1980s and 1990s to over 100 percent in the following decade.[26] Demand for housing assets rose, and housing prices escalated accordingly. Thus micro-level behavior led to increased systemic risk that was not adequately appreciated or understood, and hence was not monitored by the authorities.

Thus there are immense emerging challenges that confront financial sector regulators as a consequence of the ongoing North Atlantic financial crisis. There will be extensive debate at both the academic level and among practitioners. How will economists and policymakers change their views on the efficiency and rationality of markets, particularly financial markets? What effect will such reexamination have on financial innovation in the future? What will regulatory authorities do in the meantime while these debates are being settled at the intellectual level? Will they overreact and restrict financial growth in the months and years to come? Will this affect global GDP growth as well?

At this point I turn to the key proposals currently being made for a major overhaul of the financial regulatory architecture.

## Reforming the Regulatory Framework: The Future Perspective

There has been and is a great deal of discussion at both the national and international levels on reforming the financial regulatory system to address the various weaknesses that have emerged. At the national level, for example, both the U.S. and U.K. treasuries have released detailed proposals for regulatory reform that are now being considered by their respective legislatures.[27] At the international level, the G20 took the lead in late 2008.[28] The resulting recommendations of the G20 Working Group 1 were broadly accepted by the leaders of the countries involved and remitted for implementation to the various standard-setting bodies, with the Financial Stability Board (FSB) assigned a broad coordination role. The key objective outlined by the FSB for regulatory reform is to create a "more disciplined and less procyclical financial system that better supports balanced sustainable economic growth."[29]

There is no question, therefore, that financial regulation has to be strengthened comprehensively. The prevailing intellectual paradigm of light-touch regulation premised on the efficient markets hypothesis is being questioned. Hitherto unregulated institutions, markets, and instruments will now have to be brought under the regulatory framework, and the framework itself will need to be redesigned to address the emerging needs at both the national and international

---

26. FSA (2009b).
27. U.S. Department of the Treasury (2009); H.M. Treasury (2009).
28. G20 Working Group 1 (2009).
29. FSB (2009).

levels. As this new enthusiasm for financial regulation unfolds, it is important to keep in mind the basic functions of the financial system, and how they can be strengthened so that the needs of the real economy are better served. To reiterate: among the key objectives of regulatory reform is the emergence of a "more disciplined and less procyclical financial system that better supports balanced sustainable economic growth." Such a system would not, for example, allow leverage to increase to the extent that it did.[30]

## Financial Innovation

Reform should ensure that the financial system continues to play a vital role in intermediating savings to provide adequate levels of funding to the real sector, thereby supporting economic growth. It needs to be recognized that financial markets will remain global and interconnected, while financial innovation will remain important for fostering economic efficiency. Hence, while financial regulation and supervision must be strengthened, this process must take care not to stifle entrepreneurship and financial innovation. Still, the following question must be constantly asked: "Financial innovation toward what objective?"

As long as financial innovation is seen as promoting price discovery, greater intermediation efficiency, better risk management, and hence overall efficiency and growth, it must be encouraged, but with appropriate safeguards to maintain financial stability. Unproductive financial innovation, however, will need to be discouraged. Therefore, the debate on financial innovation and regulation has to be framed in terms of the potential and systematic relevance of such innovations in addition to the means for bringing them effectively under the regulatory umbrella.[31] The notional amounts of global derivatives relative to the nominal value of GDP exploded during the decade preceding the financial crisis. What was the economic contribution of such growth in the global economic and financial system? It clearly did not make the global financial system any safer at the macrolevel. Did market participants gain through better risk management in both the real and financial sectors? Addressing such questions will require intensive research on the utility of the kinds of financial innovation that have occurred over the past couple of decades. What has been beneficial and what has not? As work proceeds to bring new financial products and different kinds of derivatives under closer financial regulation and supervision, such reforms should be guided by the answers to such basic questions.

In general, therefore, there is a need for reform of the regulatory framework to shield the financial system from potential crises while identifying measures to mitigate the consequences of any future episodes of financial stress.

30. FSB (2009).
31. Mohan (2007); FSA (2009b); Turner (2010).

## Perimeter of Financial Regulation

The regulatory framework will need to keep pace with the associated risks in a more rapid and effective manner. Large, complex financial institutions will continue to operate in multiple jurisdictions in order to meet the needs of their large global clients, and supervision will need to be better coordinated internationally with a robust global resolution framework. To avoid regulatory arbitrage, greater consistency is needed in the regulation of similar instruments and of institutions performing similar activities, both within and across borders. As overall financial regulation is strengthened, it will be essential that it apply to *all* systemically important financial institutions. For example, if only banks are subject to tighter regulation, regulatory arbitrage will inevitably follow, with much financial sector activity shifting to other, more lightly regulated financial institutions. That is why the G20 Working Group stressed the need to regulate all systemically important financial institutions. The questions again are how much regulation, what constitutes "systemically important," how to ensure that all applicable entities, markets, and instruments are regulated, and what form should the regulation take?

There is a great degree of continuing discussion on the regulation of large, complex financial institutions. Undoubtedly they will continue to have a global presence. How will they be better regulated across borders? How can better global resolution regimes be designed that will work in practice?

In addition, capital markets will require greater emphasis on reducing counterparty risk and on ensuring that their infrastructure allows them to remain a source of funding during periods of stress. The postcrisis period is likely to be characterized by a financial system that functions with lower levels of leverage, reduced funding mismatches (both in terms of maturity and currency), less exposure to counterparty risk, and greater transparency regarding financial instruments. After credit markets recover from the crisis, it will be important to mitigate the inevitable pressure to expand profits through increased risk-taking. A more developed macroprudential approach will be important in this context.

The type, size, and cross-border exposures of institutions and markets that will emerge from this crisis are likely to be considerably different from those that existed before the crisis. As banks and financial institutions consolidate, policymakers will have to adapt prudential regulation for firms of varying degrees of size and concentration. There is now general agreement, for example, that institutions above some size threshold should be subject to higher capital requirements, possibly on an escalating basis.[32] Similarly, the design of any new or revised policy will need to ensure healthy competition. Were the high returns that the financial sector exhibited in the decade preceding the crisis due

---

32. FSB (2009); BCBS (2009b); CCMR (2009); Warwick Commission (2009).

to inadequate competition, or to excessive expansion in the trading of financial instruments, or both? Financial institutions, markets, and instruments will continue to evolve in ways that pose challenges for regulation, notwithstanding the retrenchment that is currently under way. Financial institutions, policymakers, supervisors, and regulators will all need to become better equipped to manage the interconnectedness of markets, both domestically and globally, as well as the effects of innovation and the potential for incentives to become misaligned.

It will be necessary to consider the appropriate timing for changes in the regulatory framework going forward. Recommendations should promote proportionate regulatory reaction when needed, acknowledging the possible limits of the self-regulatory approach in some contexts. For example, while ultimately capital buffers for the system should be enhanced during periods of economic expansion, in order to be drawn down as needed in downturns, changes in the current environment may have a negative impact on the real economy. A considered and comprehensive review of the consequences of reforms and harmonization, coordinated across jurisdictions, is necessary to increase the effective transition to a more stable financial system.[33]

In short, the overarching mandate of reforms is to make regulatory regimes more effective over the business cycle. This is related to many other issues, including certain aspects of compensation schemes at financial institutions, margin requirements and risk management practices focused on value-at-risk calculations based on short historical samples, the capital adequacy framework, and valuation and loan loss provisioning practices. In addition, there is a need to redefine the scope of the regulatory framework to establish appropriate oversight for the institutions and markets that may be the source of systemic risk. Risk management also must be improved to better evaluate vulnerabilities arising from low-frequency, systemwide risks and to better mitigate these risks.

Against this broad background, this section endeavors to focus on defining the priorities for action insofar as financial regulation and supervision are concerned.

## MACROPRUDENTIAL ORIENTATION

As observed, the buildup of microinstitutional risks resulted in the unfolding of massive macro risk, partly through the rise in unsustainable asset prices. Therefore, as a supplement to sound microprudential and market integrity regulation, national financial regulatory frameworks should be reinforced with a macroprudential oversight that promotes a systemwide approach to financial regulation and supervision and mitigates the buildup of observable excess risks across the system. For example, there is now increasing agreement that when credit growth exceeds certain thresholds, it should entail additional capital buffer

33. G20 Working Group 1 (2009).

requirements.[34] Such thresholds will have to vary across jurisdictions, and the challenge will remain how to identify such thresholds. Prudential regimes should encourage behavior that supports systemic stability, discourages regulatory arbitrage, and adopts the concept of "systemic" risk, factoring in the effects of leverage and funding. In most jurisdictions, this will require improved coordination mechanisms between various financial authorities, mandates for all financial authorities accountable for financial system stability, and effective tools to address systemic risks. It will also require an effective global roundtable— currently proposed to be the Financial Stability Board—to bring together national financial authorities to jointly assess systemic risks across the global financial system and to coordinate policy responses.

A number of policymaking institutions, particularly central banks, have enhanced their analysis of systemic risk in recent years. In fact, many of the systemic vulnerabilities that caused or exacerbated the current turmoil had already been identified, but mechanisms to effectively translate these analyses into policy action have been lacking. The basic idea here is to multiply the capital adequacy ratios with a systemic risk factor. This means that better measures of macroprudential risk must be found. It is argued that leverage ratios, maturity mismatches, and estimates of bank credit expansion should be taken into account. Thus highly leveraged and fast growing "systemic" institutions would be subject to higher capital requirements than the rest. Brunnermeier and others (2009) argue that when there is growing systemic risk, characterized by increasing leverage, maturity mismatches, credit expansion, and asset price increases during boom times, the required amount of banking capital should increase and conversely decrease during downturns when deleveraging takes place. These ideas are now gaining wider acceptance, and the standard setters are busy finding the ways and means to translate them into practice.

Potential macroprudential tools to be explored further could include:

—complementing risk-based capital measures with simpler indicators aimed to measure the buildup of leverage, with enhanced sensitivity to off-balance-sheet exposures;

—capital requirements that adjust over the financial cycle;

—monitoring the sectoral growth of credit to identify areas of "excess credit growth" when they arise;

—loan loss provisioning standards that incorporate all available credit information;

—use of longer historical samples to assess risk and margin requirements; and

—greater focus on loan-to-value ratios for mortgages.

In general, the challenge is to continually endeavor to strike a balance between macro- and microprudential regulation.

34. FSB (2009); BCBS (2009b); Warwick Commission (2009).

REGULATORY REGIME

With the emergence of the shadow banking system and other leveraged financial institutions, the scope of regulation and oversight needs to be expanded to include all systemically important institutions, markets, and instruments. Accordingly, the perimeter of financial sector surveillance would have to be extended, possibly with differentiated thresholds to allow institutions to graduate from simple disclosures to higher levels of prudential oversight as their contribution to systemic risks increases. Work is under way to devise practical guidelines for regulators to assess systemic importance so that regulation of all systemically important institutions can be done in a consistent manner.[35] Financial authorities will need enhanced information on all material financial institutions and markets, including private pools of capital that are leveraged. Large, complex financial institutions require particularly robust oversight given their size and global reach. Regulatory disincentives should also be included to discourage such institutions from becoming too big to fail and to reduce complexity in their group structures. The regulatory and oversight framework should strive to treat similar institutions and activities consistently, with greater emphasis on functions and activities and less emphasis on legal status.

The main bone of contention here is whether and how to regulate private pools of capital, including private equity funds and hedge funds. No doubt such funds have increased in size tremendously over the past couple of decades. The amount of money hedge funds manage has increased from around $40 billion in 1990 to $540 billion in 2001 and $2 trillion in 2008, a growth rate far in excess of any metric related to the real economy.[36] Now about 10,000 hedge funds exist. There have been differences in opinion regarding the role of these funds in the current global financial crisis. Nevertheless, there is broad agreement that private pools of capital, including hedge funds, can be a source of risk owing to their combined size in the market, their use of leverage and maturity mismatches, and their connectedness with other parts of the financial system. There is emerging agreement that all such funds need to be registered with a designated regulatory authority, but debate continues on the extent of their regulation.[37]

The widespread reliance of market participants on credit ratings of market instruments led to inadequate risk analysis. Thus credit rating agencies will also require regulatory oversight. Furthermore, there is a need to modify rating agency practices and procedures for managing conflicts of interest and for assuring the transparency and quality of the rating process, particularly the process

35. FSB (2009).
36. CCMR (2009).
37. FSB (2009); CCMR (2009).

for rating complex securitized instruments and derivatives. Certain regulatory regimes mandate the use of credit ratings for risk management and for assessment of capital requirements within institutions, leading to inadequate in-house assessment of risk by these institutions. Regulators will need to reduce or eliminate such mandates so that all financial institutions take greater responsibility for their own risk assessments. Given the global scope of some credit rating agencies, the oversight framework should be consistent across jurisdictions, with appropriate sharing of information between national authorities responsible for the oversight of credit rating agencies. Much greater independent research is also needed in assessing post facto how well credit rating agencies have fared in their credit rating practices. Since their data and methodologies are generally proprietary, including the confidential information they have on the entities and instruments being rated, such research has been difficult, if not impossible, to do. Regulators will need to find ways to make such research possible without violating the need to maintain confidentiality.

## PROCYCLICALITY

Once conditions in the financial system have recovered, international standards for capital and liquidity buffers will have to be raised, and the buildup of capital buffers and provisions in good times should be encouraged so that capital can absorb losses and be drawn down in difficult times, such as the current period. It will be necessary to develop a methodology to link the stage in the business cycle to capital requirements in a nondiscretionary way and to accounting and prudential standards. Broad agreement is now emerging in the Basel Committee on Banking Supervision (BCBS) and the FSB that capital buffers have to be built in to constrain procyclical buildup of leverage in financial institutions. In addition to the changes being proposed to raise capital adequacy norms, minimum global liquidity standards are also being explored, along with greater requirements for countercyclical provisioning. The implementation of these new standards should be effective in constraining the procyclical buildup of leverage in financial systems on an automatic basis.

Many questions have also arisen about accounting conventions and procedures that are perceived to add to procyclicality in the financial system. It should be recognized that the clock should not be turned back on fair value accounting just to address the issue of temporary market illiquidity. What is needed is to make clear the nature of price uncertainty and to do so in a manner that symmetrically addresses the potential for mispricing in illiquid markets as well as in booming markets. Improvements could include better guidance and principles for mark-to-market valuation, information on the variance around the fair value calculations, and data on historic prices.

## PRUDENTIAL OVERSIGHT

There are various dimensions of prudential oversight that require strengthening and that can play complementary roles in improving financial stability.

*Capital Adequacy Framework.* There is a clear recognition of the need for higher quantity and quality capital; this will result in minimum regulatory requirements that significantly exceed existing Basel thresholds. The emphasis is on increasing the quantity and quality of tier one capital. It is being proposed that only common equity shares and retained earnings be counted toward tier one capital. As these tougher requirements are introduced, it is understood that the transition to future standards needs to be carefully phased given the importance of maintaining bank lending in the current macroeconomic climate. In view of the serious problems that arose from lower risk weights being attached to assets in the trading book, there is also agreement that the capital required against trading book activities should be increased significantly. Published accounts could also include buffers to anticipate potential future losses, through, for instance, the creation of an "economic cycle reserve." There is also increasing agreement on the introduction of a maximum gross leverage ratio as a backstop discipline against excessive growth in absolute balance sheet size.[38] In addition, in the context of rapid financial innovation and risk-based regulatory capital requirements, a well-constructed, non-risk-based capital measure can at least partially address the problem of modeling deficiencies for the advanced approaches and ensure that a minimum level of capital is retained in the banking system.

*Liquidity Risk Management.* A new element in the future regulatory approach is the explicit recognition that liquidity regulation and supervision must be given the same emphasis as capital regulation.[39] Individual institutions have demonstrated that their own internal incentive structures are such that liquidity risk may be procyclical due to its links with market and credit risk and to accelerator factors, such as the mark-to-market effects of asset values and net worth. Structural reliance on short-term wholesale market funding, including via securitization, has increased the sensitivity of banks' balance sheets and cost of funds to procyclical elements. Some regulators were already giving attention to such issues. The Reserve Bank of India, for instance, places prudential limits on purchased overnight interbank liabilities and restricts the uncollateralized overnight market to commercial banks. It also actively monitors the ratio of wholesale purchased funding that banks have to their more stable deposit funding. Therefore, regulatory policies need to appropriately reflect the true price of funding liquidity on financial institutions' balance sheets—ensuring that the market does not

---

38. CCMR (2009); BCBS (2009b); FSB (2009); Institute of International Finance (IIF 2009).
39. BCBS (2009a).

rely excessively on the central bank's emergency liquidity support facility. Policies that could be considered include:

—improved funding-risk management by strengthening risk management and governance and control;

—introduction of minimum quantitative funding liquidity buffers of high-quality liquidity assets;

—imposition of a thirty-day liquidity coverage ratio;

—a longer-term structural liquidity ratio;

—introduction of a regulatory charge for institutions that present a higher-than-average liquidity risk, and pricing of access to central bank liquidity in order to encourage institutions holding better quality collateral; and

—requirement for global banks to have sufficient high-quality liquid assets.

An effective global framework for managing liquidity in large, cross-border financial institutions should include internationally agreed-upon levels of liquidity buffers and should encourage an increase in the quality of their composition. Such a framework needs to be comprehensive and take into account overall liquidity needs. In the ongoing discussion related to enhanced requirements for mandating liquidity buffers, there is some debate on the choice of instruments that will qualify as high-quality liquid instruments: will they include only treasuries, or will high-quality corporate bonds also qualify?[40] Again, for example, the Reserve Bank of India has long imposed a "statutory liquidity ratio" (a specified proportion, 25 percent as of 2010) on all commercial banks: their net demand and time liabilities must be invested in government securities. The financial industry would clearly like to broaden the kinds of instruments that would be acceptable, but the implication of such broadening would be that central banks would also have to broaden the collateral that they accept for their liquidity operations.

*Infrastructure for OTC Derivatives.* As documented, the explosion of credit derivatives and their offshoots (such as CDOs and CDOs-squared) has demonstrated the clear need for oversight and transparency in this market. The market for credit default swaps (CDSs) operates on a bilateral, OTC basis and has grown to many times the size of the market for the underlying credit instruments. In light of problems involving some large players in this market, attention has focused on the systemic risks posed by CDSs. There is a global consensus on the need for centralized clearing and a central counterparty (CCP) for all the OTC derivative products. Accordingly, efforts are under way in the United States, the European Union, and elsewhere to implement CCPs for CDSs. There is general agreement that standardized contracts should be conducted on designated exchanges, while the remaining OTC trades also should be cleared

40. IIF (2009).

centrally. They would then be subject to the scrutiny of a central counterparty and would have mandatory reporting requirements on a transparent platform.[41]

The development of a CCP facilitates greater market transparency, including the reporting of prices for CDSs, trading volumes, and aggregate open interest. The availability of pricing information can improve the fairness, efficiency, and competitiveness of markets—all of which enhance investor protection and facilitate capital formation. The degree of transparency, of course, depends on the extent of participation in the CCP. If needed, some incentives may be provided by national authorities, for example, by taking a higher capital charge for transactions not cleared through central counterparties. If capital requirements are related to the counterparty risk exposures that arise from derivatives, repos, and security financing activities, institutions will have incentive to increase OTC derivative exposure to CCPs and exchanges while also reducing the probability of contagion when problems arise. To foster transparency and promote the use of a CCP and of exchange trading for credit derivatives, public authorities should also encourage the financial industry to standardize contracts and use a data repository for the remaining nonstandardized contracts, and to promote fair and open access to central counterparty services. The use of a CCP will naturally lead to higher costs in OTC trading, which would itself lend some stability to the system.

A CCP mechanism already exists for clearing and settling all interbank spot forex transactions and all outright and repo transactions in government securities. Nonguaranteed settlement of OTC trades in interest rate swaps also commenced in 2008. Guaranteed settlement of interest rate swap (IRS) and forex forwards is at an advanced stage, though it remains a work in progress.

India already has an institution (the Clearing Corporation of India) for centralized clearing and settlement of all interbank spot forex transactions and all outright and repo transactions in government securities. Nonguaranteed settlement of OTC trades in IRSs has also started. Work is now under way on guaranteed settlement of IRS and forex forwards.[42]

There is also some debate on the number of CCPs that are needed to foster stability in a system. Some argue that it would be beneficial to have a competitive environment for central counterparties to mitigate systemic risk resulting from counterparty credit risk, but without imposing regulatory requirements that unduly fragment the market. Others argue that because of netting in a clearinghouse with a central counterparty, overall risk is reduced substantially, and hence only one or two clearinghouses are needed in any particular system.[43] It must be ensured, however, that the CCP is adequately funded.

41. BCBS (2009b); IIF (2009); Warwick Commission (2009).
42. Gopinath (2009).
43. CCMR (2009).

*Compensation.* Among the issues that have gained prominence as contributory factors to the emergence of the global financial crisis is the explosion of remuneration in the financial sector, particularly in comparison with trends in the rest of the economy. Much more attention is now being given to the development of sound practice principles by the international standard setters. It is important that reforms in this regard be done on an industry-wide basis so that improved risk management and compensation practices by some systemically important firms are not undermined by the unsound practices of others. Among the proposals being discussed is the principle that there must be a link between overall firm performance and individual bonuses given; this is in response to the observation that large bonuses are given even if the firm is taking losses. Another principle being enunciated is that guaranteed bonuses should be either prohibited or, at a minimum, subject to limitations. In any case, there is general agreement that bonuses should be aligned with the long-term performance of the firm rather than with short-term profits.

In view of the compensation practices that have been observed even after the financial crisis, there is no doubt that there will be greater supervisory oversight over compensation practices for some time to come. At the present time, financial institutions have returned to profitability, to a great extent due to the extraordinary official measures taken to stabilize the financial system. The market mechanism does not seem to ensure that these profits are retained in financial institutions to bolster their capital. The firms that benefited from Troubled Asset Relief Program funds have preferred to return the funds as soon as they could rather than submit to regulatory limitations on compensation that they would have been subject to otherwise. Some feel that restricting dividend payments, share buybacks, and compensation rates is an appropriate way to constrain the kind of excessive compensation practices observed.[44]

Along with the enunciation of such principles and practices, it is important to look carefully at the inherent market incentive structure that has led to the observed compensation practices in the financial sector. Acting on this flawed incentive structure is more likely to be effective than regulatory prescriptions.

There is a need to question further the focus on compensation in the financial sector: is the compensation issue actually a red herring? Is it not the explosion in intrafinancial sector transactions and excess profitability of financial institutions that has led to the very high compensation levels of their employees along with the high returns to shareholders? If a firm has such high returns, they have to go somewhere: they are either distributed to shareholders or to the employees or a combination of both, which is what has been happening. In this case, it is then difficult to restrict compensation levels, as is currently being argued. If

44. FSB (2009).

the distribution of profits goes disproportionately to management and employ-ees, then the question relates to corporate governance practices. Why do boards not act more in the interest of shareholders? Much of the discussion has veered off into the minutiae of compensation practices related to the various forms in which compensation is given. To my mind, the real question relates to the high profitability observed in recent years in segments of the financial sector.

Therefore, the question really is, is there a lack of competition in the financial sector? And if so why? Are there some regulatory provisions that restrain compe-tition, or are there some entry barriers inherent in the structure of the financial industry? If competition is not lacking, then why do these profits not compete downward? And again, if the answer is indeed that there is a lack of competition, what can be done? What kind of competition policy measures would be relevant and applicable to the financial sector? Addressing these questions is probably more useful for addressing the compensation issue than focusing narrowly on compensation patterns and levels.

*Risk Management.* The fundamental weaknesses in risk management prac-tices that the current crisis revealed were the inability of financial institutions to adequately monitor risk concentrations across products and geographic areas, shortcomings in stress testing, and inappropriate practices for managing risks arising from structured products. First and foremost, it remains the responsibil-ity of the private sector to take the lead in strengthening firmwide risk man-agement frameworks. Both management and boards of directors are responsible for instituting adequate risk management and control systems. Generally, banks are expected to have effective internal policies, systems, and controls in place to identify, measure, monitor, manage, control, and mitigate their risk concentra-tions in a timely manner and under various conditions, including stressed mar-ket situations. The supervisory authorities would have to oversee compliance of such best practices for capturing firmwide risk concentrations arising from both on- and off-balance-sheet exposures and securitization activities. For example, with respect to OTC derivative markets, it is being proposed that capital require-ments be strengthened to reflect the actual risk of OTC derivatives. In deriv-ing such capital requirements, it is also being proposed that new standards be devised to account for counterparty risks. When trading is done on an exchange or with a central counterparty, the capital requirement would naturally be lower, thereby incentivizing firms to minimize bilateral OTC trading.

*Transparency.* Given the serious problems that have arisen, there clearly needs to be greater emphasis on increasing the transparency of the techniques, data characteristics, and caveats involved in the valuation of complex financial instru-ments; improved information regarding OTC derivatives markets and clearing arrangements; and better reporting of exposures in a format that permits regu-lators to aggregate and assess risks to the system as a whole. This would help

investors perform some of the due diligence currently outsourced to credit rating
agencies while also helping the latter to do better in measuring the tail risks.

The fundamental issue here is twofold: standard setters should work with
supervisors and regulators, first, to reduce complexity in accounting standards to
facilitate better assessment of uncertainty surrounding valuation, and second, to
achieve consistency of valuation methods and a single set of accounting standards.

*Enforcement.* International standards (including those for macroprudential regulation), scope of regulation, capital adequacy, and liquidity buffers should be coordinated to ensure a common and coherent international framework that national
financial authorities should apply in their countries, consistent with national circumstances. The expanded Financial Stability Forum—now renamed the Financial
Stability Board—the International Monetary Fund, and the international standard
setters could assume this coordination role. In addition, the financial regulatory
and oversight frameworks and their implementation in all G20 countries should
be reviewed periodically, validated internationally, and made public.

## The Challenges Ahead

The agenda that is being developed for strengthening financial sector regulation
and supervision is ambitious. Contentious issues are arising both at domestic
regulatory levels and at the international level regarding regulatory cooperation.
Whereas the principles that have been outlined for this regulatory overhaul are
increasingly well-accepted, many challenges will arise regarding their modes of
implementation and their practicality.

### Regulatory Structure and Authority

First, there is much discussion in many jurisdictions on the changes needed in
regulatory structure to minimize the probability of such a financial crisis arising again. There is general agreement on the need to establish a regime of macroprudential regulation and financial stability oversight, and these regimes will
need to be more effective over the economic cycle. The issue under discussion in
different jurisdictions is, who will do it? Would it be a council of regulators, the
central bank, or the treasury? The core concern behind such discussion relates to
the location of responsibility for maintaining financial stability. Should central
banks be made responsible, and also accountable, for maintaining financial stability? Macroprudential regulation is increasingly seen as one of the key means for
maintaining financial stability. It entails the imposition of prudential regulations
whenever some macroeconomic or overall financial trends require action. If the
central bank is only a monetary authority, and a separate agency, like the Financial Services Authority of the United Kingdom, is responsible for financial regulation and supervision, how is coordination to be achieved so that such action can

be implemented? The United States has a very fragmented regulatory structure, whereas the United Kingdom placed all regulatory responsibilities for all segments of the financial sector with the unified FSA. The U.S. Federal Reserve System does have significant regulatory responsibilities, but regulatory failures were significant in all North Atlantic financial systems, with the exception of Canada. So it is difficult to cite any existing system as comprising best practice.

The ongoing efforts to undertake significant regulatory reform in the United States, the United Kingdom, and in the Euro Zone illustrate the lack of consensus on what kinds of regulatory structure constitute best practice for promoting financial stability.

The United Kingdom is abandoning its experiment of completely separating financial regulation from the central bank, and the FSA is now being folded back into the Bank of England. The governor of the Bank of England will now be responsible for monetary policy, financial regulation, and financial stability, an arrangement similar to that prevailing in India. Consequent to the crisis it is felt that the central bank can better exercise its responsibility for financial stability if financial regulation also comes within its purview. However, these proposals are yet to be formulated for legislative approval.

The U.S. Treasury had initially proposed that all banking regulation be unified in a single agency, while placing greater responsibility in the U.S. Federal Reserve for maintaining financial stability. In the reform bill that has finally been passed, systemic risk will be formally assessed by a new Financial Services Oversight Council to be composed of the main regulators and chaired by the Treasury secretary. It will focus specially on SIFIs in order to prevent institutions from getting too big to fail. Any emerging SIFIs, including non-banks, will be put under the regulation of the Federal Reserve. Regulatory jurisdiction has been simplified and clarified, with the Fed handling systemic institutions; the Office of the Controller of the Currency (OCC), national banks; and the Federal Deposit Insurance Corporation (FDIC), state banks. The only agency being eliminated is the Office of Thrift Supervision. It is yet to be seen how these new arrangements will function. What is clear, however, is that there is now much greater appreciation of the role of the central bank in maintaining financial stability and in regulating SIFIs of all varieties, not just banks.

I have perhaps a biased view, having been in a central bank, though I have also worked in the treasury. I really do not believe that effective macroprudential oversight or financial stability oversight can be done without the central bank being at the helm of this activity. Any kind of group can be set up, depending on the country's overall regulatory framework, and can include the treasury and the heads of the other regulatory entities. The central bank is the lender of last resort; it is also the only agency that has an overall view of the economy, along with exceptional stability in terms of staffing and continuity in thinking, relative to most treasuries. It should carefully monitor evolving developments in all financial markets if it is doing its job well as a monetary authority.

Since the Reserve Bank of India is the monetary authority and also the financial sector regulator, it has been able to supplement its monetary policy very effectively with prudential actions on a consistent basis. It regularly monitors credit aggregates, including movements in sectoral credit. Consequently, it took action when it observed excess credit growth, both on an aggregate basis and in particular sectors, such as real estate and housing. So it increased the cash reserve ratio to curb overall credit growth and imposed higher risk weights for lending in the effected sectors. As part of its supervisory activities, it also monitors the incremental credit deposit ratio carefully and cautions banks when such a ratio is found to exceed acceptable norms. It is also able to do forward-looking countercyclical capital buffering through increases in loan loss provisioning when needed. In addition, when it observed regulatory arbitrage being practiced by the lightly regulated nonbank finance companies during 2005–07, it took measures to tighten their regulation so as to reduce their capacity to take on excess leverage. This experience is a valuable example for practicing the kind of proposals being put forward for implementing macroprudential polices as supplements to monetary policy as normally practiced in a narrow fashion.

I do believe that given different countries with large variations in institutional legacies, traditions, and systems, no one size can fit all. But at the same time, I think that the central bank does need to have a lead role as far as financial stability is concerned within any kind of arrangement that is deemed fit in a particular country. As a recent IMF paper notes: "If one accepts the notion that, together, monetary policy and regulation provide a large set of cyclical tools, this raises the issue of how coordination is achieved between the monetary and the regulatory authorities, or whether the central bank should be in charge of both. The increasing trend toward separation of the two may well have to be reversed. Central banks are obvious candidates as macro prudential regulators."[45] In any case, there is a clear need for a comprehensive approach to regulatory risk in the financial sector, particularly as the perimeter of financial regulation is widened to encompass hitherto unregulated or lightly regulated entities such as hedge funds, credit rating agencies, and other nonbank financial companies.[46]

## Impact of Proposed Regulatory Changes

The various proposals currently under discussion with respect to enhanced capital requirements will lead to increased levels of regulatory capital over the economic cycle, and the extension of such capital requirements to bank-like institutions

---

45. Blanchard, Dell'Ariccia, and Mauro (2010).
46. CCMR (2009).

that are currently unregulated or lightly regulated will inevitably lead to lower profitability for equity investors. In addition to the increases in basic capital adequacy that are being considered, other proposals under discussion include:

—higher quality tier one capital to consist of only common shares and reserves,

—maintenance of countercyclical capital buffers,

—countercyclical provisioning,

—higher risk weights for trading instruments, and

—higher capital requirements for systemically important financial institutions (for example, institutions with assets exceeding $250 billion).

The bargaining power of banking institutions had become weak in the wake of the financial crisis; hence there was little initial observable protest regarding such proposals. As the financial crisis is resolved and as some semblance of normalcy and profitability begins to return to the financial sector, the financial industry is likely to do its utmost to resist the requirements for higher capital. It will be a challenge for regulators and governments to resist demands for relaxation of the new capital requirements, both the enhanced minimum levels and the capital buffers proposed for good times. The lobbying power of the financial industry will be restored by that time, and therefore authorities will need to be prepared for such challenges.[47] Lower systemic profitability levels will also be effective endogenously in limiting compensation levels in the financial sector.

Everyone seems to agree that there is need for increased levels of regulatory capital. The key problem that requires further analysis is that such a change implies lower profitability for the financial sector. That in itself may not be such a bad idea for the maintenance of financial stability. But there is still need for greater understanding of its implications for the financial sector as a whole. Would more stringent capital requirements imply a slower pace of credit intermediation and overall lower economic growth? Or does it just mean that there will be less intrafinancial sector activity, with negligible implications for the real economy? There is clearly a great need to work out the overall economic effects of the current recommendations related to the proposed regulatory overhaul. Such impact studies are now being conducted by the BCBS before the new capital standards are put in place.

## Implementing Countercyclical Capital Requirements

The proposal for provision of countercyclical capital will face significant implementation issues. Regulators will need to do significant technical work on understanding business cycles so that turning points can be recognized. What would be the triggers for changing these capital buffers in either direction? Would these changes commence in anticipation of business cycle turns or post facto? How

47. For example, see IIF (2009).

formal or rule-based would these changes be so that regulated institutions know in advance what they need to do? An additional issue in this sphere arises from the possibility of economic cycles occurring at different times in different jurisdictions. This would necessitate greater cross-border cooperation between home and host regulators in terms of applicable capital requirements for different segments of the same international financial conglomerate. An additional problem for EMEs would be the lack of adequate data for business cycle identification.

## Identifying and Addressing Systemic Risks

There is general agreement on the need for macroprudential regulations and the identification of systemic risks such as the buildup of asset bubbles. However, considerable technical work will need to be done at both national and international levels on identifying what such risks are, what is systemic and what is not, and what kind of regulatory actions would be effective. In the recent experience, for example, there was ample awareness of the buildup of both global financial imbalances and the asset price bubble, but there was little agreement on what needed to be done. Even if adequate work is done to identify systemic risk and determine the regulatory measures necessary, what will the enforcement methodology look like internationally? Within national regulatory systems, issues relating to interregulatory cooperation will also arise: who will be in charge of issuing early warnings, and who will listen to them?

## Defining What Is Systemically Important

There is also general agreement on extending regulation to all systemically important institutions, markets, and instruments. But here again there is an implementation issue: how to decide what is systemically important. Certainly, all financial institutions that have access to the central bank liquidity window or to whom the central bank can act as lender of last resort should be subject to capital regulation. Considerable debate has ranged around the regulation of hedge funds, which come in all sizes and forms. Some are large but not leveraged, others can be both large and leveraged, and yet others can be small and leveraged. Whereas it may be that individual hedge funds or other equity pools are not systemically important, they may be so collectively. Furthermore, they could be collectively not important systemically in good times but become so in times of extensive leveraging. A similar story applies to markets and instruments. Thus national and international regulatory systems have their work cut out for them in this regard, especially since excessive regulation could indeed snuff out entrepreneurship.

## Handling Securitized Credit

A great deal of debate has emerged around the issue of securitized credit and its offshoots. Were financial innovations in this area largely unproductive and dysfunctional, and do they need to be discouraged? That the explosion in the magnitude of such derivative instruments did not provide any benefit to the financial system or the economy as a whole is now clear. However, securitization is a time-honored practice that has done much to lubricate the financial system and helped fund real-economy needs at competitive costs. So how these instruments are regulated and how the "good" financial innovations will be winnowed from the "bad" will be a challenge.

### International Regulatory Cooperation Regulating Large, Complex Global Firms

As the current global crisis has shown, whereas many of the large, complex financial institutions operate on a worldwide scale, their regulation is national. There is currently much discussion about how international regulatory cooperation can be improved, and there appears to be a good degree of consensus emerging in the standard-setting bodies regarding the contours of enhanced regulation for global firms.[48] But implementation of their recommendations will rest with national authorities and their respective legislatures. The domestic debates within national jurisdictions are much more fractious than those within the international standard-setting bodies, and the financial industry has much greater lobbying power within national borders and their respective legislatures and governments than among the largely technocratic standard setters. Apart from the regulatory problems associated with ongoing institutions, even more difficult are the problems associated with cross-border resolution of failing institutions. The discussion on these issues has just begun.

There is also increasing debate on institutions being too big to fail.[49] In the United States, there has been renewed debate on whether to reinstitute some Glass-Steagall type restrictions on the activities that are allowed for banking institutions. Should banking be boring? Whereas there would appear to be little support for bringing back the full separation between commercial and investment banks, broker-dealers, and insurance companies, there is emerging consensus that banks' activities in proprietary trading should be curbed.[50] Banks have deposit insurance protection and also have access to lender of last resort facilities from the central bank. In times of liquidity stress, they can receive liquidity assistance from the central bank, whereas in times of insolvency, it is deposit insurance that comes to their rescue. Thus, if banks' risk-taking activities result in stress, their losses are effectively socialized. Therefore some curb on their excessive risk-taking activities is justified. The recent experience has shown that in times of extreme crisis and panic, as happened in late 2008 in the United States, even institutions

---

48. BCBS (2009b); FSB (2009); G20 Working Group 1 (2009).
49. Scott, Shultz, and Taylor (2010).
50. See Volcker (2010); Brady (2010); Shultz (2010).

that are, ex ante, not entitled to central bank liquidity support effectively receive it if they are deemed to be systemically important and hence too big to fail. So apart from the issue of restrictions on banks' speculative activities, there is a general issue of financial institutions becoming too big on a global scale.

### Capital Account Management

From the perspective of emerging market economies, the volatility in capital flows has led to severe problems in both macroeconomic management and financial regulation.[51] These capital flows have been influenced significantly by the extant monetary policy regimes in developed countries, and hence their volatility is not necessarily related to economic conditions in the receiving economies. Excess flows, sudden stops, and reversals have significant effects on EME financial sectors, the working of their capital markets, and asset prices, and hence on their economies as a whole. Management of this volatility involves action in monetary policy, fiscal management, capital account management, and also financial market regulation. This will remain a challenge since there is little international discussion on this issue. There is, however, increasing recognition that some degree of capital control may be desirable in such circumstances.[52]

### Exiting Accommodative Monetary Policy

In response to the crisis, monetary policy has been loosened substantially in major advanced economies since the second half of 2007. Policy rates have been cut to near-zero levels, even lower than those in 2003–04, and financial systems have been flooded with large liquidity. Abundant liquidity is already being reflected in return of capital flows to EMEs, and this excess liquidity, if not withdrawn quickly, runs the risk of inducing the same excesses and imbalances that were witnessed during 2003–07, including the likely recycling of capital back to the advanced economies. As the global economy starts its recovery, a calibrated exit from this unprecedented accommodative monetary policy will have to be ensured to avoid the recurrence of the financial crisis being experienced now.

## Conclusion

To summarize, the emergence of the global financial crisis has led to a new wave of thinking on all issues related to both monetary policy and financial regulation. The practice of both monetary policy and financial regulation had become too formula bound and hence predictable. While these new principles are being debated, it is important to realize that in the face of unexpected developments

---

51. Committee on the Global Financial System (2009).
52. For example, see Commission on Growth and Development (2010); Ostry and others (2010).

that always arise in the financial sector, there is an important role for the exercise of judgment by both monetary authorities and financial regulators. Whereas considerable progress has been achieved on the principles governing this regulatory overhaul, very significant challenges remain on the implementation issues that will arise as a new regime takes hold globally.

# References

Bank for International Settlements. 2008. *78th Annual Report, 2007–08.* Basel.

Basel Committee on Banking Supervision (BCBS). 2009a. "International Framework for Liquidity Risk Measurement, Standards and Monitoring." Consultative document. Basel: Bank for International Settlements (www.bis.org/publ/bcbs165. pdf?noframes=1).

———. 2009b. "Strengthening the Resilience of the Banking Sector." Consultative document. Basel: Bank for International Settlements (www.bis.org/publ/bcbs164. pdf?noframes=1).

Blanchard, Olivier, Giovanni Dell'Ariccia, and Paolo Mauro. 2010. "Rethinking Macroeconomic Policy." Staff Position Note SPN/10/03. Washington, D.C.: International Monetary Fund.

Borio, Claudio. 2009. "The Financial Crisis of 2007– ?: Macroeconomic Origins and Policy Lessons." Paper prepared for the G20 Workshop on the Global Economy. Reserve Bank of India and the Bank of England, Mumbai, May 24–26 (www.g20. org/pub_further_pubs.aspx).

Brady, Nicholas. 2010. "Fifty Years in Business: From Wall Street to the Treasury and Beyond." In *Ending Government Bailouts as We Know Them,* edited by Kenneth Scott, George P. Shultz, and John B. Taylor, pp. 21–32. Stanford: Hoover Institution Press.

Brunnermeier, Markus, and others. (Geneva Report). 2009. *The Fundamental Principles of Financial Regulation.* London: Center for Economic Policy Research.

Committee on Capital Markets Regulation (CCMR). 2009. *The Global Financial Crisis: A Plan for Regulatory Reform.* New York.

Committee on the Global Financial System. 2009. *Report of the Working Group on Capital Flows to Emerging Market Economies.* Basel: Bank for International Settlements.

Commission on Growth and Development. 2010. *Post-Crisis Growth in Developing Countries: A Special Report of the Commission on Growth and Development on the Implications of the 2008 Financial Crisis.* Washington, D.C.: World Bank

De Larosière Group. 2009. *Report of the High-Level Group on Financial Supervision in the EU.* (Chairman: Jacques de Larosiere). Brussels (http://ec.europa.eu/commission_barroso/president/pdf/statement_20090225_en.pdf).

Financial Services Authority (FSA). 2009a. "A Regulatory Response to the Global Banking Crisis." Discussion Paper 09/02. London.

———. 2009b. *The Turner Review: A Regulatory Response to the Global Banking Crisis.* London (www.fsa.gov.uk/pubs/other/turner_review.pdf).

Financial Stability Board (FSB). 2009. "Improving Financial Regulation: Report of the Financial Stability Board to G20 Leaders." September (www.financialstabilityboard. org/publications/r_090925b.pdf).

Gopinath, Shyamala. 2009. "Emerging Blueprint for Prudential Regulation: Assessment and Challenges." *Reserve Bank of India Bulletin*, December (www.rbi.org.in/scripts/ BS_SpeechesView.aspx?Id=449).

Group of Thirty. 2008. *The Structure of Financial Supervision: Approaches and Challenges in a Global Market Place.* Washington, D.C.

Group of Twenty (G20), Working Group 1. 2009. "Enhancing Sound Regulation and Strengthening Transparency" (Co-Chairs: Tiff Macklem and Rakesh Mohan). (www. g20.org/Documents/g20_wg1_010409.pdf).

H.M. Treasury. 2009. *Reforming Financial Markets.* London: Stationery Office (www. hm-treasury.gov.uk/d/reforming_financial_markets080709.pdf).

Institute of International Finance (IIF). 2009. *Reform in the Financial Services Industry: Strengthening Practices for a More Stable System.* Washington, D.C.

International Monetary Fund. 2008 "Global Slowdown and Rising Inflation." *World Economic Outlook Update* (July).

———. 2009a. "Contractionary Forces Receding but Weak Recovery Ahead." *World Economic Outlook Update* (July).

———. 2009b. *Global Financial Stability Report: Navigating the Financial Challenges Ahead.* Washington D.C. (October).

———. 2009c. "Initial Lessons of the Crisis." Washington, D.C. (February).

———. 2009d. "The State of Public Finances Cross-Country Fiscal Monitor: November 2009." Staff Position Note SPN/09/25.Washington, D.C.

———. 2010a. "Financial System Stabilized, but Exit, Reform, and Fiscal Challenges Lie Ahead." *Global Financial Stability Report: Market Update*, January (www.imf.org/ external/pubs/ft/fmu/eng/2010/01/index.htm).

———.2010b. "A Policy-Driven, Multispeed Recovery." *World Economic Outlook Update* (January).

Kindleberger, Charles P., and Robert Z. Aliber. 2005. *Manias Panics and Crashes: A History of Financial Crises.* Basingstoke, England: Palgrave Macmillan.

Mohan, Rakesh. 2007. "Recent Financial Market Developments and Implications for Monetary Policy." *Reserve Bank of India Bulletin*, October.

Ostry, Jonathan D., and others. 2010. "Capital Inflows: The Role of Controls." Staff Position Note SPN/10/04. Washington, D.C.: International Monetary Fund.

Reddy, Y. V. 2008. "Global Financial Turbulence and Financial Sector in India: A Practitioner's Perspective." *Reserve Bank of India Bulletin*, August.

Reinhart, Carmen M., and Kenneth S Rogoff. 2009. *This Time Is Different.* Princeton University Press.

Scott, Kenneth, George P. Shultz, and John B. Taylor, eds. 2010. *Ending Government Bailouts as We Know Them.* Stanford, Calif.: Hoover Institution Press.

Shultz, George P. 2010. "Make Failure Tolerable." In *Ending Government Bailouts as We Know Them,* edited by Kenneth Scott, George P. Shultz, and John B. Taylor, pp. 3–10. Stanford, Calif.: Hoover Institution Press.

Taylor, John. 2009. "The Financial Crisis and the Policy Responses: An Empirical Analysis of What Went Wrong." Working Paper 14631. Cambridge, Mass.: National Bureau of Economic Research (January).

Turner, Adair. 2010. "After the Crises: Assessing the Costs and Benefits of Financial Liberalisation." Fourteenth Chintaman Deshmukh Memorial Lecture. Reserve Bank of India, February 15 (http://rbidocs.rbi.org.in/rdocs/Speeches/PDFs/ISRT12022010.pdf).

United Nations. 2009. *Report of the Commission of Experts of the President of the United Nations General Assembly on Reforms of the International Monetary and Financial System.* (Chairman: Joseph Stiglitz). New York (www.un.org/ga/econcrisissummit/docs/FinalReport_CoE.pdf).

U.S. Department of the Treasury. 2009. *Financial Regulatory Reform: A New Foundation* (www.financialstability.gov/docs/regs/FinalReport_web.pdf).

Volcker, Paul. 2010. "Financial Reforms to End Government Bailouts as We Know Them." In *Ending Government Bailouts as We Know Them,* edited by Kenneth Scott, George P. Shultz, and John B. Taylor, pp. 11–20. Stanford, Calif.: Hoover Institution Press.

Warwick Commission. 2009. *The Warwick Commission on International Financial Reform: In Praise of Unlevel Playing Fields.* University of Warwick.

Yellen, Janet L. 2009. "A Minsky Meltdown: Lessons for Central Bankers." Presentation to the Eighteenth Annual Hyman P. Minsky Conference on the State of the U.S. and World Economies. Levy Economics Institute of Bard College, New York, April 16 (www.frbsf.org/news/speeches/2009/0416.html).

# 5

## What Regulatory Policies Work for Emerging Markets?

LUO PING

This chapter discusses the banking regulatory and supervisory practices in China with reference to the international standard for banking supervision, namely, the Basel Core Principles for Effective Banking Supervision (BCPs).[1] While China has incorporated many sound practices advocated by the BCPs, there are quite a few areas where significant differences can be observed with respect to qualification review of senior management, broader regulation at the product level, prescriptive rules, and guidance for risk management.

The findings presented here are intended to further enhance the understanding of the international standard on banking supervision as well as its implementation in emerging markets. Based on this analysis, I argue that general principles and a principle-based approach to regulation do not seem to work well for emerging markets. Indeed, the current financial crisis has revealed some shortcomings in the existing international standards on banking supervision. Perhaps this standard can be improved by greater specificity and by incorporating more aspects of the experiences in emerging markets.

### Banking Sector Reform in China

Banking sector reform is the most important part of financial sector reform in China. It started as early as 1978, when the monobank system was replaced with

The views expressed in this paper are those of the author and do not reflect the views of the commission.
1. See Appendix 5A.

a multilayered system that separates commercial lending operations and central banking. However, the most recent major reform initiatives to improve the functioning of the banking sector and banking regulatory system started in late 2003 when, after the success in corporate sector reform, the government decided to recapitalize all the state-owned banks and establish the China Banking Regulatory Commission (CRBC), which is devoted exclusively to regulation and supervision of the banking industry. By this time, China had completed the process of introducing an institutional approach to financial regulation, while the central bank, the People's Bank of China, continued to be responsible for monetary policy.

The CBRC is fully committed to building up a strong and robust banking sector and an effective supervisory system. The bank restructuring over the years has been successful. At present the entire banking sector has restored its solvency, and banks have become financially sound and better managed financial institutions. A comparison of data from 2003 to 2008 reveals the remarkable change in the financial strength and resilience of the banking industry. Over this period, the total assets have increased by RMB 34.7 trillion, up 1.3 times; bank capital has increased by RMB 2.72 trillion, up 2.6 times; and profits have increased by RMB 521.8 billion, up seventeen times. The nonperforming loan ratio of major commercial banks was reduced by 15.5 percentage points, while the number of banks in compliance with the minimum capital requirement of 8 percent has increased from 8 to 204, with their assets accounting for 99.9 percent of the total banking assets. The average capital adequacy ratio is 12 percent for all commercial banks.

On the regulatory and supervisory side, since its establishment the CBRC has benchmarked to international standards and sound practices in banking supervision and has worked hard to develop a clear roadmap for the future. In its early days the CBRC provided significant input into the drafting of the Law of the People's Republic of China on Banking Regulation and Supervision (hereafter referred to as the Law), which was issued shortly after the CBRC began operation in late 2003. While recommending the Basel Core Principles for Effective Supervision as the most relevant framework for banking supervision, the CBRC helped to ensure that the Law clearly defines not only the objectives of banking supervision and the responsibilities of the banking supervisor but also detailed approaches to banking supervision. Indeed, over 50 percent of the provisions under the Law closely reflect various principles of the BCPs document.[2] Moreover, the BCPs document is included as an appendix in the interpretation notes of the above Law, together with other relevant rules and regulations issued by the government, which is unprecedented in the rule-making process in China.[3]

---

2. The Law contains six chapters and fifty provisions.
3. People's Republic of China (2004).

Although the BCPs have helped to significantly shape the banking regulatory framework in China, there are quite a few areas where the regulatory and supervisory practices in China differ from the supervisory practices as endorsed by the BCPs.

Generally speaking, principles stand for a basic or general truth. Specifically, "the Core Principles are a framework of minimum standards for sound supervisory practices and are considered universally applicable. . . . The Core Principles are neutral with regard to different approaches to supervision, so long as the overriding goals are achieved."[4] Throughout the BCPs document, many principles are defined in very general terms. Indeed, many principles are phrased in such a way that they are close to the principles defined by the U.K. regulators in spirit, namely, a principle-based approach to regulation.

Such an approach has been well defined by the U.K. Financial Services Authority (FSA). The FSA states in its 2007 report that "principles-based regulation means, where possible, moving away from dictating through detailed, prescriptive rules and supervisory actions how firms should operate their business. We want to give firms the responsibility to decide how best to align their business objectives and processes with the regulatory outcomes we have specified."[5] In contrast to the United Kingdom and, more broadly speaking, some other highly developed markets, supervisors in emerging markets continue to share a preference for adopting specific rules and regulations. China's approach to regulation and supervisors provides an example that clearly suggests that a rules-based approach is the most appropriate way to go for emerging markets for now and into the future.

## Regulatory and Supervisory Practices in China

Discussed below are some differences between the supervisory practices in China and sound practices advocated by the BCPs. For the sake of convenience the discussion follows the BCPs' framework and is intended to shed light on how international standards can be improved by incorporating more of the experiences from emerging markets.

### Objectives, Independence, Powers, Transparency, and Cooperation (Principle One)

The objectives of banking supervision and powers of the supervisors are very important, and more often than not they are defined by law. For emerging markets such as China, these issues must be made clear and specific. In the BCPs

---

4. Basel Committee (2006a).
5. FSA (2007).

document, Principle One states at the outset that "an effective system of banking supervision will have clear responsibilities and objectives for each authority involved in the supervision of banks."[6] Here Principle One focuses on the clarity of the responsibility and objectives of supervisory agencies and is silent on the specific objectives of banking supervision. In contrast, the 1997 version clearly identifies the objectives of banking supervision: "The key objective of supervision is to maintain stability and confidence in the financial system, thereby reducing the risk of loss to depositors and other creditors."[7]

As a fundamental issue, the objectives of banking supervision should be clearly defined in specific terms for supervisors in all countries. In practice, a specific definition of objectives will help each authority involved in banking supervision to better define its role and responsibilities. The law governing banking supervision in China clearly states at the outset that the objective of banking supervision is to protect the interests of depositors and other consumers. As China follows an institutional approach to regulating different sectors of the financial services industry, these objectives are critical as they provide clarity and a sense of purpose for the CBRC, as the sole government agency authorized for the pursuit of these objectives.

In reality, a supervisory agency might define its responsibilities and objectives so as to simply justify its existence. In some countries, several supervisors are involved in banking supervision, and they all have a set of responsibilities and objectives, but this does not necessarily contribute to effective supervision and partly explains why an overview of global implementation of the BCPs indicates that compliance with this component of Principle One is close to 90 percent, almost the highest level among all the principles (International Monetary Fund [IMF] and World Bank 2002). Therefore, it could be concluded that the revised statement "an effective system of banking supervision will have clear responsibilities and objectives for each authority involved in the supervision of banks" is still too general to be considered a minimum standard (see Appendix 5A). Ideally, the guidance on the issue should be as specific as possible by listing a number of commonly agreed-upon objectives, such as protection of the interest of depositors and consumers, and ensuring the stability the banking system. Indeed, following the current financial crisis, governments in a number of countries recently stated publicly that all bank deposits would be safe or that deposit insurance coverage would be unlimited. These actions were successful in avoiding retail bank runs and highlighted the importance of protection of depositors in maintaining financial stability. Given these developments, there is good

6. Appendix 5A lists the revised 2006 version of the Basel Core Principles (see also Basel Committee 2006a).

7. Basel Committee (1997).

reason to suggest that the BCPs need to be more specific with the objectives of banking supervision. The silence regarding the overall objectives of banking supervision may well be a way to accommodate differing national practices, but it also indicates a more principles-based approach to supervision, a characteristic that becomes increasingly evident in a number of principles concerning risk management.

## Licensing and Structure (Principles Two–Five)

The entire supervisory cycle starts with the definition of banks and the permissible activities of banking institutions. It is in these areas that significant differences can be seen between China's approach and the practices endorsed by the BCPs document. In the BCPs, four principles relate to the permissible activities of banks, authorization of banking establishments, prior regulatory approval for transfer of significant ownership, and major acquisitions. The BCPs clearly state that the permissible activities of banks must be clearly defined, without suggesting whether there is any need for further regulation. This may well be typical of the general practices in developed markets, where "product regulation" does not exist.

For example, the U.K. FSA has been reluctant to accept the idea that it should regulate products in either retail or wholesale markets. Its regulatory philosophy is based on the following set of assumptions. First, firms must be subject to prudential regulation to ensure financial soundness. Second, firms must be subject to business conduct regulation, including regulation of sales practices, to ensure that customers are treated fairly and are well informed. And finally, product regulation is not required because well-managed firms will not develop products that are excessively risky, and because well-informed customers will only choose products that serve their needs.[8]

In contrast, the Law on Banking Regulation and Supervision in China states that the banking supervisor is empowered to determine the business scope of banks (that is, permissible activities). Based on the Law, the CBRC has issued a set of detailed procedures governing the review of permissible activities. Under these procedures, banks need to have prior supervisory approval for all new products or services, such as foreign exchange transactions, issue of subordinated debt, derivative transactions, asset management, custodian services for investment funds, and offshore banking transactions. Moreover, any new activities that are not defined by the current regulations will also be subject to supervisory approval as specified in the future by the supervisor. Another example lies in how problems related to securitization are addressed: the CBRC recently ruled that banks should never use low-quality assets as underlying assets for securitization.

8. FSA (2009).

While the CBRC recognizes that such approval processes may have the potential to slow the pace of financial innovation, the supervisor strongly believes that such an approach does help to reduce the business risks of banks—particularly those that do not have sound risk management procedures and processes—and thus contributes to the system's stability.

It is interesting to note that supervisors in some developed markets also have come to recognize that "financial innovations can sometimes achieve economic rent extraction, rather than delivering valuable customer and economic benefits . . . contributing significantly to increased systemic risk."[9] One implication is that regulators may well need to consider the direct regulation of products at both the retail and wholesale level. This development is worth noting in the update of international guidance on banking supervision.

## Prudential Regulation and Requirements (Principles Six–Eighteen)

Development of prudential rules and regulations as well as their implementation represent a large part of a supervisor's day-to-day activities. Among all supervisory tasks, capital regulation is the most important. There seems to be general agreement among emerging markets that as it stands now Principle Six, on capital regulation, is too general to be really helpful in that it falls short in endorsing the Basel Accord of 1988 (Basel I) as the international standard for capital regulation, let alone the Basel Accord of 2004 (Basel II). Promoting international convergence for capital regulation has been the focus of the Basel Committee from the late 1980s to the present, with an emphasis on strengthening capital requirements for securitization and trading book exposures. In addition, the reference to "internationally active banks" in Principle Six remains unclear and further narrows the scope of application for "the applicable Basel requirement." The president of the Deutsche Bundesbank recognized the same issue recently when he stated, "The main achievements of the first Basel Capital Accord were that it represented a significant step toward international harmonization of banking regulation—it was later applied by more than 100 countries."[10]

Furthermore, according to one survey of non–Basel Committee countries, out of 115 jurisdictions in Africa, Asia, the Caribbean, Latin America, the Middle East, and Europe, 95 are currently planning to implement Basel II.[11] It is a bit difficult to understand why the Basel Accord has not been duly recognized in the BCPs—with necessary modification, of course—as the de facto capital standard in light of its widespread adoption and clear support by some Group of Ten supervisors as well.

9. FSA (2009).
10. Weber (2009).
11. Financial Stability Institute (2008).

Current capital regulation in China is based largely on a modified version of Basel I with some elements of Basel II, replacing the club approach of the Organization for Economic Cooperation and Development with a more sensible alternative. By the end of 2008 the average capital of banks in China was 12 percent, with 82 percent of the regulatory capital being tier one without allowing for innovative capital instruments one way or another. In fact, the supervisor did not consider inclusion of short-term subordinated debt as tier three capital since such an approach does not make any intuitive sense given its very limited power to absorb losses resulting from the trading book (in addition to the lack of such instruments in the market).

Furthermore, in contrast to Basel I, the current capital rule does not place any constraint on the amount of provisions that may count as part of capital. Given that general provisions are not tax deductible and are no different than retained earnings, they are included in tier one capital rather than tier two capital and, more important, subject to no limit. This approach has gained more acceptance nowadays. Recently, the Financial Stability Board (FSB) noted that the Basel Committee should consider the allocation of general provisions in banks' regulatory capital and examine whether the removal or modification of the caps that limit the amount of provisions that may count as capital is warranted.[12]

The FSB also suggested that the Basel Committee should further enhance capital regulation by making it more risk-sensitive and by raising the quality, consistency, and transparency standards for the capital base, as well as by introducing a leverage ratio, a minimum global standard for funding liquidity ratio, and a framework for countercyclical capital buffers.[13] Many of these issues will need to be harmonized internationally. As the role of capital has become increasingly important following the current financial crisis, the international supervisory community may need to revisit the international guidance on capital regulation as presented in Principle Six.

All supervisors agree that capital regulation is not a panacea; sound risk management is just as important. The BCPs document is right to devote a large share of its content—namely, Principles Seven to Sixteen—to guidance on risk management, covering credit risk, market risk, liquidity risk, operational risk, and interest rate risk in the banking book. By stressing that banks and banking groups have in place a comprehensive risk management process for all material risks, subject to supervisors' satisfaction, the BCPs again demonstrate a clear preference for a principle-based approach to supervision.

As discussed earlier, China's approach is rules-based and in most cases is prescriptive and even intrusive, covering not only licensing but also all risk

---

12. FSB (2009).
13. FSB (2009).

management–related issues. Indeed, there are no general principles in China governing banking supervision, although the idea of a principles-based approach has been adopted in a limited way for licensing requirements for innovative financial products only.[14] In some cases, the risk management rules and regulations are highly prescriptive, yet they are accepted by the industry. For example, a set of rules governing bank financing of fixed asset investments was recently issued and went into effect as of November 2009. The rules provide specific guidance on processing loan requirements, loan evaluation, signing of contracts, disbursement of loan proceeds, and loan monitoring after disbursement. One provision is so specific that it requires that all disbursement of loan proceeds over 5 percent of the investment, regardless of the size of investment, or higher than RMB five million be wired by banks directly to service providers as the beneficiaries instead of to the borrowers. The rationale for such a specific approach is to help strengthen banks' credit risk management in addition to addressing the immediate concern of using loan proceeds for purposes outside the loan covenants. Noncompliance will result in supervisory sanctions. The feedback from the industry so far has been positive.

Undoubtedly, one of the weaknesses of a principles-based approach is that it makes the assessment of compliance rather subjective and difficult, both at the national and international level. Indeed "experience has already shown that the Principles may be interpreted in widely diverging ways, and incorrect interpretations may result in inconsistencies among assessments."[15] With this in mind, the Basel Committee took the initiative to have a document prepared for use in compliance assessments at its October 1998 meeting. This document, *The Core Principles Methodology,* introduces a more rules-based approach to assessing the effectiveness of banking supervision, providing more specificity and partly addressing the weakness of the principle-based approach in the main document. This shift in the approach to supervision can be seen most clearly in Essential Criterion Ten, relating to Principle Seven, which requires that "the supervisor issues standards related to, in particular, credit risk, market risk, liquidity risk, interest rate risk in the banking book and operational risk."[16]

A set of clear rules has always been important for emerging markets. As far as China is concerned, the very starting point is for the supervisor to issue rules and guidance for all material risks, and then check banks' compliance as the next step, so as to ensure compliance with the rules, both in spirit and to the letter.

---

14. The Principles on Loan Classification, issued in 1998 and revised subsequently, are basically very specific rules governing banks' practice for valuation of loans rather than a set of general principles.

15. See Basel Committee (1999).

16. Basel Committee (1999).

In light of the lessons learned from the current financial crisis, a global trend has begun toward establishing regulation that is more prescriptive and intrusive. This will have implications for the approach to banking supervision when the time comes for updating the international guidelines.

This shift in emphasis is occurring in some developed markets as well. For example,

> The UK FSA's regulatory and supervisory approach, before the current crisis, was based on a sometimes implicit but at times quite overt philosophy which believed . . . that the primary responsibility for managing risks lies with the senior management and boards of the individual firms, who are better placed to assess business model risk than bank regulators and who can be relied on to make appropriate decisions about the balance between risks and return.[17]

However, the FSA's new approach is significantly different and guided by a different philosophy of regulation. This new approach is more intrusive than before, to say the least.

Another important concept of the BCPs, one that runs through the entire document, is proportionality. This concept first appears in Principle Seven with the reference that "these [risk management] processes should be commensurate with the size and complexity of the institution." This concept is extremely relevant to China's banking sector. To some extent, the current banking sector is a reflection of a dual economy where the level of development between various regions, sectors, and industries diverges significantly. In such a dual banking sector, almost all large banks are publicly listed and are aggressively introducing sophisticated statistical analytical tools for risk management, while many small banks are still having difficulty establishing traditional risk management procedures and processes. Against this background, the enforcement of supervisory rules naturally has to be differentiated or proportionate. In fact, a differentiated supervisory approach or the use of the proportionality concept (分类监管 or *fen lei jian guan*—different supervisory treatment of different banking institutions) has been very popular among supervisors, and previously, separate rules were even issued to accommodate financial and operational differences among banks depending on their status of incorporation, that is, foreign, state-owned, shareholding, or city commercial banks. Until quite recently the supervisor clearly indicated that there should be a uniform set of rules applicable to all banks, irrespective of incorporation and other factors. Increasingly more and more rules and regulations have converged to cover the entire banking sector while only the rural credit cooperative sector, given its sector challenges and target client group, remains largely under a

17. FSA (2009).

different set of rules. The concept of proportionality is revisited in the conclusion with regard to international assessments of compliance.

## Methods of Ongoing Banking Supervision (Principles Nineteen–Twenty-One)

Among both emerging and developed markets there is a lot of commonality in the way supervisors conduct both on-site and off-site supervision. This may be attributed to the nature of banking supervision, namely, the need to enforce rules and check compliance. Principle Twenty states that "an effective banking supervisory system should consist of on-site and off-site supervision" and also requires specifically that the supervisor keep "regular contacts with bank management." The language of this principle is a big improvement over the previous version, which stated that "an effective supervision should consist of some form of both on-site and off-site supervision." The earlier version does not give due weight to on-site examination by supervisors in order to accommodate the practices of some highly developed markets.

While maintaining regular contacts may well be an important issue for some developed markets, it does not appear to be so important as to constitute part of an international standard for banking supervision. In China the banking supervisor expects to have regular contact with management since such an arrangement is clearly embedded in the supervisory process. As a general practice, the supervisor calls for regular meetings with banks on general supervisory issues, and at least once a year there are tripartite meetings among supervisors, banks, and external auditors, as well as meetings with the board members and supervisory board members. Under the rules-based system in China, lack of regular contact with banks is totally out of the question.

Interestingly enough, one of the lessons from the current financial situation is that supervisors should seriously address the lack of regular contact with bank management. Such "light-touch" supervision is a factor in the problems associated with some developed markets. Going forward, the right approach is probably to balance the practices in emerging markets and developed markets so that "regular contact" is treated as an essential criterion and thus receives the emphasis it deserves.

## Accounting and Disclosure (Principle Twenty-Two)

China's experience supports the view of the assessors that principles on loan classification and provisioning should be complemented with more precise guidelines on loan evaluation, income recognition, collateral valuation, establishment of loan loss allowances, and credit risk disclosure.[18] This issue has gained atten-

---

18. IMF and World Bank (2002).

tion following the adoption of international accounting standards. Recently, the revision of international accounting standards by the International Accounting Standards Board has reflected, to a large extent, the concerns of banking supervisors. However, although the revised asset impairment rules are likely closer to the expected loss concept advocated by supervisors, these accounting rules still fall short of supervisors' expectations because of the differences between the accounting profession and prudential regulation. Therefore, there is a great need for more and specific supervisory guidance on loan loss provisioning to encourage banks to recognize losses as early as possible and to provision sufficiently for loan losses.

At the present, the most urgent task for the supervisor in China is to ensure that banks build up their provisions and reserves in good times so as to strengthen the resilience of the individual banks and the banking system in general. Such an initiative was introduced two years ago, when banks reported high profits and low levels of nonperforming loans. However, before a more rules-based system is put in place—such as the Spanish dynamic provisioning system supported by a powerful database of bank loss experience—the supervisor in China has taken the approach of using its discretion and judgment in urging banks to build strong provisions buffers. Taking into account the average loss of around 75 percent for nonperforming loans disposed by asset management corporations, the supervisor has asked banks to increase the provisioning coverage ratio. From a 2009 value of 130 percent, the ratio was expected to reach 150 percent by the end of 2010, reflecting both forward-looking and countercyclical considerations, even though the underlying supervisory provisioning rules remain unchanged. Clearly, more specific guidance from the international supervisory community would help national supervisors in further strengthening their provisioning policies, especially given the need to develop a set of countercyclical supervisory standards covering both capital and provisions. Standard setters should give due consideration to alternative approaches to recognizing and measuring loan losses that incorporate a broader range of available credit information, including a fair value model, an expected loss model, and dynamic provisioning.[19] However, an expected loss model and dynamic provisioning are extremely data-intensive and may prove to be quite difficult for emerging markets, while a fair value model can hardly be an option for the foreseeable future. The overall direction is clear: provisions for loan losses should cover estimated loan losses that have been identified for individual loans, as well as estimated losses for loans in a company's portfolio that have likely been incurred but not yet been individually identified. Estimation of loan losses that have not yet been individually identified is a subjective process and therefore requires judgment. Such judgment factors could

19. Financial Stability Forum (2009).

include changes in relevant economic and environmental trends, lending policies and procedures, and changes related to new loan segments and products. It is advisable to stress the importance of exercising supervisory judgment in light of the market conditions for emerging markets rather than emphasizing unnecessarily an overreliance on analytical tools.

## Corrective and Remedial Powers of Supervisors (Principle Twenty-Three)

As stated in Principle Twenty-Three, "Supervisors must have at their disposal an adequate range of supervisory tools to bring about timely corrective actions." The guidance from the BCPs is very definitive in this regard and supports at least some form of product regulation, as referred to in the discussion of the permissible activities of banks. Such supervisory actions include "restricting the current activities of the banks, withholding approval of new activities or acquisitions and restricting or suspending payments to shareholders."[20] Supervisory practice in China confirms the importance of taking various supervisory actions, and again, the supervisor in China is in a much better position to do so as the role is prescribed by the Law as part of the authorization process for new products. This approach complements other supervisory sanctions, making another useful weapon readily available to the banking supervisor. Therefore, there may be a need to recognize at the global level that approval of new activities, in addition to approval of acquisitions, is important, be it part of the authorization process or part of the corrective actions that the supervisor may have at his or her disposal.

## Consolidated and Cross-Border Banking Supervision (Principles Twenty-Four–Twenty-Five)

Consolidated supervision is clearly set to a high standard. It does not come as a surprise that many emerging markets would show weak compliance in this area, as shown in the IMF's 2002 report.[21] Like other emerging markets, China has just recently issued a set of rules governing consolidated supervision. Enforcement of these rules will take time as it is both a challenge for banks to manage their operations on a consolidated basis and for the supervisor to conduct consolidated supervision covering all aspects of the business conducted by the banking group worldwide.

On the cross-border issue, Principle Twenty-Five states, "Banking supervisors must require the local operations of foreign banks to be conducted to the same standards as those required of domestic institutions." Of course, the legal responsibilities of national supervisors will remain unchanged with respect to the regulation of their domestic institutions or the arrangements for consolidated

20. Basel Committee (2006a).
21. IMF and World Bank (2002).

supervision already put in place globally. However, this statement does not seem to recognize the differences in national supervision due to institutional, historical, legal, or other factors, and as a result, it may not actually work in the best interests of emerging markets.

In terms of the compliance record, the gap between developed and emerging markets can, not surprisingly, be quite significant.[22] Although a supervisor in an emerging market may require local operations of foreign banks from developed markets to conform to the same standards as apply to domestic institutions, these foreign banks are likely subject to a set of less robust standards than they would be in their home country. This will remain a reality as long as differences in supervision exist between developed and emerging markets. Perhaps the language of Principle Twenty-five is better viewed as a reference to the policy direction or, more accurately, an endgame result where in the distant future both developed and emerging markets will have equally robust supervisory systems. Perhaps a more balanced approach is to state that the supervisor should expect foreign banks to be subject to both the standards of the home supervisor and the standards of the host supervisor, particularly when the latter is considered less robust. Alternatively, the principle could directly refer to the source documents by stating that "all international banking groups and international banks should be supervised by a home country authority that capably performs consolidated supervision," or that the supervisors should ensure "that all cross-border banking operations are subject to effective home and host supervision."[23]

China's experience also supports this argument. The country began to open up its banking sector to other countries in 1979 and committed itself in 2001 to removing all geographic and customer restrictions on foreign banks. However, as far as the prudential regulatory framework is concerned, the loan classification rules were issued in 1998 while the provision policy was introduced 2002, and a well-defined capital standard was not made available until 2004. In this context, a requirement to subject foreign banks to a set of less robust rules does not seem to be in the interest of foreign banks. In fact, the idea underlying an open policy for China and for its banking sector in particular is to leverage the expertise of foreign banks to improve the operations of the local banking market and the local supervisory system as well. At present, while the supervisor is committed to a set of uniform rules applicable to all banking institutions, rules governing foreign banks continue to differ from those governing local banks in certain aspects. Despite increasing local incorporation of foreign banks and subsidiarization in China, one can not overlook the role of the home supervisor, especially

22. IMF and World Bank (2002).
23. See Basel Committee (1992) and Working Group on Cross-Border Banking (1996), respectively.

in light of the implementation of Basel II on a consolidated basis, which has yet to be introduced in China.

One last point relates to financial deregulation and the desirable business model for commercial banks. Many people, both in government and academia, strongly believe that the repeal of the Glass-Steagall Act fueled the crisis. The Glass-Steagall Act was introduced in the United States in 1933 as a response to the unsound banking practices and public anger after the stock market crash in 1929. The act prohibited commercial banks from underwriting, holding, or dealing in corporate securities, either directly or through their subsidiaries in the securities industry. Glass-Steagall had a significant impact on the business model of financial institutions and the regulation of banks, both in the United States and in other countries, including China.

Despite some enhancements to Basel II, there has been strong resistance to shifting from universal banking to narrow banking. It is the view of some major developed markets that large complex banks providing a wide range of activities will remain a feature of today's world financial system. Therefore, it does not seem at all practical to work on the assumption that there can or should be complete institutional separation of utility banking and investment banking.

In full recognition of the desire of the developed markets to maintain the status quo of universal banking and its related regulatory framework, the supervisor in China has no intention of repeating the same process of deregulation that occurred in some developed markets. Instead, the presence of firewalls will effect a clear separation between operations basically engaged in commercial banking and those that perform investment banking activities. Such a regulatory distinction has served China well in preventing the contagion of risks between the banking and capital markets. Experience has shown that the erosion of these firewalls will likely expose the banking sector to the irrationality of capital markets to the detriment of the depositors that supervisors have a legal obligation to protect in the first place.

## Conclusion

As an emerging market, China has used international standards such as the Basel Core Principles for Effective Banking Supervision as a benchmark to improve the effectiveness of banking supervision. The BCPs document has played a significant role in shaping the regulatory framework in China. While China has incorporated many sound practices endorsed by the BCPs, there are still quite a few significant differences.

Broadly speaking, China has adopted a rules-based approach to regulation; in many cases, regulations are prescriptive or even intrusive. In building a robust supervisory system, China finds specific guidance more helpful than sole reliance on principles-based approaches.

Adherence to international standards is an important agenda item globally. At present, the Financial Stability Board is working hard to promote a race to the top in standards implementation, with FSB members leading by example in disclosing their degree of compliance with these standards. China's banking supervisor has conducted a self-assessment of the implementation of the BCPs every two years since 2003. The third self-assessment in 2007 was performed using the BCPs of 2006.[24]

The IMF–World Bank Financial Sector Assessment Program is expected to evaluate China soon. Without any intention to pre-empt the result of the forthcoming FSAP, perhaps one can expect that China's compliance with international standards on banking supervision, which is an essential part of the FSAP, will be similar to its Asian peers and presumably below that of many developed markets. However, China's banking supervisory system has ensured the safety and soundness of the individual banks and the banking system in China, which is the basic objective of successful and effective banking regulation and supervision.

International financial institutions have assessed countries' compliance with the BCPs either on a stand-alone basis or as part of the FSAP. Based on their extensive experience, it is easy for assessors to formulate an overall view of a country's compliance with relevant international standards. However, the challenge is to formulate a clear view as to what level of compliance or effectiveness of banking supervision would be most appropriate for a given country in light of that country's particular circumstances, such as the level of development, sophistication of the banking system, and institutional capacity of the supervisor. In essence, this relates to the concept of proportionality. On one hand, given the gaps and weaknesses of the supervisory system, emerging markets need to continue improving the effectiveness of banking supervision. On the other hand, despite an impressive compliance record, some developed markets, as the center of the international financial system, may need to do more in order to close gaps revealed by the current financial crisis so as to improve the effectiveness of banking supervision beyond mere compliance with the international standards. The extent of supervisory actions should be in keeping with the stated supervisory objectives and be judged accordingly as well.

## Appendix 5A. Basel Core Principles for Effective Banking Supervision

The following is taken from *The Core Principles for Effective Banking Supervision* (Basel Committee 2006a).

---

24. CBRC (2008).

## Principle One—Objectives, Independence, Powers, Transparency, and Cooperation

An effective system of banking supervision will have clear responsibilities and objectives for each authority involved in the supervision of banks. Each such authority should possess operational independence, transparent processes, sound governance and adequate resources, and be accountable for the discharge of its duties. A suitable legal framework for banking supervision is also necessary, including provisions relating to authorization of banking establishments and their ongoing supervision; powers to address compliance with laws, as well as safety and soundness concerns; and legal protection for supervisors. Arrangements for sharing information between supervisors and protecting the confidentiality of such information should be in place.

## Principle Two—Permissible Activities

The permissible activities of institutions that are licensed and subject to supervision as banks must be clearly defined, and the use of the word "bank" in names should be controlled as far as possible.

## Principle Three—Licensing Criteria

The licensing authority must have the power to set criteria and reject applications for establishments that do not meet the standards set. The licensing process, at a minimum, should consist of an assessment of the ownership structure and governance of the bank and its wider group, including the fitness and propriety of Board members and senior management, its strategic and operating plan, internal controls and risk management, and its projected financial condition, including its capital base. Where the proposed owner or parent organization is a foreign bank, the prior consent of its home country supervisor should be obtained.

## Principle Four—Transfer of Significant Ownership

The supervisor has the power to review and reject any proposals to transfer significant ownership or controlling interests held directly or indirectly in existing banks to other parties.

## Principle Five—Major Acquisitions

The supervisor has the power to review major acquisitions or investments by a bank, against prescribed criteria, including the establishment of cross-border operations and confirming that corporate affiliations or structures do not expose the bank to undue risks or hinder effective supervision.

## Principle Six—Capital Adequacy

Supervisors must set prudent and appropriate minimum capital adequacy requirements for banks that reflect the risks that the bank undertakes, and must define the components of capital, bearing in mind its ability to absorb losses. At least for internationally active banks, these requirements must not be less than those established in the applicable Basel requirement.

## Principle Seven—Risk Management Process

Supervisors must be satisfied that banks and banking groups have in place a comprehensive risk management process (including Board and senior management oversight) to identify, evaluate, monitor and control or mitigate all material risks, and to assess their overall capital adequacy in relation to their risk profile. These processes should be commensurate with the size and complexity of the institution.

## Principle Eight—Credit Risk

Supervisors must be satisfied that banks have a credit risk management process that takes into account the risk profile of the institution, with prudent policies and processes to identify, measure, monitor, and control credit risk (including counterparty risk). This would include the granting of loans and making of investments, the evaluation of the quality of such loans and investments, and the ongoing management of the loan and investment portfolios.

## Principle Nine—Problem Assets, Provisions, and Reserves

Supervisors must be satisfied that banks establish and adhere to adequate policies and processes for managing problem assets and evaluating the adequacy of provisions and reserves.

## Principle Ten—Large Exposure Limits

Supervisors must be satisfied that banks have policies and processes that enable management to identify and manage concentrations within the portfolio, and supervisors must set prudential limits to restrict bank exposures to single counterparties or groups of connected counterparties.

## Principle Eleven—Exposures to Related Parties

In order to prevent abuses arising from exposures (both on-balance-sheet and off-balance-sheet) to related parties and to address conflicts of interest, supervisors must have in place requirements that banks extend exposures to related companies and individuals on an arm's length basis; these exposures are effectively monitored; appropriate steps are taken to control or mitigate the risks;

and write-offs of such exposures are made according to standard policies and processes.

### Principle Twelve—Country and Transfer Risks

Supervisors must be satisfied that banks have adequate policies and processes for identifying, measuring, monitoring and controlling country risk and transfer risk in their international lending and investment activities, and for maintaining adequate provisions and reserves against such risks.

### Principle Thirteen—Market Risks

Supervisors must be satisfied that banks have in place policies and processes that accurately identify, measure, monitor, and control market risks; supervisors should have powers to impose specific limits and/or a specific capital charge on market risk exposures, if warranted.

### Principle Fourteen—Liquidity Risk

Supervisors must be satisfied that banks have a liquidity management strategy that takes into account the risk profile of the institution, with prudent policies and processes to identify, measure, monitor, and control liquidity risk, and to manage liquidity on a day-to-day basis. Supervisors must require banks to have contingency plans for handling liquidity problems.

### Principle Fifteen—Operational Risk

Supervisors must be satisfied that banks have in place risk management policies and processes to identify, assess, monitor, and control or mitigate operational risk. These policies and processes should be commensurate with the size and complexity of the bank.

### Principle Sixteen—Interest Rate Risk in the Banking Book

Supervisors must be satisfied that banks have effective systems in place to identify, measure, monitor, and control interest rate risk in the banking book, including a well-defined strategy that has been approved by the Board and implemented by senior management; these should be appropriate to the size and complexity of such risk.

### Principle Seventeen—Internal Control and Audit

Supervisors must be satisfied that banks have in place internal controls that are adequate for the size and complexity of their businesses. These should include clear arrangements for delegating authority and responsibility; separation of the functions that involve committing the bank, paying away its funds, and accounting for its assets and liabilities; reconciliation of these processes; safeguarding the bank's assets; and appropriate independent internal audit and compliance functions to test adherence to these controls as well as applicable laws and regulations.

### Principle Eighteen—Abuse of Financial Services

Supervisors must be satisfied that banks have adequate policies and processes in place, including strict "know-your-customer" rules, that promote high ethical and professional standards in the financial sector and prevent the bank from being used, intentionally or unintentionally, for criminal activities.

### Principle Nineteen—Supervisory Approach

An effective banking supervisory system requires that supervisors develop and maintain a thorough understanding of the operations of individual banks and banking groups, and also of the banking system as a whole, focusing on safety and soundness, and the stability of the banking system.

### Principle Twenty—Supervisory Techniques

An effective banking supervisory system should consist of on-site and off-site supervision and regular contacts with bank management.

### Principle Twenty-One—Supervisory Reporting

Supervisors must have a means of collecting, reviewing and analyzing prudential reports and statistical returns from banks on both a solo and a consolidated basis, and a means of independent verification of these reports, through either on-site examinations or use of external experts.

### Principle Twenty-Two—Accounting and Disclosure

Supervisors must be satisfied that each bank maintains adequate records drawn up in accordance with accounting policies and practices that are widely accepted internationally, and publishes, on a regular basis, information that fairly reflects its financial condition and profitability.

### Principle Twenty-Three—Corrective and Remedial Powers of Supervisors

Supervisors must have at their disposal an adequate range of supervisory tools to bring about timely corrective actions. This includes the ability, where appropriate, to revoke the banking license or to recommend its revocation.

### Principle Twenty-Four—Consolidated Supervision

An essential element of banking supervision is that supervisors supervise the banking group on a consolidated basis, adequately monitoring and, as appropriate, applying prudential norms to all aspects of the business conducted by the group worldwide.

## Principle Twenty-Five—Home-Host Relationships

Cross-border consolidated supervision requires cooperation and information exchange between home supervisors and the various other supervisors involved, primarily host-country banking supervisors. Banking supervisors must require the local operations of foreign banks to be conducted according to the same standards as those required of domestic institutions.

# References

Basel Committee on Banking Supervision. 1992. *Minimum Standards for the Supervision of International Banking Groups and Their Cross-Border Establishments*. Basel: Bank for International Settlements.

———. 1997. *The Core Principles for Effective Banking Supervision*. Basel: Bank for International Settlements.

———. 1999. *The Core Principles Methodology*. Basel: Bank for International Settlements.

———. 2006a. *The Core Principles for Effective Banking Supervision* (revised). Basel: Bank for International Settlements.

———. 2006b. *The Core Principles Methodology* (revised). Basel: Bank for International Settlements.

China Banking Regulatory Commission (CBRC). 2008. *2007 Annual Report* (http://zhuanti.cbrc.gov.cn/subject/subject/nianbao2007/english/ywqb.pdf).

Financial Services Authority (FSA). 2007. *Principles-Based Regulation: Focusing on the Outcomes That Matter*. London.

———. 2009. *Turner Review: A Regulatory Response to the Global Banking Crisis*. London.

Financial Stability Board (FSB). 2009. "Financial Stability Board Meets in Paris." Press release, September (www.financialstabilityboard.org/press/pr_090915.pdf).

Financial Stability Forum. 2009. *Report of the Financial Stability Forum on Addressing Procyclicality in the Financial System*. Basel: Bank for International Settlements.

Financial Stability Institute. 2008. *2008 FSI Survey on the Implementation of the New Capital Adequacy Framework in Non-Basel Committee Member Countries*. Basel: Bank for International Settlements.

International Monetary Fund (IMF) and World Bank. 2002. "Implementation of the Basel Core Principles for Effective Banking Supervision." Washington, D.C.

People's Republic of China. 2004. "The Interpretation Notes of the Law of the People's Republic of China on Banking Regulation and Supervision." Beijing.

Weber, Axel. 2009. "The Future of Banking Regulation." Speech at the Conference on the Future of Banking Regulation. Frankfurt am Main, September 24 (http://www.bis.org/review/r090929a.pdf).

Working Group on Cross-Border Banking, Basel Committee on Banking Supervision and the Offshore Group of Banking Supervisors. 1996. *The Supervision of Cross-Border Banking*. Basel: Bank for International Settlements.

# 6

## Banking Supervision in Indonesia

ANWAR NASUTION

The focus of this discussion is on the process of building a strong system of financial supervision and regulation in Indonesia.[1] To start with, I believe that the basic principles of risk-focused supervision are highly relevant to emerging economies so as to avoid waste of resources, cost overruns, and inefficient spending in their development efforts. I also believe that a sound supervisory framework should be dynamic and reflect the realities of the financial sector for which it is created. As such, though the best practices in the market-based, advanced economies are an important starting point for considering how to enhance supervisory frameworks, one should also bear in mind that a single framework does not fit all types of financial institutions or systems.

### Applicability of Risk-Focused Supervision in Indonesia

For a number of reasons, major reform and considerable time will be required for an emerging economy like Indonesia to adopt the U.S. supervisory system and the Basel Committee on Banking and Supervision recommendation for increased reliance on the evaluation and testing of banks' risk management systems. A shift to the U.S. regulatory practices of the CAMEL system (capital adequacy, asset quality, management ability, earning quality, and liquidity level)

1. This chapter originally was presented as a note at the Conference on Financial Sector Regulation and Reform in Emerging Markets, Brookings Institution, Washington, D.C., October 22–23, 2009.

and adoption of the risk-based bank capital regime of the Basel II Accord will necessitate improvements in market infrastructure; reform of the corporate sector, including both public and private companies; and strengthening of financial sector regulatory and supervisory agencies. Such a shift in the regulatory and supervisory system will also require the retraining of bankers, supervisors, and regulators in the field of risk management in the banking industry.

The following discussion reviews in greater detail the reasons that major reform is needed, as well as the challenges it will face.

## Characteristics of the Indonesian Economy

To begin with, Indonesia has an emerging mixed economy and lacks a well-developed or full-fledged market-based system. The economy may be described as mixed because of the important role played by state-owned enterprises (SOEs) and heavy government interventions in the economy. At present, the central government owns about 150 SOEs, while local governments own about 1,223 firms. The public sector companies operate in nearly every sector of the economy, including the banking, telecommunications, aviation, plantation agriculture, petroleum, mining, and hospitality industries. Aside from exercising other policy instruments, such as exchange rate policy, a distorted licensing system in the natural resources sector, tight control over the export-import and domestic trading sectors, and financial repression, the government also intervenes directly in day-to-day operations of the state-owned companies to pursue its industrial policy and export-oriented development strategy. A significant public sector role in the economy, both as regulator and player, is also evident in other Asian countries, particularly the former socialist countries.

## Role of Banking in the Indonesian Economy

In terms of assets and branch networks, the banking industry constitutes the core of the Indonesian financial system. As a percentage of annual GDP in 2008, the total assets of the various components of the financial services industry were 48.6 percent for deposit-taking institutions and 13.7 percent for nonbank financial institutions (including insurance, pension fund, leasing, and venture capital sectors). In the same year, the ratio of market capitalization to GDP stood at 21.7 percent of GDP, while the ratio of market capitalization to total outstanding bonds amounted to 13.4 percent. The rapid growth of the mutual fund industry in recent years is the outcome of the recapitalization of collapsed banks after the financial crisis of 1997.[2] The type of assets held by the funds are mainly

2. A mutual fund is a retail investment vehicle designed to allow relatively small investors to hold a diversified portfolio of financial assets.

recapitalized bonds, short-term Bank Indonesia certificates (Sertifikat Bank Indonesia) and treasury bills, and small amounts of equity shares and corporate bonds.

Having collapsed during the Asian financial crisis in 1997, all state-owned and large privately owned domestic banks were either recapitalized or taken over by the Indonesian Bank Restructuring Agency, an institution established by the government. To satisfy the regulations on capital requirements, these financially distressed banks received capital injections in the form of recapitalized bonds from the government, some of which were non-traded. Because Basel I classifies sovereign bonds as zero-risk assets, they are categorized as tier two capital. These government bonds served as significant contributors to the revenue of the recapitalized banks.

Partly because of the availability of cheap credit with low risks from state-controlled banks during the long period of financial repression in the past, the floating of equity shares on the Jakarta Stock Exchange has not been an important source of external financing. The privatization of SOEs began after the crisis in 1997, partly due to the need to finance the national budget deficit. The government retains golden shares in some strategically important privatized SOEs, such as banks. The emergence of the bond market has been one of the unexpected outcomes of the 1997–98 financial crisis. The market is dominated by long-term domestic government bonds issued to recapitalize the banking sector, which was devastated by the crisis. For this purpose, the authorities issued Rp 430 trillion (34 percent of GDP in 2000) worth of long-term government bonds between May 1999 and October 2000. After the end of the International Monetary Fund (IMF) recovery program in 2003, the government changed its borrowing strategy for financing the budget deficit to bond sales on both the domestic and foreign markets. Previously, during the long period of President Suharto's rule (1966–98), the fiscal deficit had been financed by development aid from official sources.

A group of public sector banks controls about half of the banking market in Indonesia. This group consists of five large commercial banks owned by the central government and twenty-six regional development banks owned by the thirty-three provincial governments. By law this group of banks has a monopoly over deposits from the public sector and state-owned enterprises. The activities of these public sector banks include quasi-fiscal operations to promote government policies, and consequently they are not subject to market discipline. The state-controlled banks are implicitly guaranteed by the state and, therefore, are not allowed to fail.

## Effects of Financial Repression

During the long history of financial repression, Asian governments, including the government of Indonesia, not only set bank lending guidelines but also exercised control over both deposit and lending rates, thereby segmenting the financial markets. Foreign exchange power and access to offshore borrowing were controlled by the central bank and normally extended to state-owned banks and those owned by the politically connected. At the same time, financial repression policies and inefficient allocation of access to international borrowing created disequilibrium in the financial markets. This in turn led to distorted licensing and trading systems, and encouraged rent-seeking and corruption, collusion, and nepotism. Direct lending allowed the channeling of credits by state banks to a select few politically well-connected borrowers to enable them to build their business empires.

*Private Banking Conglomerates*

In the past, all domestic privately owned banks in Indonesia belonged to politically well-connected business groups or conglomerates. These groups usually started their businesses in the nonfinancial sector. Thanks to undervalued currencies and the availability of economic rents, including cheap financing with low risks from the state-owned banks, these privileged business groups rapidly expanded to become giant conglomerates, similar to the chaebol in South Korea. The business lines of these huge conglomerates included banking and other financial services. Like the universal banks in Germany and Japan, private banks in Indonesia were not only engaged in retail and wholesale commercial and investment banking but also held equity in commercial entities, to which they also extended loans. As in Germany and Japan, the privately owned banks in Indonesia had close relationships with affiliated commercial concerns, characterized by cross-shareholding and shared directorships.

The Asian financial crisis in 1997–98 showed that credit risks had accumulated both in the heavily regulated banking industry as well as in unregulated affiliated firms. The crisis arose from a general lack of disclosure combined with violations of legal lending limits to affiliates, shareholders, and managers. In addition, violating the regulations on net open positions, banks and nonbank corporations borrowed heavily on the short-term international market, with loans denominated in foreign currencies, to finance long-term credits, denominated in rupiah, mainly to their affiliates. Some of the external borrowings were used to finance long-term investment projects in the non-traded sectors of the economy, such as real estate and commercial property. Such practices resulted in maturity and currency mismatches. The experiences gained from the 1997–98 financial crisis indicate that the poor quality of bank assets was partly due to conflicts of interest between different businesses within the same conglomerates. As a result of this situation, banks tended to evaluate loan applications from affiliates less rigorously than would be the case for unaffiliated firms. As in the 1990s, the collapse of the small-sized Bank Century in November 2008 was also caused by excessive lending to a subsidiary, Antaboga Deltasekuritas, which traded in derivatives transactions, with such lending going undetected by banking supervisors.

## International Banking

Healthier market competition from foreign banks has only recently been allowed, following the Asian financial crisis of 1997. After gaining greater branching power, foreign institutions are now legally allowed to penetrate domestic markets. Based on rulings on the financial services industry by the World Trade Organization, foreigners can now control 99 percent of the equity shares of domestic banks. The financially troubled, large domestic private banks under receivership with the Indonesia Bank Restructuring Agency were sold to foreign buyers in the early 2000s. At present, foreign-owned and joint venture banks control about 7.3 percent of commercial bank lending. This accounts for only 0.76 percent of total lending by the regional development bank group and 0.17 percent of total lending by private national banks.

Access to international borrowing has also been rationalized by linking it to bank capitalization. During the era of financial repression, access to low-cost financing from overseas was part of the rent as explicitly and implicitly guaranteed by the government. The implicit guarantee included the adoption of foreign exchange risks embedded in the fixed exchange system applied at that time. In Indonesia, an archipelagic country with more than 17,000 islands, it is impossible to control capital flows. This is particularly so because Singapore, the regional financial center, is located close to the heart of Indonesia. Indonesia's past experience indicates that capital controls can be easily circumvented, particularly in the absence of a highly disciplined bureaucracy to enforce such controls. They can be evaded through under- and over-invoicing, arm's-length transactions, transfer pricing, shifting settlement dates, and outright smuggling of currency.

## Transparency and Valuation

With the responsibility for risk being assumed by the government as part of the financial repression policy, there was no incentive for bank managers to monitor and manage risks, upgrade transparency in corporate reporting, or provide economically relevant information. Ideally, required information should include disclosure of asset quality to assess financial positions of borrowers and by extension the loan portfolios of banks. As credits were allocated based on noneconomic considerations, the supervisors classified loans based on repayment of the credit rather than on the creditworthiness of borrowers or the market value of the collateral they pledged. Such inefficient allocation of financial resources has resulted in poor asset quality and a high level of nonperforming loans. Moreover, without reliable, up-to-date, and complete information, the markets cannot work effectively and efficiently.

The shortcoming of mark-to-market valuation of collateral is a fundamental accounting issue faced by banking regulators and supervisors all over the world. Mark-to-market accounting distorts valuations during periods of market volatility, when the long-term value of assets differs from their market prices. Forcing excessive write-downs during a period when asset prices are below their fundamental values may lead to fire sales of illiquid assets that could result in a vicious circle of spiraling asset price devaluations.

## Market Infrastructure

The basic ingredients of market infrastructure are still in the making in emerging Indonesia, including protection of property rights at least cost and availability of high-quality information to minimize market asymmetries. The legal system continues to be underdeveloped with regard to the proper application of the laws and regulations, enforcement of contracts, and the sanctioning of defaulting borrowers. As a result, it is still impossible to mitigate some banking risks because it is difficult to enforce the seizure of collateral pledged by defaulters.

## Supervisory Weaknesses

Financial and banking-sector supervision needs to be overhauled. In line with the Basel I recommendations, prudential rules and regulations and the banking supervision unit of Bank Indonesia (BI) were upgraded during the course of the IMF recovery program from 1997 to 2003. In addition to regular periodic supervision, on-site supervision also has been instituted so as to ensure tighter oversight of problem banks. Supervisory officers, however, have received little training in the field of credit analysis and risk management in banking sector organizations. The risks specific to the banking industry are divided into eight categories: capital or gearing risks, credit risks, counterparty risks, liquidity or funding risks, market or price risks (which include currency and interest rate risks), operational risks, and sovereign and political risks. Arm's-length transactions between banks and their affiliates are rarely detected by supervisors. Moreover, long-standing bad habits have proven difficult to erase. The recent Bank Century (BC) debacle also demonstrates that market infrastructure has not improved significantly and that weaknesses persist in the supervisory and regulatory system. Relevant, accurate, comprehensive, and timely information is frequently unavailable.

## Inaction

The BC case also shows that banking supervisors continue to be disinclined to take prompt corrective action. Established in December 2004, BC was the product of the merger of three small banks with histories of inadequate capital-ization, poor management, and fraudulent practices. The new bank was given the chance to correct the deficiencies it had inherited. However, it turned out that BC had to be placed under intensive supervision in February 2005, barely three months after its establishment, to ensure that it abided by its capital-raising commitments. Despite repeated warnings from the supervisors, no firm correc-tive measures were taken.

## Technical Knowledge and Integrity

Transparency and accountability are not sufficient on their own to establish pub-lic trust and a sound banking system. The expertise and experience of bankers, regulators, and supervisors during the previous era of financial repression mainly involved the bureaucratic channeling of credits to targeted economic sectors and customer classes, as provided for by government regulations and policies. Aside from suffering from inadequate technical knowledge and funding, the banking supervisory system also lacks personal integrity, with the result that the prevail-ing laws and regulations are frequently not properly enforced. It is the banking supervisors who are responsible for the application of the laws, rules, regulations, concepts, structures, procedures, and best practices. The inherent weaknesses in the regulatory and supervisory system afford little incentive to banks to provide key relevant information or to adhere strictly to prudential rules and regulations.

The prosecution of the senior Bank Indonesia officials in 2008–09 shows that the personal integrity of regulators remains problematic, even in the central bank. A little-known publication based in Jakarta devoted its February 2008 issue to reprinting classified internal memoranda and minutes of meetings of the board of governors of BI concerning the improper withdrawal of funds amount-ing to Rp 100 billion ($100 million) by BI from one of its foundations in July 2003.[3] The withdrawal of the funds was concealed by improper accounting of both BI's and the foundation's books. During a change in the foundation's legal status, the funds apparently disappeared from its accounts and were not recorded either as debt or revenue in BI's accounts. To bypass the "know-your customer" regulations and the Money Laundering Law, the funds were allegedly transferred from the foundation's accounts to BI accounts with various commercial banks, and then the entire amount was withdrawn in cash. Press reports suggest that approximately Rp 68.5 billion of the funds were apparently used to pay for "additional legal assistance" for five former members of BI's board of governors, who were facing legal difficulties at the time. These reports also suggest that the

---

3. See "Bedah kasus Aliran Dana BI (Tracing the Flow of Bank Indonesia Funds)," *Konstan News Magazine* 3, no. 60 (2008): 3–82.

remaining Rp 31.5 billion was given to members of the Indonesian parliament to facilitate the passage of a new Bank Indonesia Law.

## Procedures for Problem Banks

There is a lack of technical expertise in handling problem banks. To protect depositors, the Lembaga Penjamin Simpanan (LPS), the state deposit insurance company, was established in 2004. This was followed by the establishment of a financial safety net under the auspices of the Financial Stability Forum (FSF), which is chaired by the minister of finance. Ceilings on the amount of deposits guaranteed by the LPS were introduced to replace the blanket guarantee scheme introduced during the financial crisis in 1997.

At present, both the FSF and the LPS lack established operating procedures for the handling of problem banks, as well as early warning indicators for individual banks. As shown by the current BC debacle, both the FSF and the LPS rely solely on stress tests designed by BI, based on incomplete and outdated information and unrealistic scenarios. CAMEL-style sets of indicators for individual institutions are not available. Neither the FSF nor the LSP has supervisory powers over banks, and they rely solely on BI for information on the financial circumstances of insured banks. The LPS has no direct access to the computer systems of the insured banks and the detailed structure of their deposits. So if something goes wrong, it cannot act rapidly in transferring insured deposits to bridge banks or to other institutions.

## Interagency Coordination

Inadequate interagency coordination also is a factor in the failure to deal with problem banks in a timely manner. This is shown by a lack of information exchange, and inadequate coordination and cooperation among the supervisors of the financial system: BI, Bapepam (the Capital Market and Financial Institutions Supervisory Agency), the LPS, and the FSF. To address this interagency problem, the 2004 BI Law envisaged the transferring of responsibility for banking supervision from the central bank to an independent Financial Sector Supervisory Agency, to be established no later than the end of 2010, which would take over responsibility for the supervision of the entire financial services industry. Until such time as this agency comes into being, BI remains the sole institution responsible for regulating and supervising banks. In addition to these responsibilities, BI has multiple other functions: setting monetary policy, acting as the government's bank, holding foreign exchange reserves, serving as lender of last resort, and maintaining the payments system and financial stability. This gives rise to potential conflicts between macro- and microprudential objectives. The microprudential objective is to minimize the likelihood of the failure of an individual institution, whereas the macroprudential objective is to limit the contagion from individual bank failures to the rest of the financial system. No plan has been drawn up to date on how this independent, super-financial regulatory agency will be established.

## Recommendations

Successive phases of economic reform, deregulation, and privatization of SOEs since late 1998 have moved the Indonesian economy toward a more market-based system. Many of the distorted policies have been partly or wholly corrected, including the undervaluation of exchange rates, distorted licensing and trading regimes, and the policy of financial repression. Interest rates have been gradually deregulated, and banks' access to foreign borrowing has been rationalized.

A number of policy measures have been taken to promote the stability of the banking sector in a more market-based system that is more closely linked to the international markets. The first of these policy measures is the upgrading of market infrastructure to make it more effective and efficient. This measure includes the adoption of international standards, with some modifications to make them more suitable to Indonesia's economic structure, history, and traditions. The problem, however, lies in implementation.

Second, the authorities have started to retrain bankers, bank inspectors and supervisors, regulators, accountants, lawyers, and other relevant parties on risks that are specific to the financial services and banking industries. Progress, however, has been relatively slow due to a lack of funding and difficulties in reeducating those whose mindsets were molded during the long era of financial repression.

Aside from training programs at the national (Indonesian) level, Asia as a whole should make use of existing regional organizations to collaboratively train bankers, supervisors, and regulators from countries that face problems similar to those of Indonesia. Asia has a number of regional organizations that could play a role in this regard: the Executives' Meeting of East Asia Pacific Central Banks; the Association of Southeast Nations Plus Three; the Bank for International Settlements Asian Consultative Council; the South East Asia, New Zealand, and Australia Central Banks; and the South East Asian Central Banks. The last entity has a training center in Kuala Lumpur. Through these regional organizations, Asian nations can share knowledge, expertise, and experience and benefit from economies of scale.

A third policy measure is to increase the number of qualified bank inspectors and supervisors to cope with the expansion of the banking sector that occurred after deregulation in 1988, and with the extension of the central bank's role to include supervision of the secondary banking system, including rural credit banks. Alternatively, responsibility for the supervision of rural banks could be transferred to Bank Rakyat Indonesia, a specialized state-owned bank charged with serving the rural sector, and to the country's regional development banks. The rural credit banks operate in an informal, face-to-face manner.

The question of transferring responsibility for banking regulation and supervision from the central bank is a difficult and controversial issue all over the world. Some argue that transferring such power from the central bank—while maintaining its role as lender of last resort—will reduce the ability of the monetary authority to oversee financial vulnerabilities in specific institutions as well as systemic risks that threaten the entire system. The key is proper coordination and the exchange of information between the supervisors and regulators of the banks and other financial institutions, on the one hand, and the central bank, on the other. Due to a shortage of experts and inadequate funding, emerging markets such as Indonesia cannot afford the luxury of overlapping and fragmented regulation involving various central and local institutions, as exemplified by the system in place in the United States.

Through regional organizations and their affiliations with the Bank for International Settlements, IMF, and Group of Twenty, countries in this region can contribute to the ongoing review of the scope of global financial regulation so as to minimize systemic risks and maintain financial stability. Asia can contribute to the formulation of international accounting and prudential standards based on Asian developmental experiences, values, and traditions. What are the impacts of interlocking ownership and management, as well as concentrations of portfolios in a few large business conglomerates, on financial risks and therefore on capital adequacy requirements? How should interlocking nonbank-affiliated companies be supervised? The crises of 1997 and 2007 show that market discipline has been ineffective in constraining risks involving affiliated companies from outside the banking sector. These unregulated companies have assumed both credit and liquidity risks, funding poor-quality, long-term investment projects with high degrees of leverage.

However, the extension of the boundaries of regulation beyond the banking industry would require the sort of expertise that is frequently lacking in emerging economies such as Indonesia. In addition, new regulatory constraints raise opportunity and compliance costs in the economy, and this could have consequences for economic growth. A more complex regulatory regime could also create new opportunities for arbitrage, as well as moral hazard, if it is accompanied by an expansion of the scope of deposit insurance and government bailouts.

## Conclusion

Building a strong and sound banking sector is one the keys for the future development of emerging Asia, including Indonesia. The current global financial crisis shows that Asia needs to replace its export-led strategy with a greater focus on domestic and regional markets. The export-led strategy needs to be modified by shifting away from the traditional overvaluation of exchange rates, availability of cheap financing, and other government aid to greater reliance on increased productivity. This will require the mobilization of savings for the financing of education and training, research and development, health care, and the building of a modern, physical economic infrastructure.

The U.S. experience provides valuable reference points for the development of effective and sound banking supervision in emerging economies. The adoption of the U.S system, however, needs to be viewed within the institutional context of each economy. In building a strong and sound banking system, Indonesia needs to retrain its bankers, regulators, and supervisors in the field of risk management in the banking industry, and to develop its market infrastructure, particularly its legal and accounting systems (including the development of efficient bankruptcy procedures). The regulatory and supervisory agencies need to be strengthened by upgrading the technical knowledge and integrity of supervisors. State-owned enterprises and banks need to be freed from government interference and made more subject to the rigors of market discipline. Since the structure of privately owned conglomerates in Indonesia is akin to the universal banking model in Germany or the keiretsu system in Japan, supervising arm's-length transactions between banks and their business affiliates will require additional work on the part of supervisors.

# IV

## Financial Market Development and Stability

# 7

## *Who Should Regulate Systemic Stability Risk? The Relevance for Asia*

MASAHIRO KAWAI AND MICHAEL POMERLEANO

A review of past crises suggests that there were almost always policy mistakes leading to financial vulnerabilities, systemic risks, and eventually financial crises. Often these past crises were slow to unfold. In the case of the United States' subprime loan crisis, incipient signs of a crisis appeared in the summer of 2007. Bear Stearns collapsed in the spring of 2008. The crisis could have been spotted in its early stages. So the questions are: What is needed to prevent a systemic crisis? Who should have the responsibility to do this? How should a country establish such an arrangement to forestall a crisis? These subject matters are quite relevant to many emerging economies, particularly those in Asia.

There were several policy mistakes behind the global financial crisis. The International Monetary Fund (IMF 2009) identified three policy mistakes: mismanagement of macroeconomic policy, particularly monetary policy in the United States; flaws in financial regulations and supervision; and a weak global financial architecture. These factors all contributed to the failure to contain the buildup of financial vulnerabilities and systemic risks in the United States and some European countries.

First, the U.S. Federal Reserve took the view that no one would be able to reliably identify bubbles in asset prices and that monetary policy should not prick

The authors are thankful to Charles Calomiris, David Mayes, and Larry Wall for comments and Barnard Helman for editorial assistance. The findings, interpretations, and conclusions expressed in the paper are those of the authors and do not necessarily represent the views of the Asian Development Bank, its Institute, the World Bank, their respective executive directors, or the countries they represent.

asset price bubbles but should wait and respond to the bursting of the bubble and just mitigate its negative impact. The overall philosophy behind the Federal Reserve was that an effective post-bubble response was more important than the prevention of the bubbles, which would be difficult to accomplish using monetary policy. This philosophy may well have fed the so-called "Greenspan put" and encouraged the buildup of financial vulnerabilities.

Second, financial supervisory and regulatory frameworks around the world were weak. Neither the unified regulator of the United Kingdom nor the highly fragmented regulators of the United States were able to prevent or deal promptly with the crisis. There were regulatory gaps everywhere and a fallacy of composition—that is, while individual financial firms were deemed sound, systemic risk still built up in the system. The authorities were looking at the "trees" and not the "forest."[1] A key lesson of the crisis, therefore, is that financial policymakers need to strengthen top-down macroprudential supervision, complemented by bottom-up microprudential supervision.

Third, the global financial architecture was weak. Global organizations including the IMF, the Bank for International Settlements (BIS), and the Financial Stability Forum (FSF) did not conduct effective macroeconomic-financial surveillance of systemically important economies (United States, United Kingdom, the euro area) nor provide compelling warnings. International arrangements for the regulation, supervision, and resolution of internationally active financial firms were highly fragmented. In addition, the global discussion of the "global payments imbalance" may have diverted attention away from the buildup of U.S. domestic financial vulnerabilities toward China's exchange rate policy.

Learning from the lessons of the crisis, the United States and the United Kingdom have been shifting their regulatory structures toward empowering their respective central banks with new and greater authorities of systemic stability regulation. Now the question is how policymakers in other countries, particularly those in Asia, should formulate a strategy of systemic stability regulation to prevent a financial crisis, and how they should organize themselves to effectively implement it at the national level. Another issue is whether there is any role for regional mechanisms for financial stability to complement the national and global efforts.

## Crisis Prevention, Management, and Resolution

The most fundamental approach to a financial crisis would be to prevent one from taking place. The key principle should be: "Preventing a crisis is better

1. According to the IMF (2009), "A key failure during the boom, was the inability to spot the big picture threat of a growing asset price bubble. Policymakers only focused on their own pieces of the puzzle, overlooking the larger problem."

than curing one." This entails the prevention or mitigation of the buildup of financial vulnerabilities that could lead to systemic risk and eventually a financial crisis. Once a financial crisis breaks out, the process can be very messy, calling for appropriate crisis management responses. When a financial crisis evolves into a full-blown economic crisis with systemic damages to the entire economy, crisis resolution measures are needed. See table 7-1 for a comprehensive summary of policy lessons from the global financial crisis.

## Crisis Prevention

Crisis prevention is better than any cure. The major preventive mechanisms would include: (i) establishment of effective regulation and supervision that monitors and acts on economy-wide systemic risk; (ii) a sound macroeconomic management framework (for monetary, fiscal, and exchange rate policies) that can counteract the buildup of systemic vulnerabilities such as asset price bubbles; and (iii) the creation of a strong international financial architecture that can send pointed early warnings and induce effective international policy coordination to reduce systemic risk internationally.

In the prevention exercise, every country needs an effective framework for macroeconomic-financial surveillance—which is a surveillance that focuses on macroeconomic developments, financial sector developments, and the interactions between the two—and macroprudential supervision. Both are important because they can help spot problems and trigger action to reduce economy-wide risk.

The key facet of macroprudential regulation is that it draws attention to aggregate movements in the markets that can be a threat to systemic stability, even though at the individual firm level the problem might not be evident. The present crisis revealed that macroprudential supervision was weak in many countries. The authorities failed to identify where the ultimate risks lay due to the use of various risk-shifting instruments that made it difficult to track such risks. Hence they were unable to accurately assess the system's ability to withstand a large adverse shock. In hindsight, it is evident that the authorities should have looked beyond the financial sector and examined corporate and household behavior.[2] Subsequently, they should have set limits on leverage and associated tax incentives for corporations, loan-to-value ratios for mortgages, and debt-to-income ratios for credit. Rules are only useful if they are enforced, and part of the problem appears to have been regulatory capture, which weakened adherence to traditional prudential norms.

Microprudential supervision takes a bottom-up approach that focuses on the health and soundness of individual financial firms. This approach has

2. Information on the structure of household finance is particularly critical to gain a clear idea of the problems in the sector and how these might best be tackled.

Table 7-1. *Summary of Policy Lessons from the Global Financial Crisis*

| Objective | National Measures |
| --- | --- |
| Preventing or reducing the risk of systemic crises | *Establish effective financial regulation & supervision to monitor and act on systemic risk*<br>• Establish a national systemic stability regulator or council in charge of containing systemic risk<br>• Improve information transparency and disclosure in financial and corporate sectors<br>• Strengthen macroprudential supervision, with a focus on consolidated supervision of systemically important institutions<br>• Improve monitoring of household and corporate sectors<br>• Reduce pro-cyclicality of regulation |
| | *Adopt sound macroeconomic management (monetary, fiscal, exchange rate, and public debt)*<br>• Pursue non-inflationary monetary policy<br>• Maintain sound fiscal policy<br>• Manage public debt prudently<br>• Avoid large current account deficits<br>• Use monetary policy to curtail excesses, booms, and asset price bubbles<br>*Maintain sustainable current account positions*<br>• Avoid excessive currency overvaluation<br>• Avoid persistent current account deficits and heavy reliance on short-term capital inflows |
| Managing crises | *Provide timely liquidity of sufficient magnitude*<br>• Restore market confidence through consistent policy packages<br>• Reduce moral hazard problems |
| | *Support the financial sector within a consistent framework*<br>• Extend guarantees of bank obligations<br>• Conduct stress tests to identify losses and capital needs of financial institutions<br>• Establish a consistent framework for nonperforming loan removal and recapitalization |
| | *Adopt appropriate macroeconomic policies to mitigate the adverse feedback loop between financial and real sectors*<br>• Adopt an appropriate monetary and fiscal policy mix contingent on the specific conditions of the economy<br>• Be prepared for extraordinary policies |
| Resolving systemic crises | *Establish frameworks for resolving financial firms' impaired assets, and corporate and household debt*<br>• Establish frameworks for resolving bad assets of financial institutions<br>• Introduce legal and out-of-court procedures for corporate debt workouts |
| | *Introduce rules for exit of non-viable financial institutions*<br>• Establish clear procedures for exits of financial institutions, and rehabilitation of institutions<br>• Establish legal and formal procedures for corporate insolvencies and workouts |
| | *Introduce international insolvency mechanisms for resolving internationally active financial firms*<br>• Strengthen national insolvency procedures of banks, non-bank financial institutions, and corporations |

Source: Authors.

| Global Measures | Regional Measures |
| --- | --- |
| • Strengthen capacity, resources, and effectiveness of Financial Stability Board to promote global systemic stability<br>• Support implementation of international standards and codes, and best-practice corporate governance<br>• Agree on regulations over rating agencies, hedge funds, remunerations, etc | • Establish a regional systemic stability council, such as the European Systemic Risk Board and the proposed Asian Financial Stability Dialogue<br>• Strengthen regional monitoring of financial markets<br>• Develop a regional early warning system |
| • Strengthen IMF surveillance and early earning systems, with a focus on systemically important economies<br>• Utilize private-sector monitoring agencies | • Strengthen regional macroeconomic policy dialogue and monitoring<br>• Develop a regional early warning system |
| • Coordinate policies to avoid unsustainable global payments imbalances | • Expand regional demand where savings rates are exceptionally high |
| • Strengthen IMF liquidity support, including the new Flexible Credit Line | • Strengthen a regional liquidity support facility to contain crises and contagion |
| • Establish a common international rule for public sector interventions in the distressed financial system<br>• Avoid financial protectionism | • Harmonize national interventions in the financial system—such as bank deposit guarantees—at the regional level |
| • Streamline IMF conditionality<br>• Design international fiscal support programs for fiscally constrained economies | • Strengthen the regional ability to formulate conditionality<br>• Create regional fiscal support systems |
| • Harmonize national frameworks for resolving bad assets of financial institutions<br>• Provide international support | • Finance regional programs to help accelerate bank and corporate restructuring |
| • Harmonize national resolution regimes for non-viable financial institutions | • Harmonize insolvency procedures by adopting good practices |
| • Introduce international procedures for cross-border insolvencies | • Develop regional insolvency procedures to support the global effort |

Box 7-1. *Macroprudential Supervisory Measures*

*Competition regulation*
Reduction of the "too big to fail" or "too interconnected to fail" problem through
  imposing size limits on firms

*Market conduct regulation*
Enhanced transparency and competition

*Financial firms*
Higher standards for capital requirements and risk management for systemically
  important financial institutions
Limits on financial firms' leverage, such as setting maximum leverage ratios and/
  or credit growth
Efforts to mitigate pro-cyclicality through automatic counter-cyclical provisioning, such as a form of dynamic provisioning
Limits on exposure to specific sectors, for example to corporations, households,
  and hedge funds among others

*Households*
Loan-to-value (LTV) restrictions for mortgages
Limits on consumer debt, such as debt-to-income ratios

*Corporations*
Limits on leverage, such as debt-to-equity ratios
Limits on tax advantages, such as disallowing interest deductibility for leverage
  exceeding a certain level or foreign currency–denominated debt

*External*
Limits on external debt
Limits on currency and maturity mismatches

traditionally taken the view that making each financial firm safe makes the whole
financial system safe. The focus on individual financial firms is important but
often discounts the importance of the overall system. Crisis prevention necessitates taking a macroprudential approach to complement the existing microprudential supervisory rules. Essentially, microprudential supervision is good at
looking at the "trees," while macroprudential supervision looks at the "forest."
Macroeconomic-financial surveillance examines a much wider scope.

To understand the nature of macroprudential surveillance, it is useful to consider the examples of a broad agenda to address systemic risk, outlined in box
7-1. The box lists a set of issues that effective supervisors and regulators should

bear in mind. The objects of systemic oversight should be broad, including the corporate and household sector, as well as macroeconomic elements such as external debt.

Borio and Shim (2007) suggest that macroprudential measures may be put in place in a gradual, sequenced manner in the face of a buildup of vulnerabilities and systemic risk. For example, once a sign of built-up vulnerabilities is identified, policymakers need to express coordinated warnings. When vulnerabilities worsen but the problem is largely limited to a certain sector of the economy—such as commercial real estate and/or household mortgages—precise tools can be mobilized that target those sectors, including applying sector-focused stress tests, tightening lending and underwriting standards, and limiting loan-to-value ratios. If the problem becomes more generalized and poses systemic risk, raising minimum capital requirements will be called for, and if the problem is built through markets and unregulated institutions, as opposed to banks, then tightening monetary policy by raising policy interest rates might be more effective.

## Crisis Management

Once a crisis unfolds, the macroeconomic and financial authorities need to respond and manage the process well so that the crisis does not grow to critical proportions. The crisis management tools that have been used in recent years include: (i) provision of timely and adequate liquidity; (ii) support of distressed, but viable financial firms through guarantees, nonperforming loan (NPL) removal, and recapitalization; and (iii) adoption of appropriate macroeconomic policies to mitigate the adverse feedback loop between the financial sector and the real economy, reflecting the specific conditions and reality of the economy. Many of these policies could create moral hazard problems.

However, once a systemic crisis starts, the deleveraging process sets in, and asset prices begin to decline, it is difficult to arrest this process and reverse it. In a sense, the unwinding of the high leverage and the elimination of asset price bubbles are desirable, but they have serious consequences to the financial system and the real economy. The objective of crisis management is to mitigate the negative feedback loop between the financial sector and the real economy through a comprehensive set of monetary, fiscal, and financial-sector policies.

### LIQUIDITY INJECTION AND MACROECONOMIC POLICY

During the global financial crisis, central banks have been aggressive in providing liquidity to the markets, reducing policy interest rates, and even adopting the "quantitative easing" policy—under the *de facto* zero interest rate, as was done in Japan—in the face of acute contraction of money markets globally. Major central banks have also set up currency swap-lines with the U.S. Federal Reserve to ensure adequate supply of U.S. dollar liquidity. Such operations were highly successful in calming the turbulent financial markets in the fall and winter of 2008.

Fiscal policy responses have also been made relatively quickly. The Group of Twenty (G20) consensus of providing large amounts of fiscal stimulus to support aggregate demand has been laudable. Mitigating economic contraction helps prevent the adverse economic conditions—declining housing prices, shrinking consumption, rising corporate bankruptcies, and rising unemployment—from further damaging the health of the overall financial system, even though it cannot stop the economy-wide deleveraging process.

However, one needs to be cautious in order to avoid excessive fiscal spending. One of the reasons behind the delayed response by Japanese financial authorities in addressing the banking sector problem in the 1990s was that while continuous fiscal spending supported minimum aggregate demand, it reduced the sense of urgency to directly work on bank restructuring (Kawai 2005). Fiscal stimulus should be used as an instrument to provide a cushion while the financial authority is working directly on fundamental financial sector problems.

## FINANCIAL SECTOR SUPPORT

Financial authorities need to respond to a systemic financial crisis with a set of comprehensive policy measures. These include a provision of liquidity to troubled financial firms, guarantees of deposits and interbank claims, a rigorous assessment of major financial firms' balance sheets, removal of nonperforming assets from their balance sheets, and recapitalization of viable firms, while consigning nonviable firms for orderly resolution. Prompt intervention is critical. Clearly, Japan's delayed intervention was an important factor behind its lost decade (Kawai 2005).

The initial priority of financial sector support is to stabilize the financial system by taking steps to restore market confidence—including blanket protection of bank deposits and guarantees of interbank claims and possible other assets, as well as the provision of liquidity support to troubled financial firms. The next step is to "stop the bleeding" by intervening in clearly nonviable and insolvent firms; otherwise the net liabilities and resolution costs will continue to rise.

After that, governments need to develop a strategy and plan for the recapitalization and rehabilitation of weak but viable financial firms using public funds. But to do so, several steps are needed: rigorous assessments of the balance sheets of individual financial firms, identification of the magnitude of bad assets, and capital shortfalls. Stress tests are often useful for these purposes. Recapitalization of financial firms must require recognition of losses on bad assets. After recapitalization, owners of firms must have a sufficient incentive to restructure bad assets of viable borrowers, such as a write-down.

## Crisis Resolution

Crisis resolution measures would include: (i) development of institutions and mechanisms for restructuring financial firms' impaired assets and hence corporate or household debt or both; (ii) use of national insolvency procedures for nonviable financial institutions; and (iii) use of international mechanisms for resolving nonviable internationally active financial firms, including clear burden sharing mechanisms across countries. The reality is that there is no clearly defined international regime for resolving failures of financial firms that operate across borders, and therefore the crisis management process can create international conflict leading to stalemate.

### FINANCIAL SECTOR RESOLUTION

There must be a clear resolution mechanism for dealing with nonviable financial firms. The mechanism should include closures (liquidation), mergers with healthier firms, and temporary nationalization of nonviable firms. Authorities need to put in place the clear legal and operational groundwork for these interventions to ensure the orderly exit of nonviable firms.

Another issue is to resolve the bad debt accumulated in the financial system, which may have been transferred to public asset management companies. An important principle of financial sector resolution is that the longer it takes, the larger the eventual economic costs. Assets underlying bad assets—or the bad assets themselves—should be sold in a reasonable time period so that asset markets can be cleared. Otherwise, depressed asset prices may continue indefinitely.

### COORDINATED APPROACH TO BANK AND CORPORATE RESOLUTION

To resolve troubled assets of banks, it is necessary to work on the underlying problem of bad loans to the corporate (and/or household) sector. This means that the government should forge strong links between bank and corporate restructuring. The government needs to find a credible mechanism that would encourage banks to restructure failing corporations, as an individual bank may not have sufficient incentive to adopt drastic restructuring measures such as write-downs and debt-equity swaps, leaving the "zombie" borrowers intact.[3] The problem is the "prisoners' dilemma" situation due to the absence of coordination.

The severe financial crises that devastated Asia during 1997–98 provide important lessons for addressing systemic corporate distress. Coping with it

---

3. Caballero, Hoshi, and Kashyap (2011) discussed the problem of "zombie" corporations. They proposed a model that highlights the implications of the zombie problem for restructuring. The congestion created by "zombie" corporations reduces the profits of healthy firms, discouraging their entry and investment. In this context, economic recovery is delayed significantly.

requires a host of simultaneous measures, both carrots and sticks, such as the provision of incentives for restructuring, policy approaches to the disposal of bad debts, the legal framework for corporate insolvency, efforts to strengthen bankruptcy courts, and the establishment of procedures for out-of-court workouts.[4] Governments often lack the resources and expertise required to address corporate distress on a large scale, and also policies, institutions, and legal frameworks may not be adequate to the task.

Among the crisis-affected Asian economies, Malaysia's experience is most likely the "best practice" for tackling banking and corporate restructuring in unison. The country created three agencies—Danaharta, Danamodal, and the Corporate Debt Restructuring Committee (CDRC)—for comprehensive restructuring of the banking and corporate sectors.[5] The three agencies linked their efforts effectively (see table 7-2, which also summarizes institutional arrangements in other crisis-affected Asian countries).

A bank in trouble because of nonperforming loans on its books could transfer them to Danaharta and have it sell them. Thereafter, if the bank were still in financial trouble and unable to raise sufficient capital from shareholders, it could seek assistance from Danamodal for recapitalization, diluting the original shareholders. In exchange Danamodal could facilitate consolidation of the banking sector by selling its stake to a stronger bank and thereby fostering mergers. Meanwhile, the CDRC acted as an informal mediator, facilitating dialogue between borrowers and their creditors to achieve voluntary restructuring schemes. If the CDRC could achieve this then NPLs would be resolved voluntarily. If not, Danaharta would take over the bad loans, disposing of them over the long term.

The Asian experience suggests that governments need to be actively involved in coordinating bank and corporate restructuring, possibly by establishing (or reestablishing) government-sponsored voluntary workout schemes. But to reach an optimal social outcome, the government needs to eliminate the zombie borrowers. A great deal of operational and financial restructuring would be needed in the

---

4. There is a strong consensus that corporations have a better chance of survival under a London approach or provisions similar to Chapter 11 of the U.S. bankruptcy code. In much of Europe, debt restructurings are negotiated out of court to avoid formal insolvency proceedings, which are often seen as unpredictable and lengthy, without any formal binding rules of engagement. The court-based procedure, including Chapter 11, has the advantage of being transparent in comparison to the usual out-of-court settlements.

5. Danaharta was an asset management company with functions similar to those of the U.S. Resolution Trust Corporation; Danamodal Nasional Berhad was established to recapitalize the banking sector, especially to assist banks whose capital base had been eroded by losses; and CDRC was established to reduce stress on the banking system and to repair the finances and operations of corporate borrowers.

Table 7-2. *Institutional Frameworks for Bank and Corporate Restructuring in Asia*

| Country | Major support institution | Agency for bank recapitalization | Asset management company | Agency for voluntary corporate restructuring |
|---|---|---|---|---|
| Indonesia | Indonesian Bank Restructuring Agency (IBRA) [June 1998] | Direct from Bank Indonesia (BI) or via IBRA | Indonesian Bank Restructuring Agency (IBRA) | Jakarta Initiative Task Force (JITF) [September 1998] |
| Korea | Financial Supervisory Services (FSS) | Korea Deposit Insurance Corporation (KDIC) | Korea Asset Management Corporation (KAMCO) | Corporate Restructuring Coordination Committee (CRCC) [July 1998] |
| Malaysia | Bank Negara Malaysia (BNM) | Danamodal [August 1998] | Danaharta [June 1998] | Corporate Debt Restructuring Committee (CDRC) [August 1998] |
| Thailand | Bank of Thailand (BOT) | Financial Restructuring Advisory Committee (funded by the Financial Institutions Development Fund) | FRA to take assets of closed finance companies; unsold assets moved to AMC and good assets to RAB. TAMC for commercial banks [July 2001] | Corporate Debt Restructuring Advisory Committee (CDRAC) [June 1998] |
| Japan | Financial Services Agency (FSA) | Deposit Insurance Corporation (DICJ) | RCC and IRC | None. Oversight by FSA |

Source: Kawai (2000, 2005).
FRA = Financial Sector Restructuring Authority; AMC = Asset Management Corporation; RAB = Radanasin Bank; TAMC = Thai Asset Management Corporation; RCC = Resolution and Collection Corporation; IRC = Industrial Revitalization Corporation.

present crisis, as we witnessed with the U.S. automotive industry. The U.S. government acted decisively in the restructuring and took ownership stakes in General Motors and Chrysler. It also provided "debtor-in-possession" financing and got involved in significant operational restructuring. Therefore, policymakers are well advised to undertake large-scale corporate restructuring under a government-sponsored (or industry-sponsored) out-of-court settlement. However, to establish the right incentives for sound financial behavior, this restructuring role should rely, to the extent possible, on market forces rather than government fiat.

CROSSBORDER RESOLUTION MECHANISM FOR
INTERNATIONALLY ACTIVE INSTITUTIONS
The major impediment to achieving global financial stability is the inadequate international framework for dealing with the insolvency of internationally active financial institutions. There are no international standards for cross-border bank resolution, and the existing home-country-based resolution arrangements are not sustainable.[6] The international community must agree on cross-border resolution mechanisms for failing internationally active financial institutions.

An FSF (2008) report provided principles for cross-border cooperation on crisis management. A careful read of the report leads to the conclusion that the entire set of recommendations is based on voluntary cooperation, and the FSF does not offer any roadmap for compelling action or implementation. It is useful to identify such principles, but it is unrealistic to assume that countries will follow voluntary principles and ignore self-interest in financial crises. Ultimately, self-interest will prevent the countries from adopting the principles in a real crisis. Until the issue of cross-border insolvency is addressed, it will be difficult to create a binding global financial order.[7]

## Creating a Systemic Stability Regulator

We propose that each country establish an effective, powerful systemic stability regulator that is in charge of crisis prevention, management, and resolution. There are three principles for establishing a systemic stability regulator. First, the regulator should have clear regulatory objectives and mandates for crisis prevention, management, and resolution. Second, the regulator should be given sufficient regulatory resources including political backing; legal, human, and financial resources; as well as adequate instruments and tools for effective implementation. Third, the regulatory structure has to be effective and preserve operational independence.

---

6. Hüpkes (2009) found that the cross-border framework for managing a crisis is weak and that the winding-down of a large cross-border institution is complex. The resolution is hampered by the asymmetries of exposures across jurisdictions that create a risk of asset ring-fencing and discourage the sharing of information and collaboration; multiple (and conflicting) insolvency processes across jurisdictions; resolution tools that do not work when markets are not functioning; and practical constraints such as technical competence across jurisdictions and different time zones.

7. Some authors have argued that a possible alternative is to develop an informal agreement similar to the London approach for international insolvencies.

## Objectives and Mandates

The overall mandate of the systemic stability regulator should be to contain systemic risks in the financial system and promote financial stability.

One of the most important objectives of the systemic stability regulator is to maintain financial stability through the prevention of financial crises, that is, through monitoring, anticipating, and intervening prior to crises. The regulator should aim to spot vulnerabilities in a country's financial system so that, if necessary, it would trigger actions in a timely and informed manner to prevent a rise of systemic risk and an eventual crisis from occurring. The role of the regulator would be to strengthen, not displace, examinations and supervision focused on individual institutions.

The major objectives and mandates can be summarized as:

—Monitoring systemic risks—such as large or growing credit exposure to real estate—across financial firms and markets;

—Assessing the potential for deficiencies in risk management practices, broad-based increases in financial leverage, or changes in financial markets and products, which would create systemic risk;

—Analyzing possible spillovers among financial firms or between firms and markets—for example through the mutual exposures of highly interconnected firms;

—Identifying possible regulatory gaps—including gaps in the legal regime governing the insolvency of financial institutions—that pose risks for the system as a whole;

—Curtailing systemic risks across the entire financial system encompassing corporations, households, and capital inflows as well as arrangements for crisis management and financial firm resolution through legislative action, prudential measures, issuance of early warning, advice on monetary policy, and intervention in individual firms; and

—Issuing periodic reports on the stability of the financial system.

Essentially, the systemic stability regulator must conduct a macroeconomic-financial surveillance and take a macroprudential approach to supervision that addresses risks to the financial system as a whole in an effort to enhance economy-wide financial stability and prevent systemic crises. This would include the monitoring of corporate finance and household debt, which have implications for monetary policy and financial stability, as well as international banking flows, which bear on systemic stability due to the risks of sudden stops.[8]

8. In emerging markets, a corporate sector that is highly leveraged and unprofitable or that is prone to currency mismatches (as in Indonesia and the Republic of Korea in 1997) can lead to massive problems. See Kawai (2000).

It would be desirable to produce some form of early warning system. Ideally, this warning would enable the authorities and supervised entities to avoid problems by alerting them to the need for preemptive action; even if this were not possible, the ability to activate corrective action in advance would be of considerable benefit. In order for the systemic stability regulator to predict most crises, it has to be oversensitive and predict false positives, that is, even those crises that fail to materialize.

The systemic stability regulator would also organize the immediate response to a crisis, the strategy for coordinated financial and corporate sector restructuring, and the orderly resolution of failed corporations and financial institutions. The regulator is thus charged with express responsibility for containing systemic risks in the financial system.

## Regulatory Resources and Implementation Tools

The systemic stability regulator needs sufficient political, legal, legislative, human, and financial resources to carry out its objectives and mandates effectively. It would need substantial analytical capabilities and resources to identify the types of information needed, collect the required information, analyze the information obtained, and develop and implement the necessary policy, supervisory, and regulatory responses.

### REGULATORY RESOURCES

The regulator should be allowed to obtain information from other official sources whenever possible, for example, from assessments and programs of the central bank—if the central bank does not have the full responsibility of systemic stability regulation—and other financial supervisors. It would further need broad authority to obtain information—through data collection and reports or, when necessary, examinations—from a range of financial market participants, including banking organizations, securities firms, and key financial market intermediaries.

In some countries, the systemic stability regulator might be able to rely on private companies—for example, credit bureaus and rating agencies—to collect corporate data, or might assign this responsibility to bank supervisors. To collect the necessary data the regulator would have to operate in a system that provides the capacity to enforce compliance or exact a commensurate penalty when firms are found to be in violation of laws. This includes the authority to craft an orderly resolution of systemically important financial firms and benchmarks to limit leverage. Essentially, the regulator would require knowledge and expertise across a wide range of financial firms and markets to offer a comprehensive and multi-faceted approach to systemic risk.

The need for a multi-faceted approach is exemplified by the fact that numerous systemic risks can emerge in both the formal banking and the "shadow banking" system. Central banks and banking supervisors can only offer a limited perspective on risk, and their views have to be complemented by the perspectives of regulators of securities and insurance markets, ministries of finance, as well as domestic and external debt management agencies. Formal consultation with external, independent stakeholders who have market knowledge and expertise can improve the systemic stability regulator's decision-making process as well.

## POLICY IMPLEMENTATION

The systemic stability regulator should possess the entire implementation arsenal—the instruments, tools, and techniques to be used to achieve its objectives and mandates. These include macroprudential supervisory tools to reduce systemic risk, such as the ability to impose capital and liquidity requirements, limit leverage ratios, loan-to-value ratios and debt-to-income ratios, as well as to introduce (or revise) legislation concerning insolvency regimes for nonviable financial firms. Given the importance of these matters for the aggregate level of risk within the financial system, the regulator would need to set the standards for capital, liquidity, and risk management practices for financial firms.

Monetary policy is also important as a "leaning against the wind" tool to prevent a buildup of systemic risk through the markets, because even though regulators and supervisors try to influence the market, it might be difficult for them to discern whole-market developments. For example, as a "shadow banking system" may continue to exist in the future, monetary policy would have to be mobilized in order to affect the entire economy and all market players—including those outside the traditional regulatory perimeter, or shadow banks.

### Operational Independence

In order to ensure effectiveness, the systemic stability regulator should be independent of political considerations. Any forthright, disinterested assessment of systemic stability requires two types of independence. First, the regulator must not have anything other than its own reputation riding on the assessment. Second, it must be independent of the political system and the interests of individual agencies—such as the tax authority's interest in revenues or the debt management agency's desire to mobilize debt at low interest rates—while respecting political and/or operational independence of the central bank in many cases.

The key competencies related to financial stability are:

—performing prudential regulation and supervision of individual financial institutions;

—monitoring systemic risks and pursuing actions to maintain macroprudential stability;

—providing short-term liquidity assistance to solvent banks;

—presiding over swift and orderly resolutions at troubled banks, at limited cost to both creditors and society at large;

—limiting the losses of people unable to protect themselves; and

—coordinating the activities of the various parties involved to ensure coherence and avoid gaps in the system.[9]

Clearly, as the ultimate providers of domestic currency liquidity to the market and solvent financial firms, the central bank has to be actively involved in maintaining financial stability and in restoring stability should it become impaired. The central bank should provide liquidity assistance and play an essential part of macroeconomic-financial surveillance (and in some cases macroprudential supervision), with other supervisors actively involved and playing a collaborative role. Fiscal authorities also need to be involved. Decisions regarding institutional insolvency involve property rights, important distributional considerations, wider political dimensions, as well as technical issues. Thus the systemic stability regulator should be in charge of a wide range of issues, including those related to central banking, insolvency laws, fiscal resource mobilization, and tax authorities, in addition to financial supervision and regulation.

The central bank can face potential conflicts. Macroprudential regulation and supervision inevitably involve guiding the actions of, and even determining the fate of, large systemically important individual financial firms. For instance, macroprudential regulation might warrant tightening monetary policy to abate an asset price rise, while employment considerations might dictate maintaining easy monetary policy. The independence and mandate of the central bank in the area of price stability could be undermined if it were to play a dominant role in macroprudential regulation and supervision. It is important to resolve conflicts of interest among agencies in a transparent way by the top decision-making body.

In addition to independence, substantive accountability has to be embedded in regulatory objectives, mandates, and processes covering crisis prevention as well as management and resolution. The accountability cannot be limited to reporting obligations. Sanctions, punishment, or both should be imposed on the systemic stability regulator should its performance prove inadequate. Ideally, it is desirable to create an incentive mechanism with deferred compensation. Adequate accountability warrants publishing periodic stability reports that enable the actual performance of the financial system to be compared against the warnings of the regulator.

## Organizing a Systemic Stability Regulator

The structure of the systemic stability regulator should be organized in the most effective way possible to carry out the delegated responsibilities of financial stability.

9. See Mayes, Morgan, and Lim (2010).

## A Single Agency versus a Council Approach

An important issue is whether it should be a single entity or a collective effort among different national financial authorities, each with a different specific responsibility. Key financial authorities include: the central bank, financial supervisor(s), and the finance ministry.

First, one can think of establishing a single, fully integrated national agency in charge of systemic stability regulation. Asia offers such a fully consolidated model in Singapore (see table 7-3). In Singapore, the finance ministry essentially embraces all the necessary functions, including those of the central bank, and acts as the regulator and supervisor of financial firms, and as the agent for macroprudential supervision, in addition to managing the national treasury function. Therefore it has the advantage of being able to take a very coherent approach to systemic stability regulation. For many countries this is not possible because central banks have become increasingly independent of the government and the political process.

The second option would be for the central bank to play the systemic stability regulator function by taking over macroprudential supervisory and regulatory powers and responsibilities. The recent regulatory changes in the United States and the United Kingdom have placed their respective central banks at the core of macroprudential supervision (see below), and Hong Kong, China; India; and Malaysia follow this model in Asia. However, an argument can be made that a central bank may not be in the best position to take sole responsibility for maintaining financial stability as this responsibility requires a much broader expertise and culture than traditional central banking. This arrangement could also expose the central bank to the risk of political interventions once the outbreak of a crisis requires management and resolution policies.

The third option would be to concentrate the macroprudential power into an integrated supervisory authority. In Japan and Taipei,China, a fully integrated supervisory authority is in charge of macroprudential responsibility. One of the shortcomings of this approach is that supervisory agencies are not the organizations best suited to conducting macroeconomic-financial surveillance. As a result, this model would require close coordination with the central bank for information exchange and overall economic assessment.

The fourth option is a combination of the second and third options, that is, an arrangement where the central bank and the supervisory authorities share macroprudential responsibilities. Australia, China, Korea, and the Philippines have all adopted this model in Asia. In this model, the central bank and the supervisor(s) have to coordinate with each other and with the finance ministry.

Apart from the first model, all other arrangements would require close coordination among the financial authorities. Hence it would be desirable to institutionalize the arrangement by establishing a systemic stability regulatory "council"

Table 7-3. *Structure of Financial Regulatory Supervision in Asia*

| | Entity with Regulatory Oversight | | | |
| Country | Banks | Securities and markets | Insurance | Macroprudential responsibility |
|---|---|---|---|---|
| Australia | Australian Prudential Regulation Authority (APRA) | Australian Securities and Investments Commission (ASIC) | Australian Prudential Regulation Authority (APRA) | APRA, collaborates with ASIC and Reserve Bank of Australia |
| China, People's Republic of | People's Bank of China (PBoC); China Banking Regulatory Commission (CBRC) | PBoC; China Securities Regulatory Commission (CSRC) | PBoC; China Insurance Regulatory Commission (CIRC) | PBoC Financial Stability Bureau, cooperation with CBRC |
| Hong Kong | Hong Kong Monetary Authority (HKMA) | Securities and Futures Commission (SFC) | Office of the Commissioner of Insurance (OCI) | Hong Kong Monetary Authority (HKMA) |
| India | Reserve Bank of India (RBI): Board of Financial Supervision (BFS) | Securities and Exchange Board of India (SEBI) | Insurance Regulatory and Development Authority (IRDA) | RBI Financial Stability Unit |
| Indonesia | Bank Indonesia (BI) | Indonesia Capital Market and Financial Institutions Supervisory Agency- Badan Pengawas Pasar Modal (BAPEPAM) | | Under discussion |
| Japan | Financial Services Agency (FSA) | | | |
| Korea | Financial Supervisory Service (FSS) | | | Bank of Korea (BOK) and FSS |
| Malaysia | Bank Negara Malaysia (BNM) | Securities Commission | Bank Negara Malaysia (BNM) | Bank Negara Malaysia (BNM) |
| Philippines | Bangko Sentral ng Pilipinas (BSP) | Securities and Exchange Commission (SEC) | Insurance Commission (IC) | Financial Sector Forum (FSF): BSP, SEC, IC, and Philippine Deposit Insurance Corporation |
| Singapore | Monetary Authority of Singapore (MAS) | | | |
| Taipei,China | Financial Supervisory Commission (FSC) | | | |

*Source*: Mayes, Morgan, and Lim (2010).

comprising the finance minister, the central bank governor, and the head(s) of national financial supervisor(s).[10] An independent, powerful working group that supports this council may be chaired by a renowned expert (like former Federal Reserve chair Paul Volcker) and include finance and central bank deputies, head(s) of supervisor(s), and other relevant parties as active members, and should be endowed with authority to engage in crisis prevention, management, and resolution. The working group would provide recommendations for policy actions to the council, which would make the ultimate decision. In this instance a country's central bank may assume a secretariat role, given its usual advantages in analysis of macroeconomic-financial surveillance for systemic stability.

## Global Experiences

A review of the global experience can provide us with some incisive insights. Of eighty-three countries listed in table 7-4, twenty-nine countries have a system of integrated prudential supervision, twenty countries have supervisory agencies in charge of two types of financial intermediaries, and thirty-four countries have multiple supervisors who focus on specific sectors. Central banks in forty-eight countries (close to 60 percent of the total) have the authority to supervise banks. It is interesting to observe that developing and emerging economies tend to have multiple supervisors. Also, the countries with multiple supervisors tend to have central banks with banking supervision authority.

In all G20 countries, the central bank is largely in charge of price stability and payment system stability. Most of the central banks publish financial stability reports, and close to half have financial stability committees. Price stability remains the central bank's main mandate, but now financial stability is increasingly becoming an important mandate as well.

In many countries, regulatory structure is as much a function of history as it is of a careful allocation of objectives and tasks to individual institutions to ensure that (i) all aspects of the problem are covered; (ii) no confusing overlaps exist; and (iii) the incentives of all those involved are clearly aligned with the task of preserving financial stability (Mayes, Morgan, and Lim 2010). Small countries may find it difficult to split intellectual and political resources into multiple supervisors in order to counter vested interests, particularly when there are strong financial firms. On the other hand, concentrating too much power in a single agency could be a challenge for a democratic system. Having different sector-specific regulators may both affect and reflect the structure of the financial industry. If financial conglomerates or universal banks are common,

10. Adams (2010) recommended the creation of a high-level Systemic Risk Council that would be responsible not only for monitoring and coordination, but also for undertaking preemptive and corrective macroprudential measures by the responsible agencies.

Table 7-4. Economies with Single, Semi-Integrated, and Sector-Specific Prudential Supervisory Agencies, 2009[a]

| Single prudential supervisor for the financial system (year of establishment) | Agency supervising two types of financial intermediaries | | | Multiple sector-specific supervisors (at least one for banks, one for securities firms, and one for insurers) |
|---|---|---|---|---|
| | Banks and securities firms | Banks and insurers | Securities firms and insurers | |
| Australia (1998) | Finland | Canada | Bolivia | Albania* |
| Austria (2002) | Luxembourg | Colombia | Bulgaria* | Argentina* |
| Bahrain* (2002) | Mexico | Ecuador | Chile | Bahamas* |
| Belgium (2004) | Switzerland | El Salvador | Jamaica* | Barbados* |
| Bermuda* (2002) | Uruguay | Guatemala | Mauritius* | Botswana* |
| Cayman Islands* (1997) | | Malaysia* | Slovak Republic*[b] | Brazil* |
| Denmark (1988) | | Peru | Ukraine* | China, People's Republic of (PRC) |
| Estonia (1999) | | Venezuela | | Croatia* |
| Germany (2002) | | | | Cyprus* |
| Gibraltar (1989) | | | | Czech Republic[b] |
| Guernsey (1988) | | | | Dominican Republic* |
| Hungary (2002) | | | | Egypt* |
| Iceland (1988) | | | | France* |
| Ireland* (2002) | | | | Greece* |
| Japan (2001) | | | | Hong Kong* |
| Kazakhstan* (1998) | | | | India* |
| Korea, Rep. (1997) | | | | Indonesia* |
| Latvia (1998) | | | | Israel* |
| Maldives* (1998) | | | | Italy* |
| Malta* (2002) | | | | Jordan* |
| Netherlands* (2004) | | | | Lithuania* |
| Nicaragua* (1999) | | | | New Zealand* |
| Norway (1986) | | | | Panama |
| Singapore* (1984) | | | | Philippines* |
| South Africa* (1990) | | | | Poland* |
| Sweden (1991) | | | | Portugal* |
| Taipei,China (2004) | | | | Russia* |
| United Arab Emirates* (2000) | | | | Slovenia* |
| United Kingdom (1997) | | | | Sri Lanka* |
| | | | | Spain* |
| | | | | Thailand* |
| | | | | Tunisia* |
| | | | | Uganda* |
| | | | | United States* |
| Total: 29 | Total: 5 | Total: 8 | Total: 7 | Total: 34 |

Source: Čihák and Podpiera (2006). Updated by the authors.

a. The table focuses on prudential supervision, not on business supervision (which can be carried out by the same agencies or by separate agencies, even in the integrated model). Also, the table does not consider deposit insurers, even though they play an important role in banking supervision in a number of countries and can do so under any regulatory model.

b. The authorities announced plans to integrate prudential supervision in their central banks in 2006.

*An asterisk indicates that banking supervision is conducted by the central bank.

the argument for a universal regulator becomes stronger, as supervision of the institution as a whole does not simply represent the sum of its parts (Wall 2009).

There is also the issue of whether the same institution should be responsible for ex ante systemic stability regulation and ex post crisis management and regulation. Adams (2010) argued in favor of a single organization doing both, but the tendency in some countries has been to separate these functions so that the latter is not tainted by the mistakes of the former, and the risk of avoiding the problem is reduced. The question of whether one institution or multiple institutions with a single coordinating body is more efficient depends on the context and leadership.

## Relevance for Asia

### New Developments in the United States and the United Kingdom

FINANCIAL STABILITY REFORM IN THE UNITED STATES

The Dodd-Frank legislation in the United States is designed to minimize the threats from financial firms that are so big or interconnected that they pose a "systemic risk" to the overall economy. It also sets forth a plan to wind down troubled non-financial firms, blunting the impact that the failure of those firms could have on the economy. Indicative of increased regulatory involvement in the financial sector, Dodd-Frank makes it easier for regulators to dismantle a failing nonbank financial firm. It sets up a council of regulators charged with identifying systemic risks and gives the government and the Federal Reserve sweeping powers over financial firms at home and abroad.

The newly created Financial Services Oversight Council is chaired by the secretary of the Treasury and also includes the chair of the Federal Reserve (see box 7-2) and the heads of key regulatory agencies (the Securities and Exchange Commission, the Commodity Futures Trading Commission, the Federal Deposit Insurance Corporation, the Office of the Comptroller of the Currency, the Federal Housing Finance Agency, and the National Credit Union Administration). One state insurance regulator and one state bank regulator are expected to also get a nonvoting seat each.[11]

The council is mandated to monitor the financial services marketplace to identify potential threats to the stability of the U.S. financial system—in other words, to watch out for financial crises and stop them before they begin. A key part of this task is identifying firms that could pose a threat to financial stability, that is, firms that are considered "too big to fail." Financial firms would be placed in this category if the council deems that material financial distress at the

---

11. Only one regulator, the Office of Thrift Supervision, would be dissolved.

company could pose a threat to financial stability or the economy. The council would identify these firms and ask their respective regulators to tighten oversight.

Although commendable, there are some doubts as to whether the council can play an effective role:

—While the council brings all regulators to the table,[12] it does not cover other systemic risks that are prone to arise in the U.S. economy; these risks may be related to commercial real estate, corporate and consumer debt overhang, and the level of government debt.

—Despite its mandate, the council does not have the authority to make binding decisions and does not have an explicit process for authorizing the use of fiscal resources. It might end up relying on the used (and abused) clause of the Fed 13(3), which invokes "unusual and exigent."

—The council has adequate tools to develop "heightened prudential standards" for individual firms, but it is not clear if it has the tools needed to address systemic risks, such as the ability to rein in the excessively indebted consumer sector through "heightened prudential standards," including changing the deductibility of interest or imposing system-wide ratios of loan to value.

One of the key problems during the crisis was how to unwind troubled nonbank financial firms, such as American International Group, Bear Stearns, and Lehman Brothers, that posed a threat to the economy. Traditional bankruptcy procedures would be drawn out, which could endanger the overall financial system. In addition, banking regulators did not have the legal authority to "resolve" the failure of a non-financial firm. Dodd-Frank aims to solve this dilemma. The Federal Deposit Insurance Corporation would be able to take over a failing firm so that taxpayers would not have to foot the bill for a bailout.

A troubled firm's shareholders and creditors would be responsible for bearing the costs of its resolution, but the government would also establish a Systemic Resolution Fund within the Treasury Department to help cover any additional costs. Financial firms with more than US$10 billion in assets would be required to repay any taxpayer money used to seize or wind up the failed firms.

## Financial Regulation Reform in the United Kingdom

The new government in the United Kingdom has decided to overhaul its regulatory system. The Financial Services Authority (FSA) will be split into a Prudential Regulation Authority (PRA); the Macro Prudential Regulation Authority (MPRA); and a Consumer Protection and Markets Authority. Within the MPRA, a Financial Policy Committee (FPC) will be established under the

---

12. The council of regulators is remarkably similar to an advisory council that already exists: the President's Working Group on Financial Markets, which includes the Treasury secretary, Federal Reserve chair, and the heads of the Securities and Exchange Commission and the Commodity Futures Trading Commission.

---

**Box 7-2.** *Increased Powers of the U.S. Federal Reserve*

The Federal Reserve would require systemically significant firms, including foreign groups that own a large or risky U.S. subsidiary, to abide by "heightened prudential standards." These include leverage limits, liquidity rules, and the need to draft a resolution plan or "living will." This tighter oversight would mostly mean requiring banks to keep more liquid capital on hand. It could also take the form of limiting bank exposure to another firm or requiring a financial firm to change its risk management practices.

The Federal Reserve would be able to require any systemically important financial firm to "sell or otherwise transfer assets or off-balance-sheet items to unaffiliated firms, to terminate one or more activities, or to impose conditions on the manner in which the identified financial holding company conducts one or more activities." The Federal Reserve could order a financial firm to sell a risky division or stop dangerous trading activity if the central bank determines that there is a threat to the U.S. financial system. If that does not save a firm, the government could seize it.

---

authority of the Bank of England (BoE). The reason for this drastic overhaul is that the government has been of the view that the tripartite system—comprised of BoE, FSA, and Her Majesty's Treasury—failed to prevent the financial crisis (see box 7-3), leading to massive state intervention in the banking system and the deepest recession in the post–WWII era.

As a result of this regulatory change, the BoE will have statutory responsibilities for financial stability—in addition to price stability—and be in charge of macroprudential supervision. The FPC, which will function along the lines of the BoE's Monetary Policy Committee, will be responsible for maintaining financial stability by monitoring systemic risks and vulnerabilities that threaten the financial system as a whole, and acting in response. The PRA will be in charge of microprudential supervision of banks, investment banks, building societies, and insurance companies.

## Emerging Examples of a Systemic Stability Regulation Council in Asia

Several examples of a systemic stability regulation council can be found in Australia, Korea, India, and Indonesia.

### COUNCIL OF FINANCIAL REGULATORS IN AUSTRALIA

The Australian economy weathered the financial crisis better than that of many other advanced countries. Australia owes much of its better-than-average performance during the financial crisis to sound policies and effective financial

Box 7-3.  *Tripartite Financial Authorities in the United Kingdom until the Financial Crisis*

The United Kingdom has had tripartite authorities in promoting financial stability for more than ten years. In 1997 the Financial Services Authority (FSA) was created as a single regulator for all financial firms with sole authority to regulate banks and nonbank financial firms, covering both prudential regulation and conduct-of-business regulation. The Bank of England (BoE) was given independent control over monetary policy. With the FSA overseeing all types of financial regulation, the BoE has been responsible for maintaining market stability, and Her Majesty's Treasury has been responsible for financial and economic policy and the institutional structure of the overall financial system.

These three authorities have employed a memorandum of understanding (MOU) that delineated their respective roles and, in particular, what would occur during a financial crisis. The memorandum specifically states that during a crisis the FSA is responsible for "the conduct of operations in response to problem cases affecting firms, markets, and clearing and settlements systems" and can change "capital or other regulatory requirements and [facilitate] a market solution involving, for example, an introduction of new capital into a troubled firm by one or more third parties."

However, the FSA model and the tripartite authorities' MOU could not prevent the financial crisis from hitting the United Kingdom. More than any other country other than the United States, the United Kingdom has suffered as a result of the financial crisis. The country's largest banks—including the Royal Bank of Scotland, Barclays, HSBC, and Lloyds—were rescued, with no end in sight to the fiscal burden designed to keep the banking system afloat and facilitate lending.

Therefore, the experience of the United Kingdom raised important questions about the effectiveness of the approach. It is surprising that the extensive regulatory reforms undertaken in the late 1990s did not insulate the country from the effects of the financial crisis, and it is not clear how Northern Rock could fail under the watch of the FSA. During the collapse of Northern Rock in September 2007, with a run on the bank, the authorities—FSA and BoE—stood by until nationalization took place early the following year. The FSA admitted to significant failings over Northern Rock. An internal FSA report cited inadequate oversight resources, including high personnel turnover and limited direct contact with the firm (no one had visited the bank for three years), the ignorance or suppression of adverse findings about the firm, and the failure to push management at the bank to modify a disastrous business model that relied on short-term wholesale funding to acquire long-term assets.

The FSA's failings have put it in the line of fire for criticism, which has focused on the haste with which the FSA was formed and the failure of the new integrated regulator to overcome the institutional divisions of its former approach to regulation.

regulation. There was not the same erosion in lending standards as occurred in the United States or the United Kingdom. This was in part due to stricter regulation of mortgage lending. For instance, Australia's prudential regulator raised the capital requirements for banks investing in riskier mortgage products. Consumer protection laws and foreclosure laws also discouraged borrowers from taking out mortgages that they could not afford. Finally, Australian tax law encouraged early loan repayment and provided a means of precautionary saving, thus buffering against lost equity.

The Council of Financial Regulators, comprising the Reserve Bank of Australia (RBA) as the chair, the Australian Prudential Regulation Authority (APRA), the Australian Securities and Investments Commission (ASIC), and the Australian Treasury, has been coordinating for Australia's main financial regulatory agencies. The RBA has the dual mandate of price stability and financial system stability;[13] the APRA deals with prudential regulation of all financial institutions; and the ASIC deals with market integrity, consumer protection, and corporations. The RBA retains no regulatory authority. The Australian approach—regulation by objectives (prudential, market conduct, consumer protection, competition)—is often cited as a model for other countries.

The Council's role is to contribute to the efficiency and effectiveness of financial regulation by providing a high-level forum for cooperation and collaboration among its members. It operates as an informal body in which members can share information and views, discuss regulatory reforms or issues where responsibilities overlap, and if the need arises coordinate responses to potential threats to financial stability. The Council also has a role in advising the government on the adequacy of Australia's financial system architecture in light of ongoing developments. It is non-statutory and has no regulatory functions separate from those of its members.

FINANCIAL STABILITY AND DEVELOPMENT COUNCIL IN INDIA

In India, the task of maintaining financial stability has been with an informal inter-regulatory body, the High Level Coordination Committee on Financial Markets (HLCCFM), which is chaired by the governor of the Reserve Bank of India (RBI) and includes representatives of other regulatory agencies. This arrangement has been informal, and the mandate, authority, resources, and tools have not been explicitly vested by law in the HLCCFM.

The government has decided to establish a Financial Stability and Development Council (FSDC), which would be in charge of macroprudential supervision of the economy, including the functioning of large financial conglomerates,

13. With the mandate of financial system stability, the RBA publishes the Financial System Stability Report even though its responsibility for banks was transferred to a newly integrated regulator, APRA, in 1998.

and address inter-agency coordination issues, as well as focus on financial literacy and financial inclusion. The FSDC is expected to have a more explicit arrangement and more authority than the HLCCFM.

There will be a sub-committee of the FSDC that will be responsible for financial stability and regulatory coordination. This sub-committee would be the first stop for sorting out any discord between the regulators to address the concern that the council may undermine the autonomy of the financial sector regulators. The sub-committee will have all regulators and senior finance ministry officials as members and the Governor of RBI as chair, a structure akin to that of the HLCCFM. However, instead of just taking over the HLCCFM's function of regulatory coordination, this sub-committee would also be responsible for financial stability.

## Financial System Stability Committee in Indonesia

Indonesia has established the Financial System Stability Committee (KSSK), based on a memorandum of understanding between the Ministry of Finance and Bank Indonesia. The minister of finance serves as chair, and the governor of Bank Indonesia serves as a member of KSSK. The objective of the KSSK is to evaluate the scale and dimension of a liquidity or solvency problem involving a bank or a nonbank financial firm to assess whether the problem poses a systemic or non-systemic risk and determine the steps necessary to prevent or resolve a crisis, including the use of fiscal resources. The Financial System Safety Net (FSSN), which provides the underlying framework for the deposit insurance scheme and the emergency financial facility under the central bank's lender-of-last-resort function, would also form the basis for crisis resolution policy. The FSSN's foremost objective is crisis prevention, but it also includes crafting mechanisms to control the fiscal costs of resolution.

Bridging the gap between the Ministry of Finance and Bank Indonesia is highly desirable. However, the approach taken is not comprehensive in coverage; it does not cover other systemic risks, such as consumer debt or corporate distress.

## Korea's West Wing Meeting

The Korean government has established a framework for preemptive risk management to enable policymakers to monitor the developments of both the financial markets and the real economy and to take preemptive policy measures. The centerpiece of the preemptive program has been the informal, but high-level, meetings on financial issues regularly held in the West Wing Room of the Blue House, hence dubbed the "West Wing Meeting." The chair of these financial policy coordination meetings is the minister of strategy and finance; other members include the chair of the Financial Supervisory Commission (FSC), the governor of the Bank of Korea, and the advisor to the president on economic policies. Each member organization has a different role to play. The Ministry of Strategy and

Finance is responsible for formulating policies to promote financial market stability, the FSC (and the Financial Supervisory Service [FSS]) is responsible for the soundness of the financial sector, and the Bank of Korea is responsible for analyzing and responding to developments of the financial and currency markets. Policymakers have been working together to improve monitoring of financial markets and preempt potential problems in the financial system.[14] The Bank of Korea and the FSS share macroprudential supervisory responsibility.

SUMMARY

A study of these council arrangements in various countries is useful. What we find is that it is often the case that the council is non-statutory and has no regulatory powers separate from those of its members. In most cases it operates as an informal body in which members share information and views, discuss regulatory reforms or issues where responsibilities overlap, and, if the need arises, coordinate responses to potential threats to financial stability. The systemic stability regulatory council we propose should have clear mandates and a division of labor among the authorities, analytical resources and capacity collectively, and all the necessary macroprudential tools, backed by a high degree of authority and accountability. All financial authorities—the central bank, the finance ministry, and regulators and supervisors—should act as if they formed a single systemic stability regulator.[15]

The central bank usually has a comparative advantage in macroeconomic-financial surveillance and may or may not have macroprudential authority. If the central bank does not have the macroprudential authority, it could suggest to the regulators and supervisors that have such an authority to take certain macroprudential actions, such as an increase in required capital adequacy ratios, a reduction of allowable loan-to-value ratios, heightened prudential standards for individual banks, among other measures, to limit a significant rise in systemic risk. Similarly, there should be two-way communication. If regulators and supervisors find it difficult to contain a buildup of vulnerabilities, they can suggest that the central bank use monetary policy. Of course, the decision has to be left to the monetary policy committee of an independent central bank.

---

14. For instance, the government tightened the prudential regulations on mortgage lending by lowering the maximum loan-to-value (LTV) ratio to 60% and the maximum debt-to-income (DTI) ratio to 40% for certain speculative areas. Such measures slowed mortgage lending and stabilized the real estate market. We are thankful to Yong-Duk Kim and Changyong Rhee for this information.

15. In the case of Japan, there is a problem in information exchange because the information collected by the Financial Services Agency, which is part of the government, cannot be transmitted to non-governmental entities, including the Bank of Japan.

## Regional Approaches

Effective crisis prevention, management, and resolution clearly require a strong national framework and need to be complemented by global and regional initiatives. Table 7-1 identified policy requirements at global and regional levels. The global initiatives are led by the IMF and the Financial Stability Board (FSB). This subsection considers regional initiatives, particularly from the Asian perspective.

### EUROPEAN UNION REFORMS

In Europe, forging a robust approach to coordination is a major challenge, in particular on issues related to regional financial and macroeconomic stability. Following the proposal made by a high-level expert group headed by Jacques de Larosière (2009), the European Union has decided to establish a supranational structure to deal with the region-wide financial stability issue and enhance cooperative arrangements:

—Establishing common basic technical rules to be applied and enforced consistently;

—Identifying systemic risks at an early stage; and

—Improving the ability to act more effectively in emerging situations and resolve disagreements among national regulators.

These goals are addressed in a new comprehensive regulatory framework by establishing (i) a European Systemic Risk Board (ESRB), which would be charged with monitoring, identifying, and assessing systemic risks and implementing pan-European rapid responses to such risks, and (ii) a European System of Financial Supervisors, which would bring together existing national supervisors with three new sector-specific EU-level authorities (for banking, securities and markets, and insurance and pension, respectively).

To support the second element, three new European Supervisory Authorities (ESAs) would be set up: the European Banking Authority (in London); the European Securities and Markets Authority (in Paris); and the European Insurance and Occupational Pensions Authority (in Frankfurt). The ESAs would oversee and coordinate the day-to-day activities of national supervisors to ensure consistency and implementation of EU law, and have the power of legally binding mediation in the case of disputes.

The ESRB is an entirely new European body, with no precedent. It is responsible for macroprudential oversight and has three objectives:

—To develop a European macroprudential perspective to address the problem of fragmented individual risk analysis at the national level;

—To enhance the effectiveness of early-warning mechanisms by improving the interaction between microprudential and macroprudential analysis; and

—To help risk assessments be translated into action by the relevant authorities.

An essential role of the ESRB is to identify risks with a systemic dimension and prevent or mitigate their impact on the financial system within the European Union. To this end, the ESRB can issue risk warnings that would prompt early responses to avoid the buildup of wider problems and the risk of a future crisis. The ESRB would have the power to issue recommendations for specific actions to address any identified risks to member states including national supervisors and to the ESAs, which would have to comply or explain why they have not taken certain actions. Nonetheless, the ESRB does not have any binding powers to impose measures on member states or national authorities. It is conceived as a "reputational" body composed of high-level members capable of influencing the actions of policy makers and supervisors by means of its moral authority.

## ASIAN FINANCIAL STABILITY DIALOGUE

Asian policymakers are now discussing the possibility of establishing an Asian Financial Stability Dialogue (AFSD) among the region's financial authorities. Although it is still in the discussion stage, the objective of the AFSD is to detect financial sector vulnerabilities emerging in the region through collective monitoring of key financial products, systemically important firms and markets, as well as regional macroeconomic and financial links, and take concerted actions to contain them. This forum would bring together all responsible authorities— including finance ministries, central banks, and financial supervisors and regulators—to discuss regional financial market vulnerabilities, regional capital flows, common issues for financial-sector supervision and regulation, and efforts at regional financial integration through greater harmonization of standards and market practices.

Once such a forum is established and the financial authorities from different countries feel more comfortable working together and deepening collaboration, the AFSD would be encouraged to transform itself into a more systematic body, like an Asian FSB.

Finally, it is important to remember that after the Asian financial crisis of 1997–98, many economies in the region started building foreign exchange reserves as self-insurance, a protection against possible currency crises. For these governments, going to the IMF for financial rescue would be political suicide because of the public's lingering memory of the "IMF crisis." These economies have had every incentive to accumulate foreign exchange reserves by running large current account surpluses or intervening in the currency markets so as to protect their financial systems from external shocks and so avoid IMF interventions. Countries in the region would welcome the correction of payments surpluses if an Asian monetary fund (AMF), an advanced form of the current Chiang Mai Initiative Multilateralization, could help reduce financial turbulence and act as a regional lender of last resort. A future AMF should work closely with the AFSD to conduct regional economic and financial surveillance and early warning exercises, as the IMF and FSB are expected to do at the global level.

## Conclusion

The starting point of this paper is that a financial crisis builds up over time in response to policy mistakes and to investor herd behavior or to both. While markets tend to be forgiving for a long time, the unsustainable imbalance will eventually be corrected. By identifying and dealing with systemic risk—or sources of financial vulnerabilities—before it creates critical instability, policymakers can potentially prevent a financial crisis. For this purpose, macroeconomic-financial surveillance and macroprudential supervision are vital, and a systemic stability regulator, or relevant financial authorities under a collective framework for systemic stability regulation, must act to avoid the buildup of large vulnerabilities and imbalances in each jurisdiction. In our view, prevention is far more desirable than cure, and we recommend the establishment of a systemic stability regulator.

Several proposed models for creating a systemic stability regulator are discussed. The most coherent model for this would be to combine all the functions—central banking, supervision and regulation, and treasury—into one powerful organization. We can observe such an arrangement in Singapore. For most countries, however, a more realistic model would be to take a "council" approach where (i) all financial authorities (central bank, supervisors, and finance ministry) work in a coordinated manner, including intensive information exchange and consultation, (ii) the central bank conducts macroeconomic-financial surveillance and sets monetary policy, taking into account financial stability even if this is not its explicit mandate, and (iii) the authorities in charge of macroprudential responsibilities take the needed policy actions in consultation with other financial authorities. When a framework for financial stability is established, a successful systemic stability regulator should meet the binding set of criteria proposed in the paper.

Some Asian economies need to carefully assess the recent regulatory changes in the United Kingdom and, to some extent, the United States, where the respective central banks will shoulder the systemic stability regulation function. In many Southeast Asian economies, the central banks already assume macroprudential responsibilities. In Northeast Asia, with the exception of China, fully integrated financial supervisors assume, or share with the central bank, macroprudential responsibilities. In China, the central bank and the bank regulator share the responsibility of macroprudential policies. Asian economies need to set up the best organizational structure, but whatever they choose, they need to ensure that all the financial authorities must work very closely in a coordinated manner for crisis prevention, management, and resolution. We also argue that a regional mechanism for financial stability—to complement the national and global efforts—should be introduced.

## References

Acharya, V. V., and M. Richardson, eds. 2009. *Restoring Financial Stability*. NYU-Stern Report. New York: John Wiley and Sons.

Adams, Charles. 2010. "The Role of the State in Managing and Forestalling Systemic Financial Crises: Some Issues and Perspectives." Working Paper Series 242 (August). Tokyo: Asian Development Bank Institute.

Bernanke, B. S. 2009. "Financial Reform to Address Systemic Risk." Speech at the Council on Foreign Relations, Washington, D.C., March 10.

Borio, C. E. V., and I. Shim. 2007. "What Can (Macro-) Prudential Policy Do to Support Monetary Policy?" Working Paper 242. Geneva: Bank for International Settlements.

Caballero, Ricardo J., Takeo Hoshi, and Anil K. Kashyap. 2011. "Zombie Lending and Depressed Restructuring in Japan." *American Economic Review*.

Čihák, M., and R. Podpiera. 2006. "Is One Watchdog Better Than Three? International Experience with Integrated Financial Sector Supervision." IMF Working Paper WP/06/57. Washington, D.C.: IMF.

Cho, Yoon-Je. 2010. "The Role of State Intervention in the Financial Sector: Crisis Prevention, Containment, and Resolution." Working Paper Series 196 (February). Tokyo: Asian Development Bank Institute.

De Larosière Group. 2009. *Report of the High-Level Group on Financial Supervision in the EU* (February) (http://ec.europa.eu/internal_market/finances/docs/de_larosiere_report_en.pdf).

Financial Stability Forum. 2008. *Report of the Financial Stability Forum on Enhancing Market and Institutional Resilience*. Basel (April 7).

Fujii, Mariko, and Masahiro Kawai. 2010. "Lessons from Japan's Banking Crisis, 1991–2005." Working Paper Series 222 (June). Tokyo: Asian Development Bank Institute.

Group of Thirty. 2009. *Financial Reform: A Framework for Financial Stability*. Washington, D.C. (January 15) (www.group30/pubs/reformreport.pdf).

Hsu, Chen-Min, and Chih-Feng Liao. 2010. "Financial Turmoil in the Banking Sector and the Asian Lamfalussy Process: The Case of Four Economies." Working Paper Series 221 (June). Tokyo: Asian Development Bank Institute.

Hüpkes, E. 2009. "Crisis Resolution: Where We Stand and How to Improve It?" A paper for After the Storm: The Future Face of Europe's Financial System (March 23), Brussels.

International Monetary Fund (IMF), Strategy, Policy, and Review Department. 2009. "Initial Lessons of the Crisis for the Global Architecture and the IMF" (February), Washington, D.C. (www.imf.org/external/np/pp/eng/2009/021809.pdf).

Kawai, Masahiro. 2000. "The Resolution of the East Asian Crisis: Financial and Corporate Sector Restructuring." *Journal of Asian Economics* 11: 133–68.

————. 2005. Reform of the Japanese Banking System. *International Economics and Economic Policy* 2: 307–35.

Kawai, Masahiro, and Mario B. Lamberte. 2008. "Managing Capital Flows in Asia: Policy Issues and Challenges." Research Policy Brief 26. Tokyo: Asian Development Bank Institute.

Kawai, Masahiro, and Michael Pomerleano. 2010. "Regulating Systemic Risk." Working Paper Series 189 (January). Tokyo: Asian Development Bank Institute.

King, M. 2009. Mansion House speech, presented at the Lord Mayor's Banquet for Bankers and Merchants of the City of London at the Mansion House. London, June 18.

Mayes, David G., Peter J. Morgan, and Hank Lim. 2010. "Deepening the Financial System." In Masahiro Kawai and Jong-Wha Lee, eds., *Rebalancing for Sustainable Growth: Asia's Postcrisis Challenge*. Tokyo: Asian Development Bank Institute.

Mohan, Rakesh, and Muneesh Kapur. 2010. "Liberalization and Regulation of Capital Flows: Lessons for Emerging Market Economies." Working Paper Series 186 (January). Tokyo: Asian Development Bank Institute.

Wall, Larry D. 2009. "Prudential Discipline for Financial Firms: Micro, Macro, and Market Structures." Working Paper Series 176 (December). Tokyo: Asian Development Bank Institute.

Winkler, Adalbert. 2010. "The Financial Crisis: A Wake-Up Call for Strengthening Regional Monitoring of Financial Markets and Regional Coordination of Financial Sector Policies?" Working Paper Series 199 (February). Tokyo: Asian Development Bank Institute.

# 8

## Financial Development:
## A Broader Perspective

RICHARD REID

Although the latest bout of financial turmoil has sparked renewed interest in the desirability of financial development, and the optimal size and structure of the financial system, the debate over the relationship between financial development and economic growth has, of course, been active for many years. This topic has been of intense relevance for emerging economies, particularly against the backdrop of increased capital flows in recent years. Exposure to high capital flows carries both potential benefits and risks, and the ability to deal with these flows successfully will depend partly on the level of sophistication of the domestic financial system.

It can in turn be argued that openness to international capital flows can, under certain circumstances, encourage the broadening and deepening of domestic financial systems. Often, but not always, the growth of the financial system will also be associated with the emergence of a dominant—or even several dominant—financial centers.

This chapter aims to contribute to these broader debates by looking at how different financial systems evolve; how and why financial structures change during various stages of development; how best to measure them, that is, setting a

The author would like to thank Brian Cullen of the ICFR for his help with the research and drafting of this chapter. The findings, interpretations, and conclusions expressed here are entirely those of the author. They do not necessarily represent the views of the International Centre for Financial Regulation and its affiliated organizations and members.

framework for further analysis; and seeing what practical policy lessons can be drawn out of the historical experience of financial development. Analysis suggests that while some financial structures may be better suited to growth at certain stages of development, they may be less suited to change and innovation. Thus they may hamper growth at other stages or be more prone to—or less resistant to—shocks and the instability that follows. So, for example, there may be models of financial structure better suited to the development of infrastructure, or yet other alternatives that allow for more effective technological diffusion. The potential for variety and individuality should not be neglected.

It is also important to consider not just the demand for financial intermediation in an economy but also its supply. The history of financial development seems to be littered with gaps in the provision of financial services, not all of which have been filled either quickly or robustly. Unsurprisingly, therefore, government involvement has been evident at many levels in financial development throughout history, sometimes as a direct result of the failure of the private sector and sometimes when the primary, or at least immediate, objective does not seem to be consistent with the most technically efficient allocation of capital.

There can also be the danger of developing financial systems that are merely "convenient" from a regulatory perspective but can lead to *suboptimal* financial intermediation. As the last few years have demonstrated, the aims of regulatory emphasis can change quite substantially, as perceptions about risks inherent in financial intermediation change and as challenges to the "conventional wisdom" grow stronger. As the International Monetary Fund's John Lipsky recently noted, "The critical question is where the proper balance lies between the positive impact of financial development against the risks of instability and distortions. An associated issue is to what extent regulatory reforms—together with more effective supervision—can improve that balance by strengthening market safeguards."[1]

To address these issues, the first part of this chapter attempts to set out an up-to-date framework for classifying financial development, looking not just at the size of the financial system over time but also at the composition of instruments and institutions, the structure of financial flows, and the interplay of markets. These all have important regulatory implications and affect factors such as transparency, risk, and remuneration.

The second part of the paper illustrates some of these theoretical considerations with examples of the problems that have arisen during financial development in the past. The discussion draws on the experiences of a wide range of countries (and studies) and examines how these problems have been resolved or what unwelcome or unintended consequences there have been.

1. Lipsky (2009).

The final part of the study draws some conclusions about financial structure for the developing world in terms of avoiding pitfalls, dealing with mistakes, and thinking about areas for further study.

## Financial Development: Thinking and Approaches

It is useful to begin with a review of the literature on the relationship between financial development and real economic activity, along with a review of different approaches to financial market development.

### Financial Development and the Real Economy

The correlation between financial development and economic growth is under constant examination by economists and policymakers alike. In particular, there continues to be considerable debate over the causal link between the two. The literature on this subject is, naturally, closely linked to that on "endogeneity" in economic growth.

In broad terms, there can be said to be three camps. The first proposes that financial evolution *depends on* real growth, with the range of financial instruments and institutions responding to needs as they arise.

The second position suggests that financial development *precedes* economic growth, encouraging economic activity by offering new products and initiatives. Schumpeter (1933) regarded finance as being one of two key elements. Gurley and Shaw (1960) emphasized the importance of the role of finance in growth, Goldsmith (1969) came close to asserting that financial systems actively promoted real growth, and Gerschenkron (1962) considered that finance played a key role in the process of development, particularly for countries in a relatively backward situation.

The third view is that finance and real activity accompany each other in a *simultaneous, interactive* way, each responding to signals from the other. But there is some argument to be made that the relative importance of finance grows as GDP increases. As Wai and Patrick wrote, "In general, financial development proceeds concomitantly with economic development, with finance playing an increasingly important role."[2]

More recently, King and Levine (1993) acknowledged those scholars who are wary of drawing links between finance and growth.[3] However, in their own work, they have gone on to develop more sophisticated methods for measuring the linkages between financial development and growth. In particular, by

---

2. Wai and Patrick (1973).

3. For example, Lucas (1988) claimed that the linkages between financial and economic developments could be "overstressed."

examining a longer-term data set, they have been able to demonstrate more forcefully than others (such as Goldsmith, 1969) the apparent causal effect of finance on growth:

> The link between growth and financial development is not just a contemporaneous association. Finance does not only follow growth; finance seems importantly to lead economic growth. Furthermore, a positive association between contemporaneous shocks to financial development and economic growth does not fully account for the finance-growth link. When countries have relatively high levels of financial development, economic growth tends to be relatively faster over the next 10 to 30 years."[4]

However, as Rajan and Zingales have pointed out, this process is diverse and complex.[5] They demonstrate that on a range of measures, many countries were more financially developed in 1913 (after the first great wave of financial globalization) than they were in 1980. In their "interest group" theory of financial development, a "stalling"—or even a reversal—of financial development may occur when "incumbent" groups, which fear the competitive impact of financial deepening, erect barriers to change.

History is littered with examples where the structure of the financial system and its operation are considered to have helped or hindered growth. Adam Smith, for example, observed that the expansion of Scottish trade in the eighteenth century owed something to the establishment of the two public banks.

## How Best to Measure Financial Systems

Over the last fifty years, the literature on the measurement of financial systems has grown substantially. One of the earliest attempts to quantify size and change in the financial system was Goldsmith's financial interrelations ratio (FIR), which was also an early attempt to move from stock to flow indicators in financial measurement.[6] The FIR—the ratio of the market value of the flow of instruments to total tangible wealth—did indeed confirm the long-term tendency for financial and economic growth to go in parallel, although Goldsmith remained uncertain of the direction of causality.

Goldsmith identified three basic stages of financial development. The first consists of countries with a low FIR, typically in Europe and North America in the mid-eighteenth to mid-nineteenth century, for example. The second group has a similarly low FIR but a much bigger role for government and government-owned institutions, for example, Germany or even Russia in the late nineteenth

---

4. King and Levine (1993, p. 730).
5. Rajan and Zingales (2009).
6. Goldsmith (1969).

century. The third group possesses a much higher FIR, typified by a much higher ratio of equities to debt, a higher share of financial institutions or financial assets, and a relative decline in the share of banking institutions compared to other financial institutions; this might be described as the current "Anglo-Saxon model."

The FIR in Great Britain, for example, was around 0.35 in 1880, increasing to 1.70 by the 1960s. In the United States it went from less than 0.5 in the 1880s to around 1.27 in the 1960s. Goldsmith's analysis has been criticized in recent years over its shortcomings.[7] However, he did recognize the FIR's limitations when it came to analyzing why systems developed in particular ways, saying that "the study of financial structure involves, of course, more than the classification of financial instruments and of institutions into rather broad and rough categories."[8]

Another early approach to financial measurement was to think about the mix of financial instruments that bridged the gap between borrower and lender at the optimal level of risk, return, and maturity. This involves a more direct examination of the fundamentals of the financial system: intermediation, reallocation of current savings, asset transformation, easing of the transfer of ownership and control of the stock and flow of wealth, and transformation of maturities.

Gurley and Shaw were early proponents of attempts to measure the flow and stock of primary and secondary financial instruments in relation to national income.[9] Their work raised questions about the distribution of spending between sectors relative to the distribution of income, or savings, and also focused attention on the *form* of economic development and its interrelationship with financial structure.

Gurley's financial ratio—the ratio of total financial assets to GNP—is limited in that it compares stocks to flows.[10] His results correlate with Goldsmith's findings, suggesting a relationship between the rise in per capita income and the size of the financial system. However, Gurley was also keen to stress that there were different paths to achieving growth. For example, some economies might make minimal use of financial markets and may rely more on central planning and the pooling of funds. In such systems, the tax structure could be used to channel funds, and he even suggests inflation as a means of affecting the generation and flows of funds. He suggests, in addition, that it may even be rational for a country that has embarked on a particular course for financial development to stick with it for a prolonged period rather than attempt to transfer to a different development path.

7. See for example, Levine (1997).
8. Goldsmith (1969, p. 35).
9. Gurley and Shaw (1960).
10. Gurley (1967).

Figure 8-1. *Financial Paths Based on Gurley's Analysis*[a]

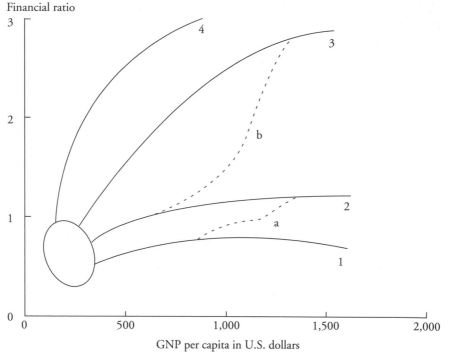

Financial ratio

GNP per capita in U.S. dollars

Source: Gurley (1967, p. 69).

a. Solid lines represent alternative financial paths; dotted lines represent shift in paths (*a,* gradual; *b,* sudden). See text for explanation of numbers.

Gurley's analysis is presented in figure 8-1, which shows these illustrative paths for financial development. He suggests that path three would be typical of the United States, whereas paths one or two would be more representative of centrally planned economies, or inflationary or fiscally oriented systems, as these tend to rely on smaller financial superstructures. Path four might be typical of an economy such as Switzerland, which specialized in the development of its financial sector.

The choice of financial development from these paths will vary over time and, as the last few years have shown, will be subject to social and political pressure. Moreover, technological advances can affect the viability of choices, the most recent of these, obviously, being computerization.

In the figure, the dotted lines *a* and *b* illustrate that it is possible for countries to shift from their previously established paths. This might be a relatively gradual and protracted process (*a*) and therefore less disruptive and less prone to abuse. However, it also may be more sudden (*b*) and more distorting and violent.

More recent studies have sought to update the analysis of financial structure and make it more sophisticated and rigorous. King and Levine built on the approach of several studies through the 1980s and early 1990s, which confirm the correlation between real per capita income growth and the average level of financial development, using data over the 1960–89 period.[11]

They also seek to examine the process of intermediation more subtly by looking at the specific channels through which financial development and growth operate. In keeping with Gurley's observations that the pace of financial development goes through various phases, King and Levine's results are summarized under growth headings: very slow, slow, fast, and very fast. Their findings show that as countries move in stages from very slow to very fast, there is indeed a corresponding increase in financial depth, the importance of banks relative to the central bank, the fraction of credit allocated to the private sector, and the ratio of private sector credit to GDP.

Conversely, Arestis, Demetriades, and Luintel focus on the link between real growth and stock market development.[12] Their emphasis on time-series analysis rather than cross-country analysis leads to the observation that long-run causality may change and that long-run relationships tend to show substantial variation.[13] Their study also points to the need for careful consideration of the sequencing of financial development, both in relation to the real economy and with regard to the structure of the financial system itself. There may even be arguments for maintaining some degree of financial repression at various stages until other prerequisites are in place for a sustainable shift to a new structure without too much disruption.

More recently still, other studies have sought to return more closely to first principles, withdrawing from the banks-versus-markets debate and refocusing on the ultimate purpose of a financial system—to bring savings into contact with opportunities for "productive" investment. These studies, therefore, link the structure of growth to the structure of the financial intermediation process. Some recent studies also have sought to link financial systems more directly to their functional efficiency in serving the needs of the real economy.[14]

Closely linked to this approach, and related to the debate on systemic risk and sector analysis, would be an analysis of financial systems based on flows of funds. This method highlights the links between the financial system and the surpluses and deficits within the real economy.

---

11. King and Levine (1993).

12. Arestis, Demetriades, and Luintel (2001).

13. One of the criticisms of the current literature on financial structure in developing countries is that it is too focused on cross-country analysis, neglecting some of the more country-specific issues.

14. For example, see Lin, Sun, and Jiang (2009).

At different phases of the growth cycle, these surpluses and deficits may vary widely, and in cases where domestic savings may be in short supply, the external sector may be the provider of capital. Such flow-of-funds types of analyses can be very useful for tracking and perhaps predicting where the pressure points in the intermediation process might arise. Such methods might also allow a more sophisticated level of analysis of the financial system by breaking it down by instrument. As the European Central Bank said in 2009, "In particular, these types of tools allow the early identification of risks that may not be easily recognisable when the focus of analysis is only on measures of leverage and volatility within individual sectors." [15]

Overall, therefore, financial measurement techniques may have become more sophisticated over the years, but in essence they continue to address the same issues: the types of financial instruments and how they have arisen (*instrumental factors*); the form and organization of financial intermediaries and markets (*structural factors*); how institutions actually operate, kinds of credit granted, and types of resources generated (*operational factors*); and—finally—*process-related factors*, that is, what has been the interplay of forces shaping the financial system.

## Factors Affecting the Supply of Financial Services

Consistent within the theme here of going "back to basics," it is worth noting that the factors influencing developing financial systems today have resonance with developments in the "developed" world between roughly 1800 and 1950. Therefore, this section provides a brief overview of the key factors affecting financial structure. More important, it attempts to relate past experience with some of these issues to their current relevance for emerging markets.

In some cases it is a matter of judgment and no doubt argument as to how certain factors should be characterized, and some factors have tended to receive more attention than others. For example, studies of financial history tend to be dominated by analysis of how shocks have affected financial development. Similarly, a good deal of attention has been focused lately on the comparison between the late nineteenth century era of financial globalization and the increased capital flows of the last thirty years. [16]

Table 8-1 groups these factors under two main headings: first, those that have always been deemed crucial to financial development, and second, those factors that seem to have more bearing on issues facing emerging markets now (although, in one form or another, they also applied in earlier phases of financial development).

15. European Central Bank (2009, p. 156).
16. See, for example, Obstfeld (2009) and Eichengreen and Bordo (2002).

Table 8-1. *Factors in Financial Development, Then versus Now*

| Then | Now |
|------|-----|
| Type of economy | Incentives for innovation |
| Stage of development | Financial infrastructure |
| Macroeconomic shocks | Access to global investors |
| Social and political influences | Fiscal and exchange rate regimes |
| Legal and regulatory constraints | |
| Individuals | |

## Type of Economy

Different economies with particular biases and factor endowments tend to put different demands on their financial sectors and thus affect their structure. For example, agricultural economies might have quite limited requirements, ones heavily geared to the seasonal and erratic nature of the business.

Cameron suggests that one reason why the Austrian financial system did not develop ties with industry to the same degree that Germany did was because Austria had no Ruhr Valley; thus it had little or no heavy industrial sector requiring capital on a much greater scale than could be provided by mutual, cooperative, and private banking institutions.[17] Economies that are more trade and commerce oriented would be more likely to develop arm's-length financing, letters of credit, bills and acceptances, insurance provisions, and merchant banking facilities.

## Stage of Development

Many less-developed countries today pursue growth strategies in parallel with agrarian change. At the same time, many attempt to construct and encourage an appropriate financial system consistent with broader macroeconomic aims. The contrast with the eighteenth and nineteenth centuries, of course, is that there were no precedents then, and the concept of planning financial development through growth phases was much less evident. There were examples of national pushes for growth (for example, Germany starting in 1870), but on the whole, such changes occurred on a more piecemeal and ad hoc basis.

Few economies remain wedded to a particular structure for a very long time. As the structure of growth changes, so do the needs of financial intermediation. Sometimes the transition between stages is gradual; sometimes it is violent. One early (now criticized) view of the importance of the stage of development to the structure of finance and policy was Gerschenkron's idea that the structure

17. Cameron (1967).

of the financial system was a function of "relative backwardness."[18] The later an economy industrialized relative to Great Britain, the more its financial structure was dominated by institutional factors aimed at increasing the supply of capital. This could include large-scale government involvement. His analysis has been somewhat criticized on a number of fronts, not least with regard to the difficulty of actually defining stages of development. His work also seems to be based on a narrow range of case studies and does not hold up well to scrutiny.[19]

Nevertheless, as economies move between phases of growth driven by, for example, agriculture, trade, investment, or consumption, the nature of the demand for financial services changes. More sophisticated economies tend to require greater choice, such as for housing finance and insurance services.

But the argument is by no means straightforward, and there may be occasions when an apparently "unsophisticated" system both suits the need of the economy and is perhaps the only viable option available. Goldsmith (1969) noted that in the 1945–60 period, FIRs were significantly higher in the United States and Great Britain than in Germany. However, one of the factors behind Germany's successful postwar recovery was undoubtedly the role of the banking system and its ability to take a long-term view of financing the corporate sector. Would a higher FIR in the postwar period, reflecting more involvement of nonbanking intermediation, have actually hindered growth during the "golden age"? Much would have depended on exactly how the financial pie could have been enlarged, and in this particular case, it is quite possible that there was no truly viable alternative.

But the appropriateness of the structure will change over time. Some years ago, the Bundesbank acknowledged that perhaps the bank-dominated system that served Germany so well in the postwar period was less well suited in an environment of much higher and more mobile capital flows.[20] As the World Bank's chief economist recently noted in a paper on optimal financial structure, "There exists some optimal financial structure for the economy at every stage of development."[21]

## Macroeconomic Shocks

Shocks, which seriously affect an economy's fundamentals, can come in various forms. Bouts of severe or hyper-inflation have been a common destabilizing factor, whether in Germany in 1923, Argentina in the 1980s, or Zimbabwe in the last few years. This can wipe out savings, redistribute economic power, strongly

18. Gerschenkron (1962).
19. See, for example, O'Brien (1986).
20. Gessler Commission (1979).
21. Lin, Sun, and Jiang (2009).

affect liquidity preferences, cause currency instability, and, of course, undermine confidence generally.

Wars and war financing can greatly affect financial stability, and for years afterwards, they affect institutions' ability to intermediate due to constraints on their balance sheets. Sometimes new institutions are created for the purposes of facilitating public financing in the wake of the fiscal strain war can put on an economy (for example, the Caisse de Dépôts et Consignations in France, established in 1816).

History shows that severe business cycles can affect the banking system's attitudes toward types of financing for a prolonged period afterwards. Some argue that the 1873–75 depression in France left so many banks with devalued corporate securities on their books that they shied away from such financing for many years afterwards. It is unclear whether today's recession will lead to changes as structurally important as those of the 1930s (such as the long-enduring Glass-Steagall Act in the United States).

Fraud can also have an impact on intermediation. For example, recent cases such as Bernard Madoff's Ponzi scheme have certainly had an impact on the public response to the latest financial crisis, although it's hard to say what the longer-term fundamental effects on regulation and the financial structure might be. A classic, historical example of the impact of fraud again comes from France. In the aftermath of John Law's irregular method for financing government debt through the Mississippi Company bubble (1719–20), the use of the word "banque" in the title of banking institutions became unpopular.[22] Combined with the financial problems of the French Revolution, there developed a tendency for financial institutions to adopt other names such as *crédit, caisse, comptoir,* and *société.*

## Political Pressures

Political forces can have a great bearing on financial structure.[23] This influence could take the form of a command-type economy, with a large proportion of financing occurring via government or government-controlled institutions. This would include the overriding of market mechanisms by state planning and bureaucracy. It could determine political structure: for example, the existence of a federal structure of government or transforming from a federal structure to a more unified structure. Some observers felt that the move toward a customs union in nineteenth-century Germany presaged the 1870 shift toward national cooperation and the push for growth. Politics can be an important influence in terms of the ownership and therefore objectives of financial institutions. The

---

22. For more on John Law, see, for example, Murphy (1997).
23. See Rajan and Zingales (2003), among others.

waves of nationalization a number of countries experienced at various stages were not always the result of a financial shock but rather a response to shifting political attitudes. For example, the nationalizations in France under Mitterrand were more of a political statement compared to the recent trend of government involvement in banks today.

This factor is worth considering, especially in the wake of the current financial crisis. There has been a widespread political backlash against large parts of the financial system. This has brought forth a welter of proposals on capital regulation, liquidity and leverage controls, governance, and remuneration issues, and has provoked fundamental questions about the social usefulness of significant parts of the financial system.

It remains to be seen how this reaction and subsequent regulatory and supervisory responses fundamentally affect financial structure and the behavior of borrowers and lenders. It may be, for example, that many of the competitive forces shaped by the new regulatory architecture may not become fully apparent until after the authorities have actually begun to implement their exit strategies. When this starts to happen, it may expose some of the less robust business models.

## Social Factors

Closely associated with political factors are social factors. This can be seen in the modern-day debate with regard to access, be it about financial inclusion or exclusion. In the past, many mutual and cooperative institutions were established and encouraged in order to provide basic saving and lending services for groups who either would not have had access to the more exclusive financial facilities elsewhere in the system, or for whom such facilities were less suited to their particular small, local needs. Of course, local knowledge is also a way to reduce risk.

Some countries and political systems also embraced the concept of comprehensive social security systems, often operating on a pay-as-you-go basis. This arrangement would be less likely to support the growth of long-term contractual savings products and certain types of capital markets. Hyperinflation, as already mentioned, can also contain the development of long-term contractual savings markets.

## Incentives for Innovation

Incentives tend to fall into two broad camps. Constrictions, unfulfilled demands, gaps in financial provision, and new technology all tend to act as positive incentives for innovation. Negative incentives tend to come in the form of tightly controlled allocation of resources, chiefly by government authorities but also possibly by entrenched or incumbent groups. Particular economic conditions may encourage innovation. A good example here has been the recent period of extraordinarily low interest rates, the search for yield, and the abundance of emerging economies' savings circulating in the global economy. This recent experience has, of course, raised the question of innovation outpacing the capacities of regulatory and supervisory authorities.

As Sundaresan notes, light-touch regulation can lead to powerful flows of innovation but also high, or even excessive, risk taking.[24] Heavy-touch regulation may stifle innovation, although it could, of course, stimulate financial intermediation outside the formal financial structure.

It is also worth noting here that technological advance and innovation in other sectors may spark innovation in the financial sector. A classic example of this in emerging markets has been the growth of mobile telephone banking.

## Legal and Regulatory Constraints

Legal and regulatory forces can come in many shapes and forms. Financial companies can be regulated by having their functions controlled—for example, long- versus short-term business, types of deposits they might supply, composition of portfolios they might hold, restricted access to individual market segments (for example, mortgage markets), and restrictions on the amount of loans. Institutions may even be restricted by geographic limits.

Restrictions can also be applied for regulatory and supervisory purposes, for solvency reasons, and in support of fiscal and monetary goals. This can generate conflict if the need to build capital buffers clashes with the need to provide credit during periods of economic stress.

Some have suggested that as a result of legislation, barriers to entry and constraints on the activity of banks had a major impact in the United States for part of the nineteenth and early twentieth centuries. This meant that the supply of financial services simply could not keep pace with demand for those services.[25]

Laws relating to accounting standards, definitions, incorporation rules, bankruptcy, solvency, and transparency can all have an impact on financial structure. Some have argued, for example, that the legacy of common law in some former colonies in Asia had an important influence on their bankruptcy regimes. At the very least, changes in all of these factors will have transitional cost effects. Hence the benefits of "regulatory convenience" must be weighed against the costs of inefficient allocation of capital.

## Individuals

There can be little doubt that individuals can influence financial development significantly, although care must be taken to distinguish between those whose reputations stand out because of fraud or incompetence versus those who have

24. Sundaresan (2009).
25. See for example, White (1982).

had a more material and long-term effect on structural developments. As mentioned above, there is no shortage of candidates for the former category in the latest phase of economic development. History, too, is littered with characters who have had an impact, usually bad, on financial development, such as the aforementioned John Law.

However, one should be careful when attributing the impact of financial changes to one person alone. For example, was the emergence of trustee banks in Scotland and cooperative banks in Germany attributable to particular clergymen in those countries, or was the involvement of those individuals "only" a contributory factor to the development of a set of institutions whose emergence was already in progress? Wall Street at the end of the nineteenth century was associated with a flurry of colorful characters, but were they merely products of underlying economic conditions or were they, in fact, the drivers of those conditions?

A modern-day example for emerging markets might be Muhammad Yunus, widely regarded as the "founder" of the microfinance movement. Was the development of microfinance an inevitable result of economic and financial pressures, or did it require the impetus of figures such as Yunus and the Grameen Bank?

Politicians, in particular, often can have an impact on financial development. This can be achieved either by instituting economic goals that call forth a financial response from a hitherto reluctant financial sector, or more directly by encouraging the establishment of specific financial institutions aimed at filling perceived gaps in the intermediation process or in line with new or redrawn political objectives.

## Financial Infrastructure

Fixing the so-called plumbing of the financial system, some would argue, lies at the heart of current efforts to apply efficient and effective regulation and supervision. Indeed, the Group of Twenty has charged the Financial Stability Board with pressing ahead on many fronts dealing with the harmonization of definitions, standards, and calibrations. As the recent crisis has shown, the ability to value, clear, and settle in financial markets is a vital part of being able to implement successful resolution plans. A principal problem here is a lack of transparency. Transparency, of course, brings greater competition and may remove or alleviate barriers to change.

In this context, the current questions over the merits of conventional trading facilities versus the newer alternative trading platforms are partly a debate about the quality, accessibility, and flexibility of the infrastructure.

## Access to Global Capital

At the turn of the nineteenth century, the issue of financial globalization was seen more in terms of deploying the surplus savings of developed regions in the (then) emerging economies, rather than as a means to spur development of financial markets in the receiving countries. Nevertheless, the flood of capital into North and South America and parts of Asia did enhance growth and the development of financial centers. Conversely, sudden stops in capital flows also had severe effects in sparking and compounding banking and financial crises.[26]

In the context of today's emerging markets, there is probably a greater realization on the part of governments that access to foreign investors, be it through banking flows, portfolio flows, or foreign direct investment flows, can be of substantial economic benefit. But, in general, there probably is also a greater awareness now of the potential negative effects of fostering large-scale inward investment, both in terms of lopsided growth and the often unequal distribution of this capital, and in terms of conflicts between short-term and longer-term objectives.

## Fiscal and Exchange Rate Regimes

A number of modern, emerging economies are finding that the existence of well-organized capital markets and financial structures can greatly assist in the pursuit of their objectives with regard to fiscal policies and exchange rate regimes. An example from the past was the establishment of the Caisse de Dépôts et Consignations (CDC) in France in 1816. Effectively, the CDC was set up to distance government from borrowing from the household sector by empowering it to collect up all the small deposits of post banks, savings banks, notaries, and others and use them for the purchase of government securities. The CDC became the dominant player in this market.

It could be argued that by opening more financing to market forces—as opposed to the imposition of more bureaucratic rationing mechanisms—a country would improve the economic efficiency of its capital usage. A counterargument is that at certain stages of development, it makes sense for a country that has embarked on one path of development to apply a degree of financial repression, since a rapid move to too much market openness may leave the system open to abuse.

One recent study emphasized the need to think carefully about the sequencing of financial reforms as part of a liberalization process, particularly in connection with exchange rate and tax policies.[27] It highlighted the experience of the Nordic countries in the 1980s, where this was not done: "The Nordic record of financial liberalization demonstrates that the sequencing of financial reforms, internally and externally, on the route to financial liberalization is of the utmost importance in determining macroeconomic performance. It is the key to the

---

26. See for example, Eichengreen and Bordo (2002).
27. Chen, Jonung, and Unteroberdoerster (2009).

ruinous record of Finland and Sweden."[28] In effect, a bout of financial liberalization, combined with certain tax incentives and a fixed exchange rate regime, created a powerfully procyclical environment that was not sufficiently offset by tight enough fiscal policy.

## What Is the Future for Financial Development, and What Can the Past Tell Us?

It is apparent that financial development and the determination of financial structure are not simple processes. I have identified eleven elements above, and clearly, depending on classification, many more could be added. What, if any, lessons could future policymakers draw from history? Some of these lessons are dealt with below.

### Is There an Optimal Size and Structure for the Financial System?

This question has taken on an added dimension given the current debate about "socially reasonable" financial intermediation.[29] No matter what measures are used, there is great variation in the size of the financial system between countries at similar stages of development and within countries at different stages of development. There are also clearly periods when the pace of growth is beyond any previously experienced, and there will be occasions when the size of the financial system, the volume of financial instruments exchanged, the numbers of people involved, and even perhaps the share-price performance of its quoted financial companies are out of keeping with any previous experience.

However, it is very hard to say with certainty if there is an optimal size or what it might be. If one definition of the optimal size is that all borrowers and lenders find access to financial intermediation on their preferred conditions, then there may never be an optimal size, as this will always be changing and there will always be leads and lags involved in the adjustment process.

Perhaps a more fruitful approach is to think instead about the degree to which the financial system is suited to the current needs of the real economy, and whether it addresses the tasks that it faces adequately and with a risk profile acceptable to that society. Part of the current debate is about finding out where that balance lies. Clearly, this is an area where further research is required.

One possible approach in this regard, and one that helps identify the burden placed on the financial system in terms of both the supply of and demand for funding, is to develop more comprehensive flow of funds analyses. Such work depends upon data availability, and more studies are being pursued along these

---

28. Chen, Jonung and Unteroberdoerster (2009, p. 34).
29. See for example, Turner (2009).

Figure 8-2. *Euro Area Flow of Funds, 1999 versus 2008*[a]

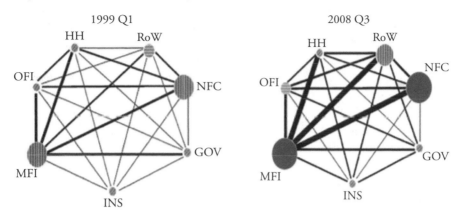

Source: European Central Bank calculations and *Financial Stability Review June 2009* (European Central Bank 2009). Reproduced with permission from the European Central Bank.

a. The thickness of the lines shows the size of the gross balance sheet exposures (assets plus liabilities) between two sectors. The size of the circles illustrates the amount of gross exposures within sectors. NFC, nonfinancial corporations sector; MFI, monetary financial institutions sector; OFI, other financial intermediaries sector; INS, insurance sector; GOV, government sector; HH, households sector; RoW, rest of the world.

lines as the information flows improve, especially in emerging markets. Flow of funds studies, looking at the financial surpluses and deficits of economic sectors within the economy and between the domestic economy and outside economies, can also be used in the context of network analysis and investigations into systemic risk analysis because they help identify phases of growth in the financial system that are out of step with historic experience. This is of use to policymakers and regulators.

In its June 2009 Financial Stability Review, the European Central Bank highlighted the benefits of such an approach within the context of the euro area.[30] As can be seen in figure 8-2, the size in financial surpluses and deficits (as indicated by the size of the nodes in the graph) and the volume of flows between the sectors (as indicated by the thickness of the lines) within the euro area grew substantially between 1999 and 2008.

*What Is the Best Way to Deal with Gaps in Financial Provision?*

The issue of access to financial services is currently much talked about and clearly is one of the key areas for ongoing research. This raises the issue of how best to plug gaps in the supply of financial services. However, this is not necessarily an

30. European Central Bank (2009).

easy task. One way to begin approaching the problem is by looking at information asymmetries between borrowers and financial intermediaries.

A recent paper by Columba, Gambacorta, and Mistrulli summarized some of these issues: "Informational asymmetries between small firms and banks may be so pronounced that profitable investment opportunities are not financed. Small enterprises may mitigate this problem by posting collateral or building close relationships with lenders. Nevertheless, these solutions are of little help to firms which have little collateral or credit history."[31]

The paper notes that, in response, borrowers may then join together and share a joint responsibility for default. Such mutual guarantee schemes may help firms achieve joint responsibility and improve their access to credit. History suggests that this should not be discounted as a viable financial model. For example, mutual guarantee institutions have proved common and successful (for a variety of historical reasons) in Germany, France, Spain, and Italy.

The value of these sorts of institutions becomes even more apparent when one considers that, post crisis, a variety of "developed" world countries are looking to more local or mutually based systems. For example, recent reports suggest that pension funds are turning away from traditional forms of finance and embracing low-risk microfinance.

The key to ascertaining the efficiency or effectiveness of a financial system rests on the degree to which it performs the functions of asset transformation and intermediation. When barriers to intermediation arise, either on the lending or borrowing side, they often call forth measures that create further rigidities at a later date.[32] Is it important then that a system be able to evolve in a framework where restrictions on the nature of business assets and liabilities are kept to a minimum, consistent with regulatory and prudential objectives?

There can be occasions when the creation of a directly controlled government agency has great merit when the existing system is unable to meet one or some of the tasks imposed upon it. This is usually most appropriate when there is a wide gap between the maturity of the funds available and the maturity of loans desired, that is, when there is a need to use short-term resources for long-term lending.

### It Is Possible to Assign Broad Categorizations to Financial Structures? Is It Worth Trying?

A number of analysts have tried to label financial structures: "Anglo-Saxon," "East Asian," "Continental," "Scandinavian," ad infinitum. These run the gamut from the basic bank-dominated universal model to the specialist model;

---

31. Columba, Gambacorta, and Mistrulli (2009, p. 1).
32. For example, the financial policies that were suitable for postwar France were in need of change by the 1960s.

government-dominated financing, informal or shadow intermediation, or formal intermediation; market-based classifications, such as centralized versus decentralized (over-the-counter) markets and the (arguably) less regulated private equity and venture capital–hedge fund type systems. But is this categorization necessarily worthwhile?

Once again the broad brush of history tends to indicate that while many financial systems exhibit strong characteristics similar to one type of system or another, particularly in earlier stages of development, the mix of institutions and instruments tend to broaden and deepen as those economies evolve.

Nonetheless, there can be very dominant, common features among even well-developed economies. This goes beyond institutional structure and can, for example, include attitudes to liquidity or borrowing. It is still true to say that savings and cooperative banks are a major component of the German banking sector (and that of other European countries). Some economies have a much bigger (relatively) contractual savings industry, and some developed countries continue to have a significant weight of government or government-sponsored financial intermediaries.

In a recent speech, Charles Goodhart referred to the susceptibility of the "Anglo-Saxon" financial model in the latest crisis in contrast to the "Asian model," which at least in this crisis has held up much more robustly.[33] Goodhart characterizes the Asian model as representing a readiness to keep a significant part of the financial system under state control, with private banks being predominantly family-owned or part of an industrial combine or some combination of both.[34] Lending is more allied to central planning, but innovation, on the other hand, may be stifled.

The premise of the Anglo-Saxon model is that public sector intervention is economically inefficient, perhaps dampens the growth of external control mechanisms (for example, transparency and market forces), and thus may adversely affect management selection. Hence the Anglo-Saxon model is more associated with market forces but may also require more activist regulation. The so-called Asian model has a more straightforward regulatory architecture and therefore tends toward less regulatory arbitrage.

Given that one result of the recent financial crisis has been the huge intervention by public authorities in some of the Anglo-Saxon model economies, Goodhart muses on the possibility of convergence between the two systems as the Anglo-Saxon one reels from the current crisis. Of course, much of this intervention is an emergency response, a lot of which will be unwound, and does not in most cases involve a fundamental shift in attitude toward ownership issues. But

33. Goodhart (2009).
34. The industrial combine, of course, was also a very common form in many parts of Europe in the nineteenth century.

there is some debate in the West about the role of the public sector versus the private sector. At the microlevel, there is some refocusing on more traditional channels of credit, such as credit unions and cooperatives, since some groups are being excluded from the more formal financial sectors.

## Are Financial Systems Converging?

Forty years ago, there was also a considerable debate about what the correct or most efficient financial structure should be. The Gessler Commission in Germany examined the universal bank model.[35] Similarly, in the 1970s the United Kingdom commissioned the Wilson Committee Report to look into, among other issues, a lack of competition in deposit taking (which was felt to be stifling innovation) and whether or not the financing needs of small and medium-size nonfinancial institutions were being adequately met.[36] There was much debate about the merits of the universal banking system versus the then specialist U.K. banking system, as well as speculation as to how much convergence there would be between the two types.

Now, in contrast, these sorts of debates are focused on what type of system emerging markets should be aiming for. Some evidence suggests that there *is* a narrowing of the gap in the structure between developed and emerging financial systems. One need only observe that papers are being published now on the development of derivatives markets in sub-Saharan Africa to appreciate that there is, in some of the literature, an implicit assumption that emerging markets should develop more "Western" financial systems, even if the actual convergence has been minimal so far.

## What Is the Role of "Financial Centers," and Are They a Priority Objective?

Having one's own strong and competitive financial center is sometimes seen as indicative of economic and political importance and hence as being a desirable policy objective in its own right. A study of financial history tends to show that the combination of factors that leads to the successful and durable establishment of a major financial center takes a very long time to develop. It is not just the economic weight of the country in which the aspiring center is sited that is important; it is also the financial structure and surrounding legal and regulatory structure and reputational record that underpin a country's importance as a portal for finance.

Recent analysis of international capital flows has confirmed the increasing role of financial centers in the developing world and the increased importance of capital flows between emerging economies (the South-to-South capital flows).[37]

35. Gessler Commission (1979).
36. Wilson Committee (1980).
37. See, for example, Haldane (2009).

Figure 8-3. *Global Flow of Funds, 1985 versus 2005*[a]

1985                                                    2008

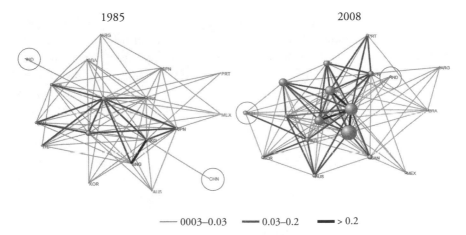

—— 0003–0.03    —— 0.03–0.2    ▬▬▶ > 0.2

Source: Haldane (2009). Reproduced with permission from the Bank of England.

a. Nodes are scaled and in proportion to a country's gross external stocks; the thickness of the lines is proportional to the bilateral external financial stocks relative to the nodes' combined GDP.

As shown in figure 8-3, China and India are barely represented in the graph for 1985, whereas by 2005 their financial centers carry much greater weight and are much more interconnected with other financial centers. Given that the developing world has weathered this financial crisis more robustly than many Western countries and that growth in emerging markets is set to continue to outpace that of developed markets for some years to come, it is logical to expect the importance of financial centers in the developing world to increase. But this will require continued effort to develop all the factors that add to the attractiveness of a financial center.

Perhaps, rather than making the achievement of a large financial center a primary objective, it makes more sense to focus instead on matching the structure of the financial system to needs of the economy it serves and perhaps, too, to ways of dealing smoothly with high levels of global capital flows. History tends to suggest that large financial centers will evolve in their own time when these conditions are met.

## Conclusion

Despite the obvious historic correlation between financial development and higher GDP levels, emerging economies *should not* necessarily be seeking to emulate all aspects of Western financial structure. A variety of factors influences the structure of a financial system, and these usually have a gradual impact over many years. It may be more useful for developing economies to focus, at a more "micro" level, on which financial instruments and institutions can service the demands of their domestic economy. An illustrative analogy might be the experience of the developing world in pursuing import substitution policies in the 1950s through 1970s. Now generally viewed with skepticism, these programs sought to introduce the infrastructure, firms, and dynamics of industrialized economies via government policy (sometimes through financial repression as well), regardless of whether they were appropriate for the economy at the time.

Perhaps the major lesson for emerging markets from a consideration of types of financial structures should be more focus on the transition from one phase to the next and the risks and pitfalls associated with such transitions. With reference to figure 8-1, a trajectory such as *a* may be gentle enough to accommodate all the necessary political, regulatory, supervisory, and educational adjustments, whereas one such as *b* might outrun the development of the rest of the real economy and be more susceptible to instabilities.

## References

Arestis, P., P. O. Demetriades, and K.B. Luintel. 2001. "Financial Development and Economic Growth: The Role of Stock Markets."*Journal of Money, Credit and Banking* 33, no. 1: 16–41.

Cameron, R. 1967. *Banking in the Early Stages of Industrialization—A Study in Comparative Economic History*. Oxford University Press.

Chen, H., L. Jonung, and O. Unteroberdoerster. 2009. "Lessons for China from Financial Liberalization in Scandinavia." *European Commission Economic Papers*, no. 383.

Columba, F., L. Gambacorta, and P.E. Mistrulli. 2009. "Mutual Guarantee Institutions and Small Business Finance." Working Paper 290. Basel: Bank for International Settlements (October).

Eichengreen, B., and M. D. Bordo. 2002. "Crises Now and Then: What Lessons from the Last Era of Financial Globalization." Discussion Paper w8716. Cambridge, Mass.: National Bureau of Economic Research (January).

European Central Bank. 2009. *Financial Stability Review June 2009*. Frankfurt am Main.

Gerschenkron, A. 1962. *Economic Backwardness in Historical Perspective*. Cambridge, Mass.: Belknap Press of Harvard University Press.

Gessler Commission. 1979. *Grundsatzfragen der Kreditwirtschaft: Bericht der Studienkommission*. Schriftenreihe des Bundesministeriums der Finanzen, Heft 28. Bonn: W. Stollfuss.

Goldsmith, R. W. 1969. *Financial Structure and Development*. Yale University Press.

Goodhart, C. A. E. 2009. "Banks and the Public Sector Authorities." Paper presented at the People's Bank of China–Bank for International Settlements Research Conference on the International Financial Crisis and Policy Challenges in Asia and the Pacific. Shanghai, August 6–8.

Gurley, J. G. 1967. "Financial Structures in Developing Economies." In *Fiscal and Monetary Problems in Developing States*, edited by D. Krivine, pp. 99–120. New York: Praeger.

Gurley, J. G., and E. S. Shaw. 1960. *Money in a Theory of Finance*. Washington, D.C.: Brookings.

Haldane, A. G. 2009. "Rethinking the Financial Network." Speech delivered to the Financial Student Association, Amsterdam (www.bankofengland.co.uk/publications/speeches/2009/speech386.pdf).

King, R. G., and R. Levine. 1993. "Finance and Growth: Schumpeter Might Be Right." *Quarterly Journal of Economics* 108, no. 3: 717–37.

Levine, R. 1997. "Financial Development and Economic Growth: Views and Agenda." *Journal of Economic Literature* 35, no. 2: 688–726.

Lin, J. Y., X. Sun, and Y. Jiang. 2009. "Toward a Theory of Optimal Financial Structure." Policy Research Working Paper WPS5038. Washington, D.C.: World Bank (September).

Lipsky, J. 2009. "Finance and Economic Growth." Remarks at the Bank of Mexico Conference on Challenges and Strategies for Promoting Economic Growth. Mexico City, October 19.

Lucas, R. E., Jr. 1988. "On the Mechanics of Economic Development." *Journal of Monetary Economics* 22, no. 1: 3–42.

Murphy, A. E. 1997. *John Law: Economic Theorist and Policy-Maker*. Oxford University Press.

O'Brien, P. K. 1986. "Do We Have a Typology for the Study of European Industrialization in the Nineteenth Century?" *Journal of European Economic History* 15, no. 2: 291–334.

Obstfeld, M. 2009. "International Finance and Growth in Developing Countries: What Have We Learned?" *IMF Staff Papers* 56, no. 1: 63–111.

Rajan, R. G., and L. Zingales. 2003. "The Great Reversals: The Politics of Financial Development in the 20th Century." *Journal of Financial Economics* 69, no. 1: 5–50.

Schumpeter, J. 1933. *The Theory of Economic Development*. Harvard University Press.

Sundaresan, S. 2009. "Development of Financial Markets in Asia and the Pacific." Paper presented at the People's Bank of China–Bank for International Settlements Research Conference on the International Financial Crisis and Policy Challenges in Asia and the Pacific. Shanghai, August 6–8.

Turner, A. 2009. "How to Tame Global Finance." *Prospect Magazine,* no. 162, August 27.

Wai, U., and H. Patrick. 1973. "Stock and Bond Issues and Capital Markets in less Developed Countries." *IMF Staff Papers* 20, no. 2.

White, E. N. 1982. "The Political Economy of Banking Regulation." *Journal of Economic History* 42, no. 1: 33–40.

Wilson Committee. 1980. *Report of the Committee to Review the Functioning of Financial Institutions*. Cmnd. 7937. London: Her Majesty's Stationery Office.

# 9

## Financial Development in Emerging Markets: The Indian Experience

K. P. KRISHNAN

I t is broadly recognized in economic literature that efficient and developed financial markets can lead to increased economic growth by improving the efficiency of allocation and utilization of savings in the economy. Better functioning financial systems ease the external financing constraints that impede firm and industrial expansion. There is a growing body of empirical analyses, including firm-level studies, industry-level studies, individual country studies, and cross-country comparisons, that prove this strong, positive link between the functioning of the financial system and long-term economic growth. Specifically, financial systems facilitate the trading, hedging, diversifying, and pooling of risk. In addition, they better allocate resources, monitor managers and exert corporate control, mobilize savings, and facilitate the exchange of goods and services.[1] Thus well-functioning financial markets are critical, especially for emerging market economies (EMEs).

India is one of the five countries classified as big emerging market economies by the World Bank. This list also includes China, Indonesia, Brazil, and Russia. These countries have made the critical transition from a developing country

The views expressed here are those of the author and do not necessarily represent the views of the Government of India. The author wishes to acknowledge the tremendous assistance of Anuradha Guru in preparing this manuscript and Shefali Dhingra for performing background research. Acknowledgments also are due to a number of colleagues who reviewed and commented on the chapter as well as to those conference participants who made many useful suggestions.

1. Levine (1997).

to an emerging market. The World Bank has predicted that these five biggest emerging markets' share of world output will have more than doubled from 7.8 percent in 1992 to 16.1 percent by 2020.[2] On account of its size and improved economic performance in the last decade or so, India is contributing significantly to the increase in trade and economic activity, and thus to world economic growth. Hence it is important to look at the manner in which financial development has occurred in India, and how it has been instrumental in shaping the contours of India's economic progress and has in turn been shaped by it. It will also be instructive to study what more India must do to join the league of countries known for their efficient financial sectors and markets.

The first section of this chapter explores how the financial development of an economy can be measured. Using mainly the World Economic Forum (WEF) financial development indicators, one can see where EMEs stand in terms of domestic financial development vis-à-vis the developed economies and where India stands among the EMEs in the area of financial development. The second section traces the financial development of India from the 1990s to the present, looking at each segment of the financial markets and comparing development indicators with those of peer countries. This analysis highlights the dualistic development of the financial sector in India. The final section attempts to explain this dualism and sets a roadmap for future development of financial markets in India.

## Measuring Financial Development

Different sets of indicators have been used in attempts to measure the financial development of economies. Starting in 1999, the World Bank began publishing a database on financial development and structure across countries. The most recent World Bank study updates and expands the financial development and structure database.[3] This database has a select number of financial system indicators (around thirty) including:

—indicators for the size of the financial system, including liquid liabilities to GDP, currency outside the banking system to base money, financial system deposits to GDP, and so forth;

—banking system indicators for size, structure, and stability;

—indicators for capital markets and the insurance sector; and

—indicators for financial globalization, such as international debt to GDP and remittance inflow to GDP.

2. World Bank (1997).
3. Beck and Demirgüç-Kunt (2009).

However, this database does not rank countries on financial development indicators.

Other studies by the World Bank provide indicators on regulation and supervision of banks, coverage and structure of deposit insurance schemes, and indicators of barriers to banking access in developing and developed countries.[4]

In another attempt to measure financial development, an occasional paper of the European Central Bank, using original methodology and database, constructs composite indexes that measure domestic financial development in twenty-six emerging economies for 2008, using mature economies as a benchmark.[5] The study uses twenty-two variables, grouped according to three broad dimensions: institutions and regulations, size of and access to financial markets, and market performance. According to this index, South Korea is ranked sixth among thirty countries, China is fourteenth, and India ranks twenty-second. This paper finds that India performed relatively better as regards its financial markets and nonbank institutions but requires improvements in the business environment as well as bigger and more efficient banks.[6]

Recognizing that there is a lack of consensus on how to define and measure financial system development, the WEF released its first annual Financial Development Report (FDR), which provides an index and ranking of fifty-two of the world's leading financial systems.[7] The 2009 FDR ranks fifty-five countries based on over 120 variables spanning institutional and business environments, financial stability, and size and depth of capital markets, among others, and is thus one of the most comprehensive databases available on financial development.[8]

For the purposes of the 2009 FDR and its index, financial development is defined as "the factors, policies, and institutions that lead to effective financial

---

4. One of the databases of the World Bank Group (of the International Financial Corporation) is the Doing Business database, which provides a quantitative measure of regulations for starting a business, getting credit, protecting investors, and the like. This database has a number of limitations and hence does not fully capture the financial development of a country. See www.doing business.org.

5. Dorrucci, Meyer-Cirkel, and Santabárbara (2009).

6. The domestic financial development index calculated in Dorrucci, Meyer-Cirkel, and Santabárbara (2009) captures three dimensions of financial markets. First, there is the institutional dimension, which includes the regulatory and judicial framework and the quality of institutions. Second is the market dimension, which includes the traditional measures of size and access to finance (stock market value as a percentage of GDP, private bond market as a percentage of GDP, total bank claims as a percentage of GDP, and assets of nonbank financial institutions as a percentage of GDP); financial innovation; and residents' access to finance. The third dimension is market performance, including measures of technical efficiency, liquidity, and distribution of domestic assets base.

7. WEF (2008).

8. WEF (2009).

intermediation and markets, and deep and broad access to capital and financial services."[9] In accordance with this definition, the FDR recognizes various aspects of development of a financial system, presenting them as the "seven pillars" of the financial development index (FDI). These fall into three broad categories:

—*Factors, policies, and institutions:* the "inputs" that allow the development of financial intermediaries, markets, instruments, and services. This is comprised of three pillars: institutional environment, business environment, and financial stability.

—*Financial intermediation:* the variety, size, depth, and efficiency of the financial intermediaries and markets that provide financial services. This includes three more pillars: banks, nonbank entities, and financial markets.

—*Financial access:* the last pillar, related to access of individuals and businesses to different forms of capital and financial services.[10]

One of the key design principles of the FDI is the inclusion of a large number of variables relevant to the financial development of both emerging and developed economies. Emphasis is placed on the component parts of the FDI as a framework for analysis, following which a very conservative approach has been taken to the weighting of variables. The FDR has generally weighted different components of the index equally. Standardization is done to permit aggregation and cross-country comparisons. This is accomplished by rescaling the variables on a 1–7 scale, with 1 being the least advantageous to financial development and 7 being the most advantageous. In some instances, the interaction among different variables is also captured because certain variables can be considered more beneficial in impact in the presence of others.

The FDI developed by the WEF, like other such indexes on financial development, has many limitations, both conceptual and methodological as well as data related. The FDR recognizes that limitations also exist due to the rapidly changing environment and the unique circumstances of some of the economies covered. Yet in its attempt to establish a comprehensive framework and a means for benchmarking, it provides a useful starting point. The FDR is unique in the comprehensiveness of the framework it provides and the richness of relevant data it brings to bear on financial system development.

9. WEF (2009, p. xiii)

10. WEF (2009, appendix A). The sub-pillars under each of the seven pillars of the FDI are, for the *institutional environment:* financial sector liberalization, corporate governance, legal and regulatory issues, and contract enforcement; for the *business environment:* human capital, taxes, infrastructure, and cost of doing business; for *financial stability:* currency stability, banking system stability, and risk of sovereign debt crisis; for *banking financial services:* size index, efficiency index, and financial information disclosure; for *nonbanking financial services:* initial public offering activity, merger and acquisition activity, insurance, and securitization; for *financial markets:* foreign exchange markets, derivatives markets, equity market development, and bond market development; and for *financial access:* commercial access and retail access.

Table 9-1. *Rankings of Select Emerging Economies, 2009*

| Country | Overall rank | Institutional environment | Business environment | Financial stability | Banks | Nonbanking companies | Financial markets | Financial access |
|---------|------|------|------|------|------|------|------|------|
| | | Factors, policies, and institutions | | | Financial intermediation | | | |
| Malaysia | 22 | 22 | 30 | 13 | 12 | 25 | 29 | 22 |
| South Korea | 23 | 31 | 16 | 28 | 22 | 18 | 20 | 52 |
| China | 26 | 35 | 40 | 23 | 10 | 12 | 26 | 30 |
| South Africa | 32 | 27 | 36 | 31 | 30 | 32 | 30 | 47 |
| Brazil | 34 | 42 | 47 | 15 | 35 | 15 | 37 | 31 |
| Thailand | 35 | 33 | 31 | 36 | 34 | 47 | 36 | 29 |
| *India* | *38* | *48* | *48* | *46* | *39* | *17* | *22* | *48* |
| Russia | 40 | 53 | 34 | 39 | 55 | 4 | 41 | 49 |

Source: WEF (2009).

The 2009 FDR places most of the developed countries in the top rankings, with the United Kingdom holding the first rank. Among the emerging economies, Malaysia places at the top, ranking twenty-second, followed by South Korea and China. India is thirty-eighth in its overall ranking.[11] Table 9-1 presents India's rankings on various financial development parameters vis-à-vis other important emerging markets.

It would be a fair summary to say that as per these reports, based on reasonably standard and agreed upon criteria, India does not rank very high in its overall score of financial development. However, it is relatively well placed in terms of development of nonbanking financial services (seventeenth) and financial markets (twenty-second).[12] Within the financial markets, India fairs well in development of its foreign exchange markets and derivatives markets. Some of the sub-indicators in which India ranks well are regulation of securities exchanges (ninth) and currency stability (tenth). However, the country's institutional environment is considerably weaker, ranking forty-eighth, a consequence of its lower levels of financial sector liberalization as well as a low degree of contract enforcement. India's business environment is also affected by two particular challenges: an absence of adequate infrastructure and the high cost of doing business. These areas of difficulty translate into highly constrained financial access.

11. India ranked thirty-one out of fifty-two countries in the 2008 FDR (WEF 2008).
12. Nonbanking financial companies, as per the definition in the FDRs, include initial public offering activity, merger and acquisition activity, insurance, and securitization.

Table 9-2. *Select Macroeconomic Indicators, India, 1951–2009*

Percent of GDP

| Indicator | 1951–52 to 1959–60 (average) | 1990–91 to 1999–2000 (average) | 2000–01 to 2008–09 (average) |
|---|---|---|---|
| Average GDP growth | 3.6 | 5.7 | 7.2 |
| Agriculture | 53.4 | 28.4 | 20.5 |
| Services | 29.7 | 51.5 | 54.4 |
| Gross domestic saving rate | 9.8 | 23.0 | 30.3 |
| Gross fixed capital formation rate | 11.1 | 23.6 | 30.2 |
| Total foreign trade | 13.3 | 19.6 | 35.7 |
| Two-way gross capital flows | n.a. | 41.8 | 77.9 |

Source: Central Statistical Organization, Reserve Bank of India (RBI).

## Financial Development: The Indian Experience

Table 9-2 summarizes some select macroeconomic indicators of the Indian economy. The highlights of India's growth story since the 1990s have been:

—an average GDP growth rate of 7.2 percent achieved over 2000–01 to 2008–09, with an increasing share of services in GDP;

—high GDP growth driven by domestic demand, both of consumption and investment;

—a high average saving rate of 30.3 and an investment rate of 30.4 as a percentage of GDP over the 2000–01 to 2008–09 period; and

—increasingly important external trade and external capital flows, as evidenced by the share of merchandise trade to GDP increasing to 35 percent in 2007–08 from 23.7 percent in 2006–07. Likewise, two-way gross capital flows as a share of GDP were 41.8 percent during the 1990s and increased to 77.9 percent over 2000–09. They stood at 112.4 percent in 2008–09.

With acceleration in economic growth and a significant increase in savings and investments in the country, a discussion on the role of finance becomes important and can have major policy implications. To be able to appreciate the linkage between growth and financial development, I first trace the historical evolution of financial markets in the country.

### Historical Evolution of Financial Markets

The financial system and infrastructure of a country, at a given point in time, are the result of their own peculiar historical evolution. This evolution is shaped by the continuous interaction between all the players in the system and public policy interventions over time. These policy interventions are also a reflection of the thinking of regulators and governments of the time as to the acceptable and desirable balance between innovation and stability, and between the role of the state and the markets.

The evolution of Indian financial markets and the regulatory system has followed a similar path. For instance, India began with the central bank, Reserve Bank of India (RBI), as the banking sector regulator, and the Ministry of Finance as the regulator for all other financial sectors. Today, most financial service providers and their regulatory agencies are in place. The role of regulators has evolved over time from that of an instrument for planned development in the initial stage to that of a referee of a relatively more modern and complex financial sector.

Over this period, a variety of financial sector reform measures have been undertaken in India, with many important successes. A key feature of these reforms has been the attempt of the authorities to align the regulatory framework with international best practices, keeping in view the needs of the country and domestic factors. These reforms can be broadly classified as steps taken toward

—liberalizing the overall macroeconomic and regulatory environment within which financial sector institutions function,

—strengthening the institutions and improving their efficiency and competitiveness, and

—establishing and strengthening the regulatory framework and institutions for overseeing the financial system.

The following pages display, in tabular format, the developments that have taken place in each segment of the financial market, namely, securities, debt, foreign exchange, banking, and insurance, and also make an assessment of growth and development in each of these segments.

## Securities Markets

Table 9-3 outlines the status of the securities markets before 1992 and by 2009.

### EQUITY MARKETS
Though India has, in the Bombay Stock Exchange (BSE), one of the oldest stock exchanges in Asia and the world, the country's modern securities market history really starts only in the 1990s. Starting in the mid-1990s the Indian securities market has had many "firsts" to its credit. It established one of the first demutualized stock exchanges in the world. All stock exchanges in India today are corporatized and demutualized. The Indian securities market was the first to use satellite-based communication technology for securities transactions. It was the first to introduce straight-through processing in securities transactions. The growing number of market participants; the growth in volumes in securities transactions; the reduction in transaction costs; the significant improvements in

Table 9-3. *Developments in Securities Markets, pre-1992 versus 2009*[a]

| Features | Pre-1992 | 2009 |
| --- | --- | --- |
| Regulator | No specific regulator, but central government oversight | A specialized regulator for securities market (SEBI) created in 1992, vested with the powers to protect investors' interest and to develop and regulate securities market. SROs strengthened |
| Securities | Limited number of traditional instruments | Expanded to cover government securities, units of CISs and MFs, derivatives of securities, security receipts |
| Form of securities | Physical | Dematerialized through enabling legislation (1996–97) |
| Regulatory approach | Merit-based regulation | Disclosure-based regulation (1992) |
| Intermediaries | Some of the intermediaries (stock brokers, authorized clerks) regulated by the SROs | A variety of specialized intermediaries emerged. They are registered and regulated by SEBI (also by SROs in some instances). They, as well as their employees, are required to follow a code of conduct and are subject to a number of compliances. All participants are identified by a unique identification number |
| Access to market | Granted by the central government | Eligible issuers access the market after complying with the issue requirements as detailed in regulations under the SEBI Act, 1992 |
| Disclosure | Voluntary, vague, scanty, and non-standardized | Standardized, systematic, and on a par with the international standards |
| Pricing of securities | Determined by the central government | Determined by market, either by the issuer through fixed price or by the investors through book building (1992) |
| Access to international market | No access | Corporations allowed to issue ADRs and GDRs and raise ECBs. ADRs and GDRs have limited two-way fungibility. MFs also allowed to invest overseas<br>Foreign institutional investors allowed to trade in Indian markets |
| Corporate compliance | Very little emphasis | Emphasis on disclosures, accounting standards, and corporate governance |
| Mutual funds | Restricted to public sector | Open to private sector and emergence of a variety of funds and schemes |
| Exchange structure | Mutual not-for-profit exchanges | For-profit corporate, demutualized exchanges mandated through legislative amendments in the securities legislation (2004) |

*(continued)*

Table 9-3 *(continued)*

| Features | Pre-1992 | 2009 |
| --- | --- | --- |
| Trading mechanism | Open outcry, available at the trading rings of the exchanges; opaque, auction, or negotiated deals | Screen-based trading system; orders are matched on price-time priority; transparent trading platform accessible from all over the country |
| Aggregation of order flow | Market fragmented by geographic distance; order flow unobserved | Order flow observed. The exchanges have open electronic consolidated limit order book |
| Anonymity in trading | Absent | Complete |
| Settlement cycle | 14-day account period settlement, not always followed | Rolling settlement on T+2 basis (1999–2000) |
| Counterparty risk | Present | Absent with clearing corporations and clearing-houses acting as central counterparty |
| Form of settlement | Physical | Mostly electronic |
| Basis of settlement | Bilateral netting | Multilateral netting |
| Transfer of securities | Cumbersome. Transfer by endorsement on security and registra-tion by issuer | Securities are freely transferable. Transfers are recorded electronically in book entry form by depositories |
| Systemic risk management | No focus on risk management | Comprehensive risk management system at the exchanges encompassing capital adequacy, limits on exposure and turnover, VaR-based margining, client-level gross margining, on-line position monitoring, business continuity plans, and the like |
| Derivatives trading | Absent | A wide array of exchange-traded derivatives, such as futures and options on indexes and single stocks and futures on interest rates (available since 2000–01 and ongoing), com-modities (since 2003), and currencies (since 2008) |
| Research | Very little | Many market participants have full-fledged research departments. Some of them have schemes and initiatives to promote research |

Source: Author.
a. ADRs, American depository receipts; CISs, collective investment schemes; ECBs, external commer-cial borrowings; GDRs, global depository receipts; MFs, mutual funds; SEBI, Securities and Exchange Board of India; SROs, self-regulatory organizations; VaR, value at risk.

## Table 9-4. *Profile of Indian Securities Markets, 2000–09*[a]

Millions of U.S. dollars, unless otherwise indicated

| Description | 2000–01 | 2007–08 | 2008–09 |
|---|---|---|---|
| Amount raised by government | 27,548 | 55,763 | 46,093 |
| Amount raised domestically by corporate sector | 15,909 | 58,383 | 25,859 |
| Amount raised through euro issues | 900 | 6,644 | 940 |
| Amount raised by mutual funds | 2,387 | 38,479 | -5554 |
| Assets under management of mutual funds at the end of year | 19,423 | 126,383 | 81,904 |
| Market capitalization at the end of year | 164,851 | 1,286,307 | 607,061 |
| Turnover in cash segment | 617,708 | 1,283,667 | 756,054 |
| Impact cost (for a trade of Rs 0.5 crore at NSE), in percentages[b] | 0.28 | 0.09 | 0.08 |
| Trading costs, in basis points | 114 | 53 | 56 |
| Net cumulative investment by FIIs at the end of year, in billions of U.S. dollars[c] | 13.4 | 68 | 56.7 |
| Millions of investor accounts with depositories at the end of year | 3.8 | 14.2 | 15.2 |

Source: RBI, Securities and Exchange Board of India, and the National Stock Exchange of India (NSE).
a. All conversions from Indian rupee (Rs) to U.S. dollars for a particular fiscal year are made at the exchange rate prevailing on March 31 of that fiscal year.
b. A "crore" is an Indian unit equaling 10 million.
c. FIIs, foreign institutional investors.

efficiency, transparency, and safety; and the level of compliance with international standards have earned the Indian securities market a new respect among the securities markets in the world.

In addition to these developments, and thanks to the massive liberalization ushered in in 1992, the securities market in India has grown exponentially as measured in terms of the amount raised from the market, number of market participants, number of listed stocks, market capitalization, trading volumes and turnover on stock exchanges, and investor population. Table 9-4 presents some statistics pertaining to the securities markets in India.

According to the 2009 *Global Stock Markets Factbook*, India ranked thirteenth in the world in terms of total market capitalization (US$645 billion) and total value traded (US$1,050 billion) in 2008.[13] It ranked second in terms of the number of listed companies, exceeded only by United States. However, India is still far behind China in terms of market capitalization and turnover, while it scores well above the other EMEs on these equity market indicators.

13. Standard and Poor's (2009).

Table 9-5. *Growth in Derivative Markets, 2000–09*
Units as indicated

| Year | No. of contracts traded | Turnover (Rs millions) | Open interest (Rs millions) | Turnover (US$ millions) |
|------|------------------------|------------------------|------------------------------|--------------------------|
| 2000–01 | 168,323 | 40,380 | n.a. | 866 |
| 2003–04 | 57,269,034 | 21,431,012 | 71,891 | 493,916 |
| 2006–07 | 218,428,742 | 74,152,774 | 386,830 | 1,701,142 |
| 2008–09 | 657,906,085 | 110,227,482 | 577,050 | 2,163,444 |

Source: Securities and Exchange Board of India.

## EQUITY DERIVATIVES MARKETS

India's introduction of exchange-traded equity derivatives began only in this century. Trading first commenced in index futures contracts, followed by index options in June 2001, individual stocks options in July 2001, and single stocks futures in November 2001. Since then, equity derivatives have come a long way. An expanding list of eligible investors, rising volumes, and the best of risk management framework for exchange-traded derivatives have been the hallmarks of the history of equity derivatives in India so far.

India's experience with the launch of the equity derivatives market has been extremely positive. The derivatives turnover on the National Stock Exchange of India (NSE) has surpassed the equity market turnover within four years of the introduction of derivatives.[14] The turnover of derivatives (on the NSE and BSE) increased from Rs 40,380 million (US$0.87 billion) in 2000–01 to Rs 110,227,482 million (US$2,163 billion) in 2008–09 (table 9-5).

In terms of the number of single stock futures contracts traded in 2008, the NSE held the second position in the world in 2008; it was fourth in the number of stock index options contracts traded and third in the number of stock index futures contracts.[15] In terms of traded volumes in futures and options taken together, the NSE has been improving its worldwide ranking from fifteenth in 2006 to ninth in 2007 and eighth in 2008.[16] The traded volumes in the derivatives segment of the NSE in 2008 represented an increase of 55.4 percent over the figure for 2007.

Thus India is one of the most successful developing countries in terms of a vibrant market for exchange-traded equity derivatives. However, on the general

14. The NSE is the premier stock exchange of the country, accounting for 99 percent of trading in the derivatives segment.

15. These rankings are based on World Federation of Exchanges (2008).

16. Futures Industry Association (2009).

issue of risk mitigation products (of which equity derivatives are just one example), it is poignant to note that "innovations" have appeared in the country only after years of toil and waiting. Stock index futures took five years to be offered to the investors, from the time they were conceived. Exchange-traded fund for gold again took four years to become a reality. Interest rate derivatives, though launched in 2003, did not take off mainly due to constraints on the participation of banks in this market and had to be re-launched in 2009. These experiences highlight the adverse environment for financial innovation in the country.

Another issue that deserves attention for further development of these markets is the explicit segmentation of markets within exchanges. As an example, the equity spot market is one "segment," and the equity derivatives market is another segment. The currency derivatives market is yet another segment. Financial firms have to obtain separate memberships in each segment and suffer from a duplication of compliance costs. This separation also reduces the ability of a clearing corporation to know the full position of a financial firm or its customers and the risk that the firm poses to the system.

## Debt Markets

The following analysis evaluates the performance of three components of the debt market: money markets, government securities markets, and corporate debt markets.

### Money Markets

Table 9-6 shows the development of money markets in India in 1992 and 2009.

In comparison to the early 1990s, money markets are currently better in terms of depth, and as a result of various policy initiatives, activity in all the segments has increased significantly, especially during the last three years (table 9-7). With the development of market repo and collateralized borrowing and lending obligation segments, the call money market has been transformed into a pure interbank market since August 2005. In the interest of financial stability, uncollateralized overnight transactions are now limited to banks and primary dealers.

Volatility in call rates has declined over the years, especially after the introduction of the liquidity adjustment facility. There has also been a reduction in bid-ask spread in the overnight rates, which indicates that the Indian money market has become reasonably deep, vibrant, and liquid.

However, though the money market is free from interest rate ceilings, structural barriers and institutional factors continue to create distortions in the market. Apart from the overnight interbank (call market) rate, the other interest rates in the money market are sticky and appear to be set in customer markets rather than auction markets. A well-defined yield curve does not therefore exist in the Indian money market.

Table 9-6.  *Developments in Money Markets, 1992 versus 2009*

| Features | 1992 | 2009 |
|---|---|---|
| Pure interbank call money market | Absent | Call market transactions limited to banks and primary dealers only in the interest of financial stability, leading to development of pure interbank call money market |
| Uncollateralized call money segment versus collateralized market | Call money market largely uncollateralized | Shift of activity from uncollateralized to collateralized segments of the market |
| Repo market | Limited participants | Nonbanking financial companies, mutual funds, housing finance companies, and insurance companies not holding subsidiary general ledger accounts permitted to undertake repo transactions as of March 3, 2003<br><br>Subsequently, nonscheduled urban cooperative banks and listed companies having gilt accounts with scheduled commercial banks are allowed to participate in repo markets |
| Central counterparty | Nonexistent | Clearing Corporation of India set up as a central counterparty for all trades involving foreign exchange; government securities and other debt instruments routed through it |

Source: Author.

Table 9-7.  *Activity in the Money Market Segment, 2001–07*[a]

Millions of U.S. dollars

| Year | Average daily turnover[b] | | | | | Outstanding amounts | |
|---|---|---|---|---|---|---|---|
| | Call money market | Market repo (outside the LAF)[c] | CBLO | Term money market | Money market, total | Commercial paper | Certificates of deposit |
| 2001–02 | 7,202 | 6,181 | n.a. | 40 | 13,422 | 1,624 | 194 |
| 2005–06 | 4,030 | 4,748 | 4,492 | 187 | 13,458 | 3,875 | 6,119 |
| 2006–07 | 4,984 | 7,726 | 7,431 | 232 | 20,372 | 4,927 | 14,901 |

Source: RBI.

a. All conversions from Indian rupees to U.S. dollars for a particular fiscal year are made at the exchange rate prevailing on March 31 of that fiscal year.

b. Turnover is twice the single leg volumes in the case of call money and CBLO (collateralized borrowing and lending obligation) to capture borrowing and lending both, and four times in case of market repo to capture the borrowing and lending in the two legs of a repo.

c. LAF, liquidity adjustment facility.

Table 9-8. *Developments in Government Securities Markets, 1992 versus 2009*[a]

| Features | 1992 | 2009 |
|---|---|---|
| Securities | "Plain vanilla" cash flow securities | Expanded to include zero coupon bonds, floating rate bonds, capital indexed bonds, bonds with embedded derivatives, interest rate futures |
| Form of securities | Physical | "Demat" holding by RBI-regulated entities |
| Pricing of securities | Administered interest rates | Issue at market-related rates (auction) |
| Participation | Captive investors (mostly banks) | Expanded to allow primary dealers, FIIs, retail investors |
| Trading mechanism | Through telephone | NDS, which provides negotiation and screen-based trading |
| Counterparty risk | Present | Clearing Corporation of India provides novation and guarantees settlement |
| Technological infrastructure | Weak | A screen-based anonymous trading and reporting platform introduced in the form of NDS-OM, which enables electronic bidding in primary auctions and disseminates trading information with a minimum time lag |
| Depth and liquidity | Limited | Number of measures taken to promote liquidity, such as introduction of "when issued" trading, "short selling" of government securities and active consolidation of government debt through buy backs. |

Source: Author.

a. Demat, demarerialized account; NDS, negotiated dealing system; OM, order-matching segment.

## GOVERNMENT SECURITIES MARKETS

Table 9-8 illustrates how the government securities market has changed from 1992 to 2009.

As a result of the developmental measures undertaken, the volume of transactions in government securities has increased manyfold over the past decade (table 9-9). The investor base, which was largely determined by mandated investment requirements before reforms, has expanded slightly with the voluntary holding of government securities. Accordingly, the share of commercial banks in holding government securities has declined from about 41.5 percent in 2007 to 38.85 percent in 2009.[17]

17. Figures are from the monthly bulletins of the RBI.

Table 9-9. *Secondary Market Transactions in Government Securities,
2000–08* [a]

Millions of U.S. dollars

| Year | Turnover |
| --- | --- |
| 2000 | 129,093 |
| 2005 | 571,770 |
| 2008 | 1,237,993 |

Source: RBI.

a. All conversions from Indian rupees to U.S. dollars for a particular calendar year are made at the exchange rate prevailing on December 31 of that year.

However, a number of problems continue to confront these markets. A benchmark yield curve for government securities has not yet emerged. Liquidity of the markets is poor, which impedes the development of a yield curve that can be reliably used to price all cash flows off the curve. Only a handful of securities account for the bulk of trading. There are isolated pockets of liquidity for very short-term and very long-term securities. In addition, there are limits on foreign institutional investor (FII) investments in government securities (at this writing, US$5 billion), which limit voluntary demand for them from abroad.

A key issue for government securities markets is that the central bank is also the manager of public debt in the country, which leads to a series of conflicts. There is, to begin with, a conflict of interest between setting the short-term interest rate and selling bonds for the government. Furthermore, since the central bank administers the operational systems for these markets, it follows that the owner-administrator of these systems is also a participant in the market. In effect, the government securities market is a captive market, with the RBI mandating that banks hold a large amount of government bonds; this undermines the growth of a deep, liquid market in government securities with vibrant trading and speculative price discovery. This in turn hampers the development of the corporate bond market, as a benchmark sovereign yield curve is lacking, making it difficult to price corporate bonds.

## Corporate Debt Markets

Table 9-10 shows the change in corporate debt markets in India from 1992 to 2009.

Private bond market capitalization as percentage of GDP was 0.4 percent for India in 2001, increasing to 2.67 percent in 2007. The public bond market capitalization as percentage of GDP was 30 percent and 31 percent for these years, respectively. These figures indicate underdeveloped bond markets when compared to other emerging markets with similar financial sector depth. A

Table 9-10. *Developments in Corporate Debt Markets, 1992 versus 2009*

| Features | 1992 | 2009 |
|---|---|---|
| Issue procedures | Cumbersome | Simplified issue procedures put in place through regulations. Issuers required to make only some incremental disclosures every time they approach the market with a fresh issue either to the public or through a private placement |
| Centralized database | Nonexistent | Database for new bond issuances operational |
| Retail participation | Limited mainly due to high minimum lot size of Rs 1 million | The minimum market lot reduced to Rs 100,000 to enable better access to smaller investors |
| Exchange-traded interest rate derivatives | Not available | Exchange-traded interest rate derivatives launched in 2003 and re-launched with certain changes in 2009 |
| Trade reporting platform | Absent | Trade reporting platform operational |
| Dematerialization | Absent | Compulsory dematerialization in settlement from 2003 |
| Settlement | Arranged by counterparties | Settlement through an exchange platform (from 2009) |

Source: Author.

comparison of the size and composition of the domestic debt market in India with select emerging market countries puts India at the bottom in terms of private bond market capitalization as a percentage of GDP and ahead of South Africa and China in terms of public bond market capitalization as a percentage of GDP (table 9-11). In India, financial institutions and government or government-guaranteed instruments dominate most of the issuance in the corporate bond market, with a share of 8 percent and 90 percent of the total issuance as of the end of March 2009, respectively. The share of corporate issuers in the total bond issuance is very low at only 2 percent.

A well-developed corporate bond market is essential for financial system efficiency, stability, and overall economic growth. A well-functioning bond market provides for financial diversification and facilitates necessary financing for corporations and infrastructure development. However, as noted above, this market remains practically nonexistent in India, imposing an avoidable constraint on India's ability to finance its growing need for debt, particularly for infrastructure development. Most of the large issuers are quasi-governmental, including banks,

Table 9-11. *Private and Public Domestic Bond Market Capitalization as a Share of GDP, Various Countries, 2007*

Percent

| Country | Private bond market capitalization[a] | Public bond market capitalization[b] |
|---|---|---|
| *Emerging markets* | | |
| India | 2.67 | 30.97 |
| South Korea | 58.81 | 48.11 |
| South Africa | 15.96 | 25.77 |
| China | 24.46 | 28.13 |
| Thailand | 16 | 34.72 |
| Russia | 2.87 | 99.62 |
| Brazil | 16.92 | 46.13 |
| *Developed markets* | | |
| United States | 125.10 | 46.77 |
| United Kingdom | 15.84 | 32.09 |
| Japan | 38.79 | 159.91 |

Source: World Bank Financial Structure database, updated May 2009 (http://go.worldbank.org/X23UD9QUX0).

a. Private domestic debt securities are outstanding securities issued by financial institutions and corporations, as a share of GDP.

b. Public domestic debt securities are outstanding securities issued by government, as a share of GDP.

public sector oil companies, or government-sponsored financial institutions. Of the rest, a few known names dominate. There is very little high-yield issuance, and spreads between sovereign debt, AAA debt, and high-yield debt are high in comparison to other markets. Very few papers trade on a regular basis. Trading in most papers dries up after the first few days of issuance, during which the larger players "retail" the bonds they have picked up to smaller pension funds and cooperative banks. Most trading is between banks and the mutual fund companies.

The lack of depth in the government bond market and the absence of a yield curve for government bonds, which could serve as a benchmark for corporate bonds; a cumbersome primary issuance mechanism (to some extent addressed by recent changes in the regulations by the market regulator, the Securities and Exchange Board of India); the absence of sufficiently diversified long-term investors; and chronic illiquidity caused inter alia by absence of derivative instruments are some of the factors leading to underdeveloped bond markets. There are also limits on FII investments in corporate debt (US$15 billion at this writing), which are reviewed periodically.

## Foreign Exchange Markets

Table 9-12 compares the state of foreign exchange markets in India in 1992 and 2009.

Reforms in foreign exchange markets have been focused on market development with built-in prudential safeguards so that the market will not be destabilized in the process. The most important measures undertaken to reform these markets were the move toward a market-based exchange rate regime in 1993 and the subsequent adoption of current account convertibility. Allowing greater autonomy for banks in their foreign exchange operations, admitting new players into the markets, and permitting limited introduction of new products have been other important reforms.

As a result of various measures, the annual turnover in the foreign exchange market increased more than eightfold, from US$1,305 billion in 1997–98 to US$12,092 billion in 2008–09. During this period, there has been a steady but slow fall in the share of spot transactions in total turnover in the foreign exchange markets, implying an increase in gross turnover in the over-the-counter (OTC) derivatives (swaps and forwards) segment of currency markets. Activity in this segment has picked up, particularly in late 2007 and through 2008, following increased volatility in the U.S. dollar–rupee exchange rate. The average daily turnover, calculated on a monthly basis, reached an all-time high of US$35 billion in September 2008. The year 2008 closed with average daily volumes of US$28.63 billion in these markets over the full year.

While OTC foreign exchange markets are doing well in India, the exchange-traded currency futures market was only introduced in August 2008. This market, as it exists today, is limited exclusively to rupee–U.S. dollar contracts, with very low position limits and a ban on trading by nonresidents, including FIIs. Despite these restrictions, the currency futures market has seen a steady growth in liquidity and now matches the spreads that are seen on their much longer-lived OTC forwards counterparts. There is considerable scope for further development of these markets by removing the aforementioned restrictions.

## Banking Sector

Table 9-13 lists the developments in the banking sector from 1992 to 2009.

The reforms mentioned above have had a major impact on the overall efficiency and stability of the banking system in India. A select few reforms, which are critical, affect:

—*Capital:* The average capital to risk (weighted) assets ratio (CRAR) of all banks increased from 9.2 percent as of March 31, 1994, to 13.2 percent as of March 31, 2009. With the global range for CRAR being 10.2 to 13.2 percent, the capital adequacy of Indian banks is comparable to those at the international level.

Table 9-12.  *Developments in Foreign Exchange Markets, 1992 versus 2009*

| Features | 1992 | 2009 |
|---|---|---|
| Exchange rate regime | Single currency fixed exchange rate system | Valuation of rupee against a basket of currencies and a market-determined floating exchange rate regime |
| Convertibility of rupee | Not convertible | Full convertibility of rupee for current account transactions<br><br>De facto full capital account convertibility for nonresidents, and calibrated liberalization of transactions undertaken for capital account purposes in the case of residents |
| Regulatory framework | Restrictive Foreign Exchange Regulation Act (FERA), 1973 | FERA replaced with relatively more market-friendly Foreign Exchange Management Act, 1999 |
| Instruments in foreign exchange markets | Limited | New instruments permitted, such as rupee–foreign currency swap, foreign currency–rupee options, cross-currency options, interest rate swaps, and forward rate agreements |
| Market participants and regulations | Limitations on participation | Authorized dealers permitted to initiate trading positions, borrow, and invest in overseas market<br><br>Banks permitted to fix interest rates on nonresident deposits, use derivative products for asset-liability management, and fix overnight open position limits and gap limits in the foreign exchange market<br><br>Permission given to various participants in the foreign exchange market—including exporters, Indians investing abroad, FIIs—to use forward cover and enter into swap transactions without any limit, subject to genuine underlying exposure<br><br>FIIs and nonresident Indians permitted to trade in equity derivative contracts on exchanges, subject to certain conditions<br><br>Foreign exchange earners permitted to maintain foreign currency accounts; residents permitted to open such accounts within the general limit of US$25,000 a year |

Source: Author.

Table 9-13. *Developments in the Banking Sector, 1992 versus 2009*

| Features | 1992 | 2009 |
|---|---|---|
| Competition | Limited; predominantly government owned | Increased competition with entry of foreign and new private banks; reduction of public ownership in public sector banks by allowing them to raise capital from equity market up to 49 percent of paid-up capital |
| Interest rate structure | Administered interest rates | Interest rates largely deregulated with a few exceptions |
| Statutory pre-emption | High level of statutory pre-emption in the form of cash reserve ratio (CRR) and statutory liquidity ratio (SLR) requirements | Gradual reduction of CRR and SLR requirements |
| Diversification of activities | Limited | Banks allowed to diversify into non-traditional activities |
| Regulatory oversight | Strict oversight by RBI, including in day-to-day functioning | Greater functional autonomy and operational flexibility in day-to-day activities<br>Risk-based supervision introduced<br>Introduction of CAMELS supervisory rating system[a]<br>Streamlining of the supervision process with combination of on-site and off-site surveillance along with external auditing<br>Introduction of the process of structured and discretionary intervention for problem banks through a prompt corrective action mechanism<br>Establishment of the Board for Financial Supervision as the apex supervisory authority for commercial banks, financial institutions, and nonbanking financial companies |
| Products | Limited | New products and delivery channels introduced |
| Debt recovery process | Prolonged and tedious | *Lok adalats* (people's courts), debt recovery tribunals, asset reconstruction companies, settlement advisory committees, corporate debt restructuring mechanism set up for quicker recovery and restructuring |
| Markets for securitized assets | Underdeveloped | Promulgation of the Securitization and Reconstruction of Financial Assets and Enforcement of Securities Interest Act, 2002, and its subsequent amendment to ensure creditor rights |

Source: Author.

a. CAMELS is a rating that examines Capital adequacy, Asset quality, Management, Earnings, Liquidity, and Sensitivity to market risk.

—*Asset quality:* The RBI introduced an objective criterion for identifying nonperforming assets (NPAs) in 1992–93. While gross NPAs, as a proportion of gross advances, have been declining steadily and distinctly over the years, the level of gross NPAs in absolute terms has also decreased over the recent past. The ratio of gross NPAs to gross advances for the banking system was 14.4 percent in March 1998 but decreased to 2.33 percent in March 2009. During the same period, the ratio of net NPAs to net advances declined from 7.3 percent to 1.05 percent. The ratio of nonperforming loans to total loans was 2.3 percent in 2008 for India, lower than for most other EMEs.

—*Profitability:* The reform measures have also resulted in an improvement in the profitability of banks. The return on assets of all banks in India rose from 0.4 percent in the year 1991–92 to 1.0 percent in 2008. The return on assets of Indian banks is in the range 0.1 to 2.1 percent, which is comparable to the levels in other EMEs.

These profitability figures mask an important fact: that India is hugely under-banked. India's poor, many of whom work as agricultural and unskilled or semi-skilled wage laborers, micro-entrepreneurs, and low-salaried workers, are largely excluded from the formal financial system. Over 40 percent of India's working population earns but has no savings. The population served per bank branch in rural India is approximately 18,000, while in urban India it is 5,000.[18]

## Insurance Sector

Table 9-14 compares the development in the insurance sector in 1992 and 2009.

The life insurance business (measured in the context of first-year premiums) registered a year-on-year growth of 94.96 percent in 2006–07 and 23.88 percent in 2007–08. The general insurance business (gross direct premiums) registered a growth of 11.72 percent in 2007–08 (versus 3.52 percent achieved in 2006–07). This has resulted in increasing insurance penetration in the country. Insurance penetration for the year 2007 stood at 4 percent for life insurance and 0.6 percent for nonlife insurance.[19] The growth in the insurance industry has been spurred by product innovation, active distribution channels coupled with targeted publicity, and promotional campaigns by the insurers.

When India's insurance industry performance is compared with that of other emerging markets, it is apparent that Indian markets have the lowest insurance density.[20] However, in terms of insurance penetration, India fares better than most emerging markets. The participation of low-income groups in life

18. Committee on Financial Sector Reforms (Planning Commission 2009).

19. Premium volume as a ratio of GDP. See Insurance Regulatory and Development Authority (2008).

20. Ratio of premium (in U.S. dollars) to total population.

Table 9-14. *Developments in the Insurance Sector, 1992 versus 2009*

| Features | 1992 | 2009 |
| --- | --- | --- |
| Regulator | No specific regulator, but central government oversight | A specialized regulator for the insurance sector (IRDA) was constituted in 1999 to protect the interests of insurance policyholders and to regulate, promote, and ensure orderly growth of the insurance industry[a] |
| Products | Limited number of products available | New insurance products have been introduced, such as weather insurance, group health insurance for the poor, product liability insurance, life insurance with critical and terminal illness riders, and package insurance for small- and medium-size enterprises |
| Market structure | State-owned monopoly: only nationalized insurance companies allowed | Private insurance companies were allowed back into the business of insurance with a maximum of 26 percent of foreign holding in 1999 |
|  | Only six insurance companies operating | Number of insurers stands at forty-four as of end of March 2009 |
| Regulatory approach | Merit-based regulation | Disclosure-based regulation |

Source: Author.
a. IRDA, Insurance Regulatory and Development Authority.

insurance, the second most preferred savings instrument after bank savings deposits, is still very limited. One-third of all paid workers have some life insurance protection. However, only 14 percent of people in the lowest income quartile and 26 percent in the second quartile have life insurance, compared to 69 percent of those in the highest income quartile. While the elaborate sales and distribution model has contributed to the popularity of life insurance, this has come at considerable cost by way of high commissions and a large percentage of lapsed policies.[21] Policy lapses are low only in the highest income quartile, while in all other segments at least 20 percent of respondents have had a policy lapse.

21. For traditional life insurance products, a policyholder typically loses the entire investment if the policy lapses within the first three years. After that, only the surrender value is paid in the case of a lapse, which is less than 35 percent of the total premiums paid. The Insurance Regulatory and Development Authority reported that almost 5 percent of life insurance policies lapsed between 2000 and 2005. This number was as high as 16 percent among private providers due to the higher contribution of unit linked insurance plans and aggressive selling policies. See ISEC Securities (2007, p. 43).

The penetration of nonlife insurance products is negligible. For example, only 1 percent of the population appears to have medical insurance.[22]

The insurance industry also continues to face some basic problems. One of these is that a large part of the sale of "insurance" products is merely tax arbitrage, where a fund management product is given preferential tax treatment under the garb of a minimal insurance cover. A related issue is that much of the growth in insurance penetration is as a result of selling products such as unit linked insurance plans (ULIPs), which are essentially a mutual fund type of securities market product. The relatively superior performance of ULIPs could be attributed, inter alia, to higher commissions for insurance ULIPs than for mutual fund products. Thus there is a blurring of products wherein financial instruments are partaking of the multiple characteristics of investment, pensions, and insurance. Some basic changes in regulatory architecture would be necessary to address this, a topic revisited later in the chapter.

## An Assessment of Indian Financial Sector Reforms and the Way Ahead

Looking both at the story of growth and development of each of the segments of financial markets in India described above and the more numbers-based evidence in the first section, one cannot escape the fact that they point to two contradictory developments: the dramatic transformation of the stock market segment, but the considerably more limited progress in other segments of the markets. In other words, one could broadly say that while India has done well in terms of creating efficient equity and equity derivatives, development in the banking sector services, bond markets, retail access to finance, and general business environment leaves much to be desired.

The recently submitted report of the Government of India's Committee on Financial Sector Reforms (CFSR) summarizes the state of various segments of Indian financial markets in terms of immediacy, depth, and resilience (see table 9-15).[23]

In the view of the CFSR, resilience is found in the large stocks, their stock futures, and the index futures. All other markets in India lack resilience. Depth is found, in addition, with on-the-run government bonds and interest rate swaps. Immediacy is found in a few more markets. A well-functioning market

22. Planning Commission (2009, pp. 53–54).
23. Planning Commission (2009). Immediacy refers to the ability to execute trades of small size immediately without moving the price adversely (in the jargon, at low-impact cost). Depth refers to the impact cost suffered when doing large trades. Resilience refers to the speed with which prices and the liquidity of the market revert back to normal conditions after a large trade has taken place.

Table 9-15. *Liquidity of Indian Financial Markets*

| Market | Immediacy | Depth | Resilience |
|---|---|---|---|
| Large cap stocks and futures and index futures | Y | Y | Y |
| Other stocks | | | |
| On-the-run government bonds | Y | Y | |
| Other government bonds | | | |
| Corporate bonds | | | |
| Commercial paper and other money market instruments | | | |
| Near-money options on index and liquid stocks | Y | | |
| Other stock options | | | |
| Currency | Y | | |
| Interest rate swaps | Y | Y | |
| Metals, energies, and select agricultural commodity futures | Y | | |
| Other commodity futures | | | |

Source: CFSR (Planning Commission 2009).

is one that has all three elements. India has only one market where this has been achieved, for roughly the top 200 stocks, their derivatives, and index derivatives.

The CFSR further notes that when a financial market does not exist, or is inadequately liquid to meet the requirements at hand, or suffers from deviations from fair price, this constitutes market incompleteness. Economic agents are unable to enter into transactions that they require for conducting their optimal plans. Market incompleteness has many destructive implications for resource allocation and ultimately for GDP growth.

It is pertinent to try to look for answers to this differential and dualistic development of the Indian financial sector by understanding what was done right in reforms in the stock markets and what went wrong or was not done in other areas of finance. This will then be useful in charting out a road map for next-generation financial sector reforms in the country.

## Diagnosis

The extent and pace of reforms in a segment of financial markets in India appear to be shaped by two factors: a clearly defined regulatory framework and the extent of public sector presence. The debt markets in India illustrate this. The debt market has had a strong public sector presence. The dominant traded instruments are Government of India securities, and the dominant trading participants are banks, with a large fraction being the public sector banks. When the Securities and Exchange Board of India (SEBI) was created to regulate "securities markets," the markets for bonds did not fall within its mandate due to

Table 9-16. *Lags in Institutional Development in the Indian Debt Market*

| Institution | Original development | Adoption for debt market |
|---|---|---|
| Electronic trading on a single platform | Equity, 1994; commodity futures, 2004 | 2005, eleven years later |
| National access to trading | Equity, 1994; commodity futures, 2004 | Absent |
| Clearing corporation | Equity, 1996 | 1999, three years later |
| Independent regulator | Equity, 1992; insurance, 1999 | Not yet even considered |
| Competition between exchanges | Equity, 1994; commodities, 2004 | Absent |
| Entry barriers | Removed for equity, 1994; commodities, 2004 | Barriers present |

Source: Thomas (2006).

confusion in the financial architecture prevalent in the country. Despite the fact that the legal definition of the word securities included "bonds," due to a variety of reasons, including the fact that RBI was the investment banker to the Government of India and the regulator of the banking sector (which is the dominant player in the bond market), SEBI did not become the sole regulator for the bond market. Even now there is legal confusion over who regulates the government securities market, with the RBI exercising a lot of regulatory powers. Thus the bond market did not benefit from an independent regulator, as the equity markets did. The approach of reforms in equity markets was through an independent regulator, the SEBI. However, the development of bond markets took place in the context of this conflict of jurisdictions. There were considerable lags in institutional development in the Indian debt markets as compared to equity and commodities markets, as demonstrated in table 9-16.

Similarly, as regards the impact of public sector presence on the pace and direction of reforms, one finds that in India the pace of reforms has been the slowest where the government had a dominant presence, such as in the insurance and banking sector. The government had a lower involvement in commodity markets, and the least in the case of equity where reforms have made huge strides in institutional development and change.

Some of the other reasons for the varying pace of development in different sectors of the financial markets are bans or restrictions on products and participants. A policy environment that bans products and markets clearly hinders the development of liquid and efficient markets. As an example, exchange-traded currency futures were banned until August 2008, and commodity options are currently banned, obviously impeding the development of liquidity and efficiency in these markets. Equally problematic, a missing market can hamper the efficiency of other markets as well. For example, an efficient and deep corporate bond market is still lacking in India, inter alia, because the related markets for corporate repos, interest rate derivatives, and credit derivatives are either altogether missing or have only been allowed with multiple restrictions, which lead to stunted development.

In many cases, while an outright product ban is not in place, there are restrictions on participation. These include regulatory restrictions on some kinds of activities (for example, banks are prohibited from adopting long positions on interest rate futures) or quantitative restrictions (for example, all FIIs combined are required to keep their aggregate ownership of corporate bonds below US$15 billion).

The equity market—the only element of Indian finance that has achieved immediacy, depth, and resilience—has few restrictions on participation in both spot and derivatives markets. As a consequence, the equity market, especially for large stocks, has developed a distribution capability that reaches millions of market participants, including many around the world. All kinds of economic agents come together into a unified market to make the price. Competitive conditions hold for the most part, as no one player is large enough to distort the price. The diverse views and needs of a range of participants impart resilience, depth, and market efficiency. Competition between the NSE and BSE has helped improve technology and reduce costs. The most important feature of the equity market has been free entry and exit for financial firms that become members of the NSE and BSE, and the free entry and exit for the economic agents who trade on these markets through exchange members. Such an open environment is critically important for achieving liquidity and efficiency in all the other elements of Indian financial markets.

In a growing and increasingly complex market-oriented economy such as India's, which is experiencing increased integration with global trade and finance, the financial system would be an important element in the country's future growth trajectory. Further steps are required to make the financial markets deeper, more efficient, and well-regulated. In this regard, two recent important government committees, the High-Powered Expert Committee on Making Mumbai an International Financial Center (HPEC on MIFC) and the CFSR, have charted out the road ahead for India's financial system to prepare it for the challenges of the future. Despite differences in their scope and terms of reference, the two committee reports have a common underlying term of reference, namely, to recommend the next generation of financial sector reforms for India. They both emphasize that recognizing the deep linkages among different reforms, including broader reforms to monetary and fiscal policies, are essential to achieve real progress.[24] The reports outline the key elements of a financial system that India will need in its quest for higher growth over the next few years.

## Way Ahead

Drawing on various expert committee reports, mentioned above, certain policy actions are recommended below for further development of financial markets in India.

### REGULATORY ARCHITECTURE

As shown in figure 9-1, based on a report by the World Bank quoted in the CFSR, the current system involves half a dozen apex regulatory agencies, apart from several ministries in the government that retain direct regulatory powers. This structure leads to major regulatory overlaps and regulatory gaps. Sometimes this structure can also lead to regulatory arbitrage as similar financial services may be offered by institutions that come under different regulators and are therefore subject to different regulatory requirements. The overlapping regulatory structure also becomes a barrier to innovation as any new product might need approval from more than one regulator. In some cases, it is not even clear which regulator has primary jurisdiction over the product. In addition, this multiplicity of regulators creates severe problems with interagency coordination. In India, these coordination mechanisms are not formalized, and though these mechanisms can be effective in emergencies, they are not quite as effective at other times. Coordination problems are aggravated by the uneven skills and experience across regulators.

Regulatory structures need to be streamlined to avoid regulatory inconsistencies, gaps, overlap, and arbitrage. Steps in this direction should include reducing the number of regulators, defining their jurisdiction wherever possible in terms of functions rather than the forms of the players, and ensuring a level playing field by making all players performing a function report to the same regulator regardless of their size or ownership.

As also recommended by the HPEC on MIFC and the CFSR, there is merit in moving toward greater convergence of financial market regulation. The important gains achievable from this convergence are lower transaction costs due to economies of scale and scope, regulators being less prone to capture, elimination of gaps and weaknesses in regulation, greater focus on financial inclusion and literacy efforts, seamless market development, and better risk management for systemic stability. Another important gain of regulatory convergence is that it would ensure equal regulatory treatment of financial entities (in terms of

24. Planning Commission (2009) and HPEC on MIFC (Ministry of Finance 2007).

authorization, enforcement, or disciplinary decision) with similar risk characteristics, product lines, and operation in similar markets.

Options that can be explored to achieve greater regulatory convergence, based on
recommendations of various government committees, fall into two main categories.

The first category concerns *different degrees of convergence*. One option is convergence of the commodity derivatives and securities market, that is, one regulator for the equity, corporate debt, equity derivatives, and commodity derivatives markets. Another option is convergence of organized financial trading, that
is, one regulator for the aforementioned commodity derivatives and securities
market plus interest rate derivatives, foreign exchange derivatives, government
securities, and all derivatives thereon. The third option would be convergence
of all financial sector regulators, that is, one regulator for all of the above plus
insurance and pensions, with the central bank retaining regulatory control over
the banking sector.[25]

The second category concerns *policy level convergence*. This would mean that
all financial sector regulation and regulators would be covered under a single legislative enactment and under a single department, even with multiple regulators.

Each of these alternatives needs to be explored.

Along with streamlining the regulatory framework, there is also a need to
review the actual financial regulations, which tend to be "rule based" and overly
prescriptive, inserting every minute detail into the basic legislation and including detailed subordinated rules and regulations. The suggestion here is to move
toward more principles-based regulation to promote financial innovation and
avoid the mistake of over-regulation. However, even if the regulatory system
continues to be rules-based, then given the pace of financial innovation that a
country that is growing as fast as India requires, there should definitely be a constant revisiting of the rules that are in place. Otherwise, the system risks getting
stuck in an old set of rules that will restrict the pace of growth in the country.
Regulatory impact assessment could serve as an important tool for evaluating
the costs and benefits of various aspects of the regulatory architecture and implementation to guard against the error of over-regulation.

## FINANCIAL INCLUSION
A robust financial system is not as socially relevant if most people in the country
do not have access to it. Financial inclusion is a key priority for India, especially

---

25. The CFSR as well as the HPEC on MIFC recommend unification of all regulatory and
supervisory functions connected with organized financial trading into a single agency, that is, the
SEBI. On the issue of regulation of the banking sector, the CFSR recommends that all banks and
any other deposit-taking entities should come under one supervisor, the RBI.

Figure 9-1. *Current Regulatory Architecture*[a]

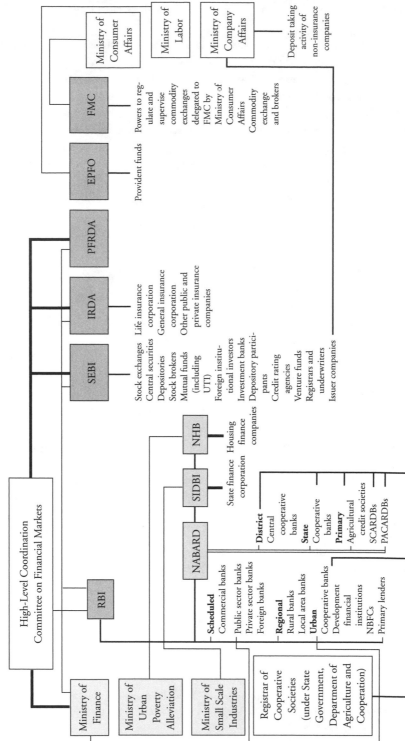

Central government agency

Tier 1 regulatory agencies each established through acts of parliament

Second tier regulator supervisory agencies, each established through acts of parliament. These institutions perform refinancing functions.

Implicit role as MoF representatives are on the Boards of SEBI, IRDA, RBI. Representatives of the MoF and MoSSI are also on the Board of SIDBI, and representatives of the MoUD are on the Board of NHB. The MoF is also represented on the boards of public sector banks, public sector Development Financial Institutions, Life Insurance Corporation, and General Insurance Corporation.

Explicit regulation and supervison

Members of the High-Level Coordination Committee on financial markets

Supervision but no regulatory role

Source: CFSR 2008, from World Bank, "India: Aligning India's Financial Regulatory and Supervisory Architecture with Country Needs, June 2005," Washington.

a. EPFO, Employees' Provident Fund Organisation; PFRDA, Pension Fund Regulatory and Development Authority; FMC, Forward Markets Commission; IRDA, Insurance Regulatory and Development Authority; MoF, Ministry of Finance; MoSSI, Ministry of Small Scale Industries; MoUD, Ministry of Urban Development; NABARD, National Bank for Agriculture and Rural Development; NBFCs, Non Bank Finance Companies; NHB, National Housing Bank; PACARDBs, primary cooperative agriculture and rural development banks; RBI, Reserve Bank of India; SCARDBs, state cooperative agriculture and rural development banks; SIDBI, Small Industries Development Bank of India; UTI, Unit Trust of India.

for rural India. The following are some recent initiatives for achieving greater financial inclusion:

—The list of banking correspondents has been expanded to include individual petty, medical, and fair price shop owners and agents of small savings schemes of the Government of India, insurance companies, and retired teachers.

—Establishment of off-site ATMs has been de-licensed.

—RBI is presently reviewing the priority sector lending guidelines and the feasibility of trading in priority sector lending certificates, as recommended by the CFSR.

—A proposal to grant a few more licenses to local area banks for a fixed period of time is also under consideration.

—A working group of RBI has recommended removing the interest rate ceiling on loans up to Rs 200,000.

Financial sector policies in India have long been driven by the objective of increasing financial inclusion, but universal inclusion is still quite some distance away. The past strategy for expanding the reach of the financial system relied primarily on expanding branching, setting up special-purpose government-sponsored institutions, and setting targets for credit to broad categories of the excluded. The success of these approaches has been mixed. A new strategy for financial inclusion is needed that builds on the lessons of the past. It needs to be recognized that financial inclusion is not only about credit but also involves providing a wide range of financial services, including savings accounts, insurance, and remittance products. Efforts at financial inclusion need to move away from sectors to segments of people that are excluded. Past efforts have focused largely on agriculture. As the Indian economy diversifies and more people move away from farming, there is an urgent need to focus on other segments as well, for instance, the poor in urban areas. Product innovation, organizational flexibility, and superior cost efficiency are essential in reaching the excluded and offering them financial services that they will want to use. Competition and technology as well as the use of low-cost, local organizations for outreach will have to play a much greater role in any such strategy.

## Government Debt Management

As mentioned earlier, a key issue confronting the government securities markets is that the central bank is also the manager of public debt in the country, which leads to a series of conflicts. There is a strong international consensus that a well-run economy should have a dedicated, consolidated public debt manager and that the central bank should not, in general, perform this role. A number of expert committees have commented on the undesirability of burdening the RBI with the task of selling bonds for the government. Both the HPEC on MIFC and the CFSR emphasize the need for creation of an independent Indian "debt management office (DMO),"operating either as an autonomous agency or an office under the Ministry of Finance.[26] The separation of debt and monetary management would provide the central bank the necessary independence in monetary management, with neither the need to provide credit to the government nor the responsibility to ensure that government borrowings are incurred at low cost. A vibrant government securities market requires the professional capability of an independent DMO for engaging with the market, building a long-term relationship with investors, and obtaining money from the market at a good price. The objective of the independent DMO should be to minimize the medium- to long-term cost of the debt, with due regard for the risks in the debt portfolio, aside from promoting development of the domestic debt market. Thus a DMO would set the stage for modernization of the bond markets and establishing of the bond-currency-derivatives nexus, complementing the strategy for financial sector reforms in the country.

### FRAMEWORK FOR INSTITUTIONAL INVESTMENTS

Various segments of the financial markets can develop and thrive only when participation in them is not artificially constrained. The most successful parts of Indian finance at present are those in which noninstitutional participants have taken a lead and engaged in speculative price discovery. This large mass of retail participation in financial markets is a unique edge that India has when compared with other international financial markets. However, considering that India is striving to develop Mumbai as an international financial center, the capabilities and strengths of institutional investors also need to be harnessed. This class of investors brings with them sophisticated analytical tools in quantitative trading systems, pools of capital, and the potential to help link Indian finance with the rest of the world. Thus the strategy should be to remove the constraints on institutional investors to allow them to reap the benefits of financial market innovations and in turn assist these markets with depth and liquidity. The regulators should move gradually to a "prudent man" principle in which the institutional investor is allowed to exercise judgment based on what a prudent man might deem to be appropriate investments.

### COMPETITION

Lack of sufficient competition in parts of the financial services industry, the pervasiveness of public ownership, and the over-compartmentalization of subsectors have resulted in suboptimal performance by existing market players. Competition needs to be across larger, more capable players rather than among a plethora

---

26. See Planning Commission (2009, pp. 38–42); Ministry of Finance (2007, pp. 191–92).

of small, weak, undercapitalized players that cannot capture economies of scale or make the kinds of investments in people, training, technology, and research into product development that supports innovation. The Indian financial sector needs a wave of consolidation—through acquisitions and mergers among private and publicly owned institutions—for its financial firms to be strong enough to compete as aggressively as they should with each other, and with foreign firms, in Indian and global markets. A license to operate in a certain area of Indian finance is, all too often, a safe sinecure with stable profits and a near-zero probability of death. There is therefore little incentive to innovate to remain competitive. This is not unlike firms in the real economy before 1992. For a shift into a high-innovation regime, both carrot and stick are required. The stick would be the introduction of competition: entry barriers in domestic finance and protectionism need to be removed. The carrot would be the significantly reduced cost of innovation that would result from a different regulatory attitude and approach. In addition, a shift from a domestically focused to an internationally focused financial sector would induce the associated carrot of enormously larger market size.

FINANCIAL STABILITY

The CFSR has especially touched upon the goal of improving financial stability as an important reason for pursuing financial sector reforms. Financial stability is the key to the sound functioning of the financial markets and the economy itself. By definition, this is a multi-agency function. Though not explicitly located by law in any agency, the task of maintaining financial stability in India at the moment lies with the interregulatory body know as the HLCCFM (High-Level Coordination Committee on Financial Markets). It is chaired by the governor of the central bank and has members from other regulatory agencies. This committee has no legal backing and hence lacks powers of enforcement.

There is also a general feeling that more needs to be done on regulation and supervision of financial conglomerates. As was evident during the recent global crisis, any financial firm whose combination of size, leverage, and interconnectedness could pose a threat to financial stability if it failed should be subject to robust consolidated supervision and regulation. The CFSR report also notes that as financial conglomerates begin to dominate the system, a consolidated system of supervision becomes more important.[27]

All this points to the need for improved inter-regulatory coordination and for strengthening and consolidating regulatory structures to deal with large, complex, systemically important financial conglomerates, on the one hand, and with the needs of the consumer, on the other. It is important to examine practices

27. Planning Commission (2009, chap. 6).

that are evolving in other jurisdictions and formalize a structure for handling issues of financial stability.

## STRENGTHENING INTERREGULATORY COORDINATION

The recent global financial crisis has drawn a lot of attention to the role of regulatory bodies. The countries of the Group of Twenty have increasingly been discussing the need for greater coordination not only between regulatory bodies but also between member countries and jurisdictions as well. India has recently become a member of the Financial Stability Board and is striving for membership in the Financial Action Task Force. Response to these international bodies has to be timely and often requires input from regulators at very short notice. As India moves in the direction of carrying out a financial sector assessment program, as per the criteria specified by international standard-setting bodies, it is in the interest of all concerned that the present arrangements are fortified to cater to the upcoming requirements.

This point can be reiterated while looking at the issues of anti–money laundering and combating the financing of terrorism (AML-CFT), which cut across the entire financial system and require a properly coordinated approach. For example, at present AML-CFT is handled by each regulator in its own way. There is a need to house the coordination of this program with an agency that can take a holistic view of the threats, vulnerabilities, and risks associated with AML-CFT, cutting across all institutions.

Similarly, issues such as financial literacy, regulation of financial and investment advisers, and reduction of products arbitrage (as in the case of ULIPs and other mutual funds) also require a more formal structure of inter-regulatory coordination than the present one. The case of entities like credit rating agencies is particularly interesting as they are regulated by one agency (SEBI) but their ratings have an impact on the entities regulated by other regulatory bodies. Inadequate inter-regulatory coordination in this area may create disharmony in the system.

The HLCCFM was a good mechanism when it was set up. However, to keep pace with subsequent developments, it needs to evolve with the times in order to be more effective, because the markets that are regulated by members of the HLCCFM have dramatically changed since 1992. It is generally agreed that over time markets have become more complex and converged and are becoming increasingly integrated. In light of these trends, if regulators do not adopt an integrated and holistic view, supervision will be suboptimal. The aforementioned issues, namely, the requirement for more organized inter-regulatory coordination, furthering of the reforms agenda, and financial stability, draw attention to the need for strengthening the present inter-regulatory coordination mechanism. The CFSR has recommended setting up a financial sector oversight agency (FSOA) by statute to focus on macroprudential as well as supervisory issues in the financial markets; develop periodic assessments of macroeconomic risks and risk concentrations, as well as risk exposures in the economy; monitor the function of large, systemically important financial conglomerates as well as large systemically important financial institutions that would otherwise be unregulated; anticipate potential risks and initiate balanced supervisory action to support efforts by the concerned regulator to address those risks; and address and defuse inter-regulatory conflicts.[28] Thus the FSOA will take over the work now done by the HLCCFM, with the advantage that it would have legal backing and the support of a permanent secretariat. This recommendation is worth taking forward.

## Conclusion

Has the global financial crisis necessitated a change in India's approach and commitment to financial sector development on the lines of recommendations of certain recent government committees? I am of the opinion that it has not. As can be seen from the discussion in the section of this chapter that traced the development of various segments of India's financial markets, the Indian approach to the development of financial markets has focused on a gradual, phased, and calibrated opening of the domestic financial and external sectors, taking into account reforms in other sectors of the economy. This continues to be the overall stand on reforms, even after the global crisis, though policies for the financial sector seem to be a little more cautious. However, given that a lot of the agenda of financial sector reforms in India has consisted of permitting formerly banned financial markets, strengthening regulation, plugging regulatory gaps, and strengthening regulatory coordination, recent global developments have in no way diluted this agenda.

An important issue that is being debated at various domestic and international forums following the crisis is the perils presented by OTC products. There is a move toward mandating a transparent trading framework for these products and more regulatory oversight. India has always favored exchange-traded financial products over OTC products due to the firm belief that OTC markets carry with them large and unknown counterparty credit risks, are not transparent, hinder competition, and, given all this, have systemic implications for financial stability.

Among the right lessons that can be drawn from the crisis are:

—Innovation in financial markets should not be strangled. However, it should be ensured that the complexities of new products are understood, especially if

---

28. Note that large, non-deposit-taking, nonbanking financial companies may borrow from both banks and mutual funds, and are properly an inter-regulatory concern, hence they would be under the purview of an FSOA.

they are traded off exchanges as OTC products. When widely distributed and poorly understood, such products are dangerous to systemic stability.

—Too much risk aversion on the part of regulators can impede growth and development.

—There is no perfect regulatory architecture, but institutional design needs to be in tune with markets and requirements.

Inclusion, growth, and stability are the three objectives of any reform process, and these objectives are contradictory. With the right reforms, the financial sector can be an enormous source of job creation both directly as well as indirectly, through the enterprise and consumption it can support with financing. Without reforms, however, the financial sector could become an increasing source of risk, as the mismatches between the capacity and the needs of the real economy and the capabilities of the financial sector widen. India has been a case study in how financial sector reforms can play a supporting role in the growth of an emerging market economy. The challenge is how to bootstrap from these past successes to escalate to the next level of financial sector development, so that it can continue to support the growth that India targets or desires going forward.

## References

Beck, Thorsten, Asli Demirgüç-Kunt, and Ross Levine. 2009. "Financial Institutions and Markets across Countries and over Time—Data and Analysis." Policy Research Working Paper 4943. Washington, D.C.: World Bank (May).

Dorrucci, Ettore, Alexis Meyer-Cirkel, and Daniel Santabárbara. 2009. "Domestic Financial Development in Emerging Economies: Evidence and Implications." Occasional Paper Series 102. Frankfurt am Main: European Central Bank (April).

Futures Industry Association. 2009. "2008: A Wild Ride—Annual Volume Survey." *Futures Industry Annual Volume Survey, Magazine of the Futures Industry* (March).

Insurance Regulatory and Development Authority. 2008. *Annual Report 2007-08*. Basheerbagh, Hyderabad.

ISEC Securities. 2007. "Indian Life Insurance." December 7, p. 43.

Levine, Ross. 1997. "Financial Development and Economic Growth: Views and Agenda." *Journal of Economic Literature* 35, no. 2: 688–726.

Ministry of Finance, Government of India. 2007. *Mumbai—An International Financial Centre. Report of the High Powered Expert Committee.* New Delhi: Sage Publications India Private Limited.

Planning Commission, Government of India. 2009. *A Hundred Small Steps. Report of the Committee on Financial Sector Reforms.* New Delhi: Sage Publications India Private Limited.

Standard & Poor's. 2009. *Standard & Poor's Global Stock Markets Factbook 2009.* New York.

Thomas, Susan. 2006. "How the Financial Sector Was Reformed." In *Documenting Reforms: Case Studies from India,* edited by S. Narayan, pp. 171–210. Bangalore: Macmillan Publishing India.

World Bank. 1997. *Global Economic Prospects and the Developing Countries: 1997.* Washington, D.C.

———. 2005. "India: Aligning India's Financial Regulatory and Supervisory Architecture with Country Needs." Washington, D.C. (June).

World Economic Forum (WEF). 2008. *The Financial Development Report 2008.* Geneva.

———. 2009. *The Financial Development Report 2009.* Geneva.

World Federation of Exchanges. 2008. *Annual Report and Statistics 2008.* Paris.

# PART V

# Improving Financial Access in Emerging Markets

# 10

## Universalizing Complete Access to Finance: Key Conceptual Issues

SUYASH RAI, BINDU ANANTH, AND NACHIKET MOR

A household's financial life can be seen as a combination of exposure to time and contingent states. Financial wealth can be seen as a combination of assets that are currently owned and the present value of future income discounted at an appropriate risk-adjusted rate. Financial services must help a household manage and increase its consumption smoothly and fully utilize its human capital, financial capital, and other resources to improve its well-being. There are, therefore, two core functions that the financial system has to fulfill for each and every household: first, management of risk by movement of resources across contingent states, and second, intertemporal consumption smoothing by movement of resources across time.

The outcomes of any financial inclusion effort must be benchmarked to these core functions. All financial products and services as well as institutions are means to achieve these outcomes in an efficient manner. Financial markets and institutions should evolve to promote complete markets that allow households to hedge future uncertainty by trading in every state of the world.[1] Consumers

All views expressed in this chapter are those of the authors alone.

1. Arrow (1964) details how risky financial securities can help in risk management by allocation of risk bearing. Arrow and Debreu (1954) develop the idea of an integrated model of production, exchange, and consumption in a complete market. Debreu (1959) captures uncertainty by expanding the characteristics in the model used to define consumption goods by making them state contingent, where all possible future states of the world are defined by unique combinations of a set of environmental variables.

should be able to bundle together securities in portfolios to choose patterns of consumption expenditure over uncertain states of nature.[2] By enabling trade in insurance policies covering factors outside the economic system, financial services can help overcome the problem of uncertainty that prevents certain markets from coming into being and allow the allocation achieved to be efficient and therefore welfare-enhancing.[3]

Financial providers can significantly help households manage idiosyncratic risks. Financial contracts at regional levels may also protect against certain regional-level idiosyncratic risks (but systemic risks for the household) such as natural disasters. At a greater scale, mechanisms could be developed that help countries globally pool and hedge risks, such as economic depression, rapid currency devaluation, inflation, and so on. It is argued that macro-securities, traded at national, regional, and industry levels, are critical aspects of a comprehensive risk management strategy.[4] Certain other risks, such as macro-longevity risk, challenge finance as a science to develop mechanisms to manage the risk without simply increasing the buffer (risk capital).[5]

The functions of a well-operating financial system would remain stable across contexts—rural and urban, developed country and developing country, rich and poor.[6] These functions are universal, and they are particularly important for low-income households, who often constitute a good part of the financially excluded population. Low resource levels merely imply that while mistakes are expensive for everyone, they are far more so for low-income households that juggle many balls to survive.[7] Though the functions remain stable, the products, delivery channels, delivery institutions, market infrastructure, and the regulatory and supervisory framework required to deliver on these functions may change significantly across contexts. The question is, how can the financial system help households fulfill these functions in an efficient and orderly manner?

In this chapter, we take the functions as a given and focus on the "how" question, considering the conceptual issues arising in an emerging market context,

---

2. Financial securities play two important roles in spreading risk: they eliminate diversifiable (individual) risk from consumption expenditure and transfer non-diversifiable (market) risk across consumers.

3. Arrow (2009).

4. See Shiller (2003) for detailed discussions on such systemic risk and the macro securities to manage them.

5. For a discussion on the importance of macro-longevity risk and the extent of buffer required by pension funds to reduce the probability of underfunding, see Hari and others (2008).

6. On the functional perspective of finance, see Bodie and Merton (1993); Merton and Bodie (1993, 1995, 2005); Merton (1995).

7. See Collins and others (2009) for detailed discussions on households' financial diaries that document financial activities at the household level.

especially those related to product design, product delivery, and channel design. (Taking this to the next level of detail would require considering national and sub-national contexts.) In the next section, we discuss two stylized approaches for delivering financial services, both with different implications for the roles and responsibilities of clients, providers, and regulators. In the subsequent sections, we highlight select issues with policy implications that should be resolved for effective financial inclusion.

## Two Contrasting Blueprints of Financial Systems

At the front end, where the interaction between the clients and the financial system happens, there are many approaches that the financial services provider could take with respect to the way services are delivered to the clients. In a stylized sense, there are two types of approaches that could be taken: on one hand, the provider could follow a hands-off approach, basically making a menu of products available; on the other hand, the provider could actively advise clients and take responsibility for that advice. Detailed descriptions of these approaches follow.

### Product Menu–Driven Approach

This approach entails design and provision of several disaggregated, stand-alone products available from a variety of "product manufacturers" with a "thin" front end between manufacturers and clients. The front end in this system is typically an agent or distributor that markets the products to the customer. There may be functional overlap across products, but each product is sold as a discrete entity. In this approach, customers choose the set of products that makes sense to them, so there is heavy dependence on customers' ability to understand a variety of products and process features.

The extent to which the products have a positive or negative impact on the customer would depend on how well the customer can choose and use the appropriate product, within the eligibility constraints. So under this approach, the need is to have a set of well-designed products and an army of agents. The mis-selling concerns (discussed in more detail later) are more around communication of information on product features. This approach characterizes most financial systems currently prevalent. It is easy to see how this scales for many products such as insurance, collateralized loans, mutual funds, and payment products. Hence this approach has dominated most efforts toward financial inclusion, which is often defined in terms of access to one or a few products. Interactions between the product and the nature of a household's financial needs have been largely overlooked.

*Customized Financial Proposition Approach*

The alternative pathway is to develop and offer financial propositions (with underlying contingent claims) tailored to individual profiles, with effective and proactive risk selection and control.[8] The back end here continues to be a variety of product manufacturers, but the customer-facing front end is a financial institution that is not defined by a product frame.

In this interface, the provider would start with this question: given the balance sheet, goals, and risk preference of this household, how can I provide a financial proposition that helps it smooth consumption over its life cycle? The process would ideally start with the provider going through an intensive, structured interaction with the household that helps it understand the household's current financial and human capital situation (see discussion below), understand the nature of uncertainties faced by the household, assess the risk and time preference, and document the goals and priorities of the household. Then the provider would create a financial proposition that would fit the household's requirements. Presuming that an exact combination of products is possible, this should provide a kind of "wrapping" around the household, to protect it from risks, while helping move resources across time to smooth consumption.[9]

The underlying structures in both these approaches are equivalent from the financial functions point of view, but they differ mainly in the *process* of designing and delivering the interface between the customer and the system. So the key difference is in whether the frontline provider's focus is on the *customer* or on the *product,* and what the assumption about the customer's *expertise* is. For example, if the household owns livestock that is a primary source of income, in both cases the mechanism to insure the animal would be available, but in the integrated proposition approach it would be fundamental to any conversation with the individual, whereas in the disaggregated approach the product would be available to be purchased at the discretion of the client.

In the disaggregated approach, the household may be presumed to be the "expert" on choosing the right option, while in the former approach, based on the household's expressed risk preferences and goals, portfolio allocation

---

8. On the possibilities of customized financial propositions, see Aaron (1999); Bodie (2003); Bodie, Hammond, and Mitchell (2001); Merton (2001, 2002, 2003).

9. As an analogy, one could take the example of a general practitioner in a health system who looks at the overall health of the people enrolled with it. The practitioner is not just selling services but actually looking at the client outcomes, with some shared responsibility with the clients and with the drug companies and other suppliers. The practitioner starts by understanding the clients' health status, past illnesses, lifestyle, risk factors (like diabetes), and so on. Then she considers all these and the available solutions she is aware of, and prescribes a set of solutions that she believes would work for the client.

expertise is provided by the provider. This distinction and combining of these stylized approaches can have important implications for the eventual impact on a household's financial well-being. This is an important strategic question for the future of financial inclusion, for policy as well as practice.

Chapter 11 of this volume, by Alfred Hannig and Stefan Jansen, gives a good sense of the progress made in the financial inclusion efforts worldwide and covers some of the important issues that the sector is currently dealing with to ensure expansion of financial access, as well as the implications thereof in terms of impact at the micro- and macro-level. It is being observed that in countries like India, with the rapid rise of commercial microfinance, the viability of the product menu–driven approach is increasing, and institutions are expanding the range of services being offered.[10]

In a way, this chapter complements the one by Hannig and Jansen by discussing issues related to the next stage in financial inclusion efforts and by looking beyond just making basic products available. In the next section, we discuss certain conceptual challenges and consider the two approaches for financial inclusion in light of these challenges.

## Select Conceptual Challenges in Financial Inclusion

It is important to consider the implications of the two blueprints discussed above and to evaluate their potential in terms of their implications for fulfilling the functions of finance efficiently and effectively.

### Designing Products: Simplicity and Complexity

In the wake of the "subprime crisis," there has been a lot of discussion about the complexity and simplicity of products, and how this affects usage and outcomes. The school of thought that places the onus of financial literacy on the customer is in a "race to simplify." However, we worry that, from a financial inclusion perspective, this significantly undermines the true potential of finance. Consider the following examples.

Two of the ways for a farmer to finance her sowing operation could be through a crop loan payable in equal monthly installments, or through a crop loan where principal and interest payments are linked to the amount of rainfall obtained in her region. Clearly, for the provider, the first product is simpler to design, provide, and communicate. The latter is complex because it combines a loan with insurance-like features and will require the lender to hedge the rainfall risk at its level. At the time of disbursing the loan, the provider in the second

10. See Cull, Demirgüç-Kunt, and Morduch (2008) for a discussion on commercialization of microfinance and its implications.

instance would not be able to give the farmer a "simple" fixed repayment schedule. However, from the perspective of the functionality required for a farmer to manage volatile income streams, the latter appears to be a superior alternative because the financial products absorb the volatility. In the first case, the volatility for the farmer is perhaps exacerbated by adding a fixed outflow to a very volatile cash flow, making the farmer worse off. In the second case, the provider uses its expertise to integrate a solution for the farmer, which she or he otherwise might not be able to create without such expert support.

Often there are underlying assumptions about product pricing and design that the client may not be aware of, and the client's decision may become impossibly complex to make. One example would be financing the retirement stage. The client would like to fulfill the function by entering into mechanisms that help him save money during times of income and invest it in a combination of assets so that an adequate amount is available during the retirement stage. He also would want to manage longevity risk and heath risk after retirement, because both these risks may render the savings inadequate. There is expected selection bias priced into mechanisms to manage either of these risks.[11] An annuity would be priced to take into account the fact that a person who is not well would not want to purchase it, while the health insurance is priced with the opposite logic, that is, a person who is likely to fall ill is more likely to purchase it. Both are selection biases that offset each other to some extent, and bundling an annuity with health insurance (or long-term care insurance) should bring the price down for the household. So, even though it is simple for the provider to sell stand-alone health insurance (or long-term care insurance) products, most clients would not be able to understand the underlying logic of product design and actuarial calculation, and therefore would not be able to enter into the appropriate financial contract.

Who does simplicity favor in cases like these? Disaggregated product delivery leaves households with the responsibility for making decisions about product choices. Individuals and households are essentially looking to fulfill certain functions that could be fulfilled by a number of product combinations, with varying degrees of efficiency and convenience for the household. Even if each product is individually easy to understand, together the products may pose a technically complex financial decision involving detailed asset allocation and estimates of the optimal level of goal financing required at different stages of life, including savings for the postretirement phase. This is an important design issue for financial inclusion because the eventual effectiveness of financial inclusion would depend significantly on how the products are used by the households, which in turn depends on how the products are designed.

11. See Merton (2003) for a detailed explanation of this example.

## *Fixing Responsibilities: Provider's and Client's Responsibilities for Outcomes*

There is a need for a detailed assessment of the extent to which the different stakeholders could be held accountable for client outcomes. In addition to the clients, there are four categories of stakeholders that could be held accountable:

—advisors and providers of financial services, who interface between clients and the financial system;

—risk aggregators and fund managers, who manage client portfolios;

—third party agencies like rating agencies, which minimize the market information asymmetry; and

—regulators and the central bank, which are responsible for the overall stewardship of the system.

Several debates on financial literacy have placed the onus on the customer to understand the intricacies of financial mechanisms, but there is insufficient emphasis on the capability of the provider and its preparedness for counseling customers on financial choices. How well trained is the customer representative of the provider in helping customers navigate complex life cycle finance choices? There is a case for placing much greater importance on provider and distributor financial literacy to ensure good customer outcomes.

Instead of passing the responsibility entirely onto clients, frontline finance workers could take the responsibility of analyzing household typologies based on risk profiles (high dependence on wage income, high volatility of cash flows due to rainfall risk) and use automated expert systems that match these profiles with financial portfolios (combinations of savings, investments, loans, and insurance mechanisms). The providers could use their expertise to build systems to implement a comprehensive process and support the financial decisions of their clients.

Here is a detailed example of such a process. As a first step in financial planning, the provider could help the client visualize cash flows over time. Adding uncertainty to some of these cash flows would reveal potential stress points in the lifecycle of the client. The task of the provider is then to advise the clients so that they can protect themselves against catastrophic scenarios while ensuring that their goals are financed and a basic level of consumption is maintained across the lifecycle.

Figures 10-1 through 10-3 visually represent the financial life of a household with four members: a husband (age thirty-four), a wife (age thirty-two), and two children (a boy age ten and a girl age eight). All persons except the girl (who will be married off) will be involved in wage labor from age twenty-one to age sixty. The man earns Rs150 a day; the woman, Rs 120 a day. All living, educational, and medical expenses are also included in the calculations. Figure 10-1 shows the wealth paths for this household across the best and worst "states of the

Figure 10-1.  *Life Wealth Envelope for Example Household
without Any Financial Mechanisms*[a]

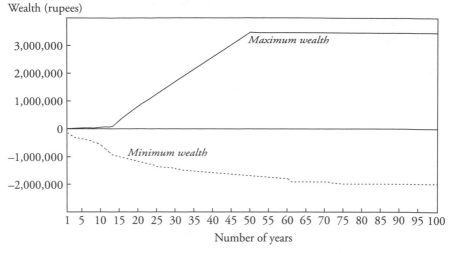

Wealth (rupees)

Source: Authors' calculations.
a. Solid and dashed lines indicate track wealth under best and worst state-of-the-world scenarios, respectively.

world" without any financial mechanisms. Please note that the x-axis represents years, while the y-axis represents the wealth level at a point in time.

Figure 10-2 shows the cash flow paths for this household across the best and the worst states of the world if life insurance is purchased for the earning members up to the extent of their human capital, and disability insurance is purchased to the extent of loss of human capital plus living expenses for the remaining years. As can be seen, the life-wealth "envelope" becomes narrower and shifts upward, with the financial situation in the worst state of the world improving because the risks are insured against.

Figure 10-3 shows the cash flow paths for the example household across the best and the worst states of the world if the family also buys an asset worth Rs 100,000 fifteen years hence and makes Rs 30,000 annually out of it, in a way extending its earning life beyond the working years of the earning member.

This example illustrates how a provider could use its expertise and household information to model the financial lives of clients and take responsibility for advising them about their financial decisions. Now, in this example, if the provider had advised this household to take a big loan without purchasing an adequate insurance policy, would this amount to mis-selling? Perhaps it would because even a cursory analysis by the provider could have shown the need for insurance in the household. In this instance, the situation is somewhat clear, but there may be cases where things are somewhat ambiguous. Defining the

Figure 10-2. *Life Wealth Envelope for Example Household with Life and Disability Insurance*

Wealth (rupees)

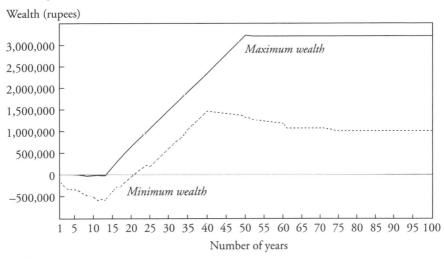

Source: Authors' calculations.

provider's responsibility would require a detailed assessment of what the provider can help the household with. The example just discussed shows that a provider may be able to do much more than what is presently being offered. This issue is further explored later in the context of communication between providers and clients.

Provider skills and capability are one aspect of the story. Directly following from this is the issue of providers' accountability, based on the roles they play vis-à-vis the financial decision-making by clients, especially if a bad customer outcome obtains.

Most product liability regimens go by the Latin maxim *volenti non fit injuria*, or "a person is not wronged by that to which he or she consents."[12] Lack of consent is seen as the main ground for pressing legal liability against the provider. This paradigm has to be nuanced in the context of financial services. Unlike physical products, financial products lack visibility, and unlike many services, they reveal their real outcomes some time down the line from the time of purchase. The client has limited ability to assess ex ante the quality of the product and its impact. Consenting to a thirty-page contract written in complex language when all providers have similar looking contracts does not mean much. So the regulation has to start by setting fair ground rules to enable truly informed

12. Geistfeld (2010).

Figure 10-3. *Life Wealth Envelope for Example Household with Insurance and Financial Asset*

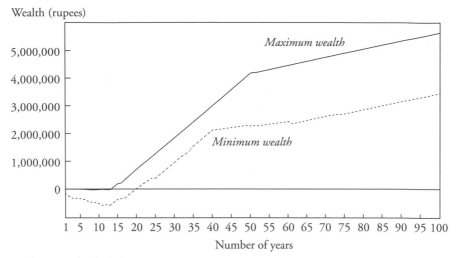

Source: Authors' calculations.

consent. There also may be a case for ex-post liability regimes in the context of financial service providers.

There are factors in financial service delivery that might lead to bad customer outcomes if provider liability is lacking in the system. For example, there are financial products in which returns to the clients may suffer due to excessive speculation by the provider.[13] Also, there are situations where the complicated underlying design of the product challenges the client's ability to understand and analyze the risks associated with the product. There is also the possibility of a provider not disclosing the risks or losses clearly, that is, not making clients aware of losses that might occur in certain states of the world, or informing clients about the losses much later, when nothing can be done about them. Hence provider liability is critical when it comes to transparency and information dissemination of financial products. Some of these factors probably can be controlled by enhancing providers' liability, both ex ante and ex post, and therefore the regulations have to be set accordingly to bolster the financial system.

However, the imposition of excessive product liability may become so expensive for the providers that it impedes their active efforts to innovate for a client's benefit.[14] Similarly, as in any product liability mechanism, the regulators would

13. Bankers' Trust is an example here, where speculation to increase returns led to losses for several clients.

14. This issue has been debated in other industries subject to rigid product liability regimes.

need to minimize misuse of the liability for making unreasonable claims. How can the incentives of the providers be aligned with the long-term implications for the clients in an efficient manner? The real challenge lies in ensuring that the products are well designed and that communication between the provider and the client is high quality from the customer's perspective. How can one tell ex post whether a purchase was preceded by adequate understanding, and to what extent can the provider be held accountable for failure on this front? Clearly, the policymakers would need to start by closely examining how the industry manages the risks and uncertainty inherent in designing and commercializing products and processes. Subsequent to this, they should try to carefully draw lines between the liabilities of various stakeholders, including the regulators.

It is not just the risk aggregators and providers of products that are liable; there are also other agencies playing important roles in connecting clients with the financial system. For example, the rating agencies' role has come under much scrutiny in recent times. How can liability be fixed on them for their rating, which has advice implicitly embedded in the "product"?

The role of regulators and policymakers is to consider the overall financial system and ensure that its development proceeds in a stable and sustainable manner. Poor regulation can lead to inadequate management of systemic risk, which can lead to unfavorable outcomes at various levels in the system, including for the households. So, in some such cases, the responsibility would belong to the regulator and policymakers, and these players must find a way to compensate the household's losses, after a due process of establishing responsibility.[15] This can be seen as a part of the responsibility of the regulator.

The clients themselves have to be held responsible for the decisions that they do make in full cognizance. Here the key issues that may confound provider liability are, first, how to ensure that this regulation does not amplify moral hazard on the clients' part, and second, how to know that clients' behavioral biases did not lead to suboptimal outcomes.

## Communication about Product Features

As discussed earlier, the availability of multiple financial products presumes a fair amount of expertise on the part of the clients.[16] Most clients are not trained in finance, and the increasing complexity underlying the product contracts is difficult even for trained people to understand. Moreover, product contracts have not done much to help the clients make the right choices. For example, credit

---

15. See Giesen (2006) for an argument for treating the liability of supervisors as a regular form of civil law liability (either in tort or contract).

16. For more on the challenges faced by customers in dealing with complex non customized products, see Merton and Bodie (2005) and Willis (2008).

card contracts have become so incomprehensible that the cost of understanding them may be quite high.[17] These challenges will be faced by those who are going to be financially included.

Understanding the process of communication between the provider and the client is important. There are essentially four ways in which the provider can communicate with the customer:

—information: explaining the product features;

—computation: helping the customer understand the implications of a certain product or set of products in the specific context of the household;

—advice: offering an integrated financial proposition to the client as advice; and

—decision: deciding on behalf of the client.

In the first instance, the provider may just share appropriate product details with the clients in a transparent, easy-to-understand format. However, even if these details are provided, the household still faces the task of estimating the impact of certain product decisions on its life. This is primarily a challenge of estimation (of optimal liquidity requirements at different stages of life) and computation (the math about implications). In the second way of communicating with a customer, the provider may help the customer understand the implications of specific product decisions by doing the computation and simulation based on inputs received from the household. In the preceding section's discussion on the responsibility of providers, a detailed example of such a computation and simulation tool is presented. Both of these kinds of communication exist in the product menu–driven approach to product design.

The third kind of communication entails the provider developing an integrated financial proposition on behalf of the client, offering it as advice, and letting the client decide. In this alternative, the onus will be on the provider to explain the rationale for the advice. This kind of communication necessarily builds on "computation" that supports the development of advice to be given to the clients.

In the fourth approach to communication, the provider decides on behalf of the clients. This alternative is actually not rare. It is crucial to highlight that *defaults* in products and *bundling* of products have advice built into them, in a manner that decisions are made on behalf of the clients. This is conceptually different from offering customized financial propositions wherein the proposition is provided as an expert's "advice" and the decision is made by the clients. The rationale for the last approach is often put in terms of the household's limitation in making the right decisions. For example, a self-control bias is given as a rationale for putting defaults in saving plans. Similarly, the microfinance institutions that

---

17. See Warren (2007) for a discussion on increasing complexity in product communication.

bundle the life insurance product with the loan presume that the client would not purchase it and thus leave the lender and family exposed to mortality risk.

Since the household's decisions may be shaped significantly by the method of communication, this issue is an important one when considering financial inclusion.[18] Though the product menu–driven approach based simply on information may be easier for the provider, the client perspective needs to be carefully considered. Just providing information on products leaves the entire process of computation and (self) advice with the clients, who often lack the expertise or time to fulfill these functions comprehensively. In the integrated proposition approach, the providers would need to modify their client communication strategy by expanding the scope of communication from just offering product information to providing computational support and advice to clients. The decision itself may be left with the clients, but the support from the providers would enable more optimal decisions.

## Behavioral Issues in Product Design and Delivery

There is some evidence indicating that individuals may not be perfect consumption smoothers. People may not be smoothing consumption over individual lifetimes but rather letting it track income through the life cycle, spending more when earning more and spending less when earning less, even over the short term.[19] Various reasons have been cited for this observed suboptimal pattern. An increasing body of literature argues that clients' behavioral biases lead to suboptimal outcomes for them, challenging the assumption that individuals make perfectly rational decisions given their observable constraints.[20] One of the most prominent of these is the self-control bias that leads to suboptimal saving and borrowing decisions for the client. Such behavioral biases also may lead to suboptimal outcomes from financial access, even when the providers have ostensibly done their job.

Presuming for the time being that certain behavioral biases do exist, what then can be the response of the financial system? It could be argued that even when individuals do not behave in their own best interests, institutions may

18. Engelmann and others (2009) provide some evidence from neuro economics that people may follow "expert" advice on financial decisions even if it is suboptimal. Cole and others (2009) show how psychological manipulation in product communication affects purchase decisions.

19. See the study by Carroll and Summers (1991) on the relationship between income growth and consumption growth. For evidence on failure to smooth consumption over the short term, see Stephens (2003); Shapiro (2005); Huffman and Barenstein (2005).

20. On behavioral issues that may impede optimal financial decisions, see Tversky and Kahneman (1974); Laibson (1997); Loewenstein, O'Donoghue, and Rabin (2003); Thaler and Sunstein (2008); O'Donoghue and Rabin (2006).

evolve to offset this behavior and produce a net result that is equivalent to the individuals behaving optimally.[21] This could be done by designing products and processes that respond to the behavioral biases in a manner that induces individuals to select the right products to suit their behavioral profile. For example, commitment savings products and welfare-enhancing defaults in products may work for individuals facing self-control problems. Notwithstanding the potential merits of these possibilities, there are challenges inherent in this approach. It often entails making certain decisions on behalf of clients, and every such decision would require taking a normative stand on what will improve outcomes for individuals. For example, it is not obvious that a reduction of consumption to increase savings is necessarily a good thing, and it is difficult to estimate when that would be the case without having a clear understanding of discount factors specific to individuals.[22] Since there is diversity in the client group, clients should always be given a choice to self-select the right option.

Between the two alternative approaches to financial services delivery discussed earlier on, the integrated proposition approach seems more capable of customizing solutions that would fit the characteristics of the household. Just as the provider would assess the risk preference of the household, it could also find ways to interact with clients who are sophisticated about their biases and offer solutions that help these clients manage their portfolios in an optimal way.[23] An individual who is sophisticated about his or her biases could benefit from such arrangements, but those who are naive about their biases may end up using these mechanisms suboptimally, and may even give the provider opportunity to exploit that naiveté, with adverse effects on the client's welfare.[24] This is a much debated issue in the realm of financial services delivery and requires some kind of resolution for defining the role of the provider in ensuring effective financial inclusion.

### Defining the Household's Portfolio: Human Capital and Financial Capital

The current frameworks of financial planning and portfolio allocation are almost always limited to financial assets. However, the financially excluded are often also the financially poor, for many of whom the most important asset for much of their lifetime is their human capital. It would be important to formally

---

21. See Merton and Bodie (2005) for a conceptual discussion on how institutions can endogenously respond to behavioral limitations. See Thaler and Sunstein (2003) for examples and ideas on how "libertarian paternalism" could help individuals and households enhance their well-being.

22. Karlan and Morduch (2009) provide a detailed argument on this. Also see Mitchell (2005) for a broader set of arguments regarding the trade-off between welfare and liberty in a provider approach that preempts client behavior.

23. On sophistication and naiveté in behavioral biases, see O'Donoghue and Rabin (2001).

24. See DellaVigna and Malmendier (2004) on how sophistication or naiveté about self-control can affect contract design.

recognize the value and risk characteristics of human capital in portfolio alloca-tion decisions.[25] A landless laborer's human capital will be very different from that of a schoolteacher, both in terms of economic value and risk profiles. The human capital of many workers in rural areas may be fairly uncorrelated with the stock market trends, and this provides diversification opportunity for the household. At the same time, the worker's return on human capital is usually quite volatile, with equity-like features (but with low average returns as well), thus making it better for the worker to invest in debt instruments.

These human capital characteristics should be incorporated in any portfolio allocation decision. The design challenge is how to ensure that this happens. If the menu-driven approach is taken, the household is expected to factor in the human capital characteristics while making portfolio allocation decisions, whereas in the customized proposition approach, the characteristics would be understood by the provider and incorporated into the proposition. Even though the household is in the best position to understand its own human capital, it may not have the expertise to understand how this capital rates with financial capi-tal and how it can optimize the overall portfolio. The household may not have access to the data and tools that could help establish the relationship between various components of its portfolio, including human capital. Here again, exper-tise may be required to understand the characteristics of the household's human capital and advise the household on the basis of the overall portfolio it is manag-ing, thus offering a customized financial proposition.

*Features of the Delivery Channel*

Though the functions of finance may be stable, the products, channels, and institutions required to fulfill these functions keep changing. The exact features of the ideal channel may change based on the combination of functions and product to be provided, but there are certain features of the delivery channel that may be synonymous with high-quality financial inclusion. It is almost axiomatic that the financial services channel should be able to provide the services in a con-venient, flexible, reliable, and continuous manner.[26] Convenience and flexibility are required to make sure the delivery channel "fits" the needs of the clients. For example, low-income households have significant short-term consumption-smoothing needs, which could be fulfilled if they had convenient access to credit or saving facilities.[27] Low-income clients also seem highly time sensitive and

25. For discussions on this paradigm, see Bodie, Merton, and Samuelson (1992); Bodie (2002); Ibbotson and others (2007).

26. Morduch and Rutherford (2003) discuss these features of the delivery channel.

27. See Collins and others (2009) for a set of examples based on the financial diaries of poor households.

often prefer to pay relatively high interest rates for convenient and "doorstep" services. Reliability and continuity help the clients actively use the channel for implementing long-term financial decisions, especially when the clients are taking a risk on the institution (investment, insurance).

The presence of a well-designed channel induces important "state-of-mind effects," both among customers and noncustomers. The fact that there is an easily accessible branch with a trained person offering services may signal reliability and continuity of access that could have a direct impact on the way households would make decisions. Inclusion is not just the opportunity to make explicit use of services but also the state of the mind that results from feeling completely included. This notion of inclusion may lead to effects even among non-clients that are attributable to the presence of the institution. Even for the basic model of traditional banking, there is some evidence from India that increased branch presence in previously excluded areas led to a decrease in poverty.[28]

It may be argued that for complete financial inclusion, proximity of the channel to the clients is important to truly ensure high-quality access. Physical proximity could be seen as a prerequisite to ensuring flexibility, reliability, and convenience. Now, if one juxtaposes this notion of a "proximate" financial services delivery channel with the two blueprints for a financial system, it seems that this channel design may be consistent with the design required to enable the integrated financial proposition approach. Such a financial services delivery channel would enable providers to think innovatively about customer needs, the type of products and services made available, and the design of these products and services. Even though the product menu–driven approach could very well operate via such channels, the true potential of proximity would be realized better if the provider uses this proximity to apply the integrated financial proposition approach; otherwise, the understanding gained from such localization would be underutilized.

The channel essentially comprises technology and people. Technology should be secure and efficient, and the same holds true for people. Much of the human resources used to reach out to the underserved in the emerging markets is characterized by underskilled and untrained agents acting as interfaces between the provider and the customer. There are issues around incentive alignment, but there are also issues regarding the skills and capabilities of the front-end providers. Even if the role of the provider is just to sell the products, the front-end staff should be fully versed in what is being sold. If advice is being given to the clients, the provider's front end should have appropriately trained personnel.

---

28. Burgess and Pande (2005).

## Summing Up

Financial services are unlike physical products in their potential for customization and malleability. Inter-temporal consumption smoothing can be provided either through savings or loans, with or without collateral. A loan can involve weekly repayment or bullet repayment; a loan when combined with rainfall insurance can allow for skipping a payment when the monsoon fails; a remittance inflow can be swept instantaneously as an account balance into a money market mutual fund. This malleable feature of financial services is what makes them so important for enabling people, particularly those who are low income, to be financially included in formal systems.

In this chapter, we have presented two stylized models of financial systems. We make the case that in order to live up to the standards of a well-functioning, complete financial market (in an Arrow-Debreu sense of the term), designers will need to think about ways to deliver financial propositions that are customized to individual households by responding to their unique circumstances.[29] This will entail the presence of proximate, well-trained providers that intermediate between the customer and those large "product manufacturers" whose goal is financial well-being and not merely product sales. These providers would need to use expertise in financial advice or wealth management to develop integrated financial propositions for their clients. We have also highlighted some of the important debates that arise in making this stylized financial system a reality.

## References

Aaron, H., ed. 1999. *Behavioral Dimensions of Retirement Economics*. Brookings.

Arrow, K. J. 1964. "The Role of Securities in the Optimal Allocation of Risk-Bearing." *Review of Economic Studies* 31 (April): 91–96.

———. 2009. "Economic Theory and Financial Crisis." Speech at the Beijing Forum, November 7 (www.beijingforum.org/en/ShowArticle.asp?ArticleID=1450).

Arrow, K. J., and G. Debreu. 1954. "Existence of an Equilibrium for a Competitive Economy." *Econometrica* 22 (July): 265–90.

Bodie, Z. 2002. "Life-Cycle Finance in Theory and in Practice." Working Paper 2002-02. Boston University, School of Management.

———. 2003. "Thoughts on the Future: Life-Cycle Investing in Theory and Practice." *Financial Analysts Journal* 59, no. 1: 24–29.

Bodie, Z., P. B. Hammond, and O. S. Mitchell. 2001. "New Approaches to Analyzing and Managing Retirement Risks." *Benefits Quarterly* 17, no. 4: 72–83.

29. Arrow and Debreu (1954).

Bodie, Z., and R. C. Merton. 1993. "Pension Benefit Guarantees in the United States: A Functional Approach." In *The Future of Pensions in the United States*, edited by R. Schmitt, pp. 194–234. University of Pennsylvania Press.

Bodie, Z., R. C. Merton, and W. Samuelson. 1992. "Labor Supply Flexibility and Portfolio Choice in a Lifecycle Model." *Journal of Economic Dynamics and Control* 16 (July–October): 427–49.

Burgess, R., and R. Pande. 2005. "Do Rural Banks Matter? Evidence from the Indian Social Banking Experiment." *American Economic Review* 95, no. 3: 780–95.

Carroll, C. D., and L. H. Summers. 1991. "Consumption Growth Parallels Income Growth: Some New Evidence." In *National Saving and Economic Performance*, edited by B.D. Bernheim and J.B. Shoven, pp. 305–43. University of Chicago Press.

Cole, S. A., and others. 2009. "Barriers to Household Risk Management: Evidence from India." Working Paper 09-116. Harvard Business School.

Collins, D., and others. 2009. *Portfolios of the Poor: How the World's Poor Live on $2 a Day*. Princeton University Press.

Cull, R., A. Demirgüç-Kunt, and J. Morduch. 2008. "Microfinance Meets the Market." Policy Research Working Paper 4630. Washington, D.C.: World Bank (May).

Debreu, G. 1959. *Theory of Value: An Axiomatic Analysis of Economic Equilibrium*. Cowles Foundation Monograph 17. Yale University Press.

DellaVigna, S., and U. Malmendier. 2004. "Contract Design and Self-Control: Theory and Evidence." *Quarterly Journal of Economics* 119 (May): 353–402.

Engelmann, J. B., and others. 2009. "Expert Financial Advice Neurobiologically 'Offloads' Financial Decision-Making under Risk." *PLoS One* 4, no. 3: e4957 (www.plosone.org/article/info:doi%2F10.1371%2Fjournal.pone.0004957)

Geistfeld, M. 2010. "The Value of Consumer Choice in Products Liability." *Brooklyn Law Review* 74, no. 3.

Giesen, I. 2006. "Regulating Regulators through Liability—The Case for Applying Normal Tort Rules to Supervisors. *Utrecht Law Review* 2, no. 1: 8–31.

Hari, N., and others. 2008. "Longevity Risk in Portfolios of Pension Annuities." *Insurance: Mathematics and Economics* 42, no. 2: 505–19.

Huffman, D., and M. Barenstein. 2004. "Riches to Rags Every Month? The Fall in Consumption Expenditures between Paydays." Discussion Paper Series. Bonn: Institute for the Study of Labor.

Ibbotson, R., and others. 2007. *Lifetime Financial Advice: Human Capital, Asset Allocation, and Insurance*. Charlottesville, Va.: Research Foundation of CFA Institute.

Karlan, D., and J. Morduch. 2009. "Access to Finance." In *Handbook of Development Economics*, edited by D. Rodrik and M. Rosenzweig, chap. 2. Amsterdam: North-Holland.

Laibson, D. 1997. "Golden Eggs and Hyperbolic Discounting." *Quarterly Journal of Economics* 112, no. 2: 443–77.

Loewenstein, G., T. O'Donoghue, and M. Rabin. 2003. "Projection Bias in Predicting Future Utility." *Quarterly Journal of Economics* 118, no. 4: 1209–48.

Merton, R. C. 1995. "Financial Innovation and the Management and Regulation of Financial Institutions." *Journal of Banking and Finance* 19 (July): 461–81.

————. 2001. "Finance and the Role of Financial Engineering in the 21st Century." Keynote speech at the conference on Finance and the Role of Financial Engineering in the 21st Century. Kyoto University, December 12–13 (www.kier.kyoto-u.ac.jp/fetokyo/sympo_merton/merton-e.html#001).

————. 2002. "Future Possibilities in Finance Theory and Finance Practice." In *Mathematical Finance—Bachelier Congress 2000,* edited by H. Geman and others, pp. 47–74. Berlin: Springer Verlag.

————. 2003. "Thoughts on the Future: Theory and Practice in Investment Management." *Financial Analysts Journal* 59, no. 1: 17–23.

Merton, R. C., and Z. Bodie. 1993. "Deposit Insurance Reform: A Functional Approach." *Carnegie-Rochester Conference Series on Public Policy* 38 (June): 1–34.

————. 1995. "A Conceptual Framework for Analyzing the Financial System." In *The Global Financial System: A Functional Perspective,* edited by D.B. Crane and others, pp. 3–31. Harvard Business School Press.

————. 2005. "The Design of Financial Systems: Towards a Synthesis of Function and Structure." *Journal of Investment Management* 3, no. 1: 1–23.

Mitchell, G. 2005. "Libertarian Paternalism Is an Oxymoron." *Northwestern University Law Review* 99, no. 3.

Morduch, J., and S. Rutherford. 2003. "Microfinance: Analytical Issues for India" (www.nyu.edu/projects/morduch/documents/microfinance/Microfinance_Analytical_Issues_for_India.pdf).

O'Donoghue, T., and M. Rabin. 2001. "Choice and Procrastination." *Quarterly Journal of Economics* 116, no. 1: 121–60.

————. 2006. "Optimal Sin Taxes." *Journal of Public Economics* 90, no. 10-11: 1825–49.

Shapiro, J. 2005. "Is There a Daily Discount Rate? Evidence from the Food Stamp Nutrition Cycle." *Journal of Public Economics* 89, no. 2-3: 303–25.

Shiller, R. J. 2003. *The New Financial Order: Risk in the 21st Century.* Princeton University Press.

Stephens, M. 2003. "'3rd of the Month': Do Social Security Recipients Smooth Consumption between Checks?" *American Economic Review* 93, no. 1: 406–22.

Thaler, R., and C. R. Sunstein. 2003. "Libertarian Paternalism." *American Economic Review* 93, no. 2: 175

————. 2008. *Nudge: Improving Decisions on Health, Wealth, and Happiness.* Yale University Press.

Tversky, A., and D. Kahneman. 1974. "Judgment under Uncertainty: Heuristics and Biases." *Science* 185, no. 4157: 1124–31.

Warren, E. 2007. "Unsafe at Any Rate." *Democracy: A Journal of Ideas*, no. 5 (www.democracyjournal.org/article.php?ID=6528).

Willis, L. E. 2008. "Against Financial-Literacy Education." *Iowa Law Review* 94, no. 1: 197–285.

# 11

## Financial Inclusion and Financial Stability: Current Policy Issues

ALFRED HANNIG AND STEFAN JANSEN

The recent financial crisis has shown that financial innovation can have devastating systemic impacts. International standard setters' and national regulators' response has been a global concerted effort to overhaul and tighten financial regulations. However, at a time of designing stricter regulations, it is crucial to avoid a backlash against financial inclusion.

In this chapter, we argue that greater financial inclusion presents opportunities to enhance financial stability. Our arguments are based on the following insights:

—Financial inclusion poses risks at the institutional level, but these are hardly systemic in nature. Evidence suggests that low-income savers and borrowers tend to maintain solid financial behavior throughout financial crises, keeping deposits in a safe place and paying back their loans.[1]

—Institutional risk profiles at the bottom end of the financial market are characterized by large numbers of vulnerable clients who own limited balances and transact small volumes. Although this profile may raise some concerns

All views are those of the authors alone. The authors thank Lara Gidvani, Celina Lee, and David Saunders from AFI as well as Mateo Cabello from Oxford Policy Management for their valuable contributions.

1. The Bank Rakyat Indonesia units experienced unprecedented deposit growth from small customers during the worst of the financial crisis, while a conservative lending policy contributed to maintaining good loan portfolio quality. See Patten, Rosengard, and Johnston (2001) and Hannig and Jansen (2008).

regarding reputational risks for the central bank and consumer protection, in terms of financial instability, the risk posed by inclusive policies is negligible.

—In addition, risks prevalent at the institutional level are manageable with known prudential tools and more effective customer protection.

—The potential costs of financial inclusion are compensated for by important dynamic benefits that enhance financial stability over time through a deeper and more diversified financial system.

In the following pages, we present the current state of financial inclusion globally. We also explore some trends in financial inclusion and what the most effective policies are to favor it. In doing so, we suggest that innovations aimed at countering financial exclusion may help strengthen financial systems rather than weaken them.

## What Is Financial Inclusion?

Financial inclusion aims at drawing "unbanked" populations into the formal financial system so that they have the opportunity to access financial services ranging from savings, payments, and transfers to credit and insurance. Financial inclusion neither implies that everybody should make use of the supply, nor that providers should disregard risks and other costs when deciding to offer services. Both voluntary exclusion and unfavorable risk-return characteristics may preclude a household or a small firm, despite unrestrained access, from using one or more of the services. Such outcomes do not necessarily warrant policy intervention. Rather, policy initiatives should aim to correct market failures and to eliminate nonmarket barriers to accessing a broad range of financial services.[2]

Despite the considerable progress made by microfinance institutions, credit unions, and savings cooperatives over the last two decades, the majority of the world's poor remain unserved by formal financial intermediaries that can safely manage cash and intermediate between net savers and net borrowers. According to the Consultative Group to Assist the Poor (CGAP), the absolute number of savings accounts worldwide is reported to exceed the global population.[3] And yet half of the world's adult population—2.5 billion people—does not, in fact, have access to savings accounts and other formal financial services.[4]

Financial inclusion as a policy objective represents the current consensus in a long-standing debate on the contribution of finance to economic development and poverty reduction (see box 11-1). It reflects the evolution of financial sector policies in developing countries over the past decades, and embodies important insights

2. Demirgüç-Kunt, Beck, and Honohan (2008).
3. CGAP (2009a).
4. Chaia and others (2009).

Box 11-1. *Financial Development versus Inclusion*

Conventional measures of financial development reflect traditional policy objectives. The focus on aggregate capital accumulation resulted in "domestic credit to the private sector" (as a percent of GDP) being the most prominent measure of the "depth" of financial development. Its impact on growth is well established, but it is poorly correlated with "breadth" or financial access. Hence financial deepening and financial access are only weak substitutes as policy goals. Growing evidence of links from inclusion to equity, growth, and poverty alleviation have turned inclusion into a stand-alone policy objective.

into the positive impact that financial services have on the (economic) lives of the poor.[5] Financial sector policies have evolved through three stylized stages: first, fostering state-led industrial and agricultural development through directed credit; second, market-led development through liberalization and deregulation; and third, institution building that aims at balancing market and government failures.

At least until the 1980s, many developing countries channeled public funds to target groups like farmers and small enterprises, and regulated the scope of activities for which these funds could be used. These "directed credit" programs assumed that the rural poor were unable to save or to afford market rates of interest and therefore needed loans at subsidized rates to build capital. Hence development banks lent at below-market rates to selected target groups. To fund cheap loans, deposit rates were often subject to regulatory ceilings, undermining domestic resource mobilization. The results of "financial repression" were typically shallow financial systems and institutions that had little capacity to allocate resources efficiently according to risk-return characteristics. In addition, poor targeting yielded transfers through highly repressive subsidized interest rates, and subsidies weakened financial institution performance. Not only did these programs typically prove to be unsustainable, they also did not improve outreach of financial services to the poor, particularly in rural areas.

At the end of the 1980s, a new approach emerged that focused on the performance of financial institutions in delivering their services to segments of the population with little or no access to finance. The changes were substantial: the new approach shifted the discussion away from individual firms and households onto institutions and their ability to provide services on a sustainable and widespread basis. Initial experiences in Indonesia, Bangladesh, Bolivia, and some other countries demonstrated that microfinance and rural finance conceived as

---

5. The development benefits of financial services will be addressed in the section on implications for macroeconomic efficiency and welfare.

"banking with the poor" are indeed financially viable and may thus increase outreach on a sustainable basis. These encouraging examples led to a new view called
the "financial system" paradigm.[6] The underlying assumptions of this approach
were that poor people can generate an economic surplus, which enables them to
repay the real costs of loans and to save. The term microfinance came to replace
"microcredit," the former being used increasingly to refer to a variety of financial
products such as loans, deposits, insurance, payments, and remittances offered
by a variety of regulated and unregulated financial institutions.

Over the past few years, microfinance has undergone a rapid transformation
as its links to the formal financial system have been expanded. Growing theoretical and empirical evidence suggests that financial systems that serve low-income
people promote pro-poor growth.[7] Lack of access to finance, therefore, adversely
affects growth and poverty alleviation. It makes it more difficult for the poor to
accumulate savings and build assets to protect against risks, as well as to invest in
income-generating projects. As a result, the interest in financial sector development has increasingly focused on the factors that determine not only the depth
but also breadth of access, in a move toward inclusive financial systems.

With this increased attention to the poverty alleviation aspects of finance,
policy objectives are being constantly expanded to include more quality access
to a wider range of financial services.[8] This trend has been facilitated by the
development and rapid diffusion of information and communication technology that dramatically reduces the cost of connecting users to formal financial
institutions through payment systems, with potential spillovers into a broader
range of services.[9]

Against this background, financial services to the unbanked have become
a major area of interest for policymakers, practitioners, and academics, who
increasingly emphasize financial inclusion as a policy objective. The notion of
building inclusive financial systems recognizes not only the goal of incorporating
as many poor and previously excluded people as possible into the formal financial system, but it also assigns to mainstream financial institutions the role of
reaching out to the unbanked.[10] From this perspective, microfinance is now seen
as an integral part of an inclusive financial system. As a result, financial inclusion
has become an important policy goal that complements the traditional pillars
of monetary and financial stability, as well as other regulatory objectives such as
consumer protection. Policies to encourage increased access for the previously

6. Otero and Rhyne (1994).

7. Beck, Demirgüç-Kunt, and Maksimovic (2004).

8. Morduch (1999); Robinson (2001).

9 . See Demirgüç-Kunt, Beck, and Honohan (2008); UN Capital Development Fund (2006).

10. UN Capital Development Fund (2006).

unbanked must, however, take into consideration the objectives of financial stability, especially in light of the current economic and financial crisis.[11]

All these policy changes were possible because, at the microlevel, views on household behavior with respect to financial services have changed dramatically. Today, it is understood that poor households rely on a variety of financial instruments in the daily management of their cash flows and risks and in their endeavors to build assets through saving. Tools such as financial diaries show that the key challenge faced by these low-income households is the irregularity of their cash flows.[12] The average income at the international poverty line of $2 a day translates in practice into a highly variable flow that requires active management to smooth consumption and reduce vulnerability to various shocks, such as health risks, as well as to cope with major life cycle events.[13]

## How to Measure Progress?

Reliable and comprehensive data that capture various dimensions of financial inclusion are a critical condition for evidence-based policymaking.[14] That includes the definition of consistent financial inclusion indicators that not only may set a clear direction for policymaking by translating the concept of financial inclusion into operational terms but also may allow tracking progress and measuring outcomes of policy reforms.

This presents several challenges, though. Thus the definition of financial indicators has traditionally been shaped by previously formulated policy objectives. On other occasions, some indicators may introduce important distortions into the analysis prior to policymaking discussions by prioritizing aggregate volumes over numbers and characteristics of clients.

Broadly speaking, financial inclusion can be measured through the following lenses in order of complexity:

—*Access:* the ability to use available financial services and products from formal institutions. Understanding levels of access may require insight into and analysis of potential barriers to opening and using a bank account for any

11. Hawkins (2006).

12. "The Financial Diaries project is a year-long household survey that examines financial management in poor households" in South Africa. Data are "captured into a specially designed Access Database that produces customised diary questionnaires for each household, as well as a system of reports that allows for continuous data surveillance." The overall aim of the project, which is funded by the FinMark Trust, the Ford Foundation, and the Micro Finance Regulatory Council, is to get a better grasp of how poor people manage their finances. See www.financialdiaries.com.

13. Collins and others (2009).

14. This section is based on Bankable Frontier Associates (2009).

purpose, such as cost and physical proximity of bank service points (for example, branches and ATMs). A very basic proxy for access can be derived by counting the number of open accounts across financial institutions and estimating the proportion of the population with an account.

—*Quality:* the relevance of the financial service or product to the lifestyle needs of the consumer. Quality encompasses the experience of the consumer, demonstrated in attitudes and opinions toward those products that are currently available to them. The measure of quality therefore would be used to gauge the nature and depth of the relationship between the financial service provider and the consumer as well as the choices available and consumers' levels of understanding of those choices and their implications.

—*Usage:* beyond the basic adoption of banking services, usage focuses more on the permanence and depth of financial service and product use. Hence determining usage requires more details about the regularity, frequency, and duration of use over time. To measure usage, it is critical that information reflect the user's point of view, that is, data gathered through a demand-side survey.

—*Impact:* measuring changes in the lives of consumers that can be attributed to the usage of a financial device or service poses serious methodological challenges to survey design.

This information can be sourced either from the demand side, that is, at the individual, household, or firm level, or from the supply side, that is, at the level of a financial institution, or from a combination of both. The key surveys that have produced relevant data have been compiled by CGAP.[15]

With all these elements in mind, it can be stated that measurement of financial inclusion serves two primary objectives that imply different data needs: first, measuring and monitoring levels of financial inclusion, and second, deepening understanding about factors that correlate with financial inclusion and, subsequently, the impact of policies.

These primary objectives can be broken down to more basic levels (figure 11-1). Measurement data can be used to approximate the number of people who have access to or are currently using some type of financial service or product. Provided these data can be linked to other in-country factors, such as population characteristics, they can also help identify priorities and catalyze changes in policy and approach. If collected repeatedly, these data can also be used to monitor progress over time. On the other hand, data can also deepen understanding of the problem of financial inclusion. This typically entails a more complex method of design and collection. This type of data is more appropriate to support solution-building and impact measurement of policies put in place.

---

15. Kneiding, Al-Hussayni, and Mas (2009).

Figure 11-1. *Measurement Objectives*

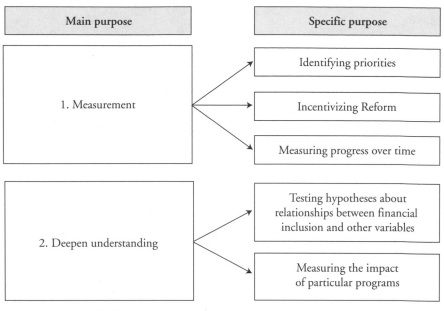

Source: Porteous (2009).

## Financial Inclusion Trends

There has been significant but uneven progress toward financial inclusion around the world in recent years. Some of these steps have been driven by market-friendly policies that will be presented in more detail in a later section.

Some countries in Asia, such as India and Indonesia, have a long tradition of emphasizing access to finance.[16] At the regional level, these policy priorities have paid off: 25 percent of households living on less than $2 a day now have access to formal or semiformal financial services, compared to 40 to 50 percent of the population as a whole.

Other success stories include:

—Mongolia: a successful turnaround of a state bank increased the number of deposit accounts by over 1.4 million since 2006, now reaching 62 percent of households.

—Philippines: mobile phone banking has expanded to serve four million clients since 2002.

—India: access to credit among the poor is up from 7 percent in 2004 to about 25 percent in 2009, as the microfinance sector added 9.9 million clients.

16. The information on Asia in this section is based on Fernando (2009).

Figure 11-2. *Financial Exclusion in Asia*[a]

Millions of people

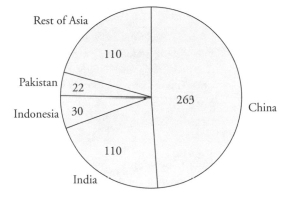

Source: Fernando (2009).
a. A total of 535 million people remain financially excluded.

—Bangladesh: Four to six million new microcredit clients have been added since 2006; financial services have reached about 55 percent of poor households, substantially expanding access to savings.

—Viet Nam: 2.1 million new microfinance clients have been added since 2006.

In contrast, access in China appears to have declined since the reforms of the rural cooperatives. Also, India's poor have little access to deposits: "no frills" accounts have increased to over twenty-eight million, but studies show that many of these are barely used.

Particularly in Asia, the poor are often served by public banks or nonbank entities, including nongovernmental organizations (NGOs), with private sector banks playing a smaller role. Key examples of these public banks and nonbank entities include:

—Pakistan: Post Savings Bank, with 3.6 million accounts in 2006.

—India: post offices, with 60.8 million savings accounts as of March 2007.

—Bangladesh: Rural Development Board, with 4.7 million active borrowers in 2007.

—Viet Nam: Bank for Agriculture and Rural Development, with ten million farmer clients in 2007, and Bank for Social Policy, with 6.79 million active borrowers in 2008.

—Thailand: Government Savings Bank, with thirty-six million accounts in 2006.

—Sri Lanka: state banks, which were used by 72 percent households by the end of 2006.

However, despite this outreach, service quality is inferior, and most institutions depend on subsidies. Furthermore, as shown in figure 11-2, despite

Table 11-1. *Level of Financial Inclusion, Asia*

Percent of adult population or households included

| Level of financial inclusion | Countries |
| --- | --- |
| High: > 50 | Thailand, Malaysia, Sri Lanka, Nepal, Mongolia |
| Intermediate: 30–49 | India, China, Indonesia, Bangladesh, Viet Nam |
| Low: < 30 | Cambodia, Myanmar, Philippines, Papua New Guinea, Pakistan, Laos, Timor-Leste, Solomon Islands, Vanuatu, Samoa, Tuvalu, Kiribati |

Source: Authors' calculations.

remarkable improvements in India and Bangladesh, an estimated 535 million people in these two countries still are excluded from financial services. Table 11-1 shows how countries in Asia are sorted by their level of financial inclusion.

Africa faces substantially larger challenges than most of Asia, mostly due to a much higher incidence of poverty.[17] FinScope household surveys that are comparable across countries illustrate this difference for eleven countries (figure 11-3). While across Asia 25 percent of poor households have access to formal financial services, individual countries in Africa rarely demonstrate such a level of household access.[18]

In Africa, Kenya has pioneered an interesting process of financial inclusion through leapfrogging to mobile phone payment solutions (discussed below). As of 2009, within only three years of its initial start up, the Kenyan telecommunications provider Safaricom has attracted 7.9 million subscribers to its short message service–based transfer scheme, with significant positive impacts on users.[19]

Latin America is home to some of the best regulatory environments for microfinance, such as Peru and Bolivia.[20] In these two countries, rapid growth over the past seven years has included six million clients in the formal financial system.

Brazilian policymakers achieved universal coverage of over 5,500 municipalities by enabling banks to use retail agents. This new low-cost delivery channel triggered a massive expansion of formal financial services to twelve million

17. Information on Africa draws on Makanjee (2009).

18. FinScope surveys (designed and managed by FinMark Trust, established in 2002 with funding from the U.K. Department for International Development) are nationally representative market segmentation studies that explore consumers' perceptions and usage from informal to formal products. See www.finscope.co.za.

19. Morawczynski and Pickens (2009); Safaricom (2009).

20. Economist Intelligence Unit (2009).

Figure 11-3. *Africa: Access by Degree of Formality*

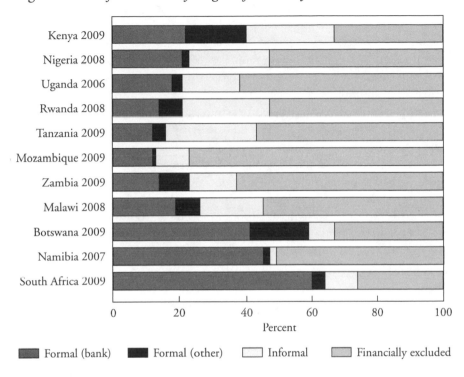

Source: Finscope 2009 brochures for South Africa, Mozambique, and Zambia. See www.finscope.co.za.

clients in only six years. Other countries, such as Colombia and Peru, are replicating this model.

Latin America has also demonstrated the potential of conditional cash transfers into simplified bank accounts as a way to connect beneficiaries to formal finance while simultaneously lowering delivery costs to the government. Transfer challenges motivated the use of agents in Brazil.[21] In Mexico, beneficiaries increased savings and investment, and more than 90 percent of households started to use banking services.[22]

Despite these impressive achievements, half of the world's population is still without access to savings accounts, insurance, and other financial services, and about 95 percent of the unbanked are in developing countries.

21. See Kumar and others (2006).
22. Zimmerman and Moury (2009).

## Impact of Financial Inclusion: Recent Evidence

As mentioned previously, collecting reliable financial data is not an easy task. A common obstacle is that both current levels and recent progress in financial inclusion vary substantially across countries. Most countries are only beginning to track financial inclusion, so data for projecting longer-term trends are not yet available. In addition, comparing survey results across countries is often difficult because methodologies used often differ from one survey to the next.

CGAP's *Financial Access 2009,* a global survey of regulators with regard to financial access, focuses on individual account holdings with regulated institutions. Using a statistical model to fill in data gaps, the survey finds 6.2 billion bank deposit accounts globally. Because of the aforementioned challenges faced by survey collectors, this number may include substantial double counting of users, which may therefore mask a rather uneven distribution. Assuming three bank accounts per banked adult, the CGAP survey arrives at an estimate of 2.6 billion unbanked adults in the developing world.[23]

Another recent survey is the World Bank's composite access indicator.[24] It suggests that financial inclusion is an issue well beyond households living on less than $2 a day (see figure 11-4). Instead, it shows how in many countries the number of financially excluded adults significantly exceeds the adult population living under the $2-a-day poverty line.[25]

Does this mean there is not a clear correlation between financial inclusion and economic development? It seems obvious that financial inclusion has some relationship to economic development. However, as figure 11-5 shows, the correlation between GDP per capita and the composite indicator is imperfect.[26] Thus, for a given income level, there is a wide variation around the conditional mean represented by the regression line. This means that many other factors play a role determining the amount of people without access to formal financial services. In this sense, more research is needed to analyze how policy, by making the environment more conducive for the expansion of financial access, plays a role in reducing financial exclusion.

This idea is reinforced by figure 11-6, which shows the correlation between domestic credit by the banking sector and financial inclusion. Again, it is possible to appreciate a wide variation in access for a given level of financial development.

---

23. CGAP (2009a).

24. See Honohan (2007). The correlation between CGAP's data on individual accounts and the World Bank composite indicator is 0.67.

25. Due to data constraints, information on poverty and inclusion is not necessarily from the same year for many countries. Both variables are relatively slow moving, though.

26. The correlation coefficient is 0.55 (significant at the 1 percent level).

Figure 11-4. *Poverty and Financial Exclusion in Absolute Numbers*

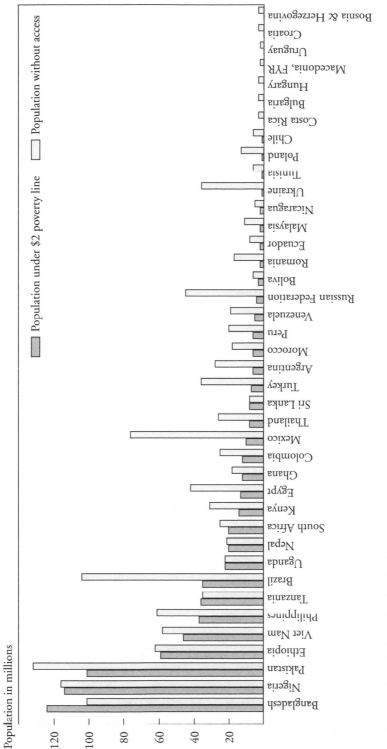

Population in millions

■ Population under $2 poverty line   □ Population without access

Source: Authors' calculations based on data from Demirgüç-Kunt, Beck, and Honohan (2008), World Bank "Finance for All" access data (http://siteresources.worldbank.org/INTRES/ Resources/PRR_Data_for_Website.xls', and World Bank World Development Indicators (http://data.worldbank.org).

Figure 11-5. *Composite Access Indicator versus GDP per Capita*[a]

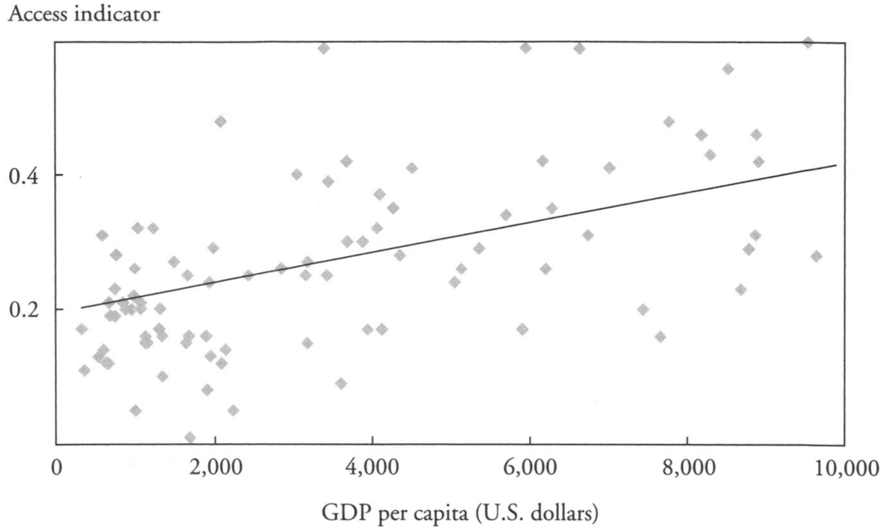

Source: See figure 11-4.
a. GDP per capita based on 2003–07 average purchasing power parity.

There is evidence for the impact of financial inclusion on both aggregate growth and individual welfare. Consistent with the evolution of policy objectives, the research focus has been first on macroeconomic aspects of financial system development; only in recent years has it begun to address the microeconomic impacts of financial inclusion.

## Macroeconomic Evidence

Financial institutions contribute to growth by reducing information asymmetries that would otherwise hinder the efficient intermediation of resources among savers and investors. There is substantial evidence that financial development has a causal impact on growth.[27] A prominent explanation is Schumpeter's view that finance fuels "creative destruction" by allocating resources to newcomers that promote innovation and possibly topple incumbents.[28] Along these lines, access to finance for new entrepreneurs is an important ingredient in the finance-growth nexus.[29]

More recently, the focus has shifted to links between finance and income inequality. Beck and others (2008) found a link between financial development,

27. Beck and de la Torre (2006); Beck, Demirgüç-Kunt, and Levine (2004); Honohan (2004); Levine (2005).
28. Beck and de la Torre (2006).
29. De la Torre, Gozzi, and Schmukler (2007).

Figure 11-6. *Implications for Macroeconomic Efficiency and Individual Welfare*[a]

Composite access indicator (percent)

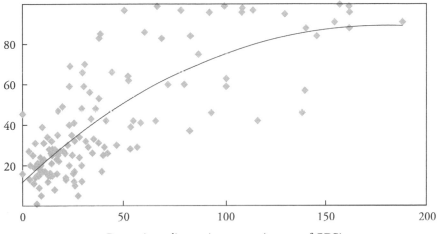

Domestic credit to private sector (percent of GDP)

Source: See figure 11-4.

a. $R^2 = 0.55$. Financial development matters, but financial inclusion varies widely at similar levels of development, suggesting that policy can make a difference.

reduced income inequality, and poverty alleviation: the aggregate usage of financial services, that is, deeper financial systems, appears to reduce Gini coefficients, a measurement of inequality.

There is also evidence at the macroeconomic level that broader financial systems enhance economic growth. Giné and Townsend (2004) show that, based on a general equilibrium model of the Thai economy, the expansion of access to the financial sector has significantly raised Thailand's growth rate. Conversely, Banerjee and others (2009) emphasize the efficiency and productivity losses associated with preferential access to finance by the better off and suggest a potential first-order effect of access on investment and growth.

Finally, Pande and Burgess (2005) find a strong positive effect on rural poverty using a "natural experiment" of new branching regulations in India that incentivized banks to expand into underserved areas. However, the high cost of this expansion policy outweighed the aggregate benefits. This result suggests large potential benefits from technology-enabled, lower-cost branch expansion.

*Microeconomic Evidence*

Until very recently, the support for financial inclusion from a microeconomic level has been solely based on plausibility, anecdotal evidence, and data that were not subject to statistical tests, such as claims that 65 percent of Grameen Bank clients cross the poverty line.[30] Establishing a causal link from the use of financial services to improvements in the lives of the poor is methodologically challenging and very expensive. It requires eliminating influences of self-selection and survivor biases in the sample, as well as numerous unobservable effects that may confound the analysis. The method of choice is field experiments that establish this link through the creation of a counterfactual by randomly dividing a subset of the population into treatment and control groups. Statistical analysis is then used to identify the differential effects of the intervention, such as exposure to a certain type of financial service.

These randomized controlled trials (RCT) are critical to underpin the claim that financial inclusion positively affects the poor. RCTs are not without shortcomings, however: while methodological rigor produces results with high levels of internal validity, it is much more difficult to generalize beyond the specific context of the experiment, that is, external validity is substantially weaker.[31]

A number of RCTs have been conducted so far. In Kenya, a randomly selected group of rural poor were offered savings accounts. The impact was found to be highly positive: uptake was very significant for female clients, and female market vendors reached higher daily expenditure levels within six months of opening an account.[32] There was no evidence that savings accounts crowd out other investments, and neither was there evidence that the savings accounts allowed for more efficient smoothing over bad shocks, particularly sickness. This study also shows a more significant positive impact of savings accounts for women than for men.

Another RCT example from India provides evidence that the effect of microcredit depends on household characteristics:

—Business owners use credit to expand their businesses, as demonstrated by an increase in spending on durables and an increase in business profits.

—Those initially identified as having a low propensity to start a business do not increase investment but rather increase consumption, such as food and transportation.

—Households with a high propensity to start a business reduce nondurable spending, increase durable spending, and reduce temptation spending.[33]

Over the eighteen-month period of study, there were no significant effects on education, health, or women's empowerment. However, business outcomes were significantly positive, including the creation of new businesses and the profits for existing business. While the impact on female welfare could not be established

---

30. Grameen Bank (2007).
31. For further criticism, see Rodrik (2008).
32. Dupas and Robinson (2009).
33. Banerjee and others (2009).

(despite frequent claims to the contrary), one has to take into account the limited time horizon.

Recent research in South Africa highlights the risk management benefits of financial inclusion.[34] Loan applicants that had been declined "at the margin" were randomly offered loans and turned out to be significantly less likely to report leaving a job after entering the experiment than those rejected clients without loans. Treated households earned more and were more likely to move out of poverty. Overall, increased access to credit appears to improve welfare. The study does present evidence that short-term loans are an important cash flow management tool and that they have largely positive impacts on people's welfare, particularly in the area of employment and income. The study also found that loans to customers at (or slightly beyond) the margin were actually profitable.

Given the difficulty with drawing generalized conclusions from RCTs, new tools will be needed to deepen understanding about which services matter most to low-income households and microenterprises, how they impact welfare metrics, and how policy tools can help relax binding constraints on the access frontier.

In conclusion, recent evaluation techniques suggest that positive effects of microfinance exist, but they may not be as overwhelming as assumed or may take more time to materialize. There is room for further research to produce more empirical evidence in support of the need to pursue financial inclusion as a policy objective.

## Financial Inclusion Policies: Recent Innovation

The financial sector is prone to market failure and, therefore, is generally heavily regulated. The low-income segment is particularly plagued by information asymmetries, as participants on the demand side often lack a track record or collateral to pacify lenders' concerns. In addition, lenders lack experience in new markets at the bottom of the pyramid and face adjustment costs regarding business processes. At the same time, the limited size of both individual transactions and the overall market pose challenges to suppliers that need to recover fixed costs.

However, once the pioneers of the microfinance revolution demonstrated tangible market opportunities, substantial business model innovation has expanded the "access possibilities frontier."[35] More recently, technological innovation has dramatically lowered the fixed costs of reaching the low-income segment and attracted a broader range of new suppliers.

Policies are a key complement to private sector innovation through regulatory frameworks, public ownership, the provision of market infrastructure, and

---

34. Karlan and Zinman (2007).
35. Beck and de la Torre (2006).

measures that lower demand-side barriers. Regulatory frameworks determine the set of institutions that are allowed to enter, shape the scope of available services, and affect institutions' cost of doing business. Prudential regulation is critical to enable financial intermediation and facilitate domestic resource mobilization and financial institution growth while simultaneously protecting savers. Furthermore, public ownership has frequently expanded outreach into segments that were considered beyond the scope of commercial approaches. Secured lending frameworks and public credit registries facilitate transactions despite asymmetric information. Finally, the low education level of poor clients suggests a need for consumer protection and financial education policies.

Policymakers have struggled to accompany rapid innovation. They have been particularly successful where they facilitated experimentation within regulatory frameworks that carefully limited the potential risks.

The rapid pace of innovation has substantially increased the complexity of policymaking. On the one hand, this calls for a rethinking of policy principles with respect to financial inclusion.[36] On the other hand, there is substantial scope for stepping up peer-to-peer advice as innovative solutions are being generated by developing country regulators.

To capture and compare emerging policy trends in developing countries, the German Gesellschaft für Technische Zusammenarbeit or GTZ (German Technical Cooperation) assessed thirty-five policy solutions geared toward promoting financial inclusion across ten countries.[37] Six solutions were found to be particularly effective. Four have improved conditions for reaching the poor through various channels, including agent banking, mobile payments, formalizing micro-saving providers, and state bank reforms. The remaining two solutions are consumer protection and financial identity policies, which play key roles in enabling financial inclusion.

## Agent Banking

Policies that enable banks to contract with nonbank retail agents as outlets for financial services have proven highly successful in advancing financial inclusion where bank branches are not economically viable. Such policies leverage existing retail infrastructure as delivery channels and turn pharmacies, post offices, or supermarkets not only into agents of banks but agents of financial inclusion.

---

36. See Claessens, Honohan, and Rojas-Suarez (2009). Most recently, at the Toronto Summit in 2009, G20 Leaders issued a set of nine principles for innovative financial inclusion (Toronto 2009).

37. See Hannig and Jansen (2008). This study laid the groundwork for creation of the Alliance for Financial Inclusion. For an overview, see APEC Business Advisory Council (2008). The Deutsche Gesellschaft für Internationale Zusammenarbeit (GIZ) was established on January 1, 2011, and brings together under one roof the Deutscher Entwicklungsdienst (DED) gGmbH (German Development Service), the Deutsche Gesellschaft für Technische Zusammenarbeit (GTZ) GmbH (German Technical Cooperation), and Inwent.

Collaboration among banks and agents has become possible as technology has reduced the costs and risks of the remote exchange of information to carry out financial transactions. Coupled with simplified account opening procedures and other incentives to use this channel, such as the delivery of cash transfers, financial system outreach and numbers of users can increase explosively, as recently observed in Brazil.

Brazil was the early leader in agent banking through the large-scale introduction of "banking correspondents" to distribute welfare grants to unbanked Brazilians. This solution addressed a key physical access barrier: only 1,600 municipalities had bank branches in 2000.[38] Today, some 95,000 correspondents cover all of the 5,500 municipalities, and nearly twelve million accounts were opened at agents over three years. The Brazilian success has inspired similar approaches in Colombia, Peru, Mexico, and Chile.[39] In 2006 Colombia passed enabling regulations allowing financial institutions to use retail agents, attracting 3,539 agents that initially focused on bill payments.[40]

Given the topography of Latin America—often a major obstacle to improving access to financial services—it is not a coincidence that agent banking schemes are blooming in the region. With a huge percentage of the population concentrated in large cities, the minority living in remote rural areas does not receive enough attention in terms of infrastructure, communications development, and services. This is particularly evident in countries like Brazil or Peru, where these minorities account for millions of people, affecting equally both poor and better-off residents. That is why, as shown in figure 11-4, in countries like Brazil, Russia, or Mexico the population without access to financial services outnumbers the population living on less than $2 a day to a greater extent than holds in smaller countries.

Critical features of the agent banking model are timely transaction settlement to minimize fraud, simplified account opening procedures, and customer due diligence compliant with international know-your-customer standards. The cost savings are substantial: according to the Peruvian Superintendence of Banks, forty banking agents may be established for roughly the same cost as one bank branch.[41]

The experience of Brazil offers valuable lessons for other countries. A Brazilian agent is a service provider of a bank or other financial institution. Any institution that is supervised by the central bank can contract an agent, and anyone can become an agent as long as the bank takes the responsibility and the relationship

38. Ivatury (2006).
39. Mas and Siedek (2008).
40. Aguirre, Dias, and Prochaska (2008).
41. Mas and Siedek (2008).

Figure 11-7. *Evolution of GSM Mobile Phone Subscribers*

Millions of subscribers

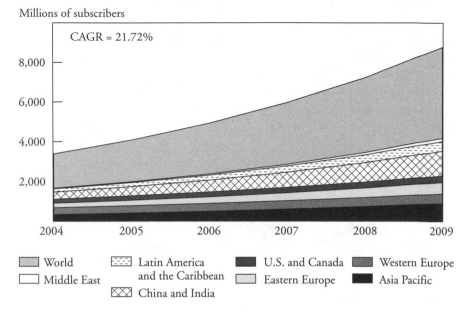

Source: Based on data obtained from International Telecommunications Union.

is governed by a public contract. The success of this model is based on its pragmatic and flexible approach. While oversight is focused on the financial institution, with the central bank getting access to all data on the agent, it also gives the financial institution enough freedom to articulate the relationship with the agent on its own terms. The Mexican case shows that know-your-customer procedures for a smaller transaction authority can also be delegated to agents.

## Mobile Payments

Globally, four billion mobile phone subscriptions were projected for 2009, well over half of them in the developing world.[42] Mobile phone penetration in developing countries has almost tripled in the past five years, with Asia in particular showing high growth rates (see figure 11-7). In Kenya, for example, 47 percent of adults own a mobile phone, and the rate of ownership rises to 73 percent in urban areas and 80 percent in Nairobi.[43]

Proliferating mobile phones open another delivery channel for basic financial services to poor people. This new technology drastically reduces the costs of convenient

42. Schulze (2008).
43. See Financial Sector Deepening Trust (2009).

and real-time financial transactions, expands access points, lessens the need to carry cash by introducing e-money, and attracts previously unbanked customers.

Several country cases illustrate the promise of mobile payments for financial inclusion. The Philippines launched the first successful mobile payment service in a developing country in 2004. Two mobile payment operators have an estimated 5.5 million customers. Mobile phone transactions cost about one-fifth of those executed through bank branches ($0.50 versus $2.50).[44]

In Kenya, the e-money transfer service M-PESA offered by mobile network operator Safaricom has achieved the most impressive outreach of mobile payments thus far. The service has experienced rapid growth and currently enjoys a subscription base of more than seven million registered customers, many previously unbanked.[45] A recent national survey illustrates the positive impact on financial inclusion: the usage of semiformal services including M-PESA has increased from 8.1 percent in 2006 to 17.9 percent in 2009, while the proportion of the population with access to only informal financial services decreased from 35 percent to 26.8 percent, respectively. Most important, the share of the population excluded from financial service decreased from 38.3 percent to 32.7 percent over the same time frame.[46]

Mobile payments challenge regulatory capacity as they cut across various regulatory domains, including banking, telecommunications, payments systems, and anti–money laundering regimes. Where mobile payments have taken root, regulators have tended to adopt a "test and see" approach that allows operators to experiment and develop their business models under close supervision. Once market innovation and learning have satisfied the needs of regulators and mobile operators, regulation has been created and implemented to provide legal certainty and to create a level playing field to allow new players.

*Formalizing Microsavings*

Policymakers have adopted various regulatory and supervisory strategies to manage the risks of licensing a wider range of institutions to offer deposit and insurance products. Strategies to adapt banking regulations to the specific nature of microfinance include:
  —licenses for specialized institutions dedicated to taking microdeposits,
  —bank licenses for successfully transforming financial NGOs, or
  —licenses for nonbank financial institutions.

44. Lyman, Pickens, and Porteous (2008).

45. M-PESA Key Performance Statistics, released by Safaricom June 8, 2009. The most recent statistics are available online at www.safaricom.co.ke/fileadmin/template/main/images/MiscUploads/M-PESA%20Statistics.pdf.

46. See also Kimenyi and Ndung'u (2009).

A tiered regulatory approach that differentiates institutions by permissible activities and limits credit risk exposure of lower-tier institutions minimizes risk from the central bank's standpoint.[47] Regardless of the strategy chosen, high-level political leadership has proven critical in catalyzing regulatory initiatives to broaden access.

In Peru, Bolivia, and Uganda, regulators have incorporated nonprofit inno-vators into the formal system by creating legal paths toward a license.[48] This has led to higher savings, benefiting not only consumers but also institutions, enabling them to weather financial crises by making them less dependent on external and wholesale funding.

In Bolivia, two microfinance NGOs that transformed into banks and six non-bank deposit-taking microfinance institutions (known as private financial funds) operating under a special regulatory framework held a combined $955 million in deposits as of June 2008. Of this amount, $458 million were held by the private financial funds, which opened almost 136,000 new savings accounts in the first half of 2008.[49] New laws, specially designed for previously unregulated NGOs, were passed in 2008.[50] The main difference from the preceding model is that NGOs will not need to be transformed into private financial funds. Instead, they will keep their nonprofit status and be allowed to collect deposits and offer extra financial services. NGOs will have the nature of nonbanking financial intermediaries but will be under the same rules as banks and financial entities.

In Indonesia, the entry barriers to the financial sector were lowered by the introduction of second-tier rural banks during financial sector liberalization in the late 1980s. After initial explosive growth due to a very liberal licensing regime and postcrisis consolidation, there are now 1,800 rural banks that hold more than $2 billion in deposits in 9.8 million accounts.[51]

## State Bank Reform

In many countries, state-owned banks still play a major role in the banking sys-tem, and in providing financial services to the poor. They are present in about 73 of 102 countries, where they hold roughly 15 percent of banking assets.[52] Public banks often are the only financial institutions in rural areas with large

47. Hawkins (2006).

48. Peru and Bolivia ranked at the top of the Economist Intelligence Unit's global microfinance index. See Economist Intelligence Unit (2009).

49. Based on data obtained from Bolivian banking supervisory authority.

50. Bolivian Superintendence of Banks and Financial Institutions, Legal Resolution SB 0034/2008.

51. See Institutions–BPR on the Promotion of Small Financial Institutions website (www.profi. or.id/images/map/scripte/).

52. CGAP (2009b).

branch networks, not least because governments have used public banks extensively to promote savings and credit in areas of less commercial interest, such as agriculture or housing, and to implement social programs.[53]

The global picture is rather mixed: some governments have closed down poorly performing state banks as the least-cost choice, as did Benin, Brazil, and Peru, while others continue to suffer from political interference and mediocre performance. More interestingly, however, some policymaker-pushed reforms have demonstrated the potential to turn financial inclusion into a new, profitable business for state banks.

Rather than restructuring the whole bank, Bank Rakyat Indonesia (BRI) and Banco do Nordeste in Brazil, for example, created separate lines of business to introduce profitable microfinance operations. Key success factors were governance reform and state-of-the-art microcredit technologies.

BRI has over 4,200 village units that serve 3.5 million borrowers and twenty-one million savers.[54] The profit of BRI's microfinance operations (27 percent of total loan portfolio) cross-subsidized the less successful banking operations during the Asian crisis.

Banco do Nordeste's "CrediAmigo" has grown rapidly, becoming the second largest microcredit program in Latin America since it was launched in the late 1990s. CrediAmigo is a microfinance line of business that operates in 2,000 municipalities, providing microcredit to 400,000 clients for a total portfolio of $155 million.[55]

*Consumer Protection and Education*

Every year 150 million new customers enter financial markets worldwide. Information asymmetry between consumers and banks regarding financial products and services puts these new customers at a disadvantage. This imbalance is greatest when customers are less experienced and the products more sophisticated. Progress on financial inclusion therefore carries the risk of producing more inexperienced and vulnerable customers.

Many financial institutions ensure that these customers are well served, but some have abused their information advantage to increase profits at the expense of consumers who found themselves overindebted, underinsured, or without a return on their investment. This was the case in Bolivia during the early 2000s, where the combination of financial illiteracy, unethical practices at some institutions, and some voids in the legal framework resulted in abuses. Preventing these situations is critical.

---

53. Young and Vogel (2005).
54. Microfinance Information eXchange (MIX) Market, December 31, 2007.
55. See Banco do Nordeste do Brasil (2010); MIX Market, December 31, 2008.

Consumer protection is generally considered to be a regulatory response to a market failure.[56] Appropriate regulation should correct information imbalances and encourage sustainable market expansion through timely information disclosure throughout the service relationship—before, during, and after the contract. Disclosure in manageable portions helps consumers better understand their rights and obligations.

Regulators need to understand the consumer perspective to ensure a level playing field. Active participation of consumer advocates helps avoid regulatory bias in favor of the financial services industry.[57] However, effective consumer advocates exist in only a handful of emerging markets.[58] Some regulators mitigate this issue by perusing consumer complaints to identify areas of concern and trends in market practices. Supervisory tools include reviewing product-related information, conducting on-site reviews, telephone interviews, and media surveillance, as well as industry and consumer surveys.

Peru has reduced the number of complaints across the financial system by 32 percent since 2004 due to the implementation of a holistic system of consumer protection. The regulatory agency supervises consumer protection policies and procedures by financial institutions but does not directly respond to complaints. In 2008, 99 percent of nearly 400,000 complaints were successfully handled by the financial institution itself. Of the remaining 4,000 complaints, two-thirds were referred to the Consumer Protection Commission, and one-third was referred to the financial ombudsman. In addition to oversight by the regulator and multiple channels for redress, Peruvian consumers have access to cost information about financial services, published daily in newspapers. When this information was first published, interest rates dropped by as much as 15 percent in six months.

Consumer education can help balance information asymmetries between consumers and providers of financial services. New, inexperienced entrants to the market are especially in need of education about their rights and responsibilities. Consumer education may be delivered by government agencies, consumer associations, or the industry, but most often consumer education programs are provided through public campaigns that use the Internet; print, radio, and television media; advertising; publications; and training.[59]

56. Eisner, Worsham, and Ringquist (2006).

57. Regulatory capture, whereby regulatory agents come to be dominated by the industry they regulate, is a recognized feature of financial markets. For an insightful take on regulatory capture, see Kay (2009).

58. Independent advocates are rare in emerging markets, where most advocates for financial customers are affiliated with either the government or the industry.

59. Examples of financial education delivery channels can be found at the International Gateway for Financial Education (www.financial-education.org), a program developed by the Organization for Economic Cooperation and Development.

## Financial Identity

In most countries, credit information is only provided above a certain loan amount, effectively excluding poor customers from the demonstrated benefits of information cost reduction provided by credit registries. More fundamentally, such clients may not even have the identification documents required to open a bank account.

Policymakers have begun to address these barriers to access by narrowing the gap between the documentation threshold associated with bank accounts and the quality of documentation prevalent among low-income clients. As a result, these policies endow clients with a financial history and transform their transaction history into a financial asset that they can use to leverage access to credit and other banking services.

In lowering documentation barriers to entry, regulators must decide on the level of risk they want to accept to promote inclusion. To reduce credit and identification risks, Indonesia has started to collect local information in the informal financial sector, especially among the pooled funds that are popular among the rural poor. This is an opportunity to capture crucial information on financial identity and financial history. In India, stringent know-your-customer norms have been relaxed to allow the creation of low-risk, basic bank accounts with a letter from the local government. In South Africa, the regulator has allowed industry to lead the way in proposing systems to identify their rural clients, as long as providers are able to ensure the proper assessments, enforcement, and consumer protection.

With regard to effective anti–money laundering (AML) and combating the financing of terrorism (CFT) regimes, although successful policy reforms (for example, in Kenya) are not yet formally compliant with the Financial Action Task Force (FATF) guidelines, regulators have adopted alternative mechanisms to ensure minimum compliance with AML-CFT approaches to client identification and verification. In the Philippines, regulators have played an active role in creating an enabling environment for mobile payments and have shown strong commitment to implementing an AML-CFT regime that allows financial inclusion.[60] However, particularly in light of rapid adoption of technological innovation, developing country policymakers and regulators increasingly report barriers to financial inclusion due to increasing identification burdens. The FATF has recognized this barrier and embarked on a process to review its recommendations on the basis that financial inclusion is complementary to financial integrity.[61]

---

60. Chatain and others (2008).

61. The FATF has recently recognized that financial inclusion and financial integrity are complementary policy objectives. Furthermore, the current president of FATF, Luis Urrutia, has reinforced this by making financial inclusion a priority area for FATF. See FATF (2010).

## Assessment

Developing-country policymakers are faced with the challenge of managing trade-offs between the objective of financial inclusion and other objectives, such as financial stability and consumer protection. The policy solutions outlined and illustrated above have been successfully implemented in this respect. To summarize, outstanding success stories include:

—Brazil, where new regulations have achieved universal access in only four years by enabling partnerships between banks and third-party agents;

—Kenya and the Philippines, where central banks have played a key role in supporting mobile phone payment schemes and left regulatory space to mobile phone operators;

—Bolivia and Uganda, which have demonstrated that microdeposit-taking can flourish in the regulated financial system with timely and appropriate policies; and

—Indonesia, which has proved how publicly owned financial institutions may become the driving force behind economic development in rural areas.

Overall, the available evidence suggests that a balance between financial stability and financial inclusion objectives can be achieved. None of the recent policy reforms promoting financial inclusion has failed in the sense that it produced deficient regulatory, supervisory, or corporate governance practices, or unsound financial performance of market participants. To the contrary, the policies discussed above have supported an accessible and stable financial sector environment.

The above policy solutions should be assessed against a widely accepted set of policy principles for expanding access to finance. These principles entail:

—promoting entry of and competition among financial firms;

—building legal and information institutions and hard infrastructure;

—stimulating informed demand;

—ensuring the safety and soundness of financial services providers;

—protecting low-income and all customers against abuses by financial services providers;

—ensuring that usury laws, if used, are effective;

—enhancing cross-regulatory agency coordination;

—balancing government's role with market provision of financial services;

—using subsidies and taxes effectively and efficiently; and

—ensuring data collection, monitoring, and evaluation.[62]

Overall, the policy solutions described above follow this widely accepted set of policy principles for expanding access to finance.

---

62. Based on the ten policy principles most recently provided by Center for Global Development. See Claessens, Honohan, and Rojas-Suarez (2009).

Finally, the policy examples discussed above belong to those countries that have demonstrated the most considerable gains in expanding financing options for the unbanked. As highlighted in the 2009 Economist Intelligence Unit survey assessing microfinance environments in fifty-five countries, the Philippines, Bolivia, Kenya, and Uganda (in this order) rank among the top ten countries that enjoy the best legal and regulatory frameworks for microfinance.[63]

## Trade-offs and Synergies between Financial Inclusion and Stability

As it happened during the 1990s with the Tequila Effect (1994) or the Asian financial crisis (1997), the current crisis has highlighted the immense value of financial stability and motivated a review of the policy tools available to prevent costly breakdowns of the financial system. Since financial inclusion has gained a much higher profile as a policy goal in recent years, it is important to inquire to what extent there are trade-offs between the objectives of maintaining systemic stability and including a growing number of users of financial services.

This appears even more relevant since the origin of the current crisis in the subprime market at least initially suggested destabilizing spillovers from the lower end of the market to the remainder of the system. And of particular concern in many developing countries is the additional regulatory uncertainty arising from the rapidly proliferating, technology-driven policy solutions that boost small-scale transactions flowing through the national payment system.

On the other hand, lessons learned suggest that past financial crises have frequently bypassed the highly localized markets at the bottom of the pyramid: the microfinance segment of BRI remained rock solid throughout the Indonesian crisis, and anecdotal evidence suggests that financial institutions catering to the lower end tend to weather macrocrises well and help sustain local economic activity.[64] Could it even be possible that a more diversified aggregate financial sector balance sheet, spread over a broader variety of economic agents, might contribute to a more resilient economy that follows a higher growth path? Jean Claude Trichet, president of the European Central Bank, seems to think so, declaring that financial stability is made up of three factors: the amount and quality of information available to players, the adequacy-inadequacy of the frameworks for crisis prevention and resolution, and the level of completeness of the market.[65]

This section aims at identifying links between financial stability and inclusion that could give rise to either policy conflicts or synergies, and outlines questions for future research. To facilitate regulatory decisionmaking, we highlight

---

63. Economist Intelligence Unit (2009).
64. Conversation with central bank officials, for example, from Rwanda.
65. Trichet (2003).

the potential costs and benefits of financial inclusion with respect to stability and stress the need to differentiate among policy tools according to their risk profiles given the desired outcome.

Financial stability is a widely accepted public goal because a sound financial system is one of the cornerstones for economic growth. However, this goal is substantially harder to define and measure than traditional policy goals, such as price stability, and disproportionately more contentious.

Financial stability has a multidimensional scope that depends on the interplay of key elements of the system and requires that the key institutions and markets in the financial system remain stable. This does not preclude occasional failures of smaller institutions and occasional substantial losses at larger institutions; these "are part and parcel of the normal functioning of the financial system."[66]

Financial inclusion changes the composition of the financial system with regard to the transactions that take place, the clients that use the various services, the new risks created, and possibly the institutions that operate in newly created or expanded markets. Does this mix tend to cause financial instability or make it more likely by multiplying the sources of potential shocks, or does it counter instability by rendering the financial system more diversified? Furthermore, once a financial crisis has occurred, how effective is financial inclusion in helping poor households cope with this particular external shock?

### Financial Inclusion: A Potential Cause of Financial Instability?

According to one definition that stresses asymmetric information, financial instability occurs when shocks to the system dramatically worsen information problems so that financial intermediation between savings and productive investment opportunities breaks down.[67] Among these shocks, those due to deteriorating financial sector or nonfinancial balance sheets appear most closely related to financial inclusion.

The exposure of financial institutions to risks from low-income markets depends on the share of their revenues that this line of business represents. Specialized microfinance institutions are most prone to these risks, although some large public banks have developed a significant footprint in the low-income segment.[68] However, microfinance clients typically have high repayment rates: when clients have few options in the formal sector, default likely implies much higher future borrowing costs in the informal sector. Hence, as formal options proliferate, credit bureaus become more important to keep these incentives intact. On the

66. Crockett (2002).
67. Mishkin (1999). Financial inclusion seems, at most, of second-order relevance for shocks due to increases in interest rates because of the limited size of the relevant market segment.
68. A good example is Bank Rakyat Indonesia.

other hand, the regulation and risk-based supervision of financial services in low-income markets appears better understood than in other segments of the market.[69]

Large numbers of clients that frequently transact small amounts put substantial strain on supervisory resources but pose limited systemic risk because they represent such a small share of overall financial sector assets. And as information technology proliferates, supervisory challenges will likely become more manageable. As a result, regulators are, in practice, more concerned with issues of consumer protection raised by the lack of sophistication among low-income clients, and with reputational risks due to the large number of clients involved if a particular institution fails.

This view is confirmed by recent research on a new macroprudential frame-work that screens instruments, markets, and institutions. The study, from the Bank for International Settlements, identifies two types of externalities as the key drivers of systemic risk: joint failures of institutions resulting from their common exposures at a single point in time, and procyclicality, the fact that the dynamics of the financial system and of the real economy reinforce each other, increasing the amplitude of booms and busts and undermining stability in both the financial sector and the real economy.[70] In addition, the research shows that the marginal contribution to systemic risk by a financial institution is correlated in a nonlinear way with its size and links with other institutions such that smaller institutions contribute disproportionately less risk.

In addition, research by the Federal Reserve demonstrates that the Community Reinvestment Act (CRA), a piece of U.S. legislation intended to incentivize banks to extend loans to low-income communities, had little impact on the subprime crisis: few of the mortgages that were originated as a result of the CRA fell into the high-risk subprime category, and those subprime mortgages that were due to the CRA performed above average.[71]

Recently, there have been reports about an incipient credit bubble in the rapidly expanding low-income sector in India, pointing to risks of excessive credit demand facilitated by lower financial education in developing countries.[72] Most observers believe excessive borrowing to be a recurrent yet locally isolated phenomenon that validates recent policy concerns with consumer protection.[73] Given the high share of nonprofit institutions in the sector, excessive lending may be driven by disbursement pressure rather than profit motives, in contradiction to the subprime crisis. In addition, vast unmet demand makes bubbles less likely to develop on a larger scale.

---

69. Christen, Lyman, and Rosenberg (2003).
70. Bank for International Settlements (2010).
71. Kroszner (2008).
72. Gokhale (2009)
73. See *The Economist* (2009).

In sum, financial inclusion introduces new lines of business with idiosyncratic risk profiles that can be appropriately regulated and supervised. The contribution to systemic risk is likely to be rather low, especially relative to consumer protection and reputational risk considerations. Especially with respect to technology -based financial inclusion policies, such as mobile phone banking, regulatory concerns have focused on financial integrity rather than stability through FATF policy frameworks to combat money laundering and terrorist financing.

The implementation of FATF standards requires a risk-based approach similar to that required for regulation and supervision of institutions serving low-income clients. It has a direct impact on financial inclusion because customer due diligence through restrictive know-your-customer rules may limit outreach potential. National regulations risk either excluding people who lack certain proofs of identity or imposing prohibitive cost of compliance on financial institutions.[74]

### Financial Inclusion: Cushioning Crisis Impact at the Local Level?

An often cited feature of past crises, especially the Asian financial crisis, has been the stability and growth of financial institutions catering to the poor amid the turmoil that toppled internationally exposed corporate lenders. As a result, local economic activities could continue, at least to some extent, or recover more quickly.

Microfinance institutions that do not mobilize deposits tend to be harder hit when a systemic crisis triggers a credit crunch, so that funds for on-lending to low-income clients are no longer forthcoming because existing credit lines cannot be rolled over. This has also been observed during the current crisis (CGAP 2009a). The transmission of a higher-level crisis through this credit channel can have severe consequences for the local economy that otherwise might be more isolated from national or even international shocks.

It remains an empirical question to confirm beyond anecdotal evidence how important local financial intermediation is as a transmission mechanism for (or protection against) an economy-wide crisis. Similarly, household use of savings for risk management during a crisis should be better researched to explore the stability of the local financial system.

## Conclusions and Recommendations: How Financial Inclusion Equips the Poor to Cope with Instability

The global economic crisis, despite its roots in financial sectors of industrial countries, will likely shift the focus of future financial inclusion policies. The fundamental rethinking of the role of government in finance triggered by the crisis has

---

74. FATF (2008).

built huge momentum for regulatory change. Policymakers should seize the current reform drive to advance financial inclusion policies that foster economic resilience.

Postcrisis opportunities to promote financial inclusion hinge on the careful analysis of the risks posed by the transactions of the poor. In the absence of such analysis, the heightened risk perception could usher in an indiscriminate restriction of innovation. In formulating financial inclusion policies, policymakers should leverage successful innovations developed by their peers that realized the benefits of financial inclusion in safe ways.

Peer-to-peer exchange among developing countries, as facilitated by the Alliance for Financial Inclusion—a global network of policymakers representing seventy developing countries—will help refine and spread these insights widely, enabling other countries to adapt and scale up successful innovations.

Most important, the crisis calls for a shift from credit to savings. Access to savings should be a top priority because it promises three important benefits:

—enhanced household capacity to manage the vulnerabilities exposed by the devastating impact of the crisis,

—diversified funding base of financial institutions to cushion the impact of a global credit crunch on domestic financial intermediation, and

—deeper financial systems that enhance economic resilience by accelerating growth, facilitating diversification, and reducing poverty.

The 2.5 billion unbanked adults are especially vulnerable to economic shocks because they are confined to the inferior risk management features of informal finance. Low-income clients that can build assets before a crash have somewhere to run for cover.

Research has revealed substantial pent-up demand for formal savings that help overcome the costly credit barriers to business expansion. As a result, income and expenditures grow, and households prove more resilient to turmoil. Better household capacity to manage risks frees up public expenditure during times of crisis. Financial inclusion also has been shown to reduce income inequality. Stronger social cohesion helps prevent political instability and permits undivided attention to crisis management. Social safety nets can simultaneously boost financial inclusion when benefits are delivered through basic bank accounts in the formal financial sector. With the subprime meltdown illustrating the dangers of reckless lending practices, consumer protection has surfaced on the policy agenda. Financial education initiatives have been gaining momentum recently; policymakers now see a stronger rationale to build financial education into high school and college curricula, and seek greater participation from the private sector in this endeavor.

However, further research is needed, especially in the following fields:

—*Key barriers to access:* at the strategic level, systematic diagnostic efforts to identify "binding constraints" to financial access will help policymakers set priorities for action.

—*Data and evidence:* updated information on levels and trends of financial inclusion is a critical step toward evidence-based policy decisions. Data collection must be tailored to objectives and available resources. Policymakers should expand collaboration with local researchers to build capacity for the collection of demand-side data.

—*Risk:* greater risk analysis of the scaling-up of technology-based financial inclusion policies with respect to financial stability is necessary to fill critical knowledge gaps due to rapid recent innovation.

Overall, a combination of showcasing of viable business models at the bottom of the pyramid, new partnerships, technological innovation that lowers transaction costs, and rapid growth and progress in poverty alleviation over the past years has helped to attract substantial private sector investment and pushed the access frontier outwards. Policymakers have facilitated strong results by adapting regulatory frameworks to financial innovation in the low-income market segment, and have been able to do so without falling short of their policy goals of financial stability or customer protection. With these recommendations in mind, there is potential to make the necessary gains in expanding financial access without compromising financial stability. The current crisis thus offers a unique opportunity for policymakers to advance financial inclusion policies that promote economic resilience.

# References

Aguirre, Ernesto, Denise Dias, and Klaus Prochaska. 2008. "Diagnostic Report on the Legal and Regulatory Environment for Branchless Banking in Colombia." Washington, D.C.: CGAP.

APEC (Asia-Pacific Economic Cooperation) Business Advisory Council. 2008. "Commercially Sustainable Microfinance: A Strategy for Promoting Financial Inclusion in APEC." Report of a workshop jointly organized by the Advisory Group on APEC Financial System Capacity Building and the APEC Business Advisory Council. Jakarta.

Banco do Nordeste do Brasil. 2010. "Background" (www.bnb.gov.br/Content/aplicacao/O_Banco/Historico_eng/gerados/hist_principal.asp).

Banerjee, Abhijeet, and others. 2009. "The Miracle of Microfinance? Evidence from a Randomized Evaluation." Working paper. MIT, Department of Economics and Abdul Latif Jameel Poverty Action Lab.

Bank for International Settlements. 2010. "Macroprudential Policy and Addressing Procyclicality." In *80th Annual Report*, chapter 7. Basel.

Bankable Frontier Associates. 2009. "Key Issues in Financial Inclusion Measurement for Regulators: Survey Design and Implementation." Commissioned draft working paper. Bangkok: Alliance for Financial Inclusion.

Beck, Thorsten, and Augusto de la Torre. 2006. "The Basic Analytics of Access to Financial Services." Policy Research Working Paper 4026. Washington, D.C.: World Bank.

Beck, Thorsten, Asli Demirgüç-Kunt, and Ross Levine. 2004. "Finance, Firm Size, and Growth." Working Paper W10983. Cambridge, Mass.: National Bureau of Economic Research.

Beck, Thorsten, Asli Demirgüç-Kunt, and Vojislav Maksimovic. 2004. "Bank Competition and Access to Finance: International Evidence." *Journal of Money, Credit, and Banking* 36, no. 3 (part 2): 627–48.

Beck, Thorsten, and others. 2008. "Finance, Firm Size, and Growth." *Journal of Money, Credit and Banking* 40, no. 7: 1379–405.

Chaia, Alberto, and others. 2009. "Half the World Is Unbanked." Framing Note. New York: Financial Access Initiative (October).

Chatain, Pierre Laurent, and others. 2008. "Integrity in Mobile Phone Financial Services." Working Paper 146. Washington, D.C.: World Bank.

Christen, Robert Peck, Timothy R. Lyman, and Richard Rosenberg. 2003. "Microfinance Consensus Guidelines: Guiding Principles on Regulation and Supervision of Microfinance." Washington, D.C.: CGAP.

Claessens, Stijn, Patrick Honohan, and Liliana Rojas-Suarez. 2009. "Policy Principles for Expanding Financial Access: Report of the CGD Task Force on Access to Financial Services." Washington, D.C.: Center for Global Development.

Collins, Daryl, and others. 2009. *Portfolios of the Poor.* Princeton University Press.

Consultative Group to Assist the Poor (CGAP). 2009a. *Financial Access 2009: Measuring Access to Financial Services around the World.* Washington, D.C.

———. 2009b. "Government's Role in Microfinance: What Is the Optimal Policy Mix?" (www.cgap.org/p/site/c/template.rc/1.26.4903/).

Crockett, Andrew. 2002. "Why Is Financial Stability a Goal of Public Policy?" In *Handbook of Monetary Policy*, edited by Jack Rabin and Glenn L. Stevens, pp. 69–86. New York: Marcel Dekker.

De la Torre, Augusto, Juan Carlos Gozzi, and Sergio Schmukler. 2007. "Innovative Experiences in Access to Finance: Market Friendly Roles for the Visible Hand?" Policy Research Working Paper 4326. Washington, D.C.: World Bank.

Demirgüç-Kunt, Asli, Thorsten Beck, and Patrick Honohan. 2008. *Finance for All? Policies and Pitfalls in Expanding Access.* World Bank Policy Research Report. Washington, D.C.: World Bank (http://go.worldbank.org/HNKL9ZHO50).

Dupas, Pascaline, and Jonathan Robinson. 2009. "Savings Constraints and Microenterprise Development: Evidence from a Field Experiment in Kenya." Working Paper 14693. Cambridge, Mass.: National Bureau of Economic Research.

Economist Intelligence Unit. 2009. *Global Microscope on the Microfinance Business Environment.* London: Economist Group.

Eisner, Marc Allen, Jeff Worsham, and Evan J. Ringquist. 2006. *Contemporary Regulatory Policy.* New York: Lynne Rienner.

Fernando, Nimal A. 2009. "The State of Financial Inclusion in Asia: An Overview." Presentation at the Alliance for Financial Inclusion Global Policy Forum. Nairobi, September 14 (www.afi-global.net/downloads/GPF_Nimal_Fernando.pdf).

Financial Action Task Force (FATF). 2008. "Guidance on Capacity Building for Mutual Evaluations and Implementation of the FATF Standards within Low Capacity Countries." Paris: Financial Access Task Force (www.fatf-gafi.org/dataoecd/61/28/40248726.pdf).

Financial Sector Deepening Trust. 2009. *FinAccess National Survey 2009: Dynamics of Kenya's Changing Financial Landscape* (www.fsdkenya.org/finaccess/documents/09-06-10_FinAccess_FA09_Report.pdf).

Giné, Xavier, and Robert Townsend. 2004. "Evaluation of Financial Liberalization: A General Equilibrium Model with Constrained Occupation Choice." *Journal of Development Economics* 74, no. 2: 269–307.

Gokhale, Ketaki. 2009. "A Global Surge in Tiny Loans Spurs Credit Bubble in a Slum." *Wall Street Journal Online*. August 13 (http://online.wsj.com/article/SB125012112518027581.html).

G20 Leaders. 2010. "The G-20 Toronto Summit Declaration." Toronto (www.g20.org/Documents/g20_declaration_en.pdf).

Grameen Bank. 2007. *Annual Report 2007*. Dhaka.

Hannig, Alfred, and Stefan Jansen. 2008. "Inclusive Financial System Reforms: What Works, What Doesn't, and Why?" Draft report. Jakarta: Deutsche Gesellschaft für Technische Zusammenarbeit (GTZ).

Hawkins, Penelope. 2006. "Financial Access and Financial Stability." Paper prepared for the Conference on Central Banks and the Challenge of Development. Bank for International Settlements, Basel, March 14–15.

Honohan, Patrick. 2004. "Financial Development, Growth and Poverty: How Close Are the Links?" World Bank Policy Research Working Paper 3203.Washington, D.C.: World Bank (February).

———. 2007. "Cross-Country Variation in Household Access to Financial Services." Paper prepared for the conference on Access to Finance. World Bank, Washington, D.C., March 15–16.

Ivatury, Gautam. 2006. "Using Technology to Build Inclusive Financial Systems." Focus Note 32. Washington, D.C.: CGAP.

Karlan, Dean, and Jonathan Zinman. 2007. "Expanding Credit Access: Using Randomized Supply Decisions to Estimate the Impacts." Working Paper 956. New Haven, Conn.: Yale University, Economic Growth Center.

Kay, John. 2009. "The Slow Drip of Faster Payments." *Financial Times*, June 16 (www.ft.com/cms/s/0/ffb86d28-5a81-11de-8c14-00144feabdc0.html).

Kimenyi, Mwangi S., and Njuguna S. Ndung'u. 2009. "Expanding the Financial Services Frontier: Lessons from Mobile Phone Banking in Kenya." Washington, D.C.: Brookings (October).

Kneiding, Christoph, Edward Al-Hussayni, and Ignacio Mas. 2009. "Multiple Country Data Sources for Access to Finance—A Technical Note." Washington, D.C.: CGAP.

Kroszner, Randall S. 2008. "The Community Reinvestment Act and the Recent Mortgage Crisis." Board of Governors of the Federal Reserve System.

Kumar, Anjali, and others. 2006. "Expanding Bank Outreach through Retail Partnerships: Correspondent Banking in Brazil." Working Paper 85. Washington, D.C.: World Bank.

Levine, Ross. 2005. "Finance and Growth: Theory and Evidence." In *Handbook of Economic Growth*, vol. 1A, edited by Philip Aghion and Steven N. Durlauf, chapter 12. Amsterdam: Elsevier.

Lyman, Timothy, Mark Pickens, and David Porteous. 2008. "Regulating Transformational Branchless Banking: Mobile Phones and Other Technology to Increase Access to Finance." Focus Note 43. Washington, D.C.: CGAP.

Makanjee, Maya. 2009. "Financial Inclusion in Africa." Presentation at the Alliance for Financial Inclusion Global Policy Forum. Nairobi, September 15.

Mas, Ignacio, and Hannah Siedek. 2008. "Banking through Networks of Retail Agents." Focus Note 47. Washington, D.C.: CGAP.

Mishkin, Frederic S. 1999. "Global Financial Instability: Framework, Events, Issues." *Journal of Economic Perspectives* 13, no. 4: 3–20.

Morawczynski, Olga, and Mark Pickens. 2009. "Poor People Using Mobile Financial Services: Observations on Customer Usage and Impact from M-PESA." Brief. Washington, D.C.: CGAP.

Morduch, Jonathan. 1999. "The Microfinance Promise." *Journal of Economic Literature* 37, no. 4: 1569–1614.

Otero, Maria, and Elisabeth Rhyne. 1994. "Financial Services for Microenterprises: Principles and Institutions." In *The New World of Microenterprise Finance*, edited by Maria Otero and Elizabeth Rhyne, pp. 11–26. Hartford, Conn.: Kumarian Press.

Pande, Rohini, and R. Burgess. 2005. "Can Rural Banks Reduce Poverty? Evidence from the Indian Social Banking Experiment." *American Economic Review* 95, no. 3: 780–95.

Patten, Richard, Jay Rosengard, and Don Johnston. 2001. "Microfinance Success amidst Macroeconomic Failure: The Experience of Bank Rakyat Indonesia during the East Asian Crisis." *World Development* 29, no. 6: 1057–69.

Porteous, David. 2009. "Key Issues in Design and Implementation of Surveys on Financial Inclusion." Presentation at the Alliance for Financial Inclusion Global Policy Forum. Nairobi, September 15 (www.afi-global.net/downloads/GPF_David_Porteous.pdf).

Robinson, Marguerite. 2001. *The Microfinance Revolution: Sustainable Banking for the Poor*. Washington, D.C.: World Bank.

Rodrik, Dani. 2008. "The New Development Economics: We Shall Experiment, but How Shall We Learn?" Working Paper RWP08-055. Harvard University, Kennedy School of Government.

Safaricom. 2009. *Annual Report*. Nairobi (October).

Schulze, Ludwig. 2008. "The Future of Mobile Banking." Presentation to the Inter-American Development Bank (www.iadb.org/am/2008/docs/MB_LudwigSchulze.pdf).

*The Economist*. 2009. "Froth at the Bottom of the Pyramid." August 25.

Trichet, Jean-Claude. 2003. "Financial Stability." Speech given at the Forum Financier Belge. Brussels, November 26 (www.bis.org/review/r031205a.pdf).

UN Capital Development Fund and UN Department of Economic and Social Affairs. 2006. *Building Inclusive Financial Sectors*. New York.

Urrutia Corral, Luis. 2010. "Keynote Address to GIABA." Speech to the Intergovernmental Action Group against Money Laundering in West Africa (GIABA). Abuja, December 10 (www.fatf-gafi.org/document/53/0,3746,en_32250379_32236879_46754677_1_1_1_1,00.html).

Vlaanderen, Paul. 2010. "Financial Inclusion and Financial Integrity: Complementary Policy Objectives." Keynote speech at Windsor III Leadership Seminar of Financial Inclusion. Windsor, UK, March 8 (www.fatf-gafi.org/document/7/0,3746,en_ 32250379_32236879_44764103_1_1_1_1,00.html).

Young, Robin, and Robert Vogel. 2005. "State-Owned Retail Banks (SORBs) in Rural and Microfinance Markets: A Framework for Considering the Constraints and Potential." U.S. Agency for International Development.

Zimmerman, Jamie M., and Yves Moury. 2009. "Savings-Linked Conditional Cash Transfers: A New Policy Approach to Global Poverty Reduction." Global Assets Project Policy Brief. Washington, D.C.: New America Foundation (www.newamerica. net/publications/policy/savings_linked_conditional_cash_transfers).

PART VI

*Cross-Border Regulation*

# 12

## Cross-Border Regulation after the Global Financial Crisis

ALEJANDRO WERNER AND GUILLERMO ZAMARRIPA

This chapter is about contagion among financial systems in a world that is global and interconnected. It argues that contagion effects from the recent financial crisis will have direct implications for reshaping the regulatory and supervisory framework.

The period of financial and economic expansion prior to the subprime crisis was underpinned by low real interest rates and excess liquidity, which facilitated robust global economic growth. Such expansion was accompanied by high leverage, excessive risk taking, and a greater openness of financial sectors to foreign investment. This contributed significantly to a more interconnected global system, thereby increasing the likelihood of contagion among financial systems. The crisis revealed four sources of contagion: losses from toxic assets, asset and liability mismatches, decoupling and recoupling effects on financial markets, and risk aversion from market participants.

The multiple sources of contagion played different roles in emerging market economies (EMEs). Toxic assets holdings did not represent a significant source of vulnerability since market participants were more risk averse and their investors less sophisticated, a situation that limited the exposure to these assets. However, the asset and liability mismatch had a differentiated effect among EMEs,

The views expressed herein are those of the authors and do not necessarily reflect the views of the Ministry of Finance, Mexico.

depending on their financial system structure and the vulnerability of the economy to capital outflows.

EMEs' financial markets were immune to the effects of the crisis in the first stage when markets decoupled, and their financial variables remained stable. However, the prevailing situation in some developed economies and the failure of Lehman Brothers resulted in a recoupling effect that generated volatility on EMEs' interest rate, foreign exchange, and securities markets. Despite the observed volatility in their financial markets, most EMEs did not experience significant outflows. Such resilience can be explained partially by the regulatory and supervisory framework that these economies developed in the years previous to the crisis.

The global financial system had become increasingly interconnected, and as a result, EMEs were subject to the effects of decisions made by risk-averse headquarters of large conglomerates operating in the region. Such decisions tried to solve liquidity or solvency problems of either the parent company or the subsidiary. For example, some of these conglomerates constrained their local lending activities to reduce their overall risk exposure.

The openness of the financial industry to foreign investors increased the level of interconnection among financial systems and allowed local contagions to become global in scope. Furthermore, regulatory and supervisory oversight evolved at a slower pace than the increasingly interconnected markets and thus was not designed to appropriately mitigate the rising risks. The same variables that previously signaled local contagions in a system, such as leverage, capitalization, or funding structure, became relevant, as they may explain the occurrence of global contagion. The interconnectedness and complexity of corporate structures, as in the case of Lehman Brothers, demonstrate the lack of a legal framework to resolve the failure of a cross-border institution of such complexity. Consequently, the contagion effects from the recent crisis reveal the need for national authorities to establish an efficient global regulatory and supervisory framework.

The design of the new global regulatory and supervisory framework should be based on a new paradigm, one that might reduce contagion in the global financial system through enhanced cross-border financial regulation and efficient coordination among national supervisors. This framework should:

—develop a supervisory structure for coordinated assessment of global risks that will enable full supervisory oversight of financial conglomerates and their subsidiaries;

—establish information exchange mechanisms for effective consolidated supervision based on mutual cooperation, consultation, and timely communication among supervisors;

—create a resolution mechanism to coordinate cross-border failures of global financial conglomerates (including ring-fencing practices);

—support effective assessment of major sources of vulnerability within the global financial system; and

—identify relevant, systemically non-cooperative jurisdictions and develop measures to limit them in order to reduce the risks they pose to the stability of the financial system.

This chapter begins with a description of the origins of the crisis and the market incentives that contributed to it, and then elaborates on the four sources of contagion. This is followed by an explanation of how these sources of contagion propagated the effects of the global crisis, with particular focus on their impact on EMEs. The fourth section assesses the impacts of contagion on Mexico and describes the measures that the Mexican government took to contain these effects and restore the financial markets. It also summarizes the lessons learned from the crisis through the perspective of Latin American EMEs. The fifth section analyzes the nature and ramifications of the complexity arising from globalization and the openness of financial markets to foreign investments. The sixth section establishes the rationale for designing a new global financial supervisory architecture, and the subsequent section elucidates five areas for reform in the redesign process. The eighth section then examines the implications of these reforms for EMEs.

## Origins of the Financial Crisis

Before the recent crisis, financial system development was driven by globalization, liberalization, deregulation, and constant innovation. This period was underpinned by a favorable financial and economic environment with low real interest rates, supported by excess liquidity in the markets and a global economic outlook that limited the volatility of macroeconomic variables. As a consequence of such a favorable environment, the markets benefited from an extensive variety of financial instruments and from enhanced conditions for financing, particularly in the terms and costs for household and corporate financing. However, during this period, the global financial system was unconsciously building up a systemic concentration of risks.

The first markets that revealed the symptoms of this potential problem were the housing and mortgage markets in the United States. In a market where mortgages were available at low interest rates, the demand for U.S. housing increased, adding pressure to market prices. Thus, from 2001 to 2005, the prices for houses appreciated significantly. This situation generated two incentives: first, as mortgage interest rates decreased, home owners had the opportunity to refinance their mortgages on better terms, and second, from the improved mortgage conditions, potential buyers enlarged their budgets to acquire new houses. Thus market conditions set the stage for increased demand for housing, which was then supported by greater availability of mortgages and by the owners' expectations to obtain a capital gain from an increase in the value of their home.

The banking industry contributed to the mortgage lending boom that laid the foundations of the crisis. Brunnermeier (2009) identified two events that led to the liquidity and credit boom. First, banks switched from holding loans on their balance sheet to an "originate and distribute" model. Instead of holding the loans, banks repackaged them and off-loaded their risk by passing it to other market participants. Second, banks increased their financing of long-term assets with instruments of shorter maturity.

In the case of the originate-and-distribute model, mortgage originators were encouraged to accelerate the off-loading of risk. Thus banks failed to ensure that loans would be serviced, and market participants failed to acknowledge the risks of the mortgages they were buying. Jiang, Nelson, and Vytlacil (2009) give evidence of such misaligned incentives. Using data from a major national bank in the United States that originated 721,767 loans between January 2004 and February 2008, the authors show a rapid expansion in the origination of mortgage loans during the boom, followed by a sharp decline during the housing bust. Mortgage volume increased from near 20,000 loans in the first half of 2004 to a peak of over 154,000 loans during the second half of 2006, and declined steeply in the second half of 2007. However, the real problem was not the number of loans but rather the deficient quality of the origination process. With flexible and reduced requirements for filing the mortgage loans, brokers were responsible for more than 70 percent of mortgage origination before the second half of 2007.

The risk off-loading was facilitated by the excess liquidity in markets and by the development of new and more complex financial instruments. Longstaff and Myers (2009) argue that innovation in financial markets focused on the design of structured investment vehicles that owned other financial assets and securities. Examples of these include collateralized debt obligations (CDOs), which offered attractive expected returns. Thus the rapid expansion of CDOs largely contributed to funding the boom in subprime mortgages.

CDOs enable a pool of mortgages of differing quality to be packaged and tranched. For instance, while the collateral of a CDO could be mainly B+ average mortgages, through enhancements (such as diversification, overcollateralization and subordination, excess spread, and active management of the pool) the final rating of that CDO could be upgraded to AAA. The CDO model assumed constant growth in the value of real estate properties to cover the credit balance in case of default. Figure 12-1 illustrates the difference between the credit ratings

Figure 12-1.  *CDO Rating versus Collateral Rating (3,912 tranches)*

Billions of U.S. dollars

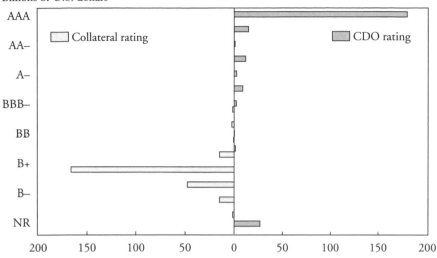

Source: Ministry of Finance, Mexico. Data based on figure 5 from Benmelech and Dlugosz (2009).

of collateralized mortgages and those of the final CDO, which after the bundling and enhancing processes usually received a AAA rating.[1]

The combination of the availability of highly rated instruments and the excess liquidity set the stage for dissemination of structured products throughout the global markets. From 2000 to mid-2007, the markets' behavior was optimistic, mainly driven by prices in housing markets. An example of this mindset can be found in a statement by Charles Prince, former CEO of Citigroup, about the prevailing mortgage market situation in July 2007: "When the music stops, in terms of liquidity, things will be complicated. But as long as the music is playing, you've got to get up and dance. We're still dancing."[2]

1. Unless indicated, the figures and tables in this chapter were elaborated by the Ministry of Finance, Mexico, with information from Bloomberg; the central banks of Argentina, Brazil, Chile, and Mexico; deposit insurance agencies of Australia, Germany, Greece, Hong Kong, Ireland, Korea, the United Kingdom, and the United States; filings on derivatives instruments and companies reports of Alfa, Bachoco, Cemex, Comerci, Femsa, GISSA, Gruma, Posadas, Sigma, and Vitro; financial reports of Grupo BBVA, Citigroup, Santander Central Hispano, the HSBC Group, and Scotiabank; International Monetary Fund; National Banking and Securities Commission of Mexico; Standard & Poor's; supervisory agencies of Chile and Colombia; and the Mexican Institute of Statistics.

2. See Nakamoto and Wighton (2007). His statement is an allusion to Keynes's analogy comparing economic bubbles to the game of musical chairs.

Figure 12-2. *Case-Shiller Home Price Indexes, 1987 to mid-2009*

Index values

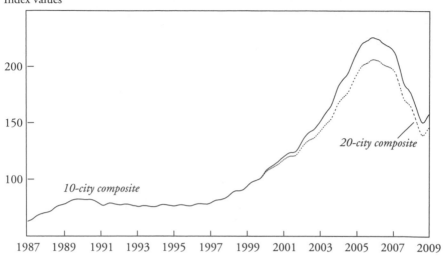

Source: Standard and Poor's, S&P Case-Shiller Home Price Indexes.

However, a few months later the U.S. housing bubble burst and everyone stopped dancing. This was reflected in a dramatic change in the mortgages' loan-to-value ratio, where the loan's outstanding balance was above the market value of the house, providing incentives to mortgage holders to default by the end of 2007. Figure 12-2 shows the downturn in housing prices in major U.S cities, which left mortgage loan holders with negative equity.

The price adjustments in the housing sector had a direct effect on the financial sector. The change in mortgage loan-to-value ratios had a negative impact on banks' balance sheets due to fair value accounting (FVA). FVA generated pressure on banks and financial institutions with large trading positions, which had to be registered and revalued at current market prices. Such revaluation reduced banks' capital. In order to avoid a financial collapse, many governments, particularly those of developed economies, bailed out a number of financial institutions. While the U.S. government led these support programs, followed by Japan and the European economies, EMEs were not directly affected by such problems, and their governments did not provide funds to capitalize their local financial institutions.

In the middle of the financial turmoil, a debate arose about whether FVA exacerbated the financial crisis or did not contribute to it. Khan (2009) argued that FVA rules themselves may not increase contagion among banks and that it is only when fair values are used as inputs in regulatory ratios or incentive contracts for management that contagion can increase. Khan finds a positive association between FVA and additional contagion when banks' fundamentals are weak, as in severe periods of market illiquidity, or when institutions are poorly capitalized or have a higher portion of fair value assets or liabilities.

Similarly, Laux and Leuz (2009) claim that FVA made only a limited contribution to exacerbating the crisis, for the following reasons:

—Market uncertainty was such that the use of either FVA or historic cost accounting would have made no difference. Even with the disclosure of fair values, investors made their inferences regarding the true value of the exposures.

—Banks can act discretionarily to decide the best timing to recognize fair values.

—Generally accepted accounting principles have a mechanism that allows for deviation from market prices under certain conditions.

—The use of FVA may have desirable incentive effects ex ante to reduce the severity of the crisis, and it may allow for early recognition of losses, making it harder for banks to hide potential problems.

Thus it is not clear that FVA exacerbated the crisis. This negative effect is more related to the excessive leverage of institutions, to the institutions' fundamentals, and to the risk perception of market participants. In the climate of uncertainty generated by the loss recognition process among financial firms, managers perceived their counterparties to be riskier and took actions that resulted in both credit and liquidity restrictions in markets. To restore confidence and maintain market function, many governments from developed economies instituted new measures, including increasing the coverage of deposit insurance. Table 12-1 provides a sample of programs implemented by developed economies to provide more stability to their systems.

Although the crisis had its origins in the U.S. mortgage lending market, the contagion effects rapidly spread to other markets, including those of developed economies, through the interconnection of the financial systems. From the analysis in this section, we can identify four main sources of contagion in the crisis: the holding of toxic assets, the mismatch between assets and liabilities, the decoupling and recoupling effects on financial markets, and the risk aversion of market participants.

## Sources of Contagion

There is evidence that the four sources of contagion affected EMEs differently: the holding of toxic assets was not a major source of vulnerability, the assets and liabilities mismatch had differentiated effects on EMEs, the recoupling effect of financial markets affected the apparent stability of their financial markets, and the risk aversion of major conglomerates operating worldwide had local effects on EMEs.

Table 12-1. *Measures Established to Increase the Amount of Deposit Coverage*

| Country | Summary | Period |
|---------|---------|--------|
| Australia | From no guarantee plan to insuring all deposits in any currency totaling up to AU$1,000,000 | October 12, 2008– October 10, 2011 |
| Germany | From a €20,000 voluntary system to an unlimited insured amount for retail banks | October 5, 2008; no due date |
| Greece | From insured amount increased to €100,000 as the maximum guarantee amount to covering all deposits of private individuals | October 8, 2008– October 8, 2011 |
| Hong Kong | Deposit insured amount raised from HK$100,000 to no set maximum to a blanket guarantee of all deposits | October 14, 2008– December 31, 2010 |
| Ireland | From a €20,000 insured amount to €100,000 as the maximum insured amount | September 30, 2008– September 29, 2010 |
| Korea | Same guarantee deposit amount—KRW 50 million—but also includes foreign currency deposits | November 3, 2008; no due date |
| United Kingdom | From a £35,000 insured amount to £50,000 as the maximum insured amount | October 3, 2008; no due date |
| United States | Increase in the maximum insured amount of all deposits, from U.S.$100,000 to U.S.$250,000 | October 3, 2008– December 31, 2013 |
| | From $250,000 limit on the insured amount of non-interest-bearing deposit transaction accounts to no maximum | October 14, 2008– June 30, 2010 |

Source: Central banks and deposit insurance agencies for each country.

## Losses from Toxic Assets

The initial concern of market participants was to assess the scale of losses from holding toxic assets. As of June 2009, several financial institutions and other market participants in developed economies recorded losses of over US$2,800 billion. Table 12-2 shows the concentration of losses in the United States, the United Kingdom, and the European region. Experiencing negative impacts on their capital structure, large global institutions were forced to raise capital initially from their national governments. Some of the major conglomerates in the United States, the United Kingdom, continental Europe, and Asia had to raise significant amounts of capital to offset their losses.

While these toxic assets were mainly located in developed economies, Latin American and other EMEs were not completely immune to their effects. The losses from holding toxic assets affected large multinational conglomerates that also have a large presence in EMEs.

Table 12-2. *Estimated Losses in Financial Institutions by Region, 2007–10*
Units as indicated

| Region | Loans (billions of U.S. dollars) | Percent of total loans | Securities (billions of U.S. dollars) | Percent of total securities | Total losses (billions of U.S. dollars) | Percent of total losses |
|---|---|---|---|---|---|---|
| U.S. banks | 654 | 34.5 | 371 | 40.5 | 1,025 | 36.5 |
| U.K. banks | 497 | 26.3 | 107 | 11.7 | 604 | 21.5 |
| Euro area banks | 480 | 25.4 | 333 | 36.4 | 813 | 28.9 |
| Other mature European banks[a] | 165 | 8.7 | 36 | 3.9 | 201 | 7.2 |
| Asian banks[b] | 97 | 5.1 | 69 | 7.5 | 166 | 5.9 |
| Total | 1,893 | 100.0 | 916 | 100.0 | 2,809 | 100.0 |

Source: International Monetary Fund.
a. Includes Denmark, Norway, Iceland, Sweden, and Switzerland.
b. Includes Australia, Hong Kong SAR, Japan, New Zealand, and Singapore.

One hypothesis is that in EME regions, like Latin America, significant losses from toxic assets in local banks did not happen because their market participants were more risk averse and their investors were less sophisticated.

*Asset-Liability Mismatch*

A financial system may be exposed to mismatches, and such a situation represents a source of vulnerability to an economy. Risk management literature argues that risks arising from asset liability mismatches may accentuate problems during periods of stress when financial institutions face illiquidity.

At an institutional level, contagion from deposit runs has always been a risk in banking systems. How deposit and interbank runs materialize is not well understood. Dupont (2007) documents the spread of a panic from insolvent and solvent banks in Kansas in 1893. The evidence provided shows that even when local newspapers disclosed official bank reports, it did not prevent deposit holders from collectively withdrawing their funds from solvent banks. The new feature is that runs are not only local but global.

In the event of a deposit or interbank run, institutions may face difficulties from a maturity mismatch between long-term assets and short-term liabilities, and from a currency mismatch between assets and liabilities, that is, markets largely dependent on foreign currency funding would become more vulnerable when the exchange rate depreciates.

An asset-liability mismatch situation is usually underpinned by the particular structure of a financial system. On a macroeconomic level, such a mismatch would reveal the degree to which an economy is vulnerable to capital flows. This situation is reflected at a microlevel on the balance sheets of the banking institutions.

To reduce vulnerability to deposit or interbank runs, the free-capital-flow model should be established only when a country has developed an institutionally and economically sound environment. Prasad and Rajan (2008) argue that countries with liberalized capital flows require a robust institutional framework that can provide confidence to foreign investors and prevent fund outflows at the first sign of price volatility.

The case of Hungary illustrates this. The banking system was mainly owned by foreign banks, and a significant proportion of its liabilities was owed to foreign institutions. After a period of credit expansion, explained by the positive economic outlook, the delinquency ratio of the loan portfolio started to deteriorate. With the increased volatility of financial variables, stockholders refused to provide additional resources to recapitalize the subsidiaries, and foreign debt holders retrieved their funds. As a result, the banking system had difficulty rolling over debt maturities, and this led to an increased perception of fragility in the financial system. In order to isolate the Hungarian problem and prevent further contagion to other EMEs, the European Central Bank, the International Monetary Fund (IMF), and the World Bank lent Hungary US$45.1 billion.[3] The experience of Hungary and other eastern European economies demonstrates how a system with vulnerabilities can contribute to a major outflow of capital.

In contrast, the financial stability of Latin American markets was partially due to the region's development of institutional frameworks that resulted from their experiences with past financial crises. Such frameworks reduced vulnerability from foreign sources of funding and allowed for a credit activity largely funded through deposits and other domestic sources.

## Decoupling and Recoupling Effects

For most EMEs contagion from the crisis showed up in the volatility of the macroeconomic variables, triggered by the announcement of Lehman Brothers' collapse on September 15, 2008. This event precipitated increased volatility in EME foreign exchange, interest rate, and securities markets. These contagion effects that increased the risk perception of EMEs occurred as a result of their interconnectedness to the global financial system. Dooley and Hutchinson (2009) identify three phases of contagion to EMEs from the subprime crisis.

The first phase began in February 2007 (the onset of the crisis) and went through May 19, 2008. During this phase, EMEs decoupled from developed economies, their stock markets outperformed U.S. stock indexes, and their currencies appreciated against the U.S. dollar.

3. Topçu (2009).

Figure 12-3. *Emerging Market Bond Index, 2008–09*

Index value

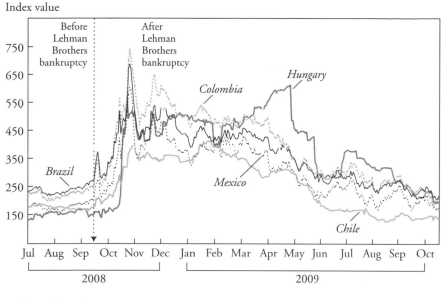

Source: Bloomberg.

A second phase, from May 19, 2008, to September 15, 2008 (the "Lehman day"), was characterized by a decline in EME main stock indexes by approximately three quarters of their outperformance relative to the U.S. stock index of the first phase. A feature of this phase was the apparent continued decoupling of credit and stock markets, reinforced by an appreciation in the value of EME currencies relative to the U.S. dollar.

In the last phase, a recoupling period from the Lehman day until the end of 2008, EME and U.S. equity markets fell to levels 40 percent below their precrisis levels, and EME currencies declined by about 10 percent. Also, EME and U.S. credit spreads increased sharply after September and by late October reached their highest levels.

The increased risk perception among foreign and local investors in EMEs after the Lehman collapse was reflected in their respective credit default swap (CDS) and emerging market bond index (EMBI) levels. After a period of intense volatility, Latin American markets returned to the levels observed before September 2008. However, this situation was different in eastern European economies, such as Hungary, which experienced a second peak in its EMBI in May 2009. Figures 12-3 and 12-4 show the EMBI and CDS levels for a sample of EMEs.

From September 2008 onward, the exchange rate of EME currencies experienced devaluation and increased volatility with respect to the U.S. dollar. Figure

Figure 12-4.  *Credit Default Swaps, 2008–09*[a]

Index value

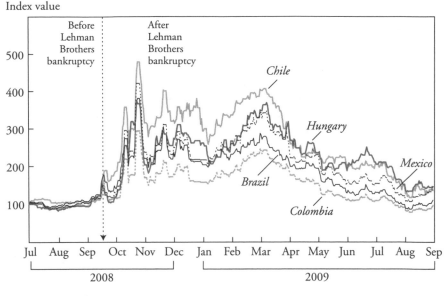

Source: Bloomberg.
a. July 1, 2008 = 100.

12-5 indicates that despite the increased volatility in the foreign exchange markets during the first quarter of 2009, the currencies of the largest economies in the region, except Argentina and Mexico, returned to the levels observed in July 2008.

Diversification strategies for investment portfolios are effective during the decoupling stage; however, during recoupling these supposed diversification strategies are unable to reduce the effects of the financial crisis. In this respect, once recoupling affected the performance of international securities markets, the effects exposed participants to price volatility and diminished investor confidence. This impact was deeper in the securities markets of developed economies, where the valuations reached their lowest level in March 2009. From this time onward, global markets began their recovery, supported by a return of confidence and a more optimistic outlook for economic growth (see figure 12-6).

Latin American EMEs recoupled after the Lehman day, as indicated by the increased volatility of their financial variables. Figures 12-3 through 12-6 show that after the Lehman bankruptcy announcement, the EMBI and CDS spreads for Brazil and Chile increased sharply, while their local currencies depreciated with respect to the U.S. dollar.

The volatility effects of financial variables had a negative impact on the capital account and reserves of most economies in the region. The responsive

Figure 12-5. *Exchange Rates in Latin America, 2008–09*[a]

Index value

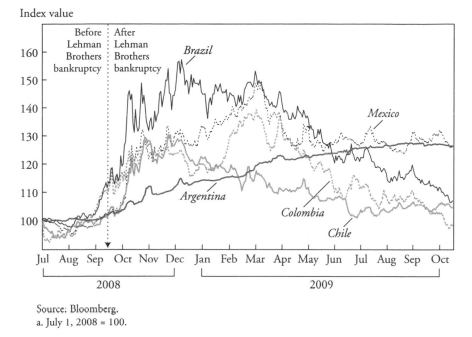

Source: Bloomberg.
a. July 1, 2008 = 100.

measures implemented to control this situation were effective for avoiding a further deterioration of international reserves. However, the effect of price volatility
had a different impact on Brazil, where the capital account registered increased
inflows. In an attempt to reduce such capital inflows, which could further appreciate the Brazilian real, the government of Brazil imposed a tax on foreign capital
inflows to its financial markets.

A detailed analysis of how the volatility of market variables affected Mexico is
presented later in the chapter, along with a description of the measures taken by
the government to mitigate the negative effects.

*Risk Aversion*

In the particular case of Latin American economies, effects of contagion materialized differently. There was not a significant impact from holding toxic assets or
an asset-liability mismatch, but there were symptoms associated with recoupling
and the risk aversion profile of large conglomerates with a presence in the region.

EMEs may experience the effects of contagion when the parent company or
another subsidiary of the group faces either illiquidity or insolvency. A subsidiary at the EME can be affected by decisions aimed to improve the overall situation of the conglomerate.

Figure 12-6. *Stock Exchange Indexes, 2008–09*[a]

Index value

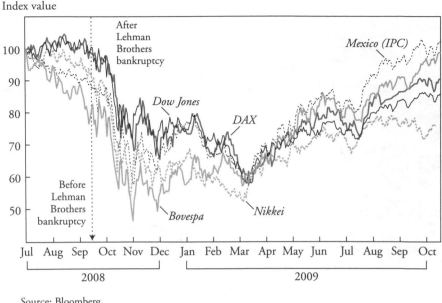

Source: Bloomberg.
a. July 1, 2008 = 100.

One concern derives from an increase in the transfer of resources from the subsidiary to the financial group through dividend payouts or through other related party transactions that might weaken the solvency of local institutions. During the crisis, EMEs' local banks represented a large share of the profits of financial conglomerates. In the case of Mexico, subsidiaries were very profitable for their holding companies, but there were no increases in dividend payouts in 2008 and 2009, except in the case of one bank (see table 12-3).

Regarding other related-party transactions, the five largest foreign-owned banks in Mexico had an average exposure to their respective conglomerate of 19 percent of the local bank net capital as of March 2009. This figure did not increase in the following months.

A second concern arises when global conglomerates limit their credit risk exposure in local markets to reduce risk-weighted assets and strengthen the global balance sheet. Despite high and stable capitalization levels in the banking system in Mexico, three large foreign banking institutions reduced their lending activity to improve the overall solvency of their conglomerates. Financing to the private sector from Santander, HSBC, and Banamex (Citigroup) subsidiaries decreased 16.7 percent, 16.5 percent, and 5.3 percent, respectively, from October 2008 to August 2009. From this it can be inferred that corporate strategies

Table 12-3. *Profits of International Bank Subsidiaries and Dividends Payouts, Mexico*

Percent

| Bank | Ratio of subsidiary profit to parent company profit | | | Ratio of dividends payout to subsidiary profit | | |
|---|---|---|---|---|---|---|
| | 2007 | 2008 | Sep-09 | 2007 | 2008 | Sep-09 |
| BBVA Bancomer | 23.9 | 26.4 | 17.7 | 78.5 | 76.0 | 60.3 |
| Banamex (Citigroup) | 43.1 | . . .ᵃ | 15.5 | 40.7 | 0 | 0 |
| Santander | 8.0 | 4.9 | 6.5 | 149.9 | 66.3 | 0 |
| HSBC | 2.7 | 5.2 | 0.9 | 0 | 75.2 | 39.8 |
| Scotiabank Inverlatᵇ | 8.8 | 8.8 | 3.1 | 23.8 | 18.1 | 66.8 |

Source: National Banking and Securities Commission of Mexico and financial statements of the parent companies.

a. Citigroup reported a net loss of $2.7 billion at the end of 2008. However, the Banamex subsidiary of Citigroup reported a net income of $921 million as of 2008.

b. Figures for the parent company of Scotiabank Inverlat are as of October 2009.

based on risk aversion may constrain the lending activity of financial subsidiaries, with impacts on the local economies. An alternative hypothesis is that large conglomerates expected their subsidiaries to achieve greater risk-adjusted returns on their capital, which led to a restrained and more selective lending activity.

## The Mexican Experience

As explained in the previous section, the recoupling effect increased volatility in the Mexican financial market. In this section, we describe the conditions prevailing in this market after Lehman's failure was announced; the consequent effects on the interest rate, securities, and foreign exchange markets; and the measures implemented by the Mexican government to reduce uncertainty, restore confidence, and maintain appropriate market functions. In addition, we summarize the main lessons learned from the crisis from the perspective of a Latin American EME.

As in other EMEs, the foreign exchange market in Mexico experienced an increase in volatility after the Lehman collapse. To reduce the volatility, the Ministry of Finance and the Bank of Mexico implemented a series of measures to promote stability and to create the conditions to prevent major capital outflows:

—Between October and November of 2008, the Bank of Mexico auctioned US$11 billion to reduce excessive volatility in the markets from the excess demand for U.S. dollars, mostly to unwind nonfinancial firms' positions on OTC derivatives.

—In October 2008 the Foreign Exchange Commission authorized daily auctions of US$400 million to increase the liquidity in the foreign exchange market. In the initial stage, the Bank of Mexico preset a minimum price of the auction at 2 percent above the fixed rate of the previous day. However, in a subsequent stage between March and June of 2009, the central bank decided to auction US$100 million, included in the initial amount, at market prices.

— The central bank was allowed to conduct additional foreign exchange auctions under extraordinary circumstances.

—In October 2008 the Bank of Mexico established a currency swap line of US$30 billion with the U.S. Federal Reserve, to provide liquidity to the peso-dollar exchange market.

—The Foreign Exchange Commission negotiated a one-year flexible credit line of US$50 billion with the IMF to support employment and give access to credit to companies and households, as well as to encourage the stability of the economy and foster growth.

—In April 2009 the Bank of Mexico provided commercial and development banks a U.S. dollar credit auction with resources from the U.S. Federal Reserve swap. This measure was implemented to give the market a signal that U.S. dollar financing from the aforementioned facilities was available.

As of October 2009, the total amount auctioned through the central bank's mechanisms was US$31 billion. The event that had the most impact on exchange rate volatility and the amount of reserves auctioned was the excess demand of foreign currency from nonfinancial firms' exposure to speculative positions on OTC derivative transactions during 2008. Their strategy, aimed at profiting from local currency appreciation, resulted in significant losses when the Mexican peso depreciated in September and October 2008. Table 12-4 shows the exposure and losses of publicly traded firms in Mexico from OTC derivatives.

The measures taken by the Ministry of Finance and the Bank of Mexico resulted in a decrease in international reserves and allowed the government to use the dollar surplus of the public sector to cover the deficit of the private sector. As shown in figure 12-7, the international reserves of Mexico started to recover one year after the decline.

The interest rate markets also showed increased volatility, particularly in longer-term rates. The Bank of Mexico, like other central banks, implemented a series of monetary policy actions that entailed a gradual reduction of the reference interest rate. From January 2009 to November 2009, the central bank reduced the interest rate from 8.25 percent to 4.5 percent (figure 12-8). In addition, the twenty-eight-day interbank offered rate (TIIE 28) decreased from 8.79 percent in September 2008 to 4.94 percent by the end November 2009. However, Mexico implemented this measure after the high-volatility period occurred in the last quarter of 2008, whereas other countries did so beforehand.

Table 12-4. *OTC Derivative Exposure of Mexican Firms, 2008*

Millions U.S. dollars

| Companies | Losses reported 4Q08 | Notional outstanding[a] | |
|---|---|---|---|
| | | 3Q08 | Types of contracts |
| Alfa | 194 | 2,159 | Cross-currency swaps and options |
| Bachoco | 97 | 528 | Knock-out puts, forwards, and TARNs[b] |
| Cemex | 911 | 5,327 | Currency swaps, forwards, and options |
| Comerci | 2,200 | 6,000[c] | Several financial derivative instruments |
| Femsa | 98 | 504 | Cross currency swaps and options |
| GISSA | 161 | 660 | Several financial derivative instruments |
| Gruma | 852 | 2,310 | Forwards, options, and structured derivatives |
| Posadas | 85 | 278 | Cross-currency swaps, principal-only swaps, and foreign exchange forwards |
| Sigma | 52 | 441 | Cross-currency swaps and options |
| Vitro | 358 | 227 | Several financial derivative instruments |
| Total | 5,008 | 18,434 | |

Sources: National Banking and Securities Commission company filings on derivative instruments, and company reports and press releases.

a. Only "derivados de negociación" (speculative contracts) are considered.

b. Targeted accrual redemption notes.

c. Figure estimated by the Ministry of Finance, Mexico.

Contrary to the gradual reduction observed in the TIIE 28 interest rate, longer-term interest rates showed significant volatility after Lehman's bankruptcy announcement in September 2008. In October 2008 the Bank of Mexico agreed to hold interest rate swap auctions to reshape the interest yield curve and mitigate the impact of fluctuations in the long-term fixed-rate curve. In these auctions, the central bank swapped TIIE 28 floating rates for long-term fixed bond rates. With the measures implemented by the Mexican government, long-term interest rates returned to a level between 8.5 percent and 9 percent, similar to that observed before the period of intense volatility (figure 12-9).

Despite the volatility of financial variables, the behavior of stock variables, like the external public and private debt, remained stable. Local issuers faced no significant restrictions on obtaining resources from foreign investors. As shown in table 12-5, the balance of public and private external debt did not decrease significantly during 2009.

Another sign of strength in the Mexican financial sector was the small share of domestic public and private debt in the hands of foreign investors with respect to the total outstanding. This share, which has remained in the range of 4 to 5 percent, limited the potential risk of an eventual run by foreign investors.

Figure 12-7. *Mexico's Net International Assets, 2008–09*[a]

Billions of U.S. dollars

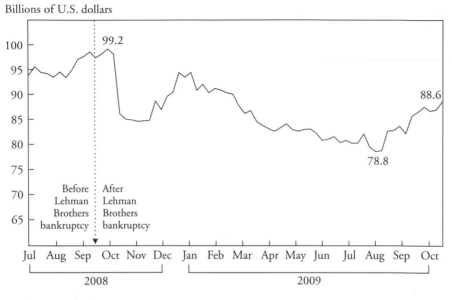

Source: Bank of Mexico.

Figure 12-8. *Mexico's Reference Interest Rates, 2008–09*[a]

Percent

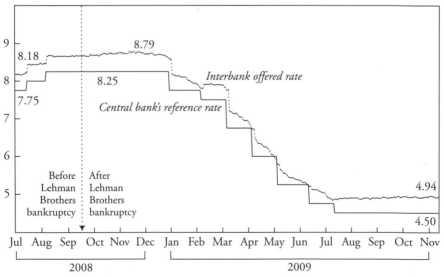

Source: Bank of Mexico.

Figure 12-9. *Domestic Fixed-Rate Bonds, 2008–09*

Percent

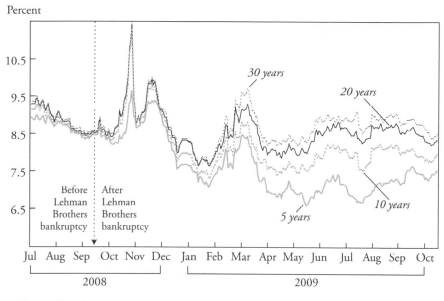

Source: Bloomberg.

Yet another factor that contributed to the stability in the capital account was the lack of need for major external financing. Domestic savings growth was supported by institutional developments, such as the creation of pensions and retirement funds and the strengthening of other institutional investors. Domestic savings have grown in a stable manner in recent years, with an increase of 9.8 percent from the second quarter of 2007 to the second quarter of 2009. The aforementioned increase in the national savings is explained by the growth in bank deposits and in pension funds from 2007 to June 2009 of 24.5 percent and 7.0 percent, respectively. As a proportion of GDP, national savings rose from 51 percent in 2007 to 59.4 percent in the second quarter of 2009 (table 12-6).

The structural components of the national savings accounts provided stability to the financial system because there is a base of domestic savings and a long-term maturity profile.

However, a deeper analysis at the institutional level reveals signs of trouble in some markets. The outstanding balance of private debt securities issued in the local market decreased 10.2 percent from September 2008 to May 2009. Such behavior is associated with investor risk aversion after a Mexican corporate default. After this default, the liquidity of the market dried up; domestic companies struggled to refinance their debt and had an increase of 300 basis points

Table 12-5.  *Public and Private Debt, 2007–09*
Millions U.S. dollars

| As of | External public debt | External private debt |
| --- | --- | --- |
| December 2007 | 55,355 | 60,432 |
| December 2008 | 56,939 | 66,817 |
| August 2009 | 52,651[a] | 63,961[b] |

Source: Ministry of Finance and Public Credit of Mexico.
a. The figure does not include US$34,500 million deferred long-term debt issued by Pemex. If it were included, the outstanding balance of the external public debt would be US$87,221 million.
b. Outstanding balance as of June 2009.

in the cost of credit. The corporate debt market did recover later in 2009, showing a growth rate in real terms of 12.2 percent from May to September of 2009 (figure 12-10).

To minimize the effects of the disruption in the debt markets, it was necessary to adopt specific public policies to avoid contagion throughout the market and the rest of the financial system. For that reason, the federal government implemented the following measures to restore confidence and maintain market function.

First, the Ministry of Finance, through Nacional Financiera and Ex-Im Bank (development banks), established mechanisms to support the refinancing of debt instruments issued by corporate firms and by nonbank intermediaries. Through these programs, the federal government provided a guarantee of 50 percent on the initial losses of corporate debt instruments that were refinanced. In the weeks after the default mentioned above, approximately less than 20 percent of the corporate debt that matured was refinanced. However, two months after this measure was implemented, corporate debt refinancing was reestablished. As of October 2009, when the program concluded, it had provided guarantees of MX$29.1 billion to thirteen companies.

Second, the Sociedad Hipotecaria Federal (SHF), a national development bank for housing, implemented a program to facilitate the refinancing of short-term maturing liabilities by mortgage-granting nonbank institutions. Furthermore, to support the growth of the mortgage industry, the SHF provided medium-term credit lines to builders and long-term financing for individual mortgages. The SHF extended a 65 percent guarantee on debt issuance of MX$6.8 billion to mortgage-granting nonbank financial institutions (Sofol Patrimonio and Sofomes Su Casita, Casa Mexicana, Vértice, and Crédito Inmobiliario) as a means to restore the market and help those nonbank companies that had a sound financial operation and responsible and transparent management.

Table 12-6. *Evolution of National Savings Accounts, Mexico, 2007–09*
Units as indicated

| Date | National savings[a] | Domestic savings (percent) | Foreign savings (percent) | National savings as percentage of GDP |
|------|---------------------|----------------------------|---------------------------|----------------------------------------|
| March 2007 | 5,228 | 98.4 | 1.6 | 49.2 |
| June 2007 | 5,344 | 98.3 | 1.7 | 48.1 |
| September 2007 | 5,547 | 98.2 | 1.8 | 49.1 |
| December 2007 | 5,713 | 98.1 | 1.9 | 51.0 |
| March 2008 | 5,928 | 98.4 | 1.6 | 51.2 |
| June 2008 | 5,975 | 98.2 | 1.8 | 48.4 |
| September 2008 | 6,210 | 98.1 | 1.9 | 50.1 |
| December 2008 | 6,703 | 98.0 | 2.0 | 55.4 |
| March 2009 | 6,751 | 98.3 | 1.7 | 60.5 |
| June 2009 | 6,777 | 98.5 | 1.5 | 59.4 |

Source: Bank of Mexico and Mexican Institute of Statistics.
a. In billions of June 2009 pesos.

Although Mexico did not experience significant liquidity problems at the local level, there were some pressures in the mutual fund industry. Domestic investors retrieved their portfolio investments from liquidity funds and moved them into bank accounts. From September to December 2008, the net assets of the mutual fund industry decreased 17 percent. Since then, net assets in the mutual fund sector have been increasing steadily (figure 12-11).

To restore confidence and liquidity in the market, the government and the central bank undertook a series of actions, such as swapping long- and medium-term government securities for short-term government debt. In addition, the following actions provided liquidity to the mutual fund market:

—The National Banking and Securities Commission issued a new rule allowing the purchase and sale of government securities among mutual funds and financial firms belonging to the same financial group during a six-month period beginning October 30, 2008. The objective of this measure was to facilitate the restructuring of mutual fund portfolios.

—The Ministry of Finance and the Deposit Insurance Agency (IPAB) modified their securities auction schemes starting in the fourth quarter of 2008, reducing placements of long-term securities from MX$3.85 billion to MX$1.85 billion weekly.

—To improve market liquidity, the Bank of Mexico introduced an auction mechanism to acquire MX$150 billion in IPAB bonds. This occurred through

Figure 12-10.  *Corporate Debt Market, Outstanding Balances, 2008–09*

Billions of pesos as of September 2009

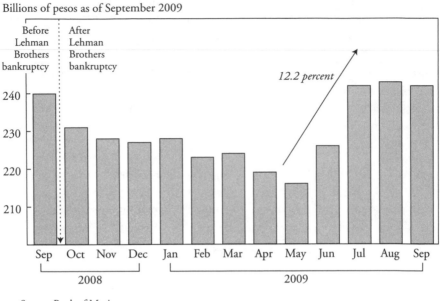

Source: Bank of Mexico.

Figure 12-11.  *Mutual Funds Debt Instruments, 2008–09*

Billions of pesos as of August 2009

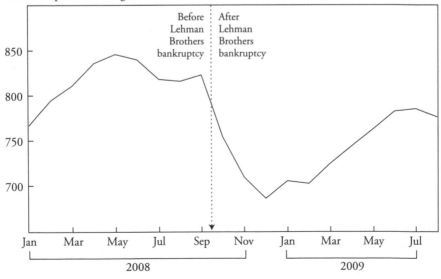

Source: Bank of Mexico.

the exchange of IPAB bonds for cash. The program ended in November 2008 with a total purchase in three auctions of MX$147 billion in bonds.

—In another effort to increase liquidity in the markets, in October 2008 the federal government announced a program in which the central bank would buy back MX$40 billion worth of medium- and long-term bonds, such as Udibonos (with maturity from three to five years, issued in units of investment that are indexed to inflation) and M bonds (maturities of three, five, seven, ten, and twenty years issued in Mexican pesos). The government acquired MX$4.3 billion of M bonds through two auctions, and 712 million investment units of Udibonos.

As a consequence of the actions taken by the government to maintain the confidence and liquidity in the domestic financial markets, there was a change in the structure of the Mexican public debt, with a larger share in the external debt and a slight decrease in the average term and duration of public debt (figure 12-12). Since 1999 the Mexican government has followed a policy of replacing foreign public debt with domestic public debt; however, during 2009 the government increased its indebtedness in foreign markets (figure 12-13).

The Mexican banking system, unlike those in other countries, remained sound and solvent during the crisis and did not require support from the federal government. Therefore it has not posed a risk to the Mexican economy. As of September 2009, the capital ratio of the commercial banking sector was 16 percent, doubling the international standard (8.0 percent). The tier one ratio was 14 percent. The capital ratio and the tier 1 ratio have both remained fairly stable from end-2007 to end-2009.

From September 2007 to September 2009, total financing from commercial banks to the private sector grew 5.2 percent in real terms. Within the last two years, commercial and industrial as well as housing portfolios showed positive growth rates. However, due to more restrictive origination criteria, the consumer loan portfolio decreased 21.9 percent (figure 12-14).

In spite of using FVA to record trading book transactions with daily mark-to-market valuations, Mexican banks did not experience major losses in their trading portfolios because they did not hold significant amounts of toxic assets. The nonperforming loan ratio of the banking system was 3.4 percent as of September 2009, 0.9 of a percentage point higher than the ratio of September 2007; nevertheless, the allowances for credit losses were 1.6 times the total nonperforming loans at the end of September 2009 (figure 12-15).

Even though the net income of the banking system has decreased 19.7 percent in real terms during the last two years, the industry continues to be profitable, with a return on equity of 12 percent as of September 2009. Such a situation allows for the maintenance of a capital base that will help restore credit growth in the future.

Figure 12-12. *Average Term and Duration of Public Debt, 2000–09*[a]

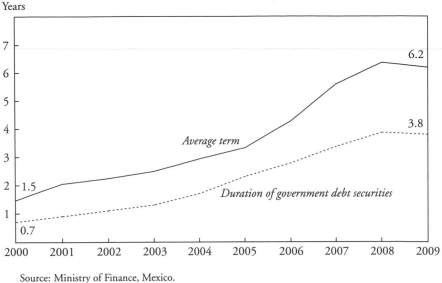

Years

Source: Ministry of Finance, Mexico.
a. Estimated for 2009.

Figure 12-13. *Net Public Debt, 1999–2009*[a]

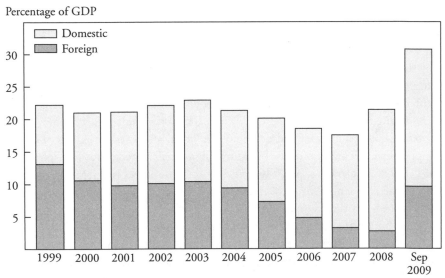

Percentage of GDP

Source: Ministry of Finance, Mexico.
a. In 2009 the federal government included the public employees pension fund.

Figure 12-14. *Performing Loans to the Private Sector by Portfolio, 2007–09*

Percentage change as of September 2009

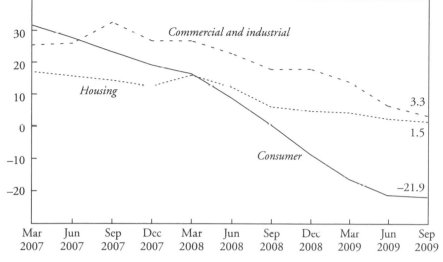

Source: National Banking and Securities Commission of Mexico.

Figure 12-15. *Asset Quality Ratios of the Banking System, 2007–09*

Nonperforming loans (percent)                    Allowances for credit losses (percent)

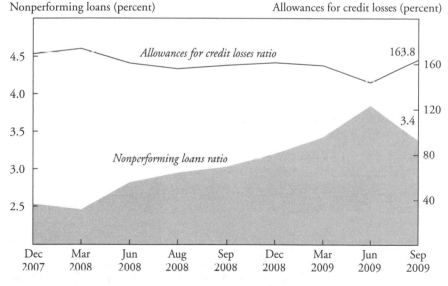

Source: National Banking and Securities Commission of Mexico.

Figure 12-16. *Banking System Funding Mix, 2007–09*

Billions of pesos as of September 2009

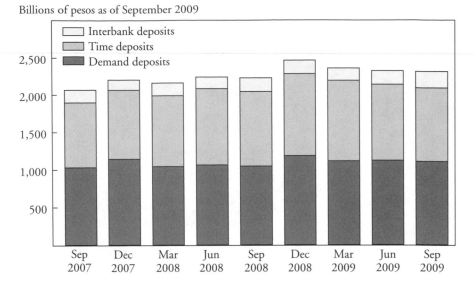

Source: National Banking and Securities Commission of Mexico.

From September 2007 to September 2009, total funding of commercial banks increased 11.85 percent in real terms; demand deposits represented 47.9 percent of the total, and time deposits constituted 42.5 percent (see figure 12-16). Most of the funding was in local currency, with foreign currency funding amounting to no more than 12 percent during this period. In the last quarter of 2008, the interbank funding market, which is less than 10 percent of the total funding, experienced pressures that constrained terms and amounts, particularly for small and medium-size banks whose business model relied on wholesale markets. (Four small and medium-size banks experienced temporary liquidity problems.)

To facilitate the process of funding, in early October 2008 the Bank of Mexico accepted new types of assets as collateral for liquidity loans at a rate of 1.1 times the one-day target rate determined by the central bank's board of governors. The new types of assets included monetary regulation deposits and securities that were formerly not accepted, such as AAA corporate bonds. In December of that same year, the liquidity program expanded to accept other collateral, such as other banks' debt securities and state and municipal governments' loans, with federal resources as guarantee of repayment. It is important to mention that despite the existence of this facility, only one medium-size bank accessed it for a short period of time.

Other Latin American countries that remained stable and solid during the crisis also had sound banking systems. One of the reasons for such resilience was

Figure 12-17. *Total Capital Ratios of Banking Systems in Latin America, 2008–09*

Percentages as of August 2009

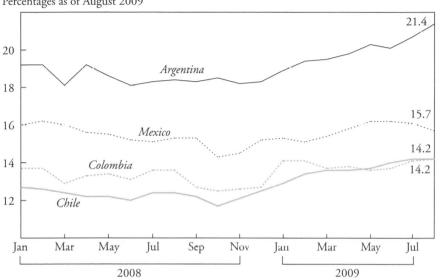

Source: Banking superintendences of Chile and Colombia, central bank of Argentina, and National Banking and Securities Commission of Mexico.

the financial systems' capital buffers built throughout the previous years (figure 12-17). Another sign of strength from the region's financial systems was the credit expansion to the private sector, which continued despite experiencing a slower pace of growth during the crisis. Similarly, the nonperforming loan ratios, which were falling in the previous years, registered a minor increase in a number of countries during 2009 (figure 12-18).

The effects of the financial crisis on Latin American EMEs materialized in a contagion to the real sectors of the economy, and were therefore expressed in reduced economic activity and, in some cases, recession. The deterioration of public finances and their need for additional monies could lead to a reduced availability of funds for private sector activities. Therefore, EME governments should develop mechanisms to allow market participants and financial intermediaries to obtain additional funding, on competitive terms, from international markets and thereby ensure that the channel for credit resources is sustained.

Foreign investment in EME financial systems should not be perceived negatively since it does not necessarily represent a source of vulnerability. The risk factors that increase the vulnerability of a system are the quality of the regulation and the structure of the participants' balance sheets. Therefore, in addition to

Figure 12-18. *Nonperforming Loan Ratios of Banking Systems in Latin America, 2008–09*

Percentages as of August 2009

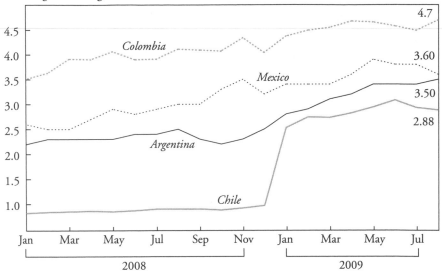

Source: : Banking superintendences of Chile and Colombia, central bank of Argentina and National Banking and Securities Commission of Mexico.

sound macroeconomic policies, there will now be a focus on microeconomic policy to build a solid prudential framework and an agency responsible for assessing the buildup of systemic risk.

Latin American countries have learned several lessons from previous crises that helped them establish a more resilient system at the microlevel. Some of the elements that have contributed to systemic resilience are:

—creation of a subsidiary regime instead of a branch regime,

—implementation of a solid prudential framework that recognizes losses as banks incur them,

—existence of long-term fixed-rate markets,

—existence of stable pension fund systems,

—limits on foreign currency risk, and

—market risk capital requirements that penalize mismatches.

## Legal Complexity of the Global Financial System

The globalization of financial markets, favored by openness to foreign investments in the financial industry, led to an increasingly interconnected system

Table 12-7. *Internationalization of Global Banks: Domestic Banks' Assets in Foreign Market, 2000 versus 2007*

Percent of GDP

| Country of origin | 2000 | 2007 |
| --- | --- | --- |
| United States | 24.3 | 47.0 |
| European Union | 13.1 | 21.4 |
| Japan | 38.9 | 68.9 |
| France | 38.6 | 76.2 |
| United Kingdom | 57.3 | 130.2 |
| Switzerland | 109.7 | 179.2 |
| Iceland | 35.4 | 364.3 |
| Austria | 31.3 | 70.8 |

Source: Bank of Mexico.

more susceptible to global contagion. In addition, industry innovation outpaced the regulatory and supervisory institutions tasked with overseeing what had become a global financial entity. Globalization was not the cause of the crisis, but it contributed to the propagation of risks.

From the industry perspective, the internationalization of financial groups meant that nations held more assets abroad than ever before. This engendered a higher degree of complexity in the corporate structure of global financial groups as well as in the assessment of risk exposures on a consolidated basis. Table 12-7 shows the increased proportion of foreign assets over time on the balance sheets of banks from developed economies.

For the past twenty years, most EMEs implemented financial policies that allowed foreign investors to participate in their banking systems. The flows of investment from foreign players to EMEs led, in most cases, to an increase in the market share of foreign institutions in national financial systems (see table 12-8). Foreign investments facilitated the development of EMEs' financial markets, but it is also true that EMEs became more vulnerable to contagion from the decisionmaking processes of parent companies.

Nier and others (2008) developed a model for a closed banking system and showed that a small increase in the interconnectivity of participants would increase the contagion effects until a threshold was reached where the connectivity in a banking system would prove efficient enough to absorb shocks. They also agree that better-capitalized banks would make a banking system more resilient to contagion effects. Other variables that affect the degree of contagion are the funding structure and the level of concentration. Such models of contagion can be applied on a global basis because the interconnection and transmission mechanisms now are global. The variables that the authors discuss lead to greater

Table 12-8. *Internationalization of EMEs' Market Share of Foreign Banks,*
*2000 versus 2007*

Assets percentages

| Country | 2000 | 2007 |
|---|---|---|
| Central and eastern Europe | 36.2 | 49.3 |
| Czech Republic | 48.9 | 97.0 |
| Estonia | 73.1 | 97.0 |
| Hungary | 63.5 | 76.5 |
| Poland | 37.8 | 70.5 |
| Russia | 11.5 | 17.2 |
| Slovakia | 54.6 | 92.0 |
| Asia, excluding China and India | 10.3 | 33.2 |
| China | 0.0 | 2.0 |
| India | 2.0 | 9.8 |
| Latin America | 28.4 | 66.9 |
| Brazil | 26.4 | 23.0 |
| Chile | 38.4 | 59.6 |
| Mexico | 28.5 | 82.0 |
| Peru | 66.1 | 48.5 |
| Venezuela | 20.7 | 26.0 |

Source: Bank of Mexico.

contagion in a domestic system and reasonably explain what happened to propa-
gate the recent crisis on a global scale.

After the use of FVA for the toxic assets, global financial conglomerates
experienced significant losses, which resulted in write-offs that reduced their
capital. Consistent with the view of Nier and others (2008), a weakly capitalized global system changed the perception of market participants about their
solvency and the market value of their investments. The recorded losses significantly affected the market capitalization of large financial conglomerates.

The behavior of financial and market variables of financial institutions
affected internal management decisionmaking, creating a new transmission
mechanism in this crisis. In this adverse scenario, managers had two incentives
driving their decisions: survival and risk aversion. The subsequent problem was
that these decisions affected financial systems around the world.

Parent companies required their subsidiaries to reduce their risk exposure
or remain at their current level of exposure. Over time the increased impact
of parent companies' centralized decisions became more evident. For example,

Citigroup's subsidiary Banamex has significantly reduced its lending activities in the last two years.

A new characteristic of the global financial system is that the costs of failure are also global. The case of Lehman Brothers illustrates the costs to the global financial system of the insolvency of a highly interconnected institution.

The corporate structure of the Lehman Brothers group was complex because of its more than 2,980 regulated and unregulated entities operating in nearly fifty countries. The design of the Lehman structure complied with the regulatory regime at each local jurisdiction while providing the flexibility to book transactions wherever it would generate maximum benefit to the overall group. Lehman generated contagion in the global markets because its structure was a collection of unregulated and regulated institutions with global presence, and when the turmoil started, its regulated entities were affected by the risk taking of its unregulated institutions.

The remaining entities, under a winding-down process for insolvency after the group's failure, generated a complex cross-border resolution coordination process among authorities. This complexity arose not only from the resolution of Lehman Brothers Holdings but also from the wind-down procedures for the insolvency of the subsidiaries, which were located at jurisdictions as diverse as Switzerland, Japan, Singapore, Hong Kong, Germany, Luxembourg, Australia, the Netherlands, and Bermuda.

The Lehman case reflects the agency problems that induced some of the behaviors that led to the current financial crisis. De la Torre and Ize (2009) argue that the coexistence of regulated and nonregulated financial institutions engaging in the same activities create the wrong incentives because regulatory arbitrage enables the unregulated entities to assume increased risk exposure and take on excessive leverage.

Understanding the global architecture of the financial system, the way contagion can happen on a worldwide basis, and the implications of the Lehman collapse leads us to conclude that the design of a new supervisory framework must include four elements:

—A global supervisory model that adequately assesses global exposure from this kind of financial institution.

—Broader information exchange agreements in case a holding company or one of its subsidiaries is in financial stress and inclusion of legal powers to limit the transfer of losses.

—A cross-border resolution mechanism to manage the bankruptcy of global financial institutions.

—Definition of what constitutes a globally systemic financial institution.

## Redesigning the Financial Supervisory Architecture

The old supervisory paradigm was built on a model where a financial holding company provided, among other things, better corporate governance and risk management policies to its subsidiaries in EMEs. Also, this model was based on the premise that the home supervisor was the main player in the supervisory processes and that the host supervisor had to provide information to the former to enable adequate assessments of the financial conglomerate's risks.

This model is consistent with one put forth by Prasad and Rajan (2008), who consider that the presence of global financial conglomerates generates benefits for EMEs. Foreign direct investment from well-regulated and well-supervised countries tends to support institutional development and governance in EMEs, and global conglomerates can provide guidance for dealing with the complex supervisory and regulatory challenges that developing countries face as they integrate into the world economy.

Contrary to the assumptions of the old paradigm, the recent financial crisis originated in developed economies, demonstrating that the actions of the parent company can have consequences for its subsidiaries. The globalization process, which allowed financial firms to expand their operations into new markets (in both developed and emerging economies), acted as a transmission mechanism that spread the contagion beyond the local level. From the supervisory perspective, there are two main lessons from the globalization process and the increased interconnectedness of the system.

First, regulation and supervision did not evolve to account for the globalization of the financial industry, thus creating deficiencies in their frameworks. They were built on two principles that were not consistent with the sector's recent development: local regulation and supervision, and the premise that only home country regulators should have an opinion on the risks of the conglomerate.

Second, market participants and regulators did not consider a scenario where a large conglomerate would need government resources in the form of capital. The participants also did not evaluate the possibility of global interconnectedness as a source of global risk and the implications of the bankruptcy of a global systemic player.

Slowing down the pace of globalization or reversing it would not solve these problems. While some economies may attempt to inoculate themselves against future global contagions by closing their borders and imposing capital controls, others are likely to recognize that the potential damage from such policies outweighs the benefits. Moreover, much of the impact of globalization, such as the emergence of global banks, the integration of bond markets, and the connectivity of financial systems, would be extremely difficult to reverse. The solution is not to eliminate the free-capital-flow model but rather to strengthen the institutional framework, based on the four elements mentioned in the previous section. There is a need for a new paradigm for cross-border financial regulation that includes concepts such as global systemic risk, the relevance of the coordination among supervisors, and the possibility of global contagion. In sum, the new paradigm in the redesign of the supervisory architecture needs to have a global perspective rather than a local one.

One element that needs to be considered is the evaluation of impacts on EMEs as a result of the policy actions of foreign governments or management decisions made abroad. The new framework should have mechanisms to prevent and limit fiscal contingencies for the different countries where the conglomerate operates in the case where a holding company becomes insolvent. This is very important, because in the event of failure the incentives of the different supervisors change and are aligned to minimize their respective losses. Until a cross-border arrangement is established to ensure legal enforceability, it should be clear which authorities would be responsible for the oversight and for the fiscal costs in case of failure.

Other elements that the new regulatory framework should address are the negative incentives operating within global conglomerates (that is, in the event of a liquidity crunch in a particular country, the parent company would be tempted to move resources within the group) and the need to create mechanisms for the global exchange of raw information, including global risk assessments for conglomerates. Consistent with this view, there is an argument by the IMF that states that host and home supervisors should consider systemic cross-border banks "global in life but national in death," and thus subsidiaries in host jurisdictions should be allowed to operate with adequate levels of capital and liquidity.

The redesign of the financial supervisory architecture for effective cross-border regulation to include the elements defined in the previous section is based on three pillars: adequate flow of information, framework efficiency, and global risk monitoring. Such redesign focuses on five areas:
  —definition of an efficient supervisory structure for global institutions,
  —an efficient information exchange mechanism,
  —an effective cross-border resolution mechanism,
  — an effective global assessment of systemic risks, and
  —identification of and measures against non-cooperative jurisdictions.

The work of the G20 and the conclusions of the Pittsburgh Summit recognized the need to reform the supervisory framework consistent with the view outlined in this section.[4] Along the same lines, the chairman of the Basel Committee on Banking Supervision (BCBS) specified that a supervisory arrangement

_____

4. G20 (2009b).

should include macroprudential and microprudential supervision, with financial supervisors stepping up for international cooperation.[5] The Financial Stability Forum also supported this view in a set of principles that outlines a series of commitments between relevant authorities, including supervisory agencies, central banks, and finance ministries, to make advance preparations for dealing with financial crises and to efficiently manage them.[6]

## Recommended Changes to the Architecture for Supervision of the Global Financial System

In the following analysis, we provide an overview of the current situation, a description of the concerns that should guide the reform, and finally, a review of the proposed solution.

### Supervisory Structure

The globalization process favored not only the growth of major cross-border financial groups in developed countries but also their expansion into EMEs. Their investments contributed to the development of EMEs' local banking systems and promoted financial innovation. Host supervisors perceived that global financial institutions provided technology and financial stability to the local system.

The supervisory architecture of the 1990s was outlined in the 1997 Core Principles for Effective Banking Supervision, which provided guidelines regarding the home-host relationship.[7] The core principles stated that home supervisors must practice global, consolidated supervision over their internationally active banks. Host supervisors had the obligation to share information about the local operations of foreign banks with the home supervisor. In 2006 the BCBS issued revised guidelines that included coordination and information exchange mechanisms between both home and host supervisors.[8] At that time, the committee did not consider the need to establish a forum in which supervisors assessed the risks to the global banking institution.

However, the losses of major global financial institutions, as a product of the recent financial crisis, exposed subsidiaries around the world to a number of potential contagion risks, demonstrating that the supervisory model was inadequate. In this regard, the G20 Working Group on Reinforcing International Cooperation and Promoting Integrity in Financial Markets (WG2) proposed the creation of supervisory colleges that should include relevant host supervisors,

5. Wellink (2009).
6. See Financial Stability Forum (2009).
7. BCBS (1997).
8. BCBS (2006).

particularly from emerging economies. The WG2 also asserted that home supervisors must ensure adequate information exchange with those host supervisors who are not members of the college of a specific institution.[9] As a result of the G20 agreements, the Financial Supervisory Board (FSB) published guidelines for supervisory colleges, including their structure, operation, and size.[10]

The new model aims to facilitate a coordinated assessment of global risks and enable host supervisors to have full visibility of the conglomerate. The creation of supervisory colleges and the shift from bilateral information exchange to a multilateral information flow model is intended to address some of the deficiencies of the old system.

In figure 12-19, the diagram on the left shows the old supervisory model with its upward flow of information to the home supervisor. The diagram on the right illustrates how the new model evolves, establishing a supervisory college and allowing the information to flow both ways, including from home to host supervisors. The flow of information in the new model is more consistent with the interconnectedness of the actual financial system.

## Information Exchange

The pre-crisis view assumed that potential risks would be limited to subsidiaries while disregarding the potential for contagion from the holding company. Therefore, the supervisory model was based on this paradigm, and existing information exchange agreements between supervisors followed the same assumption. Thus the existing agreements were bilateral in character, rigid in implementation, and potentially asymmetric given the different negotiations between supervisors.

In 2001 the BCBS released the "Essential Elements of a Statement of Cooperation between Banking Supervisors" as a reference for establishing bilateral relationships between banking supervisory authorities in different countries, and where appropriate, between banking supervisors and other financial regulators.[11] The statement recognized that information should be shared between authorities to facilitate effective consolidated supervision by home supervisors of financial institutions operating across national borders. However, this structure limited the host supervisor's ability to have an informed view of the evolution of the conglomerate.

The need for broader information sharing among EMEs can be shown in two scenarios. First, an EME would be exposed to systemic risks from its supervised intermediaries entering into OTC derivatives contracts booked in other markets.

9. WG2 (2009).
10. FSB (2009).
11. BCBS (2001).

Figure 12-19. *Redesign of the Supervisory Model*

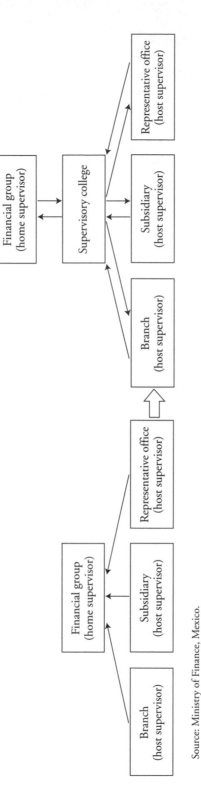

Source: Ministry of Finance, Mexico.

Without complete information sharing, the EME supervisor would be limited to assessing only those risks building up in his or her own country. Second, the Stanford and Madoff schemes underline the need to establish efficient information exchange mechanisms between national authorities for cross-border crisis management. Most EME authorities were officially informed about these two cases only after the media had already dispersed the news.

Due to increased international activity and the need for mutual cooperation and consultation, the BCBS was asked to develop a global mechanism for information exchange among banking supervisors.[12] Such information exchange should be timely and performed on a regular basis. The G20 also recognized the need for a mechanism that would allow collaboration among banking supervisors, increase the flow of information, and provide flexibility and confidentiality.[13] This is consistent with our view, which asserts that the mechanism must be comprehensive with regard to the number of supervisors and flexible about the information that can be shared in order for it to be an efficient supervisory tool.[14]

*Resolution Mechanisms*

The sudden collapse of a global conglomerate may impose significant costs to the world economy or transfer the fiscal cost from one economy to another. Therefore, it is important to establish a set of rules to contain losses at their place of origin. Concerns about the lack of a cross-border mechanism to resolve failing institutions were raised in the past. Sachs (1995) recommended establishing functional equivalents of key bankruptcy code mechanisms, such as automatic standstills, priority lending, and comprehensive reorganization plans supported by non-unanimity rules.

The design of the global supervisory model was based on the assumption that potential problems might arise in a subsidiary, not as a result of contagion from the parent company. Also, the supervisory model did not consider the existence of systemic risks since it was focused on the individual financial soundness of firms. Regulators failed to assess the moral hazard of "too-big-to-fail" firms outside their scope of regulation and the externalities caused by firms "too interconnected to fail" (as was the case with Lehman Brothers).

As recent experience shows, transnational financial institutions bear contagion risks that are potentially global in scale. Meanwhile, the existing mechanisms for crisis management and resolution arrangements are not sufficient to deal with the cross-border insolvencies of financial institutions. This implies that countries

12. WG2 (2009).

13. WG2 (2009).

14. For an example of a multilateral information exchange mechanism, see the International Organization of Securities Commissions (2002).

implement territorial approaches and use their local legal framework in the resolution of cross-border financial institutions, disregarding the effects of measures implemented by the host jurisdiction on subsidiaries of the conglomerate. In the absence of preexisting standards for sharing losses from a cross-border insolvency, the incentives of resolution authorities lie in minimizing the losses of local stakeholders (shareholders, depositors and other creditors, taxpayers, and the deposit insurer) to whom they are accountable. This underlines the need for an adequate definition and legal powers for ring-fencing to limit losses in all jurisdictions.

In the absence of an efficient mechanism to resolve the insolvency of a cross-border financial institution, the WG2 of the G20 explored a framework to coordinate regional cross-border resolution.[15] The Cross-border Bank Resolution Group of the BCBS developed an initial series of recommendations for effective and convergent bank resolutions.[16] Currently, there is an ongoing debate over the most suitable option for dealing with domestic failures, either by a universal resolution approach (which would resolve a cross-border legal entity when its failure occurs in a single jurisdiction) or by a territorial or ring-fencing approach (which allows for each jurisdiction to resolve the failure of a cross-border financial institution located within its territory).

## Effective Global Assessment of Vulnerabilities

Major financial conglomerates are established in both developed and developing countries, so it is relevant to periodically assess the major sources of vulnerabilities to the global financial system. Assessing risk only in developed countries would artificially segment an interconnected market and would limit the ability of supervisory bodies to have a comprehensive view of the system. This concept is also relevant at the local level because a supervisor should have an extended mandate to oversee systemic risk buildup at the national level.

After the crisis, the IMF and the Financial Stability Forum (now the FSB) collaborated to develop procedures for conducting regular joint early warning exercises to better integrate the regulatory and supervisory responses into the macroprudential policy framework.[17] A further analysis of the causes of the crisis, performed by the IMF and the Financial Stability Forum, revealed the need to update the international standards and guidelines, while giving attention to the impact of global capital flows on global financial stability. In addition, the Standing Committee on Assessment of Vulnerabilities was created and given the responsibility to assess vulnerabilities within the global financial system and propose policy actions to address them.

15. WG2 (2009).
16. BCBS (2009).
17. IMF (2009).

Some risk areas discussed by the FSB included the market impact of rapidly rising government debt, risks related to the timing of exit strategies from current policies, and the challenges in maintaining an appropriate balance and pace of regulatory reforms. In addition, authorities in emerging economies are assessing policy challenges related to currency mismatches on balance sheets and instability in portfolio flows.

### Measures for Non-Cooperative Jurisdictions

The strengthening of prudential standards and the establishment of efficient supervisory models and information exchange mechanisms are aimed at building a sounder global system. However, as pointed out by the de Larosière Group, any attempts to reduce risks to the stability of the financial system would be undermined by systemically relevant jurisdictions that refuse to implement international standards for anti–money laundering and combating the financing of terrorism (AML-CFT).[18] Financial system interconnectedness facilitates the smooth reallocation of funds from one jurisdiction to another, thereby exposing any financial system to the threat of unwittingly contributing to illicit activities. Therefore, it is essential to assign an equal weight to the prevention of and enforcement against such illicit activities, as well as the solvency and stability of the global financial system.

As international standards are strengthened, it will be necessary to apply them to non-cooperative jurisdictions and tax havens that have weak regulatory and governance standards, lack transparency, or fail to exchange information.[19]

At the G20 summits in Washington and London, tax authorities were requested to strengthen the exchange of tax information and address lack of transparency.[20] Countries were also asked to adhere to international standards in the prudential, tax, and AML-CFT areas and adopt the international standard for information exchange reflected in the UN Model Double Tax Convention. Furthermore, participants agreed to work on the identification of non-cooperative jurisdictions and take action against those jurisdictions that fail to meet international standards on these issues.

## Changes to the Supervisory Model: Important Issues for EMEs

The main concern from the EME perspective is that there should be equal participation in the supervisory process and timely and adequate receipt of information.

Before the crisis, national supervisors assumed that potential contagion risks could arise from the subsidiaries, and they relied on the financial strength of the

18. De Larosière Group (2009).
19. WG2 (2009).
20. G20 (2009b).

parent firm. From the perspective of the host EMEs, the supervisory colleges will enable more efficient supervision. The challenge will be to include all relevant EMEs in the supervisory colleges and for them to have an active role.

The adequate flow of relevant information from the conglomerate is important for EMEs. Such information should include interactions with the institution's top senior management, access to the conglomerate's risk assessments, and timely information regarding relevant transactions. Situations like the following should be avoided: an EME supervisor that oversees a relevant subsidiary learns about conglomerate transactions from the media rather than from the home supervisor.

EMEs should have access to information on transactions conducted abroad by both local financial institutions and public companies. In cases in which conglomerates can register transactions in several legal entities in different countries, it is important to have multilateral agreements to share information among supervisors of different relevant subsidiaries.

Other issues to consider are the negative outcomes that arise when the parent firm has financial problems or when it declines to capitalize a subsidiary. The transfer of fiscal responsibility to a host government where a subsidiary is based is a contingency for EMEs. To mitigate this risk, it is imperative that adequate mechanisms for ring-fencing be established.

As is the case for developed economies, it is necessary for EMEs to identify risk built up in their jurisdictions and prevent contagion within their systems. Therefore, EMEs need to participate in the international bodies to discuss, from their perspective, the appropriate actions to prevent contagion.

Although Mexico, Brazil, and Argentina were already members of the Financial Action Task Force, the G20 declaration further motivated EMEs to demand greater inclusion in this and other organizations.[21] The expanded membership of the FSB and the Basel Committee, among others, may enable EMEs to contribute to the design of the global regulatory and supervisory model. Broadening the membership of supervisory and regulatory standard-setting bodies is very important for EMEs. It will facilitate the inclusion of their perspectives in the setting of international regulatory standards and principles, and it will support global financial stability and help avoid unintended and undesirable consequences for the EMEs' local financial systems.

## Conclusions

The subprime crisis that originated in the United States became global because of the existence of large multinational conglomerates and global interconnectedness. This situation made the global financial system vulnerable to contagion.

21. G20 (2009a).

In the first stage of the crisis, developed economies were affected by their exposure to structured vehicles, such as CDOs, that banks used to off-load risks to the market. In the second stage, triggered by the announcement of the Lehman Brothers collapse, EMEs' financial markets recoupled with those of developed economies and experienced increased volatility in their interest rates, foreign exchanges, and stock markets.

Although developed economies experienced the most severe effects of the crisis, EMEs were not immune, because they were exposed to four sources of contagion. The first source, toxic assets, had minimal impact, because EMEs did not have significant holdings of this type of asset. The second source arose from asset-liability mismatches. These exerted differentiated effects on EMEs, mainly through the structure of their banks' balance sheets. The third source was the recoupling, during which there was an increase in the volatility of financial variables. However, despite the volatility in market prices, the capital accounts of most EMEs in the Latin American region remained stable and registered no significant outflows. The fourth source of contagion was the risk aversion of major conglomerates. These entities constrained the lending activities of their subsidiaries in EMEs in order to reduce corporate exposure to credit risk and improve their overall solvency.

The Lehman Brothers failure illustrates the potential effects from the insolvency of a globally interconnected institution and the need to establish a global model of cross-border regulation and supervision. The complex global corporate structure of Lehman comprised a mixture of regulated and unregulated entities that complied with local regulatory regimes while taking advantage of the flexibility to book transactions worldwide in order to optimize the overall group's returns.

Regulatory and supervisory oversight must be redesigned according to a new paradigm that enables it to evolve along with the increasingly interconnected markets and to appropriately mitigate the risks arising from them. Consequently, national authorities must establish an efficient *global* regulatory and supervisory framework to contain the contagion effects from systemic risks.

The new paradigm in the design of a cross-border regulatory and supervisory framework has five aspects:

—An adequate supervisory structure that will coordinate the assessment of global risks and allow home supervisors full visibility of the conglomerate's subsidiaries. This entails the creation of supervisory colleges and shifting from bilateral information exchange to a multilateral information flow model.

— An information exchange mechanism that recognizes the need for mutual cooperation and consultation and provides effective ways for timely communication and information exchange on a regular basis. Such a mechanism has to be comprehensive with regard to the number of supervisors and flexible about the information that can be shared.

—An effective resolution mechanism to contain the losses at the jurisdiction where they were originated and avoid the transfer of fiscal costs. In the absence of an efficient overall mechanism to resolve the insolvency of a cross-border financial institution, it is necessary to explore a framework for coordinating regional cross-border resolutions. This underlines the need for an adequate definition of and legal powers for ring-fencing to limit losses in all jurisdictions.

—An effective global assessment of vulnerabilities to periodically determine the major sources of vulnerability that could pose a threat to the global financial system. The resulting guidance should consider direct and indirect exposures and potential exposures to areas more correlated at times of market strain.

—The design of effective measures against systemically relevant, non-cooperative jurisdictions so as to reduce the exposure of the global financial system to their substandard practices and consequences of their failure to implement international standards for AML-CTF activities.

Finally, to maximize effectiveness and minimize unwanted outcomes, EMEs should be included in the process of redesigning the regulatory and supervisory framework of the global financial system.

## References

Basel Committee on Banking Supervision (BCBS). 1997. *The Core Principles for Effective Banking Supervision.* Basel: Bank for International Settlements.

———.2001. "Essential Elements of a Statement of Cooperation between Banking Supervisors." Basel: Bank for International Settlements.

———. 2006. *Core Principles for Effective Banking Supervision*, revised version. Basel: Bank for International Settlements.

———. 2009. "Report and Recommendations of the Cross-border Bank Resolution Group." Consultative document. Basel: Bank for International Settlements (September).

Benmelech, Efraim, and Jennifer Dlugosz. 2009. "The Alchemy of CDO Credit Ratings." Working Paper 14878. Cambridge, Mass.: National Bureau of Economic Research (April).

Brunnermeier, Markus K. 2009. "Deciphering the Liquidity and Credit Crunch 2007–08." *Journal of Economic Perspectives* 23, no. 1: 77–100.

De Larosière Group. 2009. *Report of the High-Level Group on Financial Supervision in the EU.* Brussels.

De la Torre, Augusto, and Alain Ize. 2009. "Regulatory Reform: Integrating Paradigms." Policy Research Working Paper 4842. Washington D.C.: World Bank (February).

Dooley, Michael P., and Michael M. Hutchison. 2009. "Transmission of the U.S. Subprime Crisis to Emerging Markets: Evidence on the Decoupling-Recoupling Hypothesis." Working Paper 15120. Cambridge, Mass.: National Bureau of Economic Research.

Dupont, Brandon. 2007. "Bank Runs, Information and Contagion in the Panic of 1893." *Explorations in Economic History* 44, no. 3: 411–31.

Financial Stability Board (FSB). 2009. "Next Steps on Supervisory Colleges." Note for the FSB inaugural meeting. Basel, June 26–27.

Financial Stability Forum. 2009. "Principles for Cross-border Cooperation on Crisis Management." April (www.financialstabilityboard.org/publications/r_0904c.pdf).

Group of Twenty (G20). 2009a. "Declaration on Strengthening the Financial System—London, 2 April 2009" (www.g20.org/Documents/Fin_Deps_Fin_Reg_Annex_020409_-_1615_final.pdf).

———. 2009b. "Leaders' Statement: The Pittsburgh Summit." September 24–25 (www.pittsburghsummit.gov/mediacenter/129639.htm).

G20 Working Group on Reinforcing International Cooperation and Promoting Integrity in Financial Markets (WG2). 2009. *Final Report.* March (www.g20.org/Documents/g20_wg2_010409.pdf).

International Monetary Fund (IMF). 2009. "Factsheet: IMF-FSB Early Warning Exercise." October 4 (www.imf.org/external/np/exr/facts/ewe.htm IMF).

International Organization of Securities Commissions. 2002. "Multilateral Memorandum of Understanding Concerning Consultation and Cooperation and the Exchange of Information." Madrid.

Jiang, Wei, Nelson, Ashlyn, and Vytlacil, Edward. 2009. "Liar's Loan? Effects of Loan Origination Channel and Loan Sale on Delinquency." Draft paper (June).

Khan, Urooj. 2009. "Does Fair Value Accounting Contribute to Systemic Risk in the Banking Industry?" Columbia Business School (August).

Laux, Christian, and Christian Leuz. 2009. "The Role of Fair Value Accounting in the Financial Crisis." Working Paper 15515. Cambridge, Mass.: National Bureau of Economic Research (November).

Longstaff, Francis A., and Brett Myers. 2009. "Valuing Toxic Assets: An Analysis of CDO Equity." Working Paper 14871. Cambridge, Mass.: National Bureau of Economic Research (April).

Nakamoto, Michiyo, and David Wighton. 2007. "Citigroup Chief Stays Bullish on Buy-outs." *Financial Times*, July 9 (www.ft.com/cms/s/0/80e2987a-2e50-11dc-821c-0000779fd2ac.html?nclick_check=1).

Nier, Erlend, and others. 2008. "Network Models and Financial Stability." Bank of England (April).

Prasad, Eswar S., and Raghuram Rajan. 2008. "A Pragmatic Approach to Capital Account Liberalization." Working Paper 14051. Cambridge, Mass.: National Bureau of Economic Research (June).

Sachs, Jeffrey D. 1995. "Alternative Approaches to Financial Crises in Emerging Markets." Harvard Institute for International Development (www.cid.harvard.edu/hiid/568.pdf).

Topçu, Neşe. 2009. "The Global Financial Crisis and Its Effect to Eastern Europe Countries." Paper presented at EconAnadolu 2009: Anadolu International Conference in Economics. Eskişehir, Turkey. June 17–19.

Wellink, Nout. 2009. "Supervisory Arrangements—Lessons from the Crisis." Speech prepared for the 44th SEACEN Governors' Conference. Kuala Lumpur, February 6.

## Additional Sources

The following sources, though not individually cited, were used as a basis for most of the figures and tables, as well as for certain data presented in the text of the chapter.

American Bankers Association. 2008. Letter to SEC. Washington D.C.

Ashcraft, Adam, Paul Goldsmith-Pinkham, and James Vickery. 2009. "MBS Ratings and the Mortgage Credit Boom." Federal Reserve Bank of New York, Research and Statistics Group.

Bank of Mexico. 2008. "Financial System Report 2008." Mexico City.

———. 2008. "Inflation Report: July–September 2008."

———. 2008 "Inflation Report: October–December 2008."

———. 2009. "Inflation Report: January–March 2009."

Financial Action Task Force–Groupe d'Action Financière. 2009. "FATF Report to G20 Finance Ministers and Central Bank Governors." Paris.

Financial Stability Board. 2009. "Vulnerabilities in the Global Financial System: Assessment, Prioritisation and Response." Basel.

Financial Stability Forum. 2008. "Report of the Financial Stability Forum on Enhancing Market and Institutional Resilience." Basel.

———. 2009. "Report of the Financial Stability Forum on Enhancing Market and Institutional Resilience."

González-Hermosillo, Brenda, and Heiko Hesse. 2009. "Global Market Conditions and Systemic Risk." Working Paper WP-09-230. Washington D.C.: International Monetary Fund (October).

Hall, Simon. 2009. "What Are the Main Data Issues Arising from the Crisis?" London: Bank of England.

Mayer, Christopher, and R. Glenn Hubbard. 2008. "House Prices, Interest Rates, and the Mortgage Market Meltdown" (www4.gsb.columbia.edu/null/download?&exclusive=filemgr.download&file_id=3549).

Shleifer, Andrei, and Robert W. Vishny. 2009. "Unstable Banking." Working Paper 14943. Cambridge, Mass.: National Bureau of Economic Research.

Standard & Poor's. 2009. "Industry Report Card: Latin American Banks Are Better Positioned to Face the Global Financial Crisis Than Their International Peers." New York (April).

———. 2009. "Industry Report Card: Latin American Banks Have Been Holding Up Well So Far in the Global Economic Slowdown" (October).

World Economic Forum. 2009. *The Future of the Global Financial System. A Near-Term Outlook and Long-Term Scenarios.* Geneva.

# 13

## Addressing Private Sector Currency Mismatches in Emerging Europe

JEROMIN ZETTELMEYER, PIROSKA M. NAGY, AND STEPHEN JEFFREY

The 2008–09 financial crisis has highlighted the problems associated with currency mismatches on the balance sheets of emerging market borrowers, particularly in emerging Europe. Currency mismatches aggravated the crises in countries with large currency depreciations, such as Hungary and Ukraine, complicated the crisis response, and induced highly contractionary macroeconomic policies in countries that defended their pegs, such as Latvia.

As a result, the question of how these economies can better manage their foreign exchange (FX) risk—or even "de-dollarize"—is again receiving much attention in the ongoing policy debate.[1] It also has begun to translate into

The authors are grateful to Erik Berglöf, Amar Bhattacharya, Ralph de Haas, Rika Ishii, Olivier Jeanne, Herman Kamil, Isabelle Laurent, Alex Lehmann, Axel van Neederveen, Alex Pivovarsky, Eswar Prasad, Liliana Rojas-Suarez, Christoph Rosenberg, and Peter Sanfey, and to seminar participants at the Brookings Institution, the EBRD, and the International Monetary Fund for their comments; to Anatoli Annenkov for writing and allowing us to use the material in box 13-1; and to Martin Brown, Steve Ongena, Pinar Yeşin, Christoph Rosenberg, and Marcel Tirpák for allowing us to use their data. Research support from Utku Teksoz and Katrin Weissenberg is gratefully acknowledged. The views expressed in this paper are the authors' only and do not necessarily represent the views of the EBRD.

1. Following the literature, we use the term "financial dollarization," "loan dollarization," and "liability dollarization" to denote the use of foreign currency in the financial system, and especially in bank lending to households, regardless of whether the currency used is the U.S. dollar, the euro, or other currencies. A better term for most of the countries covered in this chapter would be "financial euroization." Regarding another terminology issue, this chapter uses the terms "emerging Europe" and "transition countries" interchangeably; some of the analysis even includes Central Asian transition countries.

tougher regulation. For example, in December 2009 Hungary adopted new regulations that require higher household debt-servicing capacity and lower loan-to-value ratios for consumer and mortgage borrowing denominated in foreign exchange. Ukraine banned foreign exchange lending to households outright in late 2008 and set stringent provisioning requirements for FX lending to enterprises in June 2009. In Kazakhstan, the authorities limit FX exposures through a variety of prudential measures (for example, higher provisioning for new FX loans to unhedged borrowers), and outright prohibition of lending in FX to unhedged borrowers is also under discussion. Poland, one of the first countries in the region to regulate FX lending ("Recommendation S"; see box 13-1 on p. 388), has recently strengthened regulation further in the context of a general tightening of lending standards ("Recommendation T," passed in February 2010) . The European Commission has also contemplated introducing European Union (EU)–wide higher regulatory requirements on unhedged FX borrowers via macroprudential and capital requirements, although these are unlikely to be introduced any time soon.

Proposals to tackle the FX lending problem mainly through regulation rest on an implicit assumption that foreign currency lending in the transition region was driven by forces similar to those underlying the precrisis capital inflow and credit boom more generally, namely, a subordination of fear (of the consequences of currency devaluation) to greed (borrowers' desire for much cheaper borrowing terms, and lenders' desire to push out loans). But is this true? Our analysis provides some evidence that foreign financing was indeed a contributing factor to the FX lending boom and concludes that regulation does have a role to play in addressing the FX mismatch problem. However, even a cursory look at the data dispels the idea that financial dollarization in emerging Europe is mainly a boom phenomenon and hence it may have a simple cure based on national regulation. FX lending has been a long-standing fixture in the transition region.[2] And while it increased sharply in some countries during the precrisis boom years— most notably, in Hungary—it declined in other countries, including Russia and Kazakhstan, which were also the target of very rapid capital inflows (figure 13-1).

To put the search for policy solutions on a sounder footing, one needs a better understanding of what has driven FX lending in the first place in emerging Europe, and why some emerging market regions have managed to de-dollarize whereas in many other transition countries this has thus far proven elusive. This chapter begins with a survey of the economic literature on financial dollarization, which has grown considerably in size and quality in recent years, and by now includes several papers on eastern Europe. It next presents some evidence on the question of whether factors related to the capital inflow boom—and the

---

2. See, for example, Sahay and Végh (1996).

Figure 13-1. *Foreign Currency Lending as Share of Total Lending, 2004 and 2008*[a]

Percent of total lending, end of year

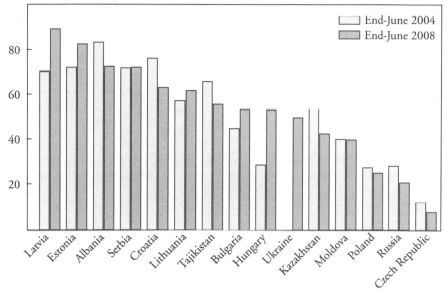

Source: CEIC database (www.ceicdata.com).

a. No comparable data available for Ukraine for 2004. In the cases of Croatia and Serbia, the values include estimated share of exchange rate–indexed local currency lending (assumed to be 74 percent in 2004 and 61 percent in 2008 in Croatia, and 57 percent in 2004 and 70 percent in 2008 in Serbia).

European model of financial integration more generally—have contributed to loan dollarization in transition economies. Finally, it analyzes the policy implications of this evidence and the de-dollarization experiences elsewhere (particularly in Latin America).

The main finding of this chapter is that financial dollarization in emerging Europe has a range of causes, from weak institutions and lack of monetary policy credibility (particularly in less advanced transition countries) to implicit guarantees associated with expectations of euro adoption, foreign funding of banking systems, and lack of local currency market infrastructure. Because these causes do not apply to all countries in the region with equal force, the right policy response will depend on country circumstances. For the purposes of making broad recommendations, three groups of countries are distinguished, based on the state of macroeconomic frameworks and institutions, and on the presence of commitments to maintain hard pegs ahead of euro membership. Depending on these characteristics, the policy response needs to focus primarily on improving macroeconomic institutions and policy credibility or on regulation or on a combination of both, together with measures to develop the legal and institutional infrastructure underlying local currency money and bond markets.

This leaves two main tasks. The first is to correctly diagnose countries. In particular, in countries that lack credible macroeconomic frameworks and institutions, attempts to develop local currency markets are unlikely to succeed, and regulatory solutions may well be counterproductive, as denominating financial contracts in FX could be an optimal response (individually and socially) to an environment of high macroeconomic, institutional, and political risk. The second task is to develop a regulatory approach to FX lending that is both effective—in particular, avoiding problems of cross-border regulatory arbitrage, which can easily arise in financially integrated Europe—and avoids large costs to financial development and access to credit. The chapter has something to say on both of these questions, but much more remains to be done.

## Theory: A Nontechnical Survey

A proximate answer to the question of why so much developing country lending is in FX, which has been emphasized by market practitioners and academics alike, points to incomplete markets—in particular, to a lack of markets for local currency debt at longer maturities.[3] However, this answer is not fully satisfactory, for two reasons. First, it begs the question of why these markets have not developed (or why they have developed in some countries but not in others of similar size and per capita income). Second, while the lack of local currency debt markets may explain why firms are pushed to borrow in foreign currency, it does not explain why a firm would not want a long-term local currency loan even when it could obtain one—a situation that an emerging market lender such as the European Bank for Reconstruction and Development (EBRD) often encounters when it attempts to lend in local currency.

Hence to fully address the puzzle of why borrowing in FX is the prevalent form of financing in many emerging market countries, one needs to explain why many borrowers seem to prefer FX loans even when they have a choice. The superficial answer is that the real interest rate of FX-denominated loans compared to local currency–denominated loans is usually much lower. But higher local interest rates compared to foreign interest rates in emerging market countries reflect exchange rate risk. Therefore, it is necessary to understand why borrowers might prefer the cheaper FX loan *even though* it comes bundled with higher currency risk.

As a matter of logic, the answer could fall in two categories. One possibility is that FX risk is mispriced in the sense that the differential between local and FX

---

3. Eichengreen and Hausmann (1999); Eichengreen, Hausmann, and Panizza (2003).

borrowing rates exceeds the expected rate of devaluation. Alternatively, it could be that the risk is, in fact, fairly priced. In this case, the answer needs to focus on the puzzle of why borrowers nonetheless prefer to pay the lower borrowing rate and take the FX risk.

From the perspective of mainstream economics, there is a problem with the first line of argument: it involves assuming that uncovered interest parity is not only violated (as an empirical matter, it often is) but is systematically violated in one direction. This would seem to be an invitation for arbitrage. If FX rates are systematically low relative to FX risk, then there should be so much FX borrowing that the imbalance disappears. For this reason, it is first worth asking how far one can get in explaining bias toward FX borrowing without assuming systematic underpricing of FX risk (we return to the underpricing idea at the end of this section).

This is actually the approach that most of the literature has taken. For the sake of determining the policy implications, the answers can be grouped in three categories: explanations that imply that (unhedged) FX borrowing is both individually and socially suboptimal, is individually optimal but may be socially suboptimal, and is optimal both individually and socially.

In the first instance, borrowers could prefer the cheaper FX loan because they ignore, underestimate, or excessively discount the FX risk that is involved. Strictly speaking, this means that borrowers behave irrationally—an unpopular assumption in economics, particularly when it involves many individuals that act independently and when the allegedly irrational phenomenon persists over time. However, there are systematic deviations from rationality that have been well documented in the recent literature on behavioral economics, and these could help explain the phenomenon at hand.[4] Consumers often tend to resolve trade-offs between current and future consumption in a way that front-loads consumption compared to what they would want to do if they could commit to a particular intertemporal path. This type of behavior could arguably explain why consumers (or small enterprises) favor a form of lending that allows higher consumption today, albeit at a cost (or risk) in the future. Consumers may realize the risks involved but nonetheless choose to borrow in foreign currency today with the intention of hedging or switching to local currency funding in the near future. But because the future always becomes present, that moment never arrives.

In the second case, foreign currency borrowing could be excessive from a social perspective but fully rational from an individual perspective, as a result of distortions such as borrower moral hazard or externalities.

—*Moral hazard* on the part of the borrower became popular as an explanation for loan dollarization after the Asian crisis, in which implicit guarantees

---

4. For a recent popular survey, see Ariely (2008), particularly chapter 6.

to borrowers and investors were widely believed to have played a role.[5] In this scenario, the borrower understands the higher risks of FX borrowing but reckons that he or she will not be forced to repay in full in the event of a depreciation-related insolvency. This could be because of limited liability or because of the existence (or expectation) of state support in the event of a devaluation.[6]

—*Externalities* could be a cause of excessive FX borrowing if the foreign currency exposures of individuals aggravate the depth of a crisis, and this effect is not taken into account when individuals choose their level and denomination of borrowing (as each individual has a negligible impact). In effect, this creates a collective action problem that gives rise to excessive FX borrowing.[7] If borrowers (or lenders) made the decision collectively, they would internalize the risks of FX borrowing and choose a lower level, but since decisions are decentralized, this is not the case.

In the third situation, borrowing in foreign currency (or alternatively, via inflation-indexed debt) could be optimal—even from a purely risk-minimizing perspective—in an environment of high and variable inflation.[8] There is a widely held presumption that it is safer for unhedged borrowers whose revenue streams are in local currency to also borrow in local currency. However, this presumption may be incorrect because it ignores the fact that the borrower commits to a *nominal* repayment in the future, while the prices of the goods that make up the firm's income stream (or the wages of a household) could change as a result of inflation or relative price shocks. Hence borrowing in local currency does not eliminate the mismatch problem: it replaces a currency mismatch with a mismatch between real and nominal units.

In a stable inflation environment, this mismatch does not matter. With volatile inflation, however, committing to a nominal repayment amount in local currency over the period of several years may be as risky as, or indeed riskier than, committing to the equivalent (at the time of borrowing) foreign currency amount. If inflation turns out to be lower than expected, it could leave the borrower saddled with unsustainable high debt (particularly if lower than expected inflation accompanies an adverse real shock, as will often be the case). The safest form of financing in this instance would normally be inflation-indexed debt, but

---

5. McKinnon and Pill (1999); Corsetti, Pesenti, and Roubini (1999).

6. For the case of limited liability, see Brown, Ongena, and Yeşin (2009). On the role of perceived or actual state support, see Dooley (2000); Burnside, Eichenbaum, and Rebelo (2001); Schneider and Tornell (2004); Rancière, Tornell, and Vamvakidis (2010).

7. Korinek (2009).

8. See Parrado and Ize (2002); Jeanne (2003). This approach is close in motivation and philosophy to the portfolio approach to *deposit* dollarization, which concludes that the optimal currency composition of the portfolio of a domestic saver will depend on the trade-off between inflation and real exchange rate volatility (Ize and Levy Yeyati 2003).

that in turn may not be feasible if low monetary credibility reflects broader institutional deficiencies, which raise doubts about the timeliness and accuracy of inflation measurement and concerns that measurements may be manipulated.[9] As a result, the safest strategy available may be to borrow in foreign currency.

Although the economic literature emphasizes inflation volatility as the principal cause of risk involved with writing financial contracts in local currency, the underlying idea is more general. From a borrower's perspective, the choice of FX versus local currency denomination involves trading off currency and real interest rate risk. One reason why real interest rates could be volatile is inflation risk. But another reason (when local currency loans involve floating interest rates that move in response to expected inflation) could be volatile interest rates in response to liquidity squeezes, unpredictable policy moves, or political instability.

The link between low policy or institutional credibility and FX borrowing emphasized in this literature represents a broader theme that runs through both corporate finance and modern international finance: "dangerous" forms of finance, such as FX borrowing or short-term borrowing, could reflect a deep policy or institutional deficiency, such as weak contract enforcement or an inability to commit to investor-friendly polices. In such circumstances, dangerous finance can be welfare improving, for two reasons.

First, dangerous financial contracts tend to be simple and hard to renegotiate. They do not involve a lot of risk sharing; it is this very fact that makes them potentially dangerous (think of simple debt as opposed to equity, or FX debt rather than debt indexed to the consumer price index). By the same token, however, they can "work" even in underdeveloped and weak institutional settings, and are much less exposed to tampering by governments. For example, unlike equity, simple debt does not require well-developed accounting standards or corporate governance in order to exist. By the same token, FX debt can thrive even in an environment in which poor economic institutions prevent the development of other debt forms.[10]

Second, dangerous finance can ameliorate some of the underlying problems (in particular, government moral hazard and its counterpart, lack of institutional commitment) by acting as a disciplining device. Dangerous debt structures such as short-term or foreign currency debt not only protect investors from the consequences of misbehavior by the borrowing country government, but they also raise the stakes for those countries precisely *because* they potentially give rise to deep crises and hence reward behavior that prevents such crises.[11] However, an inefficiency arises from the fact that the same crises could be triggered by bad

9. Rajan and Tokatlidis (2005).
10. Rajan and Tokatlidis (2005).
11. Jeanne (2000, 2009); Tirole (2003).

luck rather than bad policies. Nonetheless, the net ex ante welfare effect of dangerous debt is generally positive in these circumstances: "Dangerous forms of debt are also 'policy resistant'; they make the government more accountable, ultimately to the benefit of the country."[12]

The three explanations summarized above have vastly different implications for public policy. If FX bias is caused by borrowers who are either ill-informed or have a tendency to procrastinate, then the problem could be solved either through education or by offering low-risk instruments that are costly to refinance and hence commit borrowers to prudent behavior (many real-life loans have that feature, which makes procrastination a somewhat unconvincing explanation of FX bias). If FX bias results from externalities or simply irrational behavior, the answer lies in regulation (for example, imposing an unremunerated reserve requirement on FX bank assets, which would make FX borrowing just expensive enough to align its individual cost with its social costs). Finally, if the cause of FX bias is a lack of credible macroeconomic policies or institutions, then the only way to counter the bias is to address these institutional weaknesses directly. Thus, in this situation, making FX borrowing more expensive or prohibiting FX borrowing by unhedged borrowers will not help: rather than encouraging more local currency borrowing, it will simply lead to less overall borrowing, and it may aggravate some of the underlying institutional problems by eliminating a disciplining device.

As mentioned at the beginning of this section, all the theories we have reviewed so far "work" under the assumption that FX risk is fairly priced. Recently, however, an alternative approach has gained popularity, one that argues that banks underprice FX loans relative to local currency loans in order to match the currency structure of their assets with that of their liabilities.[13] Of course, this idea works only if bank liabilities are also biased toward FX. There could be two reasons for this:

—*FX deposits.* If this is the case, the "puzzle" is merely pushed back one step, as an FX bias in deposits would itself require explanation. This leads to a literature on deposit dollarization that argues largely along similar lines as the theories discussed above (essentially, invoking optimal portfolio choice of depositors in light of high consumer price index volatility compared to real exchange rate volatility; lack of macroeconomic credibility, and moral hazard or similar distortions).

—*Foreign currency funding from abroad.* This could take the form of subsidiary borrowing from a foreign parent (in essence drawing on parent bank deposits) or wholesale borrowing of domestic banks. In this view, financial openness, and particularly foreign bank entry (if foreign subsidiaries have cheaper access

---

12. Tirole (2003).
13. Basso, Calvo-Gonzales, and Jurgilas (2007); Luca and Petrova (2008).

to foreign funding than domestic banks), could be a driving force behind the FX bias in borrowing. Note that as long as no other distortions are assumed, this could be efficient. However, in combination with some of the other distortions described—limited rationality, moral hazard, externalities, and lack of government commitment—this channel will reinforce whatever welfare outcomes result from the initial distortion.

## Empirical Literature

There is a recent, but by now quite substantial, body of empirical work on the determinants of financial dollarization. A number of papers analyze the Latin American experience during the 1990s and the beginning of this decade.[14] Others study the correlates of liability and sometimes deposit dollarization in a broad international cross-section of countries.[15] Finally, there is a small body of work specifically on financial dollarization in transition economies.[16] Most of these papers use aggregate data (typically, with the share of foreign currency bank credit in total domestic bank loans to the private, nonfinancial sector as the main variable of interest) but a growing number are based on firm data.[17]

For the most part, these papers are not set up to discriminate between the main views on financial dollarization that we summarized in the previous section. This said, a few facts emerge from these papers that shed light on some of the theories. We briefly summarize them as follows.

First, there is consistent support for the view that macroeconomic policy credibility, and perhaps institutional quality more broadly, is a determinant of both loan and deposit dollarization. Inflation volatility tends to be associated with higher levels of FX borrowing. Proxies for institutional quality matter either in addition to or as alternative proxies for instability. In the regressions of De Nicoló, Honohan, and Ize (2003), inflation history loses significance once proxies for the quality of broad political institutions and governance indicators are included. Rajan and Tokatlidis (2005) show that dollarization is robustly related to the sensitivity with which the inflation tax reacts to growth shocks: dollarization thrives in environments in which economic fluctuations lead to macro-instability. In Guscina (2008), political instability is related to higher

14. Martinez and Werner (2002); Barajas and Morales (2003); Gelos (2003); Rossi (2004); Cowan, Hansen, and Herrera (2005); Kamil (2008).

15. De Nicoló, Honohan, and Ize (2003); Rajan and Tokatlidis (2005); Jeanne (2003); Levy Yeyati (2005); Guscina (2008).

16. Luca and Petrova (2008); Basso, Calvo-Gonzalez, and Jurgilas (2007); Brown, Ongena, and Yeşin (2009); Rosenberg and Tirpák (2008).

17. Martinez and Werner (2002); Allayannis, Brown, and Klapper (2003); Rossi (2004); Cowan, Hansen, and Herrera (2005); Kamil (2008); Brown, Ongena, and Yeşin (2009).

shares of FX debt. Brown, Ongena, and Yeşin (2009), using data from the 2005 EBRD–World Bank Business Environment and Enterprise Performance Survey (BEEPS), find a strong effect of firm security payments on their propensity to borrow in FX.

Second, the interest rate differential is a reliable predictor of loan dollarization, particularly in the cross-section.[18] This effect is found both for Latin America and particularly for transition economies.[19]

Third, there is evidence that floating exchange rates reduce dollarization. This appears to be true both for floating exchange rate *regimes* and measures of exchange rate volatility.[20] The strongest evidence in this regard comes from Latin America, but Brown, Ongena, and Yeşin (2009) also find this effect in their study of firm borrowing based on the BEEPS.

Fourth, financial development (typically proxied by credit-to-GDP or M2-to-GDP ratios) tends to be *positively* related to loan dollarization within developing country samples.[21] This runs counter to the view that lack of financial development is intrinsic to the dollarization phenomenon.[22]

Fifth, virtually all studies that use transition economy data agree that foreign funding of bank credit is a contributing factor to dollarization (the literature on Latin America does not emphasize this mechanism). There is disagreement, however, on whether foreign banks are the culprit or not. In the firm-level regressions of Brown, Ongena, and Yeşin (2009), foreign bank presence appears to contribute to dollarization, although the effect is not always robust. Basso, Calvo-Gonzalez, and Jurgilas (2007) show that the share of foreign liabilities of the banking system is a very strong predictor of loan dollarization, and they interpret this effect as reflecting the presence of foreign bank subsidiaries. However, Rosenberg and Tirpák (2008) show that once the loan-to-deposit ratio is controlled (for their measure of foreign funding), the share of foreign banks in the assets of the banking system no longer predicts dollarization. In other words, what appears to matter is foreign funding, not foreign banks per se.

Sixth, regulation appears to have some effects, but the literature does not contain a clear message on its overall importance. Many papers ignore regulation altogether. The two main exceptions are Luca and Petrova (2008) and Rosenberg and Tirpák (2008). Both papers focus on transition economies.

18. Though Rosenberg and Tirpák (2008) also show some evidence for longitudinal effects.

19. For effects in Latin American economies, see Barajas and Morales (2003); for those in transition economies, see Brown, Ongena, and Yeşin (2009); Basso, Calvo-Gonzalez, and Jurgilas (2007); and Rosenberg and Tirpák (2008).

20. See Kamil (2008) regarding floating exchange rate regimes.

21. Barajas and Morales (2003); Basso, Calvo-Gonzalez, and Jurgilas (2007).

22. Caballero and Krishnamurthy (2003).

Luca and Petrova look at measures of liberalization of foreign currency lending and deposits and at a measure of bank hedging opportunities (forward market liberalization). Only the latter seems to have an effect: a deep forward foreign exchange market lowers the level of loan dollarization for a given level of deposit dollarization. (The interpretation is that banks need not lend in dollars to stay matched but can instead cover their exposure in the forward market.)

Rosenberg and Tirpák define an "FX restriction index" based on measures that authorities could take to limit FX liabilities: requiring banks to monitor FX asset risk, requiring banks to disclose FX risk to borrowers, imposing eligibility criteria on FX customers, requiring banks to provision or hold higher reserves as a function of indirect FX exposures, and introducing a ceiling on FX exposures. The FX restriction index has a statistically significant impact on loan dollarization in their model, but the effect is economically modest (a fully restrictive regime, on average, lowers FX dollarization by about 2 percentage points). Furthermore, the size of the effect is cut in half if loan dollarization is redefined to include cross-border lending. One interpretation is that with open capital accounts, FX restrictions on banks are not very effective because they can divert borrowing to nonresident sources.

Finally, the literature confirms a robust relationship between firm-level "natural hedges"—the share of exports in firm revenue, as well as foreign ownership—and loan dollarization. Virtually every paper confirms that exporters tend to borrow more in FX than nonexporters. This said, unhedged borrowers are also significantly indebted in foreign currency. By how much? With the exception of Kamil (2008), the literature is silent on this point, reflecting data limitations.

## Reexamination of the Evidence for the Transition Region

In spite of its richness, the literature discussed in the previous section leaves a number of questions open. To ascertain the policy implications for the transition region, it is necessary to understand the role of foreign financing or foreign banks *over and above* that of the more standard causes of financial dollarization that have been identified in the literature. It also would be useful to determine the robustness of the results across methodologies and time periods for the region. Finally, it would be helpful to use at least one methodology that allows for clearer causal interpretation than is the case in most papers using macroeconomic data. Some of the "determinants" of loan dollarization identified in this literature qualify as deep causes of dollarization (for example, weak institutions). For the most part, however, they represent macroeconomic and financial outcomes that are co-determined with dollarization (for example, interest rate differentials or loan-deposit ratios). Hence regressions that attempt to uncover the effects of macroeconomic variables on economy-wide measures of dollarization are hard to interpret.

The remainder of this section takes a stab at these problems by extending the analysis of two papers in the literature, those of Brown, Ongena, and Yeşin (2009) and Rosenberg and Tirpák (2008).[23] The approach is to examine the statistical relationship between FX lending and a broad set of explanatory variables—capturing inflation history, institutional quality, exchange rate regimes, and the effects of foreign financing and foreign bank ownership, plus additional controls—using two different concepts to measure FX lending, and three data sets:

—Firm-level data based on the third (2005) BEEPS, which contains a question about the currency denomination of the last loan taken out by the firms participating in the survey.[24] The answer to this question—whether the loan was in domestic or foreign currency—is represented using a dummy variable, which is regressed on a set of firm variables and country variables, including several measures of financial integration.

—A quarterly macroeconomic dataset with the same country-level variables and the same sample period (2002–05). The dependent variable in this analysis is the FX share in banking system liabilities for each country.

—An annual macroeconomic dataset with similar variables but comprising a longer period (2000–08).

Table 13-1 highlights the main results.[25] For each of the three data sets used, it shows the results of three statistical models. All models comprise a number of potential country-level determinants of FX liabilities, including inflation volatility, a proxy for institutional quality (the EBRD governance and enterprise reform index), a dummy variable that takes the value of *one* if the country had a hard peg and *zero* otherwise, the asset share of foreign banks, and an additional variable capturing financial integration.[26] There are also a number of additional country-level control variables for which the results are not shown, as well as firm-level controls in the first group of regressions based on BEEPS data (see

23. We are very grateful to the authors of these papers for allowing us to use their data for this purpose.

24. Data are available online at EBRD, "Business Environment and Enterprise Performance Survey" (www.ebrd.com/country/sector/econo/surveys/beeps.htm).

25. For the full set of regression coefficients, see the tables in appendix 13A.

26. Note that in all cases, the variables shown in table 13-1 are measures of FX lending, not of net FX exposure (although the firm-level regressions contain some explanatory variables that control for exposure differences for given information about FX lending, such as an exporter dummy). This follows the approach used in most of the literature (exceptions include Goldstein and Turner [2004] and Kamil [2008]), reflecting lack of information about the FX composition of assets and revenue streams of FX borrowers. Very recently, Rancière, Tornell, and Vamvakidis (2010) have attempted to construct net exposure measures for transition economies by combining FX asset and liability data from banking statistics with firm-level data from the BEEPS.

Table 13-1. *Determinants of FX Lending in Transition Economies*[a]

Regression coefficients

| | Firm regression, 2002–05[c] | | | Financial integration (FI) measure[b] | | | | | |
| | | | | Quarterly dataset, 2002–05[d] | | | Annual dataset, 2000–08[e] | | |
| *Variable* | *GFI* | *BIS* | *L/D* | *GFI* | *BIS* | *L/D* | *GFI* | *BIS* | *L/D* |
|---|---|---|---|---|---|---|---|---|---|
| Inflation volatility | 0.035 | 0.026 | 0.012 | 5.986 | 5.499 | 11.040 | –1.823 | –4.648 | –1.510 |
| | (0.010) | (0.049) | (0.418) | (0.308) | (0.363) | (0.009) | (0.204) | (0.072) | (0.270) |
| Governance[f] | –0.321 | –0.228 | –0.209 | –15.800 | –13.780 | –17.070 | –20.070 | –17.070 | –22.120 |
| | (0.000) | (0.001) | (0.004) | (0.010) | (0.030) | (0.010) | (0.006) | (0.020) | (0.001) |
| Hard peg[g] | 0.013 | 0.001 | 0.075 | 32.220 | 33.300 | 23.350 | 23.020 | 24.040 | 19.500 |
| | (0.786) | (0.972) | (0.280) | (0.001) | (0.002) | (0.000) | (0.021) | (0.018) | (0.057) |
| FI measure | 0.060 | 0.000 | –0.185 | 4.625 | 0.068 | 12.940 | 2.564 | 0.016 | 3.048 |
| | (0.360) | (0.540) | (0.057) | (0.628) | (0.047) | (0.390) | (0.821) | (0.088) | (0.842) |
| Foreign banks | 0.003 | 0.001 | 0.001 | 0.122 | 0.067 | 0.131 | –0.049 | 0.024 | –0.095 |
| | (0.000) | (0.001) | (0.166) | (0.243) | (0.473) | (0.321) | (0.775) | (0.888) | (0.587) |
| Observations | 1,574 | 1,452 | 1,541 | 223 | 212 | 196 | 74 | 74 | 59 |
| Number of countries | 21 | 19 | 19 | 21 | 20 | 20 | 15 | 15 | 15 |

Sources: Brown, Ongena, and Yeşin (2009); Claessens, Kose, and Terrones (2008); Lane and Miles-Ferretti (2006); Abiad, Leigh, and Mody (2009); Basso, Calvo-Gonzalez, and Jurgilas (2007); and data from the EBRD, Bank for International Settlements (BIS), International Monetary Fund International Financial Statistics, and BEEPS III.

a. *p*-values are shown in parentheses. The table shows results from three statistical models using three datasets. For each dataset, the models differ only in terms of the financial integration measure used. The table shows only five variables of interest; additional controls are listed in the notes below.

b. GFI: level of gross financial integration (external assets + external liabilities in percent of GDP); BIS: cross-border bank lending, year-on-year change in percent; L/D: loan-to-deposit ratio.

c. Firm-level quarterly data, 2002q1–2005q2, probit estimation, marginal effects reported. The dependent variable is a dummy for whether the last loan of the firm was in a foreign currency. Following Brown, Ongena, and Yeşin (2009), additional controls used include inflation, depreciation and depreciation volatility, firm-level controls (exporter dummy, sales to multinationals, international accounting, dummy for firm size, age of firm), loan characteristics (duration, collateral) and banking sector and institutional controls (interest rate differential), FX deposits, CIS dummy, dummy for forward FX exchange market, capital controls, and foreign exchange.

d. Panel estimation, 2002q1–2005q2. The dependent variable is the share of FX loans to total loans, in percent. Estimated using generalized method of moments (GMM), using past values as instruments. Additional controls include inflation, depreciation, depreciation volatility, interest differential, and FX deposits.

e. Panel estimation, 2000–08. The dependent variable is the share of FX loans to total loans, in percent. Estimated using GMM, using past values as instruments. Additional controls include inflation, depreciation, depreciation volatility, and interest differential.

f. EBRD governance and enterprise restructuring indicator (defined from 1 to 4.3).

g. Dummy variable taking the value 1 for Bosnia-Herzegovina, Bulgaria, Estonia, Latvia, and Lithuania, and 0 otherwise.

table notes and appendix tables). The difference between the models used for each data set is in the financial integration variable, namely: gross financial integration, cross-border bank lending (using data from the Bank for International Settlements), and the loan-to-deposit ratio of the banking system. The latter two are used as alternative measures of foreign financing.

The table shows that the governance indicator is a significant and robust determinant of the FX lending share, confirming the finding of earlier studies that FX lending is more prevalent in countries with weak institutions. The economic magnitude is large, with a one-point improvement on the EBRD transition indicator scale (which runs from one to 4.3) associated with a reduction in the probability of FX borrowing by 22 to 33 percentage points (firm-level regressions), and a reduction in the share of FX lending of 12 to 22 percentage points (country-level regressions). Inflation volatility also matters in two of the three data sets, but its effects are less robust (controlling for the governance indicator). Also, the association between hard pegs and FX borrowing seems to be strong, particularly in the macroeconomic data.

Regarding the role of foreign financing and foreign banks, there is some disagreement between the firm-level and the macroeconomic regressions. In the firm-level regression, the presence of foreign banks appears to make FX borrowing more likely. The effect is statistically significant in two of the four specifications shown. Additional regressions using a broader set of financial inflow and integration controls for example reveal a statistically significant impact in ten of fourteen specifications. In contrast, the other financial integration measures do not seem to have this effect.

In the macroeconomic regressions, only bank lending inflows—but not specifically foreign banks—appear to be associated with FX borrowing. According to these regressions, what mattered is foreign financing of bank lending in transition countries, regardless of whether this took the form of parent-bank lending to a subsidiary, direct cross-border lending, or syndicated lending.

In addition, the level of gross financial integration does not seem to be associated with higher liabilities in FX.

In summary, there is some evidence that foreign financing or the presence of foreign banks or both played a role—on top of determinants such as inflation history, quality of institutions, and the exchange rate regime—in encouraging FX lending in transition economies. However, the results are not conclusive on whether foreign banks contributed to the FX lending bias beyond their role as a conduit for foreign financing. Furthermore, they imply that if there was such an effect, it was economically small, with a 10 percent increase in the share of foreign bank assets increasing the probability of FX-denominated lending and the share of FX lending by at most 3 percentage points. (See the second column of firm-level regressions in table 13-1.)

## Policy

Based on the theory and evidence presented in the previous section, we now sketch the outlines of a strategy for addressing the currency mismatch problem in the transition region. Before doing so, it is worth reviewing a success story in de-dollarization: Latin America.

### How Did Latin America De-dollarize?

Financial dollarization and currency substitution have been endemic to Latin America for many decades. Given the region's history of crises and macroeconomic volatility, this is not surprising. Most major Latin American countries experienced hyperinflation in the 1970s or 1980s (Colombia is the main exception). In some cases—including Argentina and Brazil—this lasted into the 1990s.

By the middle of the decade, however, in the wake of "Washington consensus" reform efforts and following the conclusion of Brady deals with most major countries and the resolution of the painful but brief Tequila crisis, virtually all of Latin America had stabilized to moderate or even low levels of inflation. A gradual decline in dollarization was widely expected to follow. But surprisingly, this did not happen. On the contrary, while currency substitution (use of FX in current transactions) declined in some countries, deposit and loan dollarization continued to increase. It was this astonishing fact that put financial dollarization on the map and focused the minds of policymakers and academics alike. The literature described in the previous section has its origins in this experience.

Almost immediately after the phenomenon had been understood, however, it began to recede. After peaking in the mid- to late 1990s, the FX share in total firm debt fell sharply in Latin American countries, albeit from different starting levels (figure 13-2). Progress was even more dramatic when export revenues are taken into account, with exports as a percentage of short-term dollar liabilities rising from 10 to 20 percent to over 100 percent in Colombia and Mexico by 2005, from about 50 percent to over 100 percent in Chile, and from less than 5 percent to about 50 percent in Peru. In Brazil the rise was more modest, with export coverage of dollar liabilities going from 25 to 45 percent, but this likely underestimates the extent of hedging because it ignores hedges purchased on Brazil's highly developed derivatives markets.

What happened? Roughly, Latin America's de-dollarization process seems to have been driven by five related events and policy initiatives.[27]

First, most Latin American countries experienced economic downturns and crises in the second half of the 1990s. The first of these was the home-grown

---

27. The following account is based on Borensztein and others (2004), Kamil (2008), and various International Monetary Fund reports.

Figure 13-2. *Dollarization of Liabilities of the Corporate Sector in Latin America, 1990–2007*[a]

Percent, annual average across firms (controlling for changes in sample composition)

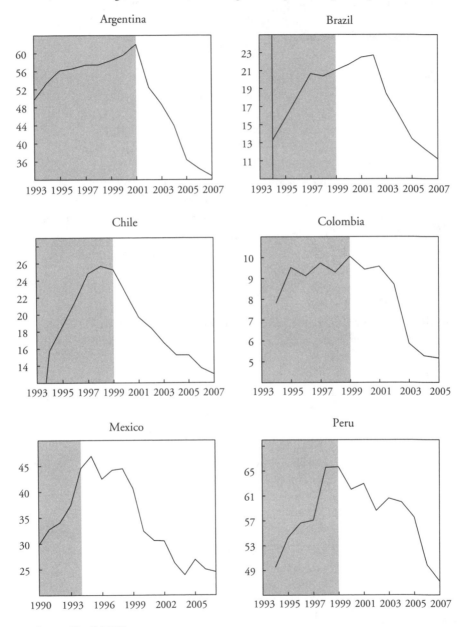

Source: Kamil (2008).

a. Darker (gray) area represents period with fixed or pegged exchange rate regime; white area, period of managed or independent floating.

1995 Mexican crisis, but most crises took place in the last years of the decade, triggered by a "sudden stop" in emerging market finance after the 1998 Russian default and devaluation. The crises ranged from relatively orderly recessions (Chile, 1999) to currency collapses, political upheaval, and sovereign default (Ecuador, 1998–2000; Argentina, 2001–02). Loan dollarization played a critical role in virtually all of these cases. In the cases of Argentina and Ecuador, sovereign debt dollarization was a contributing cause in sovereign defaults (once the devaluations occurred, public sector debt became unsustainable), and dollarization in the private sector created or magnified systemic banking crises in Argentina, Ecuador, and Uruguay (2002–03). But loan dollarization played an important role even in Chile, whose 1999 recession was in part a result of an interest rate defense of the currency in 1998. Among the major countries, only Brazil managed to escape a recession during this period, and it did so because it spent its international reserves in the final months of 1998 on removing private sector currency mismatches—much in the same way Russia did ten years later—just ahead of its January 1999 currency crisis.

Second, following these crises, the affected countries switched to flexible exchange rate regimes (except Ecuador, which adopted the U.S. dollar as legal tender). Unlike in Asia in the 1990s and in some transition economies today, these regimes for the most part were de facto and not just de jure floating exchange rates. There is convincing evidence that this move encouraged de-dollarization of corporate liabilities.[28]

Third, with the exception of Argentina, the switch to a floating exchange rate regime typically accompanied a move (albeit gradual) toward full-fledged inflation-targeting regimes and, in some cases, fiscal rules and other structural-fiscal reforms. In other words, the monetary and macroeconomic regimes changed not just in a way that made exchange rate volatility more visible but also in a way that stabilized inflation expectations and more generally made the recurrence of macroeconomically induced crises much less likely.

Fourth, a few years into the new regimes, most countries began to de-dollarize their *public* debts by issuing longer-term nominal peso bonds at gradually longer maturities in domestic markets. Mexico led the way, issuing three-year and five-year bonds in 2000, followed by seven-year and ten-year bonds in 2002, a twenty-year bond in 2003, and a thirty-year bond in 2006. Most other large Latin American countries followed suit, with Chile, Colombia, and Peru all issuing long-term, non-indexed domestic currency bonds by the middle of this decade (Argentina did so as part of its 2005 debt exchange). In several of these countries, pension reform (the creation of a private pension pillar) is believed to

---

28. See Martinez and Werner (2002) for Mexico, and Kamil (2008) for a broader group of countries.

have contributed to demand for long-term domestic currency bonds. The icing on the cake came during 2005–07, when several of these countries took advantage of favorable global liquidity conditions to issue long-term bonds in local currency in *international* markets, while at the same time buying back or prepaying FX-denominated international bonds, such as Brazilian or Mexican Brady bonds.

The fifth process factor associated with Latin American de-dollarization is the development of derivatives markets, particularly in Brazil.[29] In the middle of the decade, derivatives trading surged in the larger economies in the region, with Brazil, Mexico, Colombia, and Chile registering a combined daily trading volume of close to US$110 billion (notional) in 2006, of which US$46 billion was attributable to Brazil. Brazil and Mexico developed exchange-based derivatives markets, while over-the-counter derivatives trading was dominant in the other countries. Interest rate derivatives (swaps, options, and forward rate agreements) represented about 70 percent of total trading activity, with most of the remainder taken up by currency derivatives (FX forwards and swaps).

In contrast, there does not appear to be any direct evidence that regulation of domestic FX exposures (either directly or through regulation of the banking system) has contributed to the Latin American de-dollarization process, except in the household sector. For example, Colombia and Brazil prohibit households from holding FX deposits with resident banks.

## Main Elements of a Strategy for Emerging Europe

Like in Latin America in the 1990s, financial dollarization in emerging Europe has remained stubbornly high in the current decade despite relatively stable macroeconomic environments since the beginning of the decade (if not earlier). However, there are several factors that distinguish the recent dollarization experience in transition economies from that in Latin America, in particular, the role of foreign financing of banking systems and expectations of euro adoption. Taken together, the economic literature, the Latin American experience, and these special factors point to four policy areas that are likely to play a role—to greatly varying degrees across countries—in reducing and better managing the currency mismatch problem.

### REFORMING MACROECONOMIC REGIMES AND INSTITUTIONS

At one level, the persistence of dollarization in the EBRD region is not surprising. As we have shown, dollarization in Latin American countries did not begin to fall until countries had established credible macroeconomic policy frameworks based on floating exchange rates and inflation targeting. Very few transition countries have such regimes, namely, the Czech Republic (since 1998),

---

29. Luca and Petrova (2008).

Poland (since 1999), Albania (since 2001), Romania (since 2005), Hungary (since 2007), and Serbia (since 2009).[30] Tellingly, the two countries with the oldest and most established of these regimes, the Czech Republic and Poland, also have the lowest rates of dollarization or euroization in the region.

In emerging Europe, reforming macroeconomic frameworks and improving credibility could mean several things, depending in part on whether countries have the option to freely float their currencies or are constrained by international commitments such as participation in the European Exchange Rate Mechanism (ERM2). To the extent that there is no such commitment, countries that are serious about de-dollarizing can improve their policy and institutional credibility by building formal inflation-targeting regimes and demonstrating their success over time. Countries with weak fiscal records may also require fiscal-structural reforms to make inflation targets credible over the longer term, in addition to central bank independence. Fortunately, following the 1998–2000 crises and defaults in three transition countries (Russia, Ukraine, and Moldova), many transition countries built a track record of sound public finances, although maintaining this track record will be a challenge in light of the fiscal burdens arising from the most recent crisis.

Countries that participate in the ERM2 or have the strong intention to adopt the euro in the near term ought to focus on the credibility of eurozone entry over the targeted time frame.[31] In light of high crisis-related deficits, this will require a fiscal adjustment program to meet the Maastricht debt and deficit criteria. The European Central Bank (ECB) could support a country's path to the eurozone through currency swap arrangements against local currencies, provided that fiscal consolidation and supportive monetary policy remain on track. These arrangements would be similar to swap arrangements between the ECB and EU central banks outside the eurozone during the global financial crisis, such as those of Denmark and Sweden, except that they would be used in cases of speculative currency attacks and not financial crisis conditions, as long as good macroeconomic policies remain in place.

## Developing Local Currency Capital Markets

The economic literature does not focus on underdeveloped local currency money and bond markets as a cause of dollarization (rather, it is interpreted as a consequence of the same factors that also drive financial dollarization as commonly defined, that is, dollarization of bank loans and deposits). However,

---

30. Hungary began inflation targeting in 2001 but maintained an additional exchange rate target until late 2007.

31. Upon European Union (EU) membership, all new EU member states have agreed to eventually adopt the euro—without however committing to a timetable.

in practice, de-dollarization experiences often have been accompanied by the development of such markets. This link is not necessarily causal: for example, the government's ability to issue long-term bonds in local currency may simply be a barometer of its macroeconomic credibility, which directly affects financial dollarization.

This said, there is a plausible causal link from the development of local currency bond markets (typically, beginning with government bonds) to financial de-dollarization as follows. Moving from back to front in the causal chain, the existence of a corporate bond market could help de-dollarize bank loans and deposits by providing local currency funding opportunities to banks in an environment in which deposits are mostly dollarized. This could broaden the local currency investment opportunities of banks, enabling them to offer local currency loans at more attractive terms. Corporate bond markets will in turn require legal and market infrastructure—that is, supportive laws, regulations, and institutions. One institution that is sometimes cited as a necessary precursor is a liquid (short maturity) money market, since it may be critical in the development of a primary dealer network.[32]

Developing a corporate bond market may also require the development of a public bond market in order to overcome the "first mover" or coordination problems that are often associated with financial innovation.[33] Once a yield curve based on government bonds of various tenors has been established, corporate bonds can be priced "off" that curve, enabling potential investors to disentangle interest rate risk and corporate default risk (relative to the government). The same benchmark role can potentially be played by a large (relative to potential market entrants) and highly rated private sector borrower, or by investing international financial institutions, such as the EBRD or International Finance Corporation. To serve their purpose, benchmark bonds must be liquid, which may not be easy in markets without a developed institutional investor base. Domestic currency benchmark bonds that meet these requirements exist only in a few transition countries, namely Poland, Hungary, and Russia.

Finally, a successful corporate bond market requires a "demand side" of local institutional investors who are interested in purchasing medium- and long-term financial assets in local currency. Private institutions that might play a key role in this regard are pension funds and insurance companies. Both of them need to invest a flow of local currency receipts (contributions or premiums) to service future local currency obligations. Hence regulatory frameworks and, more generally, market conditions that help the development of nonbank financial institutions could play a critical role in building local currency capital markets.

---

32. Schinasi and Smith (1998).
33. See, for example, Allen and Gale (1994).

Derivatives markets that allow borrowers to hedge against currency and interest rate risk can also help manage currency mismatches. The most obvious channel through which this can occur is to allow FX borrowers to hedge at affordable prices. Somewhat less obviously—since one might think that the presence of affordable currency hedges may encourage firms to borrow more in FX—derivatives markets appear to contribute to the de-dollarization of corporate liabilities.[34] There could be two possible explanations. For a given deposit dollarization, FX markets can help *banks* hedge foreign currency risk and hence allow them to play the role of a buffer between deposit and loan dollarization. In addition, by allowing firms to hedge against (local currency) interest rate risk, derivatives markets may eliminate an important factor that pushes firms toward FX borrowing.

Aside from creating market institutions through their own bond issuance, should governments provide fiscal or regulatory incentives for creating local currency markets? Tax benefits in the form of preferential treatment for long-term local currency savings and lending instruments can potentially play a role in building a local currency yield curve. But more important may be the *removal* of fiscal or regulatory obstacles. For example, in Kazakhstan pension funds are obligated to hold at least 30 percent of their portfolio in long-term government bonds, many of which earn interest rates below inflation. Reducing this requirement or issuing inflation-indexed government bonds would help build a corporate bond market.

REGULATORY MEASURES
Regulation can ameliorate financial dollarization if the latter is not primarily a reflection of lack of macroeconomic credibility but instead is caused by distortions, such as moral hazard or a crisis externality, or by irrational or short-sighted behavior by corporate or household borrowers.

Regulation does not seem to have played a critical role in Latin America's de-dollarization process. However, emerging Europe may be different in this respect for two reasons. First, there is some direct evidence that cross-country differences in regulation help explain cross-country differences in loan dollarization in the new member states of the European Union.[35] Second, and more important, expectations of euro adoption and reliance on foreign funding of bank loans—the main factors that seem to distinguish dollarization in emerging Europe from dollarization in Latin America and elsewhere—imply that regulation could be a potentially important remedy in many European countries. Basic macroeconomic credibility and inflation problems are less likely to play a role in countries

34. Luca and Petrova (2008).
35. Rosenberg and Tirpák (2008).

that are in the European Union (or EU candidates) and have started their convergence with the eurozone. In addition, the convergence process may reinforce some of the underlying causes of dollarization-euroization that are best addressed by regulation, particularly a false sense that the exchange rate will remain stable throughout the convergence process (this may have played a role in Hungary; see Kiraly 2009) and that government commitments to stabilize the exchange rate give rise to implicit guarantees. Finally, if foreign funding of the banking system generates underpricing of FX loans, as some papers have suggested, this may also generate a rationale for regulation.

The appropriate form of regulation will depend on the nature of the problem, that is, the distortion that biases borrowers in favor of FX lending:

—If the problem is that borrowers are misinformed, then the right response is to force disclosure of FX risk. In light of large depreciations in some countries, this source of FX borrowing preference must have become less relevant as a result of the recent financial crisis.

—If the underlying problem is that FX interest rates are too low because borrowers and lenders do not internalize the social risk of FX borrowing in the event of a crisis, then the underlying distortion can be corrected through regulatory measures that change the relative price of FX and local currency lending. This could take the form of an unremunerated reserve requirement for FX lending by banks, higher capital requirements for FX loans, or more demanding provisioning requirements for FX loans (or, conversely, depending on the demand conditions, lower capital or provisioning requirements for local currency lending).[36] These measures will not only have the effect of protecting banks' balance sheets from the higher credit risk that they assume by lending to unhedged borrowers but also will result in relatively higher FX interest rates, hence leveling the playing field between local currency and FX loans.

—Finally, if the problem is either implicit guarantees or myopia on the part of the borrower, who focuses only on the interest rate differential, then even these more heavy-handed regulatory measures might not work unless they make the interest rate differential disappear altogether (which may, in turn, be undesirable because it *over*promotes local currency loans to borrowers that are not myopic or do not assume guarantees). In this case, the answer may be to place limits on the open FX position of *borrowers* or make some classes of borrowers ineligible for FX loans altogether.

Of the three approaches, the one described last is the least applied and the most difficult to implement. However, to the extent that one believes that myopia or implicit guarantees are really what is driving demand for FX borrowing by, for example, households or small and medium-size enterprises, it would be

36. See Korinek (2009) for more on unremunerated reserve requirements for FX lending.

well worth exploring. At the practical level, the main difficulty is that although many countries have elaborate institutions for monitoring and supervising the balance sheet risks of the banking sector, there are no equivalent institutions for supervising similar risks in the vastly more populous and fragmented corporate and household sectors. As such, instruments that try to limit the FX exposures of these sectors tend to be blunt—for example, prohibiting household borrowing in foreign currency altogether.

One way to make balance sheet regulations for corporations and households more focused without a need to create new agencies might be to impose on banks some of the burden of supervising borrower balance sheet structures. In effect, this supervision is already part of the natural due diligence process that well-run banks apply to borrowers. For example, when households apply for a mortgage loan, they typically need to disclose not only their income but also their assets and liabilities. It may not be too difficult to require banks to take account of currency risks in the balance sheet of a potential borrower in the same way. A bank would need to establish the currency exposure of a corporate borrower and would only be allowed to lend in foreign currency if that exposure remains below a certain limit. On the household side, a similar principle could be applied, or alternatively, lower loan-to-value ratios could be applied for FX borrowers, which would ensure that the borrower retains positive equity even after a devaluation of a certain size. This principle underlies Poland's "Recommendation S," which was introduced in 2006 and is credited with curbing unhedged FX lending during the peak of the boom (see box 13-1 and figure 13-3). It is also embodied in regulation that was recently introduced in Hungary.

Finally, it is important to recognize that regulation, particularly in financially integrated Europe, may not be effective unless similar regulatory principles apply across jurisdictions. Consider, for example, a tough regulation in an eastern European host country of an international banking group. If the home country does not impose similar regulation, the host country regulation can be easily circumvented (except in the presence of capital controls) by borrowing directly from the parent bank rather than the subsidiary (anecdotal evidence suggests that this occurred in some countries before the recent crisis). In addition, host countries may not want to apply tougher regulation than exists in other potential host countries to avoid discouraging capital inflows.

However, there are unlikely to be any EU-wide regulations entailing higher capital or prudential requirements in the foreseeable future, for three reasons. First, there is a recognition that the problem is partly rooted in macroeconomic factors that need to be addressed first. Second, there is a concern that under the prevailing cyclical conditions, a "tax" on FX lending would prolong the credit crunch and slow the recovery in emerging Europe. Third, it is unlikely that the twenty-seven European Union members will agree on EU-wide

Box 13-1. *Poland's "Recommendation S"*

Recommendation S on Good Practices Regarding Mortgage-Secured Credit Exposures, introduced by the Polish Commission for Banking Supervision in June 2006, comprises two essential elements to discourage FX lending. First, it recommends requiring higher creditworthiness when customers apply for a residential loan in a foreign currency than when they apply for a zloty loan of the same value. Second, and related to this point, it sets a high standard for disclosing FX-related risks. The bank is advised to first present a zloty loan offer. When a customer still wishes to take out a foreign currency loan, the bank is asked to inform the customer about the currency risk and show a simulation of the value of loan installments assuming zloty depreciation (of 20 percent and the difference between the highest and lowest zloty exchange rate in the past twelve months) and an increase of the interest rate to the level of a similar zloty-denominated loan.

Recommendation S has been credited with a rise in the share of local currency loans in new lending for the second half of 2006, although it did not affect the overall growth rate of mortgage debt. In 2007 the narrowing interest rate differential between Poland and Switzerland also may have dampened the demand for Swiss franc loans. The renewed demand for FX mortgage loans in 2008 may be attributable to the gradual easing of income criteria for FX loans and the appreciation of the zloty until the third quarter (see figure 13-3).

While Recommendation S may not have had a lasting impact on curbing FX borrowing, its real success may have been to raise the credit quality of FX loans. Data confirm that Polish FX mortgage borrowers tend to be well-educated first-time borrowers with strong employment prospects. As of the end of September 2009, the ratio of nonperforming FX mortgage loans remained low, at 0.9 percent, versus 2.4 percent for zloty-denominated mortgages.

This box was prepared by Anatoli Annenkov. For more information, see Polish Commission for Banking Supervision (2006).

regulatory changes without conducting the usual impact studies accompanying such changes.

However, there are two pragmatic short-term alternatives to EU-wide regulation. First, regulators of internationally active banking groups can affect the operations of these banks. Home country supervisors can lead this effort, in close coordination with host supervisors. The Austrian authorities, for example, have launched a new supervisory initiative restricting Austrian banks' domestic foreign currency lending to unhedged individuals, and are engaged in negotiations with the main Austrian banking groups that aim to apply similar principles to the lending of these banking groups in emerging Europe (both to direct cross-border lending and to subsidiary lending). Second, the main bank groups could

Figure 13-3. *Net New Credit to Households, Poland, 2008–10*[a]

Millions of zloty

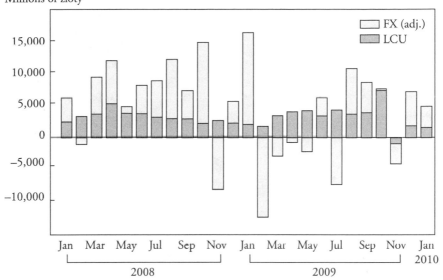

Source: Authors' calculations based on CEIC database (www.ceicdata.com).
a. LCU, local currency units.

agree among themselves to a set of lending standards that in effect embodies and preempts the main restrictions that regulators might otherwise impose. A combination of the two, with home countries setting some basic coordinated guidelines and effectively encouraging banks to incorporate them into their lending standards, would be a desirable possibility.

COUNTRY INSURANCE

The regulatory measures discussed in the previous subsection are based on acceptance of the fact that financial dollarization cannot be rooted out but instead must be managed so as to limit the risks that go along with it. One way of doing that is to manage risks at the macro-level in addition to the micro-level. This means offsetting an aggregate FX mismatch in the private sector by a long FX position (ideally, on a contingent basis) in the public sector. In the event of a "sudden stop" or other event triggering pressure on the currency, this public long FX position can then be mobilized in a way that softens the blow to the private sector. This is how Brazil (1998) and Russia (2008) managed pressures on their currencies in light of private sector open FX positions. In effect, international reserves were spent to allow the private sector to close its FX position either ahead of a devaluation (in Brazil) or accompanying a very gradual devaluation (in Russia).

The problem with this approach is that it is potentially expensive for the public sector, particularly if the "country insurance" consists of hoarding large amounts of international reserves. Even worse, if the delivery of FX (or FX risk hedges) from the public to the private sector involves a subsidy, then the country insurance mechanism could become a source of moral hazard and hence help create the very problem that it is meant to mitigate. That said, these problems are not insurmountable: for example, FX support will not create a distortion if it takes the form of (fairly priced) lending rather than a transfer. Furthermore, country insurance could be cheaper if it involves international risk sharing, either through a public institution, such as the International Monetary Fund (IMF), or through private contingent credit lines.[37] In general, a country that decides to "live with" some degree of private sector currency mismatch is well-advised to have a crisis mitigation framework in place that will allow it to cope with the consequences of pressures on the currency.

## A Framework for Country-Specific De-dollarization Strategies

Not all of the elements discussed in the previous subsection are equally suited to all emerging European countries with private sector loan dollarization. In particular, two sets of constraints or considerations need to be taken into account when defining country-specific strategies to reduce or limit the risk of FX exposures.

The first constraint is EU membership or EU candidate status. As argued in the previous section, if the expectation of euro adoption is a driver of euroization, this makes it more likely that regulation is an appropriate response. Expectations of euro adoption in small countries may also make it more difficult to develop local currency capital markets. Finally, and most obviously, international commitments and geography may limit the extent to which countries may be able to, or wish to, reform their monetary institutions in the direction of free-floating exchange rates and inflation-targeting policies. In particular, several members of the European Union have undertaken commitments under the ERM2 that limit currency flexibility, or have adopted rigid pegs in anticipation of euro adoption.

Second, attempts to address the causes of dollarization must take into account the context of a specific country. In particular, it does not make sense to push the development of local currency bond markets in countries that have not reached a minimum level of macroeconomic policy and institutional credibility (if attempted, such efforts would fail). It may make even less sense, in such countries, to try to reduce financial dollarization through regulatory measures, because financial dollarization may be a constrained-optimal response to a weak institutional environment. In other words, although regulation might

37. See Caballero and Panageas (2005), and Sturzenegger and Zettelmeyer (2007, chapter 12) for a survey.

be successful in reducing financial dollarization, it may come at the expense of precluding access to finance by unhedged borrowers and perhaps shutting down some forms of finance (for example, longer-term borrowing) altogether.

Taken together, these constraints suggest three ways of grouping countries. The first category consists of those countries with weak institutions and volatile macroeconomic environments. To address financial dollarization in this group, the strategic focus should be on building credible macroeconomic policy frameworks and institutions and allowing more exchange rate flexibility. To support this process, countries can attempt to limit external volatility, for example, through an IMF-supported arrangement or credit line. Attempts to develop local currency markets and limit financial dollarization through regulatory means can receive less emphasis during this phase.

In the second category are those countries that have built reasonably strong macroeconomic institutions and are either not candidates for the euro or not constrained by the ERM2 or by hard euro pegs. Countries in this group could mobilize all four elements of the strategy described above to varying degrees. They should continue to build macroeconomic policy credibility in the context of floating exchange rates, develop local currency markets and possibly derivatives markets (except in countries that are so small that they would not meet minimum scale and liquidity requirements), strengthen regulations, and seek country insurance to minimize risks while the de-dollarization process is ongoing.

The last group consists of EU members that participate in the ERM2 or have committed to hard pegs in anticipation of euro adoption. These countries should focus on regulatory measures to mitigate risks associated with FX mismatches on the road to the euro. Such countries could also strengthen, in collaboration with the ECB and the European Commission, their policy credibility by committing to a strong convergence program toward, and then within, the ERM2 framework to meet the Maastricht criteria. The ECB could facilitate these countries' path to the eurozone by providing genuine euro currency swap facilities against local currencies, as long as countries' convergence programs remain on track.

The question is which countries fall into which categories. This is easy to answer for some countries, but there is a "gray zone" (and judgment) involved with classifying others.

ERM2 participants or countries with hard pegs in anticipation of euro entry include the Baltic countries and Bulgaria. Countries that are outside the European Union and do not currently have candidate status make up the complementary group. This leaves highly euroized EU members or candidates such as Hungary, Romania, and possibly Croatia in a gray zone. For these countries, both choices could be on the table: to build further on past progress in improving institutions and local currency markets with the aim of reducing euroization, or to accept euroization and manage its risks, primarily through regulation.

Regardless of which "box" these countries fit in, regulation can be expected to play a role, for reasons explained in the last section. At the same time, these countries have room to strengthen both monetary and fiscal policy credibility and to improve local capital market infrastructure. Hence they should not confine themselves to a "regulation only" approach.

It is also difficult, but not impossible, to attempt to classify countries according to *monetary policy credibility*. One approach is to examine the inflation volatility data underlying the regressions shown in table 13-1. This will identify the set of countries for which inflation volatility is a key driver of dollarization, according to the regressions; however, this set is, in turn, somewhat sample specific. Another approach is to ask in which countries lending in local currency would have led to more predictability in the medium-term debt burden than lending in euros or dollars (see box 13-2 and table 13-2). Where this applies, the local currency should have proved itself a better—less risky—unit of account for financial contracts than foreign currency.

Both approaches give roughly consistent answers, suggesting that a macroeconomic credibility problem is probably not the main driving factor behind loan dollarization in central European and the Baltic countries, whereas it is more likely to be an issue in the Commonwealth of Independent States and the Balkans region. How one delineates the boundary between these groups will depend on whether memories of high inflation in the 1990s are considered to affect monetary policy credibility today, and on whether in assessing credibility, one focuses only on inflation volatility or also considers nominal interest rate volatility driven by liquidity squeezes, erratic macroeconomic policies, and political shocks. The latter approach would expand the group of countries for which policy credibility is deemed to be an issue.

Table 13-3 summarizes the discussion in this chapter. The *top right cell* shows countries for which tighter regulation and fiscal consolidation are the main options to manage the risks of currency mismatches, both because weak institutions are not the principal underlying problem in these countries and because existing policy commitments limit the options for institutional reform and for local currency capital market development.

The *bottom left cell* includes countries for which the macroeconomic and institutional credibility is probably the main issue at this point, and regulation and aggressive market development is unlikely to be useful (or could even be counterproductive) until some degree of credibility has been achieved.

Finally, the *top left cell* includes the remaining countries, which will want to use a combination of all tools to address currency mismatches. Within this heterogeneous group, the emphasis given to particular tools will vary, with more prominence given to regulation in countries with relatively advanced institutional environments and membership in, or proximity to, the European Union.

Box 13-2. *Comparing the Riskiness of Local Currencies and Euros as Currencies of Denomination*

Suppose a firm, producing one unit of real output *t* periods in the future, had been given the choice of borrowing long term, either in local currency units or in euro units, both at a fixed interest rate. Viewed from the present, the debt due at time *t* (expressed in whatever units in which it was contracted) is known with certainty. What is not known, however, is the repayment capacity of the firm expressed in the same currency unit that was used to fix the repayment amount. Suppose that uncovered interest parity holds, so that future debt constitutes the same share of *expected* firm revenue regardless of what unit debt and revenue are expressed in. Then the probability that the firm will be able to repay its debt in local currency will be higher than if it is denominated in euros, if and only if the volatility of future output in local currency units is lower than that of future output expressed in euros. Thus one way of assessing the relative riskiness of local currency debt versus euro debt is simply to compare the volatility of output expressed in the two units, as shown in table 13-2.

Table 13-2 undertakes this comparison for three different measures of volatility. First, to assess the risk faced by the borrower from not knowing precisely what the value of his production will be in the units in which the debt has been contracted, one ideally would want to compare the predictability of output, over a *t* horizon, expressed in the various units (see Borensztein and others 2004, box 1). The group of columns on the left side of the table do so by computing the standard deviations of the forecast error of cumulative GDP growth over a four-year horizon, computed as the difference of four-year-ahead *World Economic Outlook* (WEO) forecasts made for 2005 (in the 2001 WEO), for 2006 (in the 2002 WEO), and so on, and comparing them to the actual GDP values for these years.

Focusing on this measure, the results indicate (not surprisingly) that a number of central European countries (Croatia, Czech Republic, Hungary, Poland, Slovak Republic, and Slovenia) would have been better off denominating debt in local currency units versus euro units. Most other countries (including those with hard pegs, all of which have resisted a devaluation so far, and most members of the Commonwealth of Independent States and the South East Europe Program) would have fared better with euro-denominated debt. There are two anomalies: Tajikistan and the United States, which is included as a memorandum item together with a few other advanced countries. This can be attributed to the tiny sample of only five observations underlying each standard deviation.

To get around the sample size problem, we additionally compute the standard deviation of growth itself (rather than cumulative growth forecasts) over two horizons: 1994–2009, a period comprising almost the entire transition sample except for the early stabilization and liberalization years; and 2001–09 (2009 is always included to reflect crisis-related devaluations in the volatility measures). As it turns out, the longer sample is often still dominated by high inflation experiences in the first half of the 1990s. For this reason, local currency units very rarely emerge as the volatility-minimizing unit of account. This changes if the sample period is reduced to 2001–09, with local currency denominations emerging as the variance-minimizing unit in most countries. The exceptions are Belarus, Tajikistan, and Serbia (and most of the hard peg countries, as mentioned above).

Table 13-2. *GDP Volatility: Comparison of Standard Deviations across Currency Units*

| Country | Four-year forecast error (2005–09)[a] | | SD mini-mizing | SD growth (1994–2009)[b] | | SD mini-mizing | SD growth (2001–09) | | SD mini-mizing |
|---|---|---|---|---|---|---|---|---|---|
| | Local | Euro | | Local | Euro | | Local | Euro | |
| *Transition* | | | | | | | | | |
| Albania | 3.0 | 17.8 | Local | 11.9 | 17.0 | Local | 3.0 | 6.4 | Local |
| Armenia | 19.1 | 10.5 | Euro | 1,169.3 | 22.2 | Euro | 6.2 | 13.9 | Local |
| Azerbaijan | 96.0 | 12.7 | Euro | 532.5 | 23.7 | Euro | 22.3 | 24.4 | Local |
| Belarus | 149.0 | 13.2 | Euro | 416.0 | 85.1 | Euro | 22.6 | 12.1 | Euro |
| Bulgaria | 13.2 | 7.0 | Euro | 217.9 | 20.8 | Euro | 5.2 | 4.5 | Euro |
| Croatia | 6.8 | 14.7 | Local | 29.2 | 8.4 | Euro | 3.5 | 4.9 | Local |
| Czech Republic | 5.7 | 12.7 | Local | 5.3 | 7.5 | Local | 3.8 | 8.7 | Local |
| Estonia | 19.9 | 17.3 | Euro | 12.1 | 12.3 | Local | 8.5 | 8.4 | Euro |
| Georgia | 13.9 | 11.0 | Euro | 2,085.9 | 30.2 | Euro | 5.1 | 10.5 | Local |
| Hungary | 5.6 | 20.0 | Local | 8.1 | 7.0 | Euro | 4.0 | 8.1 | Local |
| Kazakhstan | 50.1 | 26.1 | Euro | 323.4 | 31.4 | Euro | 11.4 | 16.5 | Local |
| Kyrgyz Republic | 43.8 | 16.0 | Euro | 29.0 | 18.3 | Euro | 8.6 | 8.8 | Local |
| Latvia | 34.8 | 14.4 | Euro | 11.6 | 16.7 | Local | 12.6 | 12.5 | Euro |
| Lithuania | 12.4 | 7.9 | Euro | 14.6 | 14.4 | Euro | 6.8 | 6.4 | Euro |
| Macedonia, FYR | 19.7 | 11.6 | Euro | 35.4 | 8.8 | Euro | 5.1 | 5.2 | Local |
| Moldova | 32.1 | 12.8 | Euro | 36.5 | 15.6 | Euro | 6.7 | 11.0 | Local |
| Mongolia | 50.8 | 11.7 | Euro | 20.1 | 16.0 | Euro | 11.5 | 15.7 | Local |
| Poland | 15.7 | 18.2 | Local | 13.2 | 9.7 | Euro | 2.7 | 11.8 | Local |
| Romania | 22.5 | 14.5 | Euro | 39.5 | 11.1 | Euro | 11.0 | 11.3 | Local |
| Russia | 32.4 | 23.7 | Euro | 63.9 | 24.2 | Euro | 9.3 | 16.3 | Local |
| Serbia[c] | ... | ... | ... | 28.7 | 17.9 | Euro | 27.1 | 13.2 | Euro |
| Slovak Republic | 9.2 | 13.6 | Local | 12.2 | 11.1 | Euro | 3.7 | 5.9 | Local |
| Slovenia | 1.6 | 11.5 | Local | 4.2 | 3.8 | Euro | 3.6 | 3.0 | Euro |
| Tajikistan | 19.3 | 19.4 | Local | 98.6 | 25.7 | Euro | 8.5 | 7.3 | Euro |
| Turkey | 142.0 | 31.3 | Euro | 34.8 | 15.8 | Euro | 15.4 | 15.3 | Euro |
| Turkmenistan | 133.7 | 52.8 | Euro | 338.5 | 27.2 | Euro | 16.7 | 18.5 | Local |
| Ukraine | 54.2 | 40.0 | Euro | 186.1 | 18.8 | Euro | 9.6 | 18.5 | Local |
| Uzbekistan | 28.5 | 20.3 | Euro | 289.0 | 18.2 | Euro | 10.7 | 17.3 | Local |
| *Memorandum* | | | | | | | | | |
| Canada | 6.6 | 19.9 | Local | 2.9 | 9.4 | Local | 3.2 | 7.1 | Local |
| Japan | 3.7 | 6.2 | Local | 2.0 | 10.6 | Local | 2.2 | 8.0 | Local |
| United Kingdom | 5.0 | 28.1 | Local | 2.0 | 9.3 | Local | 2.5 | 8.2 | Local |
| United States | 5.1 | 4.3 | Euro | 2.1 | 9.1 | Local | 2.6 | 7.2 | Local |

Source: Authors' calculations based on data from the IMF's *World Economic Outlook,* various years.

a. Standard deviation of percentage differences between four-year-ahead GDP forecasts published in the spring 2001–05 editions of the *World Economic Outlook* (WEO) and realized (or in the case of 2009, projected) GDPs based on the April 2009 WEO.

b. Standard deviation of cumulative five-year-ahead forecast errors based on previous year's projected growth rate (that is, the 2000 rate is used to generate the cumulative forecast for 2005, the 2001 rate is used to generate the forecast for 2006, and so on).

c. For data availability reasons, the sample for Serbia starts in 1997.

Table 13-3. *Framework for Policy Responses to Liability Dollarization in Transition Economies*

| | | In ERM2, or hard peg in anticipation of euro? | |
|---|---|---|---|
| | | No | Yes |
| Macroeconomic and institutional credibility? | OK | Further reform monetary and fiscal institutions and/or build track record<br>Local market development<br>Regulation<br>Country insurance<br>*Poland, Hungary, Romania, Croatia, Serbia, Russia; possibly Kazakhstan* | Regulation<br>Fiscal consolidation and/or fiscal-structural reforms<br>*Baltic countries, Bulgaria* |
| | Low | Reform monetary and fiscal institutions and build credibility track record<br>Country insurance<br>*Ukraine, most early transition countries, some countries in the Western Balkans* | |

Furthermore, country size may limit the scope for local market development, particularly in some countries in southeastern Europe.

Note that the *bottom right cell* is empty. In a sense, countries such as Montenegro, which have unilaterally adopted the euro, fit in this area; however, their adoption of the euro precludes the need for a further policy response, at least conditional on that policy choice.

## Conclusion

As in other emerging market regions, liability dollarization in emerging Europe and in the transition economies further east has multiple causes. First among these is lack of macroeconomic credibility. In some countries, high inflation volatility may have encouraged financial contracts in foreign currency as opposed to local currency. Even in countries with more solid inflation track records, imperfect credibility has meant that FX borrowing has typically been cheaper than local currency borrowing. Whether combined with implicit guarantees associated with hard pegs, or simply the result of disregard for exchange rate risk in light of low exchange rate volatility and expected euro adoption in the medium term, this factor has created incentives for foreign currency borrowing.

Abundant foreign financing appears to have aggravated the situation, perhaps because it led to more aggressive pricing of FX loans.

Policy responses to the liability dollarization problem will be successful only if they are shaped by the correct diagnosis. In countries in which monetary and fiscal institutions are weak and there is a concern that the government might resort to the inflation tax, regulatory responses—making FX lending more expensive or banning it outright—could be counterproductive, as they may lead borrowers to take higher risks or undermine lending altogether. In these countries, the reforms must focus on the core of the problem by reforming macroeconomic institutions and strengthening public finances. In the remaining countries, regulation can play a useful role, but it should be embedded in a broader strategy that seeks to further improve macroeconomic credibility and develop local currency markets.

Regulation can be useful through two channels: first, by limiting corporate and household FX exposures and hence the risks associated with currency mismatches, even while much of the financial system remains dollarized; and second, by correcting distortions that may have made FX borrowing too cheap. At the same time, regulation to address the FX liability bias needs to be designed with care. Like any regulation, it comes at the cost of making potentially welfare-improving transactions more expensive or impeding them altogether. This is a particular concern at a time when net credit growth is still weak or negative in many emerging European countries, and many households and firms need to refinance FX debts. When introducing such regulation, policymakers will need to trade off these risks against the desire to take advantage of postcrisis political momentum favoring financial sector reforms.

Finally, attempts to introduce regulation need to address the cross-border coordination problem. In a financially integrated Europe, where cross-border banking groups own the bulk of financial system assets in many emerging European countries, regulatory discrepancies across countries could lead to regulatory arbitrage: shopping for loans where regulation is the weakest. This can be avoided through EU-wide regulation that is also adopted in the EU neighborhood. In the absence of such regulation, informal coordination between regulatory authorities can help. One good thing to emerge from the ongoing crisis is that it has created mechanisms for cross-border coordination in the context of crisis management.[38] The success of the postcrisis cleanup and reform effort could hinge on whether these mechanisms can be maintained and developed beyond the crisis.

---

38. See EBRD (2009, box 1.4).

## Appendix 13A. Regression Variables and Definitions

| Variable name | Definition |
| --- | --- |
| Age | Age of firm at time of loan disbursement, in years. |
| BIS | FX-adjusted quarterly change in the asset position of commercial banks reporting to the Bank for International Settlements, percent, from the BIS locational database. |
| ca_3 | Average current account deficit in the three years previous, percent of GDP. |
| Capital controls | 1 = country has controls on foreign borrowing by or foreign direct investment in domestic firms, 0 = otherwise. |
| CIS | 1 = country is member of Commonwealth of Independent States, 0 = otherwise. |
| Collateralized | 1 = yes, 0 = no. |
| Deprec. volatility | Variance of monthly changes in the real exchange rate versus the euro, in percentages, during the past four quarters. |
| Depreciation | Depreciation of local currency versus the euro, nominal, in percentages, during the past quarter. |
| Duration | Duration of the loan, in months. |
| EU | 1 = country is or has completed negotiations to become EU member, 0 = otherwise. |
| Exporter | 1 = firm has export revenues, 0 = otherwise. |
| fintdebl | External debt liabilities, percent of GDP. |
| fintdebt_ch | Three-year change in external debt, percent |
| fintliab | Total external liabilities, percent of GDP. |
| Foreign banks | Assets share of foreign controlled banks in domestic banking system, in percentages. |
| Forex loan | 1 = last loan of firm was in a foreign currency, 0 = last loan of firm was in local currency. |
| Forex deposits | Share of deposits in the banking sector denominated in foreign currency, in percentages. |
| Forward FX market | 1 = country has developed forward FX market, 0 = otherwise. |
| GFI | Gross financial integration, defined as stock of external assets and liabilities, percent of GDP. |
| Governance | EBRD index of enterprise reform. Scale: 1 to 4.33. |
| Income via bank | Share of firm revenues that are received through bank transfers. |

*(continued)*

## Appendix 13A *(continued)*

| Variable name | Definition |
| --- | --- |
| Inflation | Consumer price inflation in the past quarter. |
| Inflation volatility | Variance of monthly changes in the consumer price index, in percentages, during the past four quarters. |
| Interest differential | Money market rate minus euro repo rate in the past quarter. |
| International accounting | 1 = firm applies international accounting standards (IAS or USGAAP), 0 = otherwise. |
| kaopen | Chinn-Ito index of capital account liberalization. |
| L\D | Loan-to-deposit ratio. |
| Open FX position | Maximum total open FX position of banks over capital, in percentages. |
| Peg | 1 = country has crawling peg, fixed peg, or currency board exchange rate regime, 0 = otherwise. |
| Security costs | Expenses for security services over sales. |
| Small firm | 1 = less than 50 employees, 0 = otherwise. |
| State firm | 1 = at least 50 percent of ownership in state hands, 0 = otherwise. |

## Appendix 13B. Statistical Relationship between FX Lending and Explanatory Variables

Table 13B-1. *Firm-Level Regressions: Full Results, 2002–05*[a]

Regression coefficients

| Variable | Foreign financing-integration measure (FI measure) | | | | | | | |
|---|---|---|---|---|---|---|---|---|
| | GFI | BIS | L/D | fintliab | fintdebl | ca_3 | fintdeb_ch | kaopen |
| Inflation volatility | 0.0353 | 0.0255 | 0.0118 | 0.0355 | 0.0337 | 0.0629 | 0.0337 | 0.0292 |
| | (0.010) | (0.050) | (0.418) | (0.008) | (0.008) | (0.000) | (0.009) | (0.038) |
| Governance | 0.321 | -0.228 | -0.209 | -0.317 | -0.299 | -0.440 | -0.300 | -0.224 |
| | (0.000) | (0.001) | (0.004) | (0.000) | (0.000) | (0.000) | (0.000) | (0.007) |
| Hard peg | 0.013 | 0.001 | 0.075 | 0.015 | 0.009 | 0.204 | 0.007 | 0.001 |
| | (0.786) | (0.972) | (0.280) | (0.756) | (0.857) | (0.005) | (0.889) | (0.981) |
| FI measure | 0.0601 | -0.0003 | -0.1850 | 0.0008 | 0.0007 | -0.0103 | 0.0006 | -0.0061 |
| | (0.360) | (0.540) | (0.057) | (0.331) | (0.487) | (0.202) | (0.490) | (0.821) |
| Foreign banks | 0.060 | 0.000 | -0.185 | 0.001 | 0.001 | -0.010 | 0.001 | -0.006 |
| | (0.000) | (0.001) | (0.166) | (0.000) | (0.000) | (0.544) | (0.000) | (0.004) |
| Inflation | -0.001 | -0.001 | 0.000 | 0.000 | 0.000 | 0.004 | 0.000 | -0.002 |
| | (0.933) | (0.915) | (0.969) | (0.968) | (0.980) | (0.544) | (0.992) | (0.793) |
| Interest dif- ferential | -0.001 | 0.002 | 0.000 | -0.001 | -0.001 | 0.006 | -0.001 | 0.002 |
| | (0.863) | (0.477) | (0.915) | (0.760) | (0.773) | (0.051) | (0.855) | (0.501) |
| Depreciation | -0.003 | -0.001 | -0.002 | -0.003 | -0.003 | -0.005 | -0.003 | -0.001 |
| | (0.175) | (0.620) | (0.223) | (0.145) | (0.119) | (0.0163) | (0.134) | (0.621) |
| Depreciation volatility | 0.005 | 0.002 | 0.003 | 0.005 | 0.005 | 0.006 | 0.005 | 0.002 |
| | (0.234) | (0.592) | (0.355) | (0.232) | (0.254) | (0.264) | (0.252) | (0.556) |
| Exporter | 0.115 | 0.127 | 0.121 | 0.115 | 0.114 | 0.132 | 0.114 | 0.128 |
| | (0.000) | (0.000) | (0.000) | (0.000) | (0.000) | (0.000) | (0.000) | (0.000) |
| Sales to multi- nationals | 0.0349 | 0.0346 | 0.0386 | 0.0347 | 0.0361 | 0.0594 | 0.0359 | 0.0326 |
| | (0.381) | (0.411) | (0.346) | (0.382) | (0.363) | (0.211) | (0.366) | (0.439) |
| International accounting | 0.0480 | 0.0590 | 0.0627 | 0.0477 | 0.0476 | 0.0473 | 0.0475 | 0.0573 |
| | (0.270) | (0.244) | (0.176) | (0.272) | (0.273) | (0.390) | (0.275) | (0.253) |
| Small firm | -0.004 | -0.014 | -0.001 | -0.004 | -0.004 | -0.022 | -0.004 | -0.012 |
| | (0.893) | (0.671) | (0.982) | (0.908) | (0.902) | (0.603) | (0.896) | (0.701) |
| Age | -0.001 | 0.000 | -0.001 | -0.001 | -0.001 | -0.001 | -0.001 | 0.000 |
| | (0.558) | (0.691) | (0.315) | (0.561) | (0.540) | (0.414) | (0.543) | (0.696) |
| CIS | -0.128 | -0.129 | -0.0565 | -0.136 | -0.122 | -0.0551 | -0.118 | -0.140 |
| | (0.098) | (0.084) | (0.450) | (0.087) | (0.102) | (0.478) | (0.112) | (0.058) |
| Forward FX market | -0.0142 | -0.0812 | -0.0228 | -0.0129 | -0.0158 | 0.0181 | -0.0211 | -0.0734 |
| | (0.826) | (0.150) | (0.737) | (0.841) | (0.806) | (0.811) | (0.741) | (0.163) |
| Capital controls | -0.0690 | -0.0806 | -0.0857 | -0.0646 | -0.0621 | -0.0504 | -0.0644 | -0.0825 |
| | (0.059) | (0.009) | (0.015) | (0.061) | (0.063) | (0.237) | (0.064) | (0.075) |
| Open FX position | 0.004 | 0.006 | 0.004 | 0.004 | 0.004 | 0.010 | 0.004 | 0.006 |
| | (0.040) | (0.000) | (0.048) | (0.048) | (0.060) | (0.000) | (0.061) | (0.004) |

*(continued)*

## Table 13B-1 *(continued)*

| Variable | Foreign financing-integration measure (FI measure) | | | | | | | |
| --- | --- | --- | --- | --- | --- | --- | --- | --- |
| | GFI | BIS | L/D | fintliab | fintdebl | ca_3 | fintdeb_ch | kaopen |
| EU | −0.011 | 0.000 | 0.006 | −0.015 | −0.015 | 0.010 | −0.013 | 0.001 |
| | (0.842) | (0.998) | (0.914) | (0.785) | (0.790) | (0.836) | (0.820) | (0.981) |
| Forex deposits | −0.00303 | −0.00191 | −0.00154 | −0.00307 | −0.00326 | −0.00958 | −0.00326 | −0.00185 |
| | (0.032) | (0.158) | (0.345) | (0.027) | (0.015) | (0.000) | (0.017) | (0.175) |
| Collateralized | −0.0169 | −0.0102 | −0.0178 | −0.0171 | −0.0161 | −0.00614 | −0.0165 | −0.00927 |
| | (0.752) | (0.862) | (0.738) | (0.750) | (0.767) | (0.929) | (0.762) | (0.874) |
| Duration | 0.00314 | 0.00307 | 0.00291 | 0.00314 | 0.00314 | 0.00341 | 0.00313 | 0.00310 |
| | (0.000) | (0.000) | (0.000) | (0.000) | (0.000) | (0.000) | (0.000) | (0.000) |
| Number of observations | 1,574 | 1,452 | 1,541 | 1,574 | 1,574 | 1,121 | 1,574 | 1,461 |
| Number of countries | 21 | 19 | 19 | 21 | 21 | 15 | 21 | 20 |

Source: Authors' calculations based on data from Brown, Ongena, and Yeşin (2009) and Rosenberg and Tirpák (2008).

a. For variable definitions see appendix 13A. $p$-values are shown in parentheses. Dependent variable is dummy variable denoting whether firm's last loan was in FX (1) or local currency (0).

## Table 13B-2. *Quarterly Dataset, 2002–05: Full Results*[a]

Regression coefficients

| Variable | Foreign financing-integration measure (FI measure) | | | | | | | |
|---|---|---|---|---|---|---|---|---|
| | GFI | BIS | L/D | fintliab | fintdebl | ca_3 | fintdebt_ch | kaopen |
| Inflation volatility | 5.986 | 5.499 | 11.04 | 6.101 | 5.543 | 11.47 | 5.687 | 5.856 |
| | (0.308) | (0.363) | (0.009) | (0.285) | (0.255) | (0.013) | (0.276) | (0.304) |
| Governance | −15.8 | −13.78 | −17.07 | −15.08 | −15.43 | −15.13 | −14.37 | −23.47 |
| | (0.010) | (0.030) | (0.010) | (0.017) | (0.030) | (0.150) | (0.032) | (0.010) |
| Hard peg | 32.22 | 33.3 | 23.35 | 32.12 | 35.64 | 39.53 | 35.64 | 27.95 |
| | (0.001) | (0.002) | (0.000) | (0.001) | (0.001) | (0.000) | (0.001) | (0.006) |
| FI measure | 4.625 | 0.068 | 12.94 | 0.0600 | −0.177 | −0.019 | −0.110 | 4.834 |
| | (0.628) | (0.047) | (0.390) | (0.630) | (0.171) | (0.979) | (0.351) | (0.216) |
| Foreign banks | 0.122 | 0.0665 | 0.131 | 0.102 | 0.0958 | 0.0916 | 0.0652 | 0.0944 |
| | (0.243) | (0.473) | (0.321) | (0.374) | (0.314) | (0.473) | (0.484) | (0.406) |
| Inflation | −1.268 | −1.634 | −1.243 | −1.312 | −1.200 | −1.508 | −1.141 | −0.932 |
| | (0.098) | (0.047) | (0.133) | (0.082) | (0.128) | (0.018) | (0.150) | (0.283) |
| Interest differential | 0.785 | 0.919 | 0.682 | 0.747 | 0.704 | 1.823 | 0.646 | 0.473 |
| | (0.092) | (0.028) | (0.084) | (0.084) | (0.104) | (0.001) | (0.170) | (0.293) |
| Depreciation | −0.188 | 0.0255 | −0.316 | −0.196 | −0.113 | −0.386 | −0.143 | 0.0275 |
| | (0.502) | (0.922) | (0.246) | (0.490) | (0.659) | (0.281) | (0.573) | (0.918) |
| Depreciation volatility | 0.505 | 0.580 | 0.486 | 0.487 | 0.625 | 0.290 | 0.593 | 0.257 |
| | (0.389) | (0.326) | (0.437) | (0.394) | (0.231) | (0.702) | (0.285) | (0.644) |
| Forex deposits | −0.159 | −0.211 | −0.240* | −0.146 | −0.220 | −0.576 | −0.198 | −0.0998 |
| | (0.407) | (0.226) | (0.099) | (0.456) | (0.228) | (0.182) | (0.275) | (0.602) |
| Capital controls | −14.39 | −11.85 | −12.95 | −13.81 | −15.82 | −7.529 | −14.89 | −12.14 |
| | (0.010) | (0.029) | (0.017) | (0.019) | (0.0123) | (0.307) | (0.015) | (0.085) |
| Number of observations | 223 | 212 | 196 | 223 | 223 | 164 | 223 | 214 |
| Number of countries | 21 | 20 | 20 | 21 | 21 | 16 | 21 | 20 |

Source: See table 13B-1.

a. For variable definitions, see appendix 13A. *p*-values are shown in parentheses. Dependent variable is percent of FX lending in total lending. Estimated using generalized method of moments.

Table 13B-3. *Annual Dataset, 2000–08: Full Results*[a]

Regression coefficients

| Variable | Foreign financing-integration measure (FI measure) | | | | | | | |
|---|---|---|---|---|---|---|---|---|
| | *GFI* | *BIS* | *L/D* | *fintliab* | *fintdebl* | *ca_3* | *fintdebt_ch* | *kaopen* |
| Inflation volatility | −1.823 | −4.648 | −1.510 | −1.822 | −1.814 | −1.182 | −1.757 | −3.631 |
| | (0.204) | (0.072) | (0.270) | (0.180) | (0.178) | (0.361) | (0.188) | (0.137) |
| Governance | −20.07 | −17.07 | −22.12 | −20.64 | −20.7 | −21.43 | −19.73 | −21.47 |
| | (0.006) | (0.020) | (0.001) | (0.005) | (0.010) | (0.020) | (0.013) | (0.005) |
| Hard peg | 23.02 | 24.04 | 19.57 | 22.68 | 24.86 | 11.98 | 23.77 | 18.6 |
| | (0.021) | (0.018) | (0.057) | (0.018) | (0.023) | (0.211) | (0.029) | (0.031) |
| FI measure | 2.564 | 0.0164 | 3.048 | 0.106 | −0.123 | −1.339 | −0.0122 | 7.137 |
| | (0.821) | (0.088) | (0.842) | (0.487) | (0.525) | (0.424) | (0.937) | (0.000) |
| Foreign banks | −0.0486 | 0.0237 | −0.0946 | −0.0648 | −0.0107 | 0.0620 | −0.0430 | −0.0771 |
| | (0.775) | (0.888) | (0.587) | (0.714) | (0.951) | (0.722) | (0.832) | (0.642) |
| Inflation | −0.0123 | −0.0645 | −0.289 | −0.0925 | 0.0863 | 0.238 | 0.0409 | −0.0569 |
| | (0.981) | (0.961) | (0.702) | (0.864) | (0.884) | (0.748) | (0.945) | (0.963) |
| Depreciation volatility | 0.255 | 1.702 | 0.208 | 0.271 | 0.268 | −0.00621 | 0.218 | 1.425 |
| | (0.703) | (0.156) | (0.739) | (0.677) | (0.676) | (0.992) | (0.729) | (0.209) |
| Depreciation | 0.0553 | 0.0766 | 0.134 | −0.0287 | 0.178 | 0.0188 | 0.0855 | 0.00307 |
| | (0.834) | (0.775) | (0.674) | (0.906) | (0.478) | (0.939) | (0.768) | (0.992) |
| Interest differential | −0.862 | −1.059 | −0.743 | −0.937 | −0.707 | −1.325 | −0.818 | −0.606 |
| | (0.158) | (0.0406) | (0.141) | (0.101) | (0.300) | (0.044) | (0.131) | (0.190) |
| Number of observations | 79 | 74 | 64 | 79 | 79 | 61 | 79 | 74 |
| Number of countries | 16 | 15 | 16 | 16 | 16 | 13 | 16 | 15 |

Source: See table 13B-1.

a. *p*-values in parentheses. Dependent variable is percent of FX lending in total lending. Variable names as shown in appendix 13A except that inflation now denotes the previous year's consumer price index inflation; depreciation, the percent change of local currency per euro during the previous year; inflation volatility, the standard deviation of monthly inflation over the previous five years; and depreciation volatility, the standard deviation of monthly percent changes in the bilateral real exchange rate against the euro. Estimated using GMM.

# References

Abiad, A., D. Leigh, and A. Mody. 2009. "Financial Integration, Capital Mobility, and Income Convergence." *Economic Policy* 24, no. 4: 241–305.

Allayannis, G., G. W. Brown, and L. F. Klapper. 2003. "Capital Structure and Financial Risk: Evidence from Foreign Debt Use in East Asia." *Journal of Finance* 58, no. 6: 2667–710.

Allen, F., and D. Gale. 1994. "Limited Market Participation and Volatility of Asset Prices." *American Economic Review* 84, no. 4: 933–55.

Ariely, D. 2008. *Predictably Irrational.* New York: HarperCollins.

Barajas, A., and A. M. Morales. 2003. "Dollarization of Liabilities: Beyond the Usual Suspects." Working Paper 03/11. Washington D.C.: International Monetary Fund.

Basso, H. S., O. Calvo-Gonzalez, and M. Jurgilas. 2007. "Financial Dollarization—The Role of Banks and Interest Rates." Working Paper 748. Frankfurt: European Central Bank.

Borensztein, E., and others. 2004. "Sovereign Debt Structure for Crisis Prevention." Occasional Working Paper 237. Washington D.C.: International Monetary Fund.

Brown, M., S. Ongena, and P. Yeşin. 2009. "Foreign Currency Borrowing by Small Firms." Working Paper 2009-2. Zurich: Swiss National Bank.

Burnside, C., M. Eichenbaum, and S. Rebelo. 2001. "Prospective Deficits and the Asian Currency Crisis." *Journal of Political Economy* 109, no. 6: 1155–97.

Caballero, R. J., and A. Krishnamurthy. 2003. "Excessive Dollar Debt: Financial Development and Underinsurance." *Journal of Finance*, American Finance Association 58, no. 2: 867–94.

Caballero, R. J., and S. Panageas. 2005. "Contingent Reserves Management: An Applied Framework." *Economia Chilena* 8, no. 2: 45–56.

Claessens, S., A. Kose, and M. Terrones. 2008. "What Happens during Recessions, Crunches, and Busts?" Working Paper 08/274. Washington D.C.: International Monetary Fund.

Corsetti, G., P. Pesenti, and N. Roubini. 1999. "What Caused the Asian Currency and Financial Crisis?" *Japan and the World Economy* 11, no. 3: 305–73.

Cowan, K., E. Hansen, and L. O. Herrera. 2005. "Currency Mismatches, Balance Sheet Effects and Hedging in Chilean Non-Financial Corporations." RES Working Paper 4387. Washington D.C.: Inter-American Development Bank, Research Department.

De Nicoló, G., P. Honohan, and A. Ize. 2003. "Dollarization of the Banking System: Good or Bad?" Policy Research Working Paper 3116. Washington D.C.: World Bank.

Dooley, M. 2000. "A Model of Crises in Emerging Markets." *Economic Journal* 110, no. 460: 256–72.

Eichengreen, B., and R. Hausmann. 1999. "Exchange Rates and Financial Fragility." Working Paper 7418. Cambridge, Mass.: National Bureau of Economic Research.

Eichengreen, B., R. Hausmann, and U. Panizza. 2003. "Currency Mismatches, Debt Intolerance and Original Sin: Why They Are Not the Same and Why It Matters." Working Paper 10036. Cambridge, Mass.: National Bureau of Economic Research.

European Bank for Reconstruction and Development (EBRD). 2009. *Transition Report 2009: Transition in Crisis?* London.

Gelos, G. R. 2003. "Foreign Currency Debt in Emerging Markets: Firm-Level Evidence from Mexico." *Economics Letters* 78, no. 3: 323–27.

Goldstein, M., and P. Turner. 2004. *Controlling Currency Mismatches in Emerging Markets.* Washington D.C.: Peterson Institution for International Economics.

Guscina, A. 2008. "Impact of Macroeconomic, Political, and Institutional Factors on the Structure of Government Debt in Emerging Market Countries." Working Paper 08/205. Washington D.C.: International Monetary Fund.

Ize, A., and E. Levy Yeyati. 2003. "Financial Dollarization." *Journal of International Economics* 59, no. 2: 323–47.

Jeanne, O. 2000. "Foreign Currency Debt and the Global Financial Architecture." *European Economic Review* 44, no. 4-6: 719–27.

———. 2003. "Why do Emerging Economies Borrow in Foreign Currency?" Working Paper 03/177. Washington D.C.: International Monetary Fund.

———. 2009. "Debt Maturity and the International Financial Architecture." *American Economic Review* 99, no. 5: 2135–48.

Kamil, H. 2008. "How Do Exchange Rate Regimes Affect Firms' Incentives to Hedge Exchange Rate Risk?" Working paper. Washington D.C.: International Monetary Fund.

Kiraly, J. 2009. "FX Mismatches and Policy Options in Hungary." Paper presented at the EBRD Economic Policy Forum. London, May.

Korinek, A. 2009. "Excessive Dollar Borrowing in Emerging Markets: Balance Sheet Effects and Macroeconomic Externalities." Working paper. University of Maryland, Department of Economics.

Lane, P., and G. Milesi-Ferretti. 2006. "The External Wealth of Nations Mark II: Revised and Extended Estimates of Foreign Assets and Liabilities." *Journal of International Economics* 73, no. 2: 223–50.

Levy Yeyati, E. 2005. "Financial Dollarization: Evaluating the Consequences." Preliminary draft paper prepared for the *Economic Policy* Forty-First Panel Meeting. Luxembourg, April 15–16.

Luca, A., and I. Petrova. 2008. "What Drives Credit Dollarization in Transition Economies?" *Journal of Banking and Finance* 32, no. 5: 858–69.

Martinez, L., and A. Werner. 2002. "The Exchange Rate Regime and the Currency Composition of Corporate Debt: The Mexican Experience." *Journal of Development Economics* 69, no. 2: 315–34.

McKinnon, R., and H. Pill. 1999. "Exchange Rate Regimes for Emerging Markets: Moral Hazard and International Overborrowing." Working Paper 99018. Stanford University, Department of Economics.

Parrado, E. A., and A. Ize. 2002. "Dollarization, Monetary Policy, and the Pass-Through." Working Paper 02/188. Washington D.C.: International Monetary Fund.

Polish Commission for Banking Supervision. 2006. "Recommendation S on Good Practices Regarding Mortgage-Secured Credit Exposures." Warsaw.

Rajan, R., and I. Tokatlidis. 2005. "Dollar Shortages and Crises." *International Journal of Central Banking* 1, no. 2: 177–220.

Rancière, R, A. Tornell, and A. Vamvakidis. 2010 (forthcoming). "Currency Mismatch and Systemic Risk in Eastern Europe." *Economic Policy*.

Rosenberg, C., and M. Tirpák. 2008. "Determinants of Foreign Currency Borrowing in the New Member States of the EU." Working Paper 08/173. Washington D.C.: International Monetary Fund.

Rossi, J. L., Jr. 2004. "Foreign Exchange Exposure, Corporate Financial Policies and the Exchange Rate Regime: Evidence from Brazil." Working paper. Yale University, Department of Economics.

Sahay, R., and C. A. Végh, 1996. "Dollarization in Transition Economies: Evidence and Policy Implications." In *The Macroeconomics of International Currencies: Theory, Policy, and Evidence*, edited by P. Mizen and E. J. Pentecost, pp. 192–224. London: Edward Elgar.

Schneider, M., and A. Tornell. 2004. "Balance Sheet Effects, Bailout Guarantees and Financial Crises." *Review of Economic Studies* 71, no. 3: 883–913.

Schinasi, G., and T. Smith. 1998. "Fixed-Income Markets in the United States, Europe, and Japan—Some Lessons for Emerging Markets." Working Paper 98/173. Washington D.C.: International Monetary Fund.

Sturzenegger, F., and J. Zettelmeyer. 2007. *Debt Defaults and Lessons from a Decade of Crises*. MIT Press.

Tirole, J. 2003. "Inefficient Foreign Borrowing: A Dual- and Common-Agency Perspective." *American Economic Review* 93, no. 5: 1678–702.

# Contributors

VIRAL V. ACHARYA is professor of finance at the New York University Stern School of Business and a research affiliate of the Center for Economic Policy Research, European Corporate Governance Institute, and National Bureau of Economic Research.

BINDU ANANTH works for IFMR Trust.

THOMAS COOLEY is Richard R. West Dean and the Paganelli-Bull Professor of Economics at the New York University Stern School of Business.

DOUGLAS J. ELLIOTT is with the Brookings Institution.

ALFRED HANNIG is the executive director of the Alliance for Financial Inclusion.

STEFAN JANSEN is a financial sector specialist and an associate of the Alliance for Financial Inclusion.

STEPHEN JEFFREY is at Warwick University.

MASAHIRO KAWAI is dean and CEO at the Asian Development Bank Institute.

K. P. KRISHNAN serves at present as secretary of the prime minister's Economic Advisory Council in the Government of India and before this worked for many years in the Ministry of Finance of the Government of India.

RAKESH MOHAN is a nonresident senior research fellow at the Stanford Center for International Development, Stanford University.

NACHIKET MOR is the president of the ICICI Foundation for Inclusive Growth and the chair of the IFMR Trust Governing Council.

PIROSKA M. NAGY is with the Office of the Chief Economist, European Bank for Reconstruction and Development (EBRD).

ANWAR NASUTION is professor of economics at the University of Indonesia and served as the senior deputy governor of Bank Indonesia from 1999 to 2004, and chairman of the Supreme Audit Board of Indonesia from 2004 to 2009.

LUO PING is the director general of the training department of the China Banking Regulatory Commission.

MICHAEL POMERLEANO is an advisor at the World Bank.

ESWAR S. Prasad is the Tolani Senior Professor of Trade Policy at Cornell University, a senior fellow at the Brookings Institution, and a research associate at the National Bureau of Economic Research.

SUYASH RAI works for IFMR Trust.

RICHARD REID is director of research at the International Center for Financial Regulation (ICFR).

MATTHEW RICHARDSON is Charles Simon professor of applied financial economics at the New York University Stern School of Business and Sidney Homer director of the Salomon Center for Research in Financial Institutions and Markets, and a research associate of the National Bureau of Economic Research.

INGO WALTER is vice dean of faculty and Seymour Milstein professor of finance, corporate governance and ethics at the New York University Stern School of Business.

ALEJANDRO WERNER is undersecretary of the Ministry of Finance, México.

GUILLERMO ZAMARRIPA is head of the banking, Securities and Savings Unit, Ministry of Finance, México.

JEROMIN ZETTELMEYER is with the Office of the Chief Economist, European Bank for Reconstruction and Development (EBRD).

# Index

Access to financial services: barriers, 306–07; credit, 15–16, 299; increasing, 15–16; in India, 246; measuring, 229, 288–89; savings accounts, 285, 294, 298, 313. *See also* Financial inclusion

Accounting standards: fair value accounting, 326–27, 343, 350; financial regulation and, 122; international, 147–48

Acharya, Viral V., 43, 50

Adams, Charles, 191

Africa: financial inclusion, 292, 299, 303, 307; microfinance, 304, 308, 309. *See also* Kenya

AFSD. *See* Asian Financial Stability Dialogue

Agent banking, 280, 292–93, 300–02, 308

AIG, 43, 48, 51, 52, 89, 93, 192

Albania, exchange rate policies, 383

Aldrich Vreeland Act, 31

Alliance for Financial Inclusion, 313

American International Group. *See* AIG

AML-CFT. *See* Anti-money laundering and combating financing of terrorism

Anglo-Saxon financial model, 221

Antaboga Deltasekuritas, 162

Arbitrage, 369. *See also* Regulatory arbitrage

Arestis, P., 209

Argentina: financial crises, 381; government bonds, 381

Asia: banks, 20–21; capital inflows, 20–21; corporate bond markets, 13–14; exchange rate policies, 108, 243; financial inclusion, 15–16, 290–92; financial regulation, 21–22; financial repression, 160–61, 164; foreign exchange reserves, 199; institutional investors, 21, 240, 257; mobile banking, 302–03; public sector banks, 13, 68, 69, 139, 291; regional organizations, 166; systemic stability regulators, 193–97. *See also* *individual countries*

Asian Bond Fund, 14

Asian financial crisis (*1997–98*): causes, 161; effects in Indonesia, 160; lessons from, 12, 161, 167, 179–80; responses, 199

Asian Financial Stability Dialogue (AFSD), 199–200

Asian monetary fund proposal, 199–200

Asset-backed securities: AAA tranches, 43, 47–48, 60–61; commercial paper, 41, 43, 54; credit risk, 47–48; growth, 115; investors, 41; mortgage-backed, 43–44, 46–47, 49, 109–10, 113, 324; risks, 60–61. *See also* Securitization